Horn,

OR

THE

COUNTERSIDE

OF

MEDIA

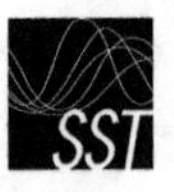

SIGN, STORAGE, TRANSMISSION

A SERIES EDITED BY JONATHAN STERNE AND LISA GITELMAN

HENNING SCHMIDGEN

Translated by Nils F. Schott

Horn,

OR THE COUNTERSIDE OF MEDIA

DUKE UNIVERSITY PRESS › DURHAM AND LONDON › 2022

Designed by Matthew Tauch
Typeset in Portrait Text and Space Grotesk by Westchester PublishingSer vices

Library of Congress Cataloging-in-Publication Data
Names: Schmidgen, Henning, author. | Schott, Nils F., translator.
Title: Horn, or the counterside of media / Henning Schmidgen ; translated by Nils F. Schott.
Other titles: Horn, oder Die Gegenseite der Medien. English. | Counterside of media | Sign, storage, transmission.
Description: Durham : Duke University Press, 2022. | Series: Sign, storage, transmission | Includes bibliographical references and index.
Identifiers: LCCN 2021014756 (print)
LCCN 2021014757 (ebook)
ISBN 9781478015109 (hardcover)
ISBN 9781478017721 (paperback)
ISBN 9781478022343 (ebook)
Subjects: LCSH: Mass media—Philosophy. | Touch—Philosophy. | Horns. | BISAC: SOCIAL SCIENCE / Media Studies | ART / Criticism & Theory
Classification: LCC P91 .S3613 2022 (print) | LCC P91 (ebook) | DDC 302.2301—dc23
LC recordavailableathttps:/ /lccn.loc.gov/2021014756
LC ebookrec ordavailableathttps:/ /lccn.loc.gov/2021014757

CONTENTS

PREFACE

This is an experimental book. In two earlier volumes, I discussed connections between humans and machines. *The Unconscious of Machines* was devoted to Félix Guattari's philosophy, which conceives of the subliminal commonalities between technics and body as a creative resource. *Brain and Time* reconstructed the scientific and technological history of experimental psychology in the nineteenth and early twentieth centuries to show how the combination of and confrontation between laboratory instruments and test subjects drove the epistemic process.[1]

Horn takes up this theme but shifts the focus to the terrain of media theory. This book is concerned not with connections between human and machine but with the in-between itself, that is, with the faces, surfaces, and interfaces that separate body and technics to reestablish contact between them in a different way. In rather unexpected ways, the COVID-19 crisis has underscored the importance of this problem. While the matter of touch and its multifaceted manifestations—from physical contact to transmissions through aerosols—is a core problem in all infectious diseases, innovative smartphone technologies can now be used for tracing and tracking potentially harmful encounters and meetings between their users. This is just one example illustrating the relevance of this book, whose central aim is to rethink the sense of touch in the age of ubiquitous computing.

I would like to thank the VolkswagenStiftung for supporting my work on this project within its funding initiative, "'Original—Isn't It?' New Options for the Humanities and Cultural Studies" in 2016. Wherever they could, Vera Szöllösi-Brenig and Sebastian Schneider provided friendly and unbureaucratic help—even when it became clear that this project would considerably outgrow its originally envisaged scope.

Support from the VolkswagenStiftung also allowed me to present the major findings of this work at an international workshop, "Symmetries of Touch," in October 2016 and discuss them with colleagues from media studies, the history of science, art history, computer science, literary studies, and sociology. I am grateful to Hanjo Berressem, Lorenz Engell, Mechthild Fend, Andrew Goffey, Eva Hornecker, Rebekka Ladewig, David Parisi, Mark Paterson, Chris Salter, Elisabeth von Samsonow, Max Stadler, Charles

Wolfe, and Siegfried Zielinski for their contributions and comments, which greatly helped me sort out my own thoughts.

Thanks are due also to the libraries, archives, museums, and other institutions that have supported my research: the Rebecca Horn Workshop, Bad König; the Collection of Plaster Casts (Glyptotheque) at the Academy of Fine Arts, Vienna; the Austrian National Library, Vienna; the Manuscript Division of the Library of Congress, Washington, DC; the Centre d'Estudis Dalinians, Figueres; the gta Archiv at the ETH, Zurich; and, finally, the University Library and the Archiv der Moderne at Bauhaus University, Weimar.

I owe a debt of gratitude to a number of people. Rebecca Horn graciously allowed me to screen several of her very early films. Andrew McLuhan and Ellen Fernandez-Sacco helped out with information on André Girard. Moreover, I would like to thank Bernhard Dotzler in Regensburg, Simon Frisch in Weimar, and Pamela Kort in Berlin (now in Zurich) for stimulating conversations and critical discussions.

Special thanks are due to my student assistants, who supported the work on this project by getting hold of texts and images, conducting research, taking care of correspondence, proofreading, and criticism: Mariann Diedrich, Mathilde Gest, Johannes Hess, Benjamin Prinz, and Isabella Triendl-Fügenschuh. Special thanks are due also to Laura Fronterré for her wonderful design of the illustration sections in this book and to Nils F. Schott for his—as always—excellent work in translating the text.

"A motorcycle mechanic," Robert M. Pirsig writes in *Zen and the Art of Motorcycle Maintenance*, "who honks the horn to see if the battery works is informally conducting a true scientific experiment."[2] It is my hope that the experiment conducted here on the horn conveys a series of interesting, stimulating, and perhaps even touching insights.

Introduction

> The new universe is neither imaginable nor conceivable, it is only touchable. The mode of action appropriate to it is fingertips pushing down on keys.
> VILÉM FLUSSER

> I had an idea in those days that textures should be very much thicker, and therefore the texture of, for instance, a rhinoceros skin would help me to think about the texture of human skin.
> FRANCIS BACON

> DON'T EVER ANTAGONIZE THE HORN.
> THOMAS PYNCHON

First, it was just telephones, then TVs with remote control, finally computers, and today smartphones and tablets, as well as watches: our daily dealings with media are characterized by a remarkable turn to the tactile. Thanks to the massive diffusion of portable touch screens, holding, pressing, and typing may not have become the dominant modes of interaction with media, but they are now certainly on the same level as hearing and seeing. In practically all places, at practically all times, we touch and handle media devices, we hold them, we fasten or in some way bring them close to our bodies, we carefully swipe across their surfaces, and in return, as it were, are attentive to their vibrations.

Yet it is not just we who increasingly touch media devices. Conversely, these devices touch and scan us—and increasingly so. We have gotten used to pressure sensors in car seats and to motion detectors in front of automatic doors or in dark stairwells as much as we have gotten used to stationary and mobile body scanners in airports, courthouses, and other public places. Today, however, we are entering a society of portable and networked media that are downright crammed with sensors: from cars and bikes via fitness trackers to glasses and shoes. Ever smaller and more lightweight, such devices are literally moving in on us, and the more they do so, and the more they are, in so doing, connected, the more intensely they scan us and our surroundings, track and trace our movements through real and virtual spaces.

At the moment, we cannot predict where the aggregation, analysis, and deployment of the immense masses of data generated by media's expanding sense of touch will lead. Yet there have long been critical voices. Long before the internet advanced to become a new mass medium, Gilles Deleuze sketched the dark vision of a control society, in which massive "electronic tagging" is combined with centralized computers. At any moment, Deleuze predicted, any person could then be located with precision and granted or denied access to certain areas of public space. The result would be a control society, in which all environments of enclosure (factories, prisons, schools, etc.) are replaced by numerical sieves whose meshes are variable, continually changing the distance between the nodes.[1]

As would be expected, today's commentators are hardly impressed by such scenarios. They depict recent developments in digital technologies as the beginning of an "age of context" full of promise. In this new age, companies no longer need to bother potential customers with unwanted advertising because, thanks to eye trackers, they can literally read their every wish in their eyes. Patients are said to be taken care of better and more quickly because wristbands, shoes, and other wearables transmit physiological data (number of steps, heart and respiratory rate, etc.) directly to hospitals, insurers, and pharmaceutical companies. And an increasing number of organisms classified as endangered or unreliable (crabs, birds, children, etc.) are to be fitted with sensors that allow for determining their locations and tracking their movements in order to, on that basis, "take better care" of them.[2]

Media theory cannot simply resolve this disproportionate relationship between two perspectives, the threatening society of control on the one hand, the promising age of context on the other. It can, however, contribute to sketching a new image of what media are or are about to become. In this regard, the recent upsurge of the tactile opens up a number of instructive perspectives. Above all, it reminds us that our dealings with media are never limited to single sense organs. They always concern the entire body. Classical media such as radio or TV might still primarily address the ear or the eye. Today's media devices, however, leave no doubt that they involve their users literally from tip to toe, from the head down to the feet, from hands and wrists via the chest to the neck and forehead.

The surface of media multiplies accordingly. It is no longer limited to speakers and screens but continues in clothes and seats, glass plates and rubber bands, walls and floors, and begins to embrace entire apartments and cities. This makes *situated relationships between technical and bodily surfaces*—what Vilém Flusser once called the encounter between the "opposing skins" of technics and body, machine and organism[3]—the concrete starting point for the work of media theory.

The productivity of an approach that seeks to rethink the concept of media starting from the sense of touch is borne out by a large number of recent studies. They range from theoretical work on the influence of remote controls on TV watching habits to historical studies on the keyboard and the mouse as the essential interfaces of computers to contributions in cultural studies on the history of the sense of touch, which also discuss the technicization of touch.[4]

Case studies on the use of scanning and sensor technology in security checks, on the automatic identification and localization of objects by means of radio waves (RFID), or on the emergence and development of haptic feedback in video game consoles and smartphones also contribute to new ways of understanding media under the auspices of the tactile. It has even been suggested that we summarize the current configuration of portable and networked media technologies under the heading "sensor society."[5]

The recent studies published by Rachel Plotnick and David Parisi confirm and reinforce the productivity of this development. From their respective points of view, Plotnick and Parisi offer substantial contributions to the emerging field of "haptic media studies." Focusing on the period between 1880 and 1925, Plotnick reconstructs the social history of pushing buttons. She shows that the rapid spread of these devices restructured human-machine relations in fundamental ways that masked both technological complexity and power relations.[6] Parisi's *Archaeologies of Touch* reconsiders the entire history of modernity, from the eighteenth to the late twentieth century, and reconstructs a wide range of scientific and technological "apparatuses" (*dispositifs*) that contributed to create the *haptic subject*. According to Parisi, the haptic subject of our present is characterized by multiple interactions with computer technology and ever more frequent experiences of vibrational feedback, which leads to further knowledge concerning the phenomenon of touch.[7]

The present book draws inspiration from these two studies, from their critical focus on human–machine relations as well as from their detailed discussion of haptic media theories in Walter Benjamin and Marshall McLuhan. At the same time, *Horn* places the emphasis on other aspects implied in the phenomenon of touch. Whereas Plotnick highlights the tactile activity of human actors and Parisi is mostly interested in feedback signals emitted by nonhuman actors, that is, reactions of media devices as they are triggered by the movements of human users, the present book is crucially interested in the *tactile agency of media technologies*.

Its ultimate goal is to sketch what, borrowing from Bruno Latour, might be called a *symmetrical theory of the tactile*.[8] This theory sets out to situate the sense of touch no longer exclusively on the side of human actors but equally also on the side of nonhuman actors, on the side, that is, of the technical objects we usually call *media*. Touch, accordingly, would not be, or at least not primarily or exclusively, a human capacity but a function increasingly taken over by scanners, trackers, and similar terminal equipment.

Symmetry here, I should emphasize, does not mean identity. Despite all progress in the field of soft robotics, most technical objects still touch and scan what they confront differently from the ways human subjects do so. While scanners' and sensors' sense of touch is usually based on light rays, X-rays, and electromagnetic waves, human touch remains committed to comparatively common conceptions of the corporeal and the material. Similarly stark is the disequilibrium between the economic, political, and administrative interests behind the scanning done by various media devices on the one hand and the motives that make individuals look at and touch the surfaces of media on the other.

These observations, however, do not change the fundamentals of the issue. "Media determine our situation." Long ago, this was the programmatic cliché in media studies.[9] Only in the age of GPS and internet are we able to attribute concrete meaning to this cliché. Today, in fact, it is media devices and infrastructures that position us, that locate and track us without our consent or contribution and, precisely in so doing, manifest their tactile agency. It is time that we take seriously and analyze this *counterside of media*.

That is the goal pursued in this experimental book, which is meant to be as much theoretically reflective as it is historically informed. This book's particular ambition is to explore and develop the symmetry of the tactile just sketched by building several bridges between media theory and media art. The technological, social, and economic conditions of the age of context thus do not occupy center stage. Instead, beginning with the phenomenology of this touch-intensive age, this study seeks to open up a simultaneously reflective and imaginative potential for engaging with a current constellation in which the things of media are ever more closely moving in on us.

To this end, the chapters that follow investigate established media theories with regard to whether and to what extent they provide concepts that facilitate the exploration of media tactility. The question of the sense of touch, of course, has been discussed exhaustively by the classic authors of media theory. As early as the 1920s, Walter Benjamin pointed to an increase in "gestures of switching, inserting, pressing" and, partly by taking up psychoanalytic insights, emphasized the transformation in modernity of all "haptic experiences."[10] Some decades later, Marshall McLuhan, in a different but similar context, gave a detailed description of "tactile man," a type produced by television, and at the same time suggested an intimate connection between tactilization and digitization.[11]

What has largely gone unnoticed in all this, however, is that Benjamin and McLuhan also thematized the tactile agency of media. In Benjamin, this is the case, for example, with the shock-like effects of film that audiences can absorb only by deploying their eye muscles as "shock absorbers" and with Dada photomontages that act like a "projectile" on the observer.[12] McLuhan uses similar terms to describe the effect of television images. The light emitted from these images "bombard[s]" viewers in their living rooms such that they themselves turn into screens. Moreover, according to McLuhan, a tactile mechanism is already at work in the TV studio, where cameras record their images by means of a "scanning finger." In this respect too, then, the sense of touch seems no longer tied exclusively to the human body.[13]

In parallel with this engagement with the classics of media theory, this book examines artistic and literary practices that have thematized the symmetry of touch in different ways. In confronting the flatness of pictorial media like photography and film, modern art has repeatedly taken up the notion, dating back to antiquity, that in the system of the senses, touch comes before and/or stands above seeing. In the late nineteenth century, this was the case for sculptor Adolf von Hildebrand, who developed a widely accepted conception of "looking [*Schauen*]" as "actual touching [*wirkliches Abtasten*]"[14]—a conception largely inspired by von Hildebrand's critique of the allegedly false depth created by the mass media of his day (photography, stereoscopy, panorama, etc.). Shortly after, painter Wassily Kandinsky depicted the artist in his entirety as transformed into a hand that in striking the keys of the scale of colors "causes the human soul to vibrate." In the early 1920s, the futurist Filippo Marinetti in his manifesto "Tactilism" even propagated a new art form centered on feeling different materials ("Rough Iron. Light brush bristles. Sponge. Wire bristles").[15]

In what follows I will show that those forms of advanced art and literature after 1945 that engaged with what in their time were new media also reflected intensively on the relationship between sight and touch. This is true for Salvador Dalí, as it is for Rebecca Horn or William Kentridge. Rebecca Horn's early performances and installations are of particular interest here. On the one hand, she implements McLuhan's thesis that media are "extensions of man" in concrete practices of producing objects and instruments meant to "extend" and "enhance" the human body and its functions. Examples include *Arm-Extensionen* (*Arm Extensions*, 1968) and *Kopf-Extension* (*Head Extension*, 1972). On the other hand, these works thematize the partly protective, partly stifling, partly downright restraining aspects of the media world thus produced. Much can also be learned from Dalí's works and performances in the 1950s, which, starting with the leitmotif of the rhinoceros, explore media surfaces with a view to biology and morphology.

Aligning media theory and media art might seem arbitrary. Yet there are many points of contact between the two fields to justify this approach. It might not be surprising that artists evoked media theory as soon as such a discourse existed, especially if they were working with new media themselves. Dalí's conception of image surfaces, for example, is indeed informed by cybernetics, while Rebecca Horn's concept of "interpersonal perception" refers, at least implicitly, to Fritz Heider's theory of media. It may then be all the more striking that inversely, classic texts in media theory pick up and work closely with artistic and art historical discourses. Benjamin, in describing the tactile agency of media, refers to Dada and to constructivism, while McLuhan in this context time and again invokes pointillism and the Bauhaus.

Combining and confronting theory and art is thus not an end in itself. It reflects the fact that media theory is not a "discipline" that, influenced by post-structuralism, simply developed from literary, especially German, studies or other humanities disciplines. Instead, this segment of theoretical work picks up substantially on the creative and experimental ways of dealing with media that are particularly salient in the field of art.[16] Today's media theory is thus confronted with the task not only of observing and processing current developments in media technology and media studies, but also of acknowledging art as an important resource—especially when it comes to outlining a new image of media in a "sensor society."

The horn serves as leitmotif for this attempt. Indeed, horns reappear in ever new variants and variations in the work of the artists considered here: in Dalí's multimedia "rhinoceros phase" in the 1950s; in the early work of Rebecca Horn, who of course is playing on her own name as well, in performances such as *Einhorn* (*Unicorn*), *Schwarze Hörner* (*Shoulder Extensions* [lit., *Black Horns*]), or *Cornucopia*; and in Kentridge, both in his drawings on Dürer's *Rhinocerus* and in his installations, which are crammed with megaphones and wind instruments.

Horns function as a simple *and* a complex motif in media art. They are evoked, in different contexts, as a natural phenomenon and as an artificial object, as a peculiar form as well as a specific material that serves a broad range of purposes: from magical symbol to animist decoration and technological object. But it is not just the history of the horn as a motif that has much to tell us. In a broader sense, horn can be conceived as something that exemplarily marks an *intermediary*. It is thus particularly suitable for guiding an investigation of the encounter of the "opposing skins" of technics and body.

On the one hand, horn is situated between the living inner world and the material outer world. As we all know, calluses (in German called *Hornhaut*, "horn skin") form on those areas of the human body where strain on the epidermis is particularly pronounced, on the palms or the heels, for example. Just as calluses, hair, and nails consist of keratin (from Greek *keras*, "horn"), so do birds' feathers and beaks and porcupines' spines.

While horn does communicate tactile sensations, it simultaneously shields the organism from the intrusion of foreign bodies. It acts as a protective shell and armor, functions as ornament and decoration, but it can also serve as tool and weapon. And although horn firmly belongs to the living body, it is not itself alive in any way. At least in humans, it is nothing but dead skin.[17]

On the other hand, "horn" stands not only for a natural material but also for an artificial object, an instrument. Naturally existing animal horns were used first as trophies, as charms, or—ground into powder—as medicine. (The powder obtained from the horns of rhinoceroses continues to be regarded in many countries as an aphrodisiac and a drug. Hunting for rhinoceroses has become a brutal business that threatens the very existence of entire species.) Formally switching between masculine tip and feminine hollow, the horns of cattle were also used as drinking vessels and wind instruments.

These latter did not just produce pleasant sounds. Even when they were still made predominantly from natural horn, they also produced practical signals, on the hunt for example. Since early modernity, this signaling function has increasingly been taken over by metal horns, among other places in that paradigmatic network of communication we still call the postal service. In high modernity, this development was continued and further developed by acoustic horns and speakers, as well as gigantic foghorns guiding maritime traffic along the coasts and no less gigantic horn antennas used in radio astronomy. Today, practically all motion detectors include miniaturized horn antennas.[18]

In other words, horn is a natural material as well as an artificial object. It is firmly tied to the living body, growing out of it, becoming visible on it and with it. Horn can be detached and separated from the body, and it can be exhibited and circulated, reencountering living bodies as an external being, a natural thing, or an artificial object. As a result, horn sheds an interesting light on the relationship between body, image, and technology. Conceived of as a literal "extension" or "projection" of the living body, it might even be understood as a medium par excellence, for it fulfills the central criterion of the definition of technical media given by Ernst Kapp, Henri Bergson, Marshall McLuhan, and others. The formation of horn in and on the human body might even be the concrete point of reference for understanding media as "extensions of man."[19]

Be this as it may, the focus on a motif that stands simultaneously for a natural material and an artificial object is extremely useful in studying the emergence and development of bodily and technical surfaces. In his engagement with the phenomena of media superficiality, Flusser has given an exemplary description of the gradual reduction of sculptures to images, of images to texts, and of texts to programs. But his depiction of this "play of abstraction" focused primarily on one side, that of media technology. His explanations of the other side, the surfaces of the body, the "body map" and the "skin atlas," however, have remained fragmentary.[20]

That is the point where our effort sets in. From the double perspective of human and machine, technics and body, this book supplements Flusser's "phenomenology of the cultural history"[21] of the outer skin of media with a natural history of surfaces—and thus contributes to achieving symmetry in this regard as well. In other words, the goal of our undertaking does not consist in reinforcing interest in the "cultural techniques" that fascinate some proponents of media theory, particularly in the German context.[22] Instead, the present study points to the existence of what might be called *natural techniques*, that is to say, biological functions and formations without which there simply would be no culture.

On this point, recent work explicitly devoted to a *biology of media* has yielded important insights. In the last few years, both Eugene Thacker and Robert Mitchell have persuasively argued that by "body," media theory should not just mean "human body." From different points of view, Thacker and Mitchell show that in the laboratories of the life sciences as well as in the installations of bio art, an entire spectrum of organisms, organs, and organic substances—from DNA sequences via individual cells to muscle tissue—function as media.[23]

Further prompts came from studies that do not or do not yet belong to the canon of media theory. Thor Hanson's wonderful book *Feathers* confirmed my intention to draw on both natural and cultural history. A particularly stimulating aspect of Hanson's account is his very detailed discussion of the fact that feathers consist of keratin. Based on a wealth of examples—from dinosaur and bird feathers via feathers for stuffing pillows to hat and writing feathers—he sketches a kind of comparative, historical keratology. The chapters that follow are devoted to this kind of horn theory, even if they do not enter into biological details to the same extent.[24]

Differently but no less intensely stimulating are the reflections on bodily limits Karen Barad develops in her philosophical elaboration of an *agential realism*. Barad explains convincingly that in looking at the outer limits of "human beings" on the one hand and of "apparatuses" (or media devices) on the other, visual clues can be quite misleading. Instead, she asserts, "human bodies, like all other bodies, are not entities with inherent boundaries and properties but phenomena that acquire specific boundaries and properties through the open-ended dynamics of intra-activity."[25] Especially because it is made not by a biologist but a physicist, this assertion does, I think, confirm my approach of looking at the genesis of bodily and technical surfaces from the inside.

The specific form this book has finally taken is that of a *fictitious exhibition*. This is not to say that from this point forward, presentation will replace explanation, indication supplant argumentation. Rather, the fiction of an exhibition is meant to underscore that what follows is not limited to engaging with texts but also brings in a multitude of different sources and materials, also and especially where the concern is not with art but with theoretical discourses: photographs of rhinoceroses and Stone Age reliefs of horns, paintings of fingernails, sculptures of horned heads, illustrations from scientific textbooks depicting the horns of rams and sheep, and unpublished manuscripts in which sketches of postal horns and megaphones surface . . .

The book's five chapters correspond to the rooms in which these texts, images, and objects are presented, commented on, and argumentatively connected in their material and semiotic "entanglement" (Barad). Each chapter-room stages an encounter between science, art, and technics. Their order is not chronological but follows different thematic emphases, highlighting media art and media theory in alternation. The first (art) chapter thus responds to the last, and the second (theory) chapter is related to the fourth, while the centrally positioned third chapter forms a passage between them and combines aspects of theorizing and artistic practice.

In coming up with and laying out these chapter-rooms, much care has been taken to respect and do justice to the qualitative differences of the various sources and materials. This is, on the one hand, the effect of a method that has led, especially in recent work in the history of science, to the exploration of local assemblages of knowledge production in their specific materiality and semioticity. In these pages, this method is, perhaps for the first time, applied in the fields of media theory and media art. On the other hand, the subject matter certainly rubs off on the method. In fact, the study of tactility has time and again drawn my attention to the different surfaces of letters and manuscripts, drawings and paintings, photos and films.

The printed book does level these differences. Nonetheless, the combination of text and images still renders it perceptible. That, precisely, is the methodological goal of this fictitious exhibition. It tries to exemplify that perceptions, also and especially in media theory, are semiotically and materially bound. It sets out to valorize the space *between* different medial representations in order to mark this space as a decisive starting point for an engaged thinking confronted with the "sensor society." It is in this sense, too, that in what follows I speak of the *counterside of media*. The term refers not just to the tactile agency of media devices. It also addresses our critical ability to reappropriate the use of existing media technologies and to both create and design new kinds of media.

A few years ago already, Katherine Hayles pointed out that the spreading of tagging and tracing technologies will require a critique of their deployment for particular economic or political purposes. At the same time, however, she pointed out that connected RFIDs, sensors, and actuators open up the possibility of "shedding the burden of long-held misconceptions about cognition and moving to a more processual, relational and accurate view of embodied human action in complex environments."[26]

The pages that follow are conceived as a contribution to the development of such a view. There is one philosopher who saw that such an undertaking cannot concern only one form of perception, that is, an aesthetics, but must take on an entire epistemology of embodiment. In this sense, Michel Serres writes about Lucretius: "Knowing [*savoir*] is not seeing [*voir*]; knowing is making contact, directly, with the things: and they, moreover, are coming to us."[27]

ONE

The Captured Unicorn

In this room, the French writer Raymond Roussel and the German artist Rebecca Horn meet. First editions of Roussel's epoch-making novels, *Impressions of Africa* and *Locus Solus*, are presented next to objects, masks, and instruments from Horn's early work. Screens display her films and performances, for example *Unicorn*, *Head Extension*, and *Finger Gloves*; hanging on the walls are Jean Ferry's and Markus Raetz's drawings and etchings of Roussel's machinic assemblages. Distributed among them are some of the models of these assemblages Harald Szeemann commissioned for his exhibition of "bachelor machines." The motto of this room comes from Lucretius: "There exist what we term images of things, which are to be called as it were their skin or bark, because the image bears a look and shape like the object, whatever it is, from whose body it is shed to go on its way."[1]

"O Rebecca"—that is the sound coming from the small horn. The listeners immediately recognize the voice. It belongs to the singer Malvina. The singing, however, does not come from Malvina's living body but from a small acoustic apparatus. In this apparatus, a golden needle follows the grooves inscribed in a wax tablet. Via a membrane and an acoustic horn, these grooves are transformed into pleasing sounds. The apparatus, however, is not simply a phonograph for recording and reproducing acoustic events. Lucius, both a gifted artist and a scientist of genius, has instead meticulously inscribed the grooves into the wax by hand: musical "groove-script" art, dated 1914.[2]

Lucius began by using an awl or graver, a tool usually employed to punch holes into leather or cardboard or to make final corrections to set type. With the help of this awl, *poinçon* in French, he applied markings to the wax. Using intense but precisely dosed rays of light that caused the surface of the wax to melt, he then connected the points thus marked to form a groove-like line.

Once inserted into the playing device, the remarkable result, according to the description in Roussel's *Locus Solus*, is a strikingly real-sounding human singing: "As the point moved over this rough path, it transmitted many vibrations to the membrane, and a woman's voice, resembling Malvina's, emerged from the horn and distinctly sang, on the correct notes: 'O Rebecca . . .'"[3]

Roussel's figure Lucius, however, is not just concerned with an exercise in virtuosity, in which the human actor (the engraving artist) performs the function of a nonhuman actor (the recording phonograph). As in Jules Verne—and Roussel's great respect for the author of *The Carpathian Castle* is well-known[4]—the artificial reproduction of the voice here has a soothing, if not magical, effect.

That is because the lengthened *a* at the end of the sung piece reminds Lucius of the first sounds emitted by his small daughter some time before she died in circumstances as violent as they were tragic. Lucius, driven into madness by the horrible event, has found refuge in Locus Solus, a park-like estate near Paris. The acoustic experience of the apparatus provokes a "salutary crisis."[5] The unexpected renewed encounter with his daughter's first uttering triggers in him the process of recovery.

Martial Canterel, owner and director of Locus Solus, is satisfied with this curious form of therapy. Its success confirms one of his rather unusual therapeutic principles, namely "to accede slavishly to the sick man's most extravagant wishes."[6] It exemplarily shows that machines can be "liberating," as Deleuze notes with regard to Roussel, that "they do not suppress difference"—the unique, the event-like, the decisive—but, to the contrary, confirm and "authenticate" it.[7] And, as we will see, it might not be a coincidence that the context in which this takes place is, in the widest sense, a psychiatric one.

Rebecca Horn has stressed how significant Raymond Roussel's oeuvre has been and continues to be for her artistic work.[8] She thereby inscribes herself in a partly Dadaistic, partly surrealist tradition that has regarded this writer as a kind of patron saint ever since Guillaume Apollinaire, Marcel Duchamp, and Francis Picabia saw his production of the stage version of

Impressions of Africa at the Théâtre Antoine. Besides Duchamp and Max Ernst, who even met Roussel once at the Galerie van Leer, Salvador Dalí, too, has emphasized the writer's importance for his work. Several paintings and texts as well as the TV movie *Impressions de la Haute Mongolie* are devoted to Dalí's explicit engagement with Roussel.[9]

Rebecca Horn underlines the significance of Roussel for her early works when she talks about having read and appreciated *Locus Solus*, especially at the time when, at the very beginning of her career, a lung infection caused by her work with toxic materials required a long hospital stay.[10] At first, of course, the differences between the two oeuvres stand out: there, the work of a writer, here, the work of an artist; there, an abounding imagination, here, precise constructions; there, a labor undertaken largely in isolation from all the currents of the avant-garde, here an entanglement in collective and performative events that allows the artist to position herself all the more clearly within contemporary art.[11] A closer look, prompted by one of Markus Raetz's Roussel etchings (fig. 1.1), however, reveals a number of things Roussel and Horn have in common.

There is, first, the theme of the closed space—in Roussel, the estate of *Locus Solus* or the "Trophy Square"[12] in *Impressions of Africa*, and in Horn, the New York apartment in *Der Eintänzer*, the Medici villa in *La Ferdinanda*, or the sanatorium in *Buster's Bedroom*; second, the motif of machinic assemblages—no more pure efficiency than pure ends-in-themselves, these assemblages in both artists emerge from the intermittent cooperation of heterogeneous elements that produce aesthetic effects; and third, the value, emphasized by both, of metamorphoses moving from art to nature, from language, image, and machine on the one hand to human being, animal, and plant on the other—in Roussel, for example, the worm who is both a wristband and a cither player, the magnetic plants and the images of water and smoke in *Impressions of Africa*,[13] and in Horn, the remarkable becoming-spider, -bird, and -snake of *Berlin Exercises*, the *Pfauenmaschine* (*Peacock Machine*), or the installations with black water and mercury.

Fourth, there is also the apparently smooth switching between genres (in Roussel, from writing to theater and film;[14] in Horn, from stories and drawings via objects and performances to Super 8 films, video, and site-specific installations); and finally, fifth, a mythologizing of their own persons, starting with their proper names (in Raymond Roussel, by means of, among other things, the assonance of Roussel and Rousseau, the splitting of the last name into *roue* ["spoke wheel" but also "peacock's fan"] and *sel* ["salt"], as well as the primordial duplication R–R, which is translated into a variety of polarities, including black/white, plus/minus, positive/negative, 1877/1933; in Horn, via numerous references to objects or entities designated as horns, for example in *Brusthorn* [*Breast Horn*] or *Schwarze Hörner* [lit., *Black Horns*, exhibited as *Shoulder Extensions*], as well as via the abundant use of horn as a material in her performances and installations, from *Haarmaske* [*Hair Mask*] via *Federinstrument* [*Feather Instrument*] and *Paradieswitwe* [*Paradise Widow*] to *Kuss der Nashörner* [*Kiss of the Rhinoceroses*]).

Given such convergences, it does not come as a surprise that Roussel—unlike, for example, Franz Kafka, Oscar Wilde, or James Joyce—does not count among the authors to whom Rebecca Horn has dedicated individual works (although the rumor persists that she has been planning a film about Roussel).[15] We are dealing with an affinity here that goes much deeper than any kind of explicit consideration or temporary influence. There is good reason to suppose that the connection with Roussel reaches down to the very foundations of her artistic work. Even the artist's origin narrative about her lung infection seems to recall an episode in *Impressions of Africa*. Roussel describes how in the course of her work on new imaging procedures, the chemist Louise Montalescot contracts a respiratory illness by breathing in "certain toxic gases."[16]

The convergences between Raymond Roussel and Rebecca Horn just sketched, which in a variety of ways shed light on the relationship between the sense of touch and media, provide an occasion to take another look at the artist's early work. Unlike art historical studies, which associate performances such as *Unicorn* (1970) or *Mit beiden Händen gleichzeitig die Wände berühren* (*Scratching Both Walls at Once*, 1974–75) with body art and video art,[17] I would like to direct our attention toward their connection with scientific contexts. The resonance between Rebecca Horn's early imagescapes and the iconography of the medical clinic has often been pointed out.[18] This chapter supplements such indications with references to experimental physiology and psychology as well as psychiatry.

Like a laboratory scientist, Rebecca Horn calls the objects used in her early works "instruments," and like one of the experimental physiologists par excellence, Claude Bernard, she deploys her instruments to *instruct* herself and others about life. At the same time, she designates the sphere at which the relevant performances and exercises are aimed as the domain of "interpersonal perception," thereby referring to Ronald D. Laing's cybernetically inspired (anti)psychiatry and Fritz Heider's psychology, which today is often read as a theory of media.

Both references contribute to gaining exemplary insights into the process of media-based experience and knowledge. These insights, not unlike what we see in Roussel, not only refer generally to the relation between body and art but concretely concern the relationship between communication and isolation, openness and limitation, freedom and imprisonment.

And indeed, Rebecca Horn's works of art have on occasion been described as "traps." In that they use certain instruments or things (rods, horns, fans) in certain situations to make certain media (light, air, etc.) perceptible, they do in fact capture their observers. Like the often-hypnotizing devices of the digital age, what becomes manifest in Rebecca Horn's increasingly complex installations is the insight that machines not only serve precisely circumscribed purposes but are always also institutions of confusion, astonishment, and cunning.[19]

Her early works, however, also show that art as a whole is based on strategies of capture and detainment in order to produce effects of a new kind in the first place. "Restraint can liberate you": this formula, coined by Rebecca Horn herself, applies to her own approach as much as to Raymond Roussel's famous procedure.

Trunk, Horn, Cone

One of Rebecca Horn's early works in particular supports the supposition of a profound connection with Roussel. The name of the piece, a contribution to a 1970 exhibition in Hamburg, is *Rüssel* (*Trunk*). The exhibition catalog contains a photograph that shows the artist from the front—standing upright, legs apart, arms to her side—wearing a fabric mask that covers her nose and mouth. The mask extends into a kind of hose that stretches along the body down to the floor and reaches about three meters forward (fig. 1.2).

The work's title, *Rüssel*, can be read as clearly hinting at the name "Roussel." At the same time, translated into French, *Rüssel* can also be read as *trompe*, which names not only the elephant's trunk but wind instruments such as the hunting horn. What the artist stages with the aid of her mask-object would then be but an object-oriented identification with Raymond Roussel that takes place on the individual-mythological level of proper names: (Rebecca) Horn—*Rüssel*—(Raymond) Roussel/trompe—(elephant) trunk/(hunting) horn.

Going one step further, we may say that *Rüssel* is a kind of reversal of the constellation in *Locus Solus*, where the sung "O Rebecca . . ." emanates from the small horn. The trunk-mask would then be a horn, and in the spot where sound usually comes out, we find, if not a singing-into, then at least the establishment of tactile contact with mouth and nose. The place of a name resounding is assumed by the body of a person who is in fact called Rebecca.

Practically in analogy with this reversal, there is a scene early in *Locus Solus* where a cat, submerged in a huge diamond receptacle filled with a special liquid called "aqua micans," sticks "its face firmly, up to its ears, into the metal horn [*cornet*]" in order to set off a subaquatic spectacle.[20]

The cat is completely "plucked" (*épilé*), and the ingestion of "bright red pills" (*pilules*) turns it into a "living electric battery" (*pile vivante*). When the cat, with the tip of the horn it is wearing, touches the prepared brain of the decapitated Danton, which is also floating in the diamond receptacle, the lip muscles attached to the specimen begin to move and utter "disjointed fragments of speech, full of vibrant patriotism"—a further example of Roussel's fantastic repetition machines.[21]

In Roussel, too, the horn thus becomes a mask, albeit one made of metal, not fabric. The significance Roussel assigned to these motifs is well known. As if seeking to underline the machinic character of his own verbal artwork, he takes them up, in modified form, at the end of *Locus Solus*. There, we not only meet the plucked cat (*chat épilé*) again in the figure of a rosary (*chapelet*), the horn (*cornet*), too, is produced once more, this time in the shape of a cone (*cône*), more precisely, of "two almost insubstantial cones of light" that take shape above an extremely flat clockwork disguised as a tarot card (fig. 1.3).[22]

We can hardly resist the temptation to compare this handy, glowing card device with one of today's portable touch screens. Yet unlike present-day smartphones and tablets, the light cones above the tarot card have the remarkable capacity to "painlessly" penetrate human body parts placed above them.[23] Canterel tries to use this means of producing cavities in "the form of a cone" to obtain "red globules" allegedly already described by Paracelsus, which in turn possibly correspond to the "bright red pills" used earlier in the novel to turn the cat into a battery . . .[24]

The horn thus becomes a cone—a form, incidentally, we also find time and again in the work of Rebecca Horn, who uses cones not only as containers for pigments (*A Rather Wild Flirtation*, *Missing Full Moon*) but also as acoustic horns (*The Turtle Sighing Tree*). In Roussel, the association of *cornet* and *cône*, moreover, refers to the narrator's activity (*conter*, *compter* [to tell or recount, to count]) and ultimately even rubs off on the name of the protagonist (Canterel).

Yet no matter how closed the linguistic system of *Locus Solus* might seem, the sliding of these allusions does not concern implicit references alone. The alignment of horn and cone can indeed also be understood as hinting at a model of memory we find in a philosopher whose work Roussel greatly admired.

In *Matter and Memory*, Henri Bergson famously introduces the image of a cone to illustrate his conception of the relationship between consciousness and memory. The drawing that accompanies his presentation seems to be purely geometric (fig. 1.4). But the explanations the text provides suggest that it might also be a simplified representation of a technical object: a scanning or writing device.

The world of the "central telephonic exchange" Bergson refers to early in the treatise to illustrate the retarding function of the brain,[25] in any case, was also a world of phonographs, kymographs, and sphygmographs. Both Roussel and Bergson were very much familiar with this world of graphic technologies—the former through his attentive reading of scientific magazines such as *La Nature*, the latter thanks to working, for a time, in experimental psychology labs.

It is certainly in keeping with the context of these technologies that Bergson uses a cone to represent the totality of recollections. In this model, the living presentness of the subject is marked by a "summit S" that "unceasingly . . . touches the moving plane P" while the base AB is "situated in the past."[26] As in Roussel, the fact of being alive is manifest at the tip of a cone that glides across a fixed or movable surface or touches down on it. The fact that Malvina's voice emanates "clearly" from the acoustic apparatus is due to the grooves Lucius artfully engraved into the wax with an awl, but it is also due to these grooves being scanned by a golden needle, while the cat touches the dura mater of Danton's brain with the tip of the metallic horn to bring Danton's head to life and thereby make the attached mouth speak.

Even if both of these are remarkably artificial forms of living presentness, the description of the memory cone in Bergson accords with both cases. In the cone, "the appeal to which memory responds" comes from the present of the "summit S."[27] Analogously, in Roussel's novel, Lucius receives an answer through the recollection of his dead daughter's first utterances, and the cat receives a response in the production of Danton's last speeches.

Seen this way, it is not just the cone moving on a geometric plane that, in Roussel, functions as a model for the connection between body, consciousness, and memory: the horn scanning or touching a surface does, too. Even the tarot card's cones of light that burrow into the skin fit into this model.

Extensions and Instruments

Rebecca Horn's 1970 work, *Rüssel*, however, is not limited to staging the connection with Roussel as such. Additionally and primarily, this work aims at exploring the possible ramifications of this association, its vectors, as it were, in the service of further artistic activity.

What comes to the fore in this context is the link between *trompe*, that is, "trunk" or "horn," and *tromper*, "to err" or "to deceive." Again and again Roussel in *Locus Solus* describes deceiving artifices. The most far-reaching example is Canterel's attempt at resurrecting corpses through chemical treatment to produce an absolute "illusion of life."[28] Moving through his park, however, we are repeatedly told about trompe l'œil, for example, with regard to a further detail of the aqua micans–filled giant diamond, where iron filings form words that become legible only "by an optical illusion depending on a series of winding cracks" or, at a later stop of the tour through the park, with regard to the Hotel de l'Europe whose windows, unlike the awning, are "merely painted in *trompe l'œil*."[29]

Nowhere in her work does Rebecca Horn aim for illusionistic painting. Rather, what has interested her since the beginning are the organic and material preconditions for illusions like painting to arise in the first place. Her early work in particular is characterized by an intense exploration of the transitions from body to art or, put differently, from skin to image.[30] Hence her pronounced interest in body painting, clothes, and various kinds of hair and feathers; hence also the early discussions of her works in terms of a "recuperation" and "return" of fashion and cosmetics to the domain of art.[31]

The text that accompanies *Rüssel* seems to point in the same direction: "Among certain South Sea islanders, we find a need for ornament that relates to the sexual organs in particular. This need, I feel it, too."[32] Remarkably, however, this does not simply make the sexual connotations of the elongated mask-object (the trunk as phallus, etc.) explicit. Slightly offset from such connotations, this short statement evokes anthropological, ethnographic, and psychoanalytic discourses that had been inquiring into the origins of art since the turn of the century.

Concretely, we may think of a treatise by Ernst Grosse published in 1894, which conceives of cosmetics as a preliminary stage of ornamentation and art and explicitly describes "primitive body painting" as ornament, not as clothing or cover,[33] or of Eckart von Sydow's 1927 study *Primitive Art and Psychoanalysis*, which thematizes the emergence of art in its autoerotic application to the figure of the body. In this connection, Sydow observes, among other things, how "pushing the need for ornamentation forward, from painting and tattooing" creates its own "domain of ornamental decoration."[34]

Just how much Rebecca Horn's early works are centered on the question of the beginnings of art becomes clear in the 1971 film *Körperfarbe* (*Body Painting*), which documents painting performances in which paint is applied directly onto naked skin. The comment on *Rüssel* specifies this interest since it articulates a concrete and, if you like, feminist counterposition to the thesis defended by traditional South Sea anthropologists that in the art of that region, "woman herself and everything that could recall her sex . . . is completely absent."[35] Rebecca Horn's short text explicitly points to the female sex and, together with the pictured mask-object, suggests that in fact, it is women who stand at the beginnings of art.

A closer look at *Rüssel* shows that this mask-object sheds light on the transition from body to art in yet another way. Anatomically, the elephant's trunk is nothing but an *extension* of the nose, and Rebecca Horn often uses the term "extension" to describe her early works. Physiologically, however, this extension refers not only to the sense of smell but to the sense of touch as well. In fact, the trunk is above all a tool for touching and grasping (a point emphasized by the way the mask bearer's arms are hanging down at her side, as if unconcerned), and there has been no shortage of attempts to turn the enormous versatility of this combined sensing and grasping organ into the objective reason for elephants' proverbial wisdom.[36]

The combination of these two aspects—extension and tactility—turns *Rüssel* into a particularly succinct statement of the program that animates Rebecca Horn's artistic work, at least in the years 1968–72. Most of the works dating from this period can indeed be understood primarily as tactile extensions.

Some of these works suggest as much in their very titles, such as *Arm-Extensionen* (*Arm Extensions*, 1968) and *Kopf-Extension* (*Head Extension*, 1972). Others do so more obliquely, such as *Bewegliche Schulterstäbe* (1971), whose title is rendered in English as *Movable Shoulder-Extensions*, or *Handschuhfinger* (*Finger Gloves*, 1972), described in the English caption as an "instrument to extend the manual sensibility" (fig. 1.5).[37] In terms of subject matter, however, other works such as *Überströmer* (*Overflowing Blood Machine*) and *Messkasten* (*Measure Box*, both 1970), too, can be understood as representations of body extensions, the former, for example, as externalizing blood circulation, the latter as objectifying and multiplying the hand.

It is unclear whether in her choice of the term Rebecca Horn picks up on McLuhan, who defined media, insofar as they are technical objects, as "extensions of man" (and who in turn picked up a figure of thought very much present in discourse since Ernst Kapp, Sigmund Freud, and Henri Bergson).[38] If this were the case, then her early works would be media art not only in the sense that the artist early on was working with Super 8 and video film to document her performances. They would be media art already because the objects they create (masks, gloves, horns, etc.) are themselves to be regarded as rudimentary or archaic bodily media—as media in the making.

However, this is not the only terminology Rebecca Horn uses to describe the objects she fabricates. Even more frequently than "extensions," she uses the term "instruments." She is thus going back before McLuhan and even Kapp, namely to the already mentioned physiologist Claude Bernard. For Bernard and other mid-nineteenth-century laboratory scientists, it was self-evident that the capacities of human sense organs were insufficient and therefore had to be amplified by scientific instruments. In this sense, at the very beginning of his 1865 *Introduction to the Study of Experimental Medicine*, he writes, "Only within very narrow boundaries can man observe the phenomena which surround him. . . . To extend his knowledge, he has had to increase the power of his organs by means of special appliances; at the same time he has equipped himself with various instruments enabling him to penetrate inside of bodies, to dissociate them and to study their hidden parts."[39] As we will see in greater detail later, it is possible, time and again, to make connections between the iconography of the experimental life sciences and the works of Rebecca Horn. On occasion, the artist herself even speaks of "performance experiments [*Aktions-Experimente*],"[40] and, like Bernard's experiments, these performances are concerned not merely with *showing* but with *instructing* herself and the participants as to the perceptions that become possible in specific constellations.[41] "Instruments" would thus have to be understood to mean not just tools but, in a strong sense, means of instruction through the senses.

What the instruments developed by Rebecca Horn all share is that they attach directly to the surface of the body. In that respect, they have a natural model in the formation of keratinous horn as we observe it in the growth of a fingernail or a feather. This is another reason why it does not come as a surprise that the point of convergence of the early works is an exploration of the sense of touch. In the already mentioned *Finger Gloves*, whose leverage intensifies the various "sense-data of the hand," this is openly manifest, as it is in *Federfinger* (*Feather Fingers*), where the installation of individual goose feathers on the fingers turns the hand into a "living instrument" of a new kind.[42]

The sense of touch also plays a central role in *Scratching Both Walls at Once*, where the tubular finger extensions are used to scan the walls of a room. Other instruments and performances of this creative period, too, have a tactile orientation, for example the already mentioned *Arm Extensions*, where the arms of the actor are extended down to the floor to touch it, or the *Head Extension* (fig. 1.6), in which both eyes of the actor are covered thus that he can "advance only by slowly feeling his way"[43]—resembling the physiologist Bernard, whose advance in knowledge takes place only through "groping experiments."[44]

A Cybernetic Ontology

Yet even here, in the overarching tendency quite literally to tie the production of art back to the surface of the body, we see a reprise of a leitmotif of Roussel's. Even if many of Roussel's machines aim at replacing the human hand (of the artist, of the musician), that is, at avoiding bodily touch where possible,[45] *Locus Solus* praises the skin as a "clairvoyant entity," and long stretches of the novel develop themes and motifs that shed light on the specific form of *its* art, the act of writing, with regard to its pertinent surfaces.[46]

The virtuosity of Lucius, who with his awl is able to draw tracks into the wax that in being played by an acoustic apparatus turn out to be recordings of song, is only one example. In *Locus Solus*, we also find writing being done directly *on* or *into* human skin. Toward the end of the novel, a poet named Lelutour beats the underarms of a boy named Luc with a bunch of nettles. Soon, "red blotches" appear on Luc's skin that turn out to be decipherable capital letters. Elsewhere, we find a description of how an "internal stellar monogram in dark grey," which is subject to a mysterious attraction to the North, is tattooed with magnetic needles onto the neck of a medieval hero.[47]

Roussel does not leave it at these extravagant "text-bearer[s]."[48] On the one hand, he lays out an entire spectrum of the most varied writing surfaces, which stretches from bones and wax via slate tablets, silk, parchment, and paper to metal and gold plates. On the other hand, in describing the various stops of the tour through the park, he introduces several other skin-related surface materials to explain the aesthetic effects of Canterel's machinic assemblages—for example, fingernails that are combined with tinfoil to become brilliant mirrors, or hair that, like the strings of an instrument, is made to vibrate and produce music.[49] The cone-shaped cavities drilled into the skin in the final chapter by the optical and aerial effect of the tarot cards to obtain explosive globules belong in this context as well.[50]

These are the kinds of descriptions that Rebecca Horn takes up when she ties the production of art back to the surface of the living body. This does not happen without discontinuities, though. Roussel does not speak of extensions and, bar some short passages, pays no attention to the human sense of touch. His machines, moreover, remain fictitious, objects of literature, whereas Rebecca Horn is working with factual instruments made of wood, fabric, and other materials.

That might be the reason why, time and again, her early works seem like excerpts or snapshots of the complex assemblages described in *Locus Solus*. Even "object-machines" like *Overflowing Blood Machine* are situated outside the extreme dimensions typical of Roussel's machines. Whereas these latter oscillate with almost no restrictions between micro- and macrocosm, Rebecca Horn's instruments and objects are practically all midsize objects. Unlike later works, they also refrain from using any kind of electromagnetic or chemical effects, which play a decisive role in *Locus Solus*. On the whole, Rebecca Horn's early machines are also significantly less heterogeneously composed than Roussel's machines.

Yet it is just these limitations that inversely allow the artist to contextualize her instruments and performances in an even more radical way than Roussel does. While Roussel is working with a language that represents a comparatively anonymous and atemporal space, Rebecca Horn in her performances employs specific people (actors) that act with the objects she has fabricated in a precisely circumscribed landscape and often at precisely defined times of the day.

Roussel, to be sure, also linked his machinic assemblages with external factors like the weather (the floating demoiselle in *Locus Solus*, the thunderstorm and Jizme's bed in *Impressions of Africa*). Yet Rebecca Horn has the components of the *inner* milieu of her performances enter into so intensive an interaction with each other that the interactions with the outer milieu of these performances multiply as well. The transition from body to art thus becomes a collective "intra-active" process that is simultaneously irreversible and open-ended.[51] We are indeed dealing with "performance experiments."

This is also due to the fact that Rebecca Horn in the late 1960s had access to a program that was out of reach for Roussel. Her works, to put it succinctly, feature specific aspects of *cybernetics*—provided that for once, we do not mean by that term the science of "command and control" instituted by Norbert Wiener but the tradition of a performative, nonmodern ontology that developed in the postwar years, particularly in Great Britain.[52]

It is in fact possible that during her stay in London in 1971–72, the artist became familiar with the work of the (anti)psychiatrist Ronald D. Laing, who was inspired by, among others, Gregory Bateson. As early as the mid-1960s, Laing had given lectures at the Institute of Contemporary Art in London, and in his already popular books he had associated the experience of psychosis with the becoming-creative of artists.

In *Politics of Experience*, for example, Laing describes the psychotic phase of the sculptor Jesse Watkins, which, besides extraordinary creativity, also included the extraordinary experience of becoming a rhinoceros. In the early 1970s, moreover, a former patient of Laing's had published an autobiographical report. There, Mary Barnes describes how, via a *Journey through Madness*, she had found her way to art.[53]

In 1972, in the context of the legendary *documenta 5* organized by Harald Szeemann, Rebecca Horn points to her links with this kind of cybernetics when she says about her artistic activity that "experiences in the domain of interpersonal perception are the basis of my work."[54] This statement is at least an implicit reference to Laing, who coined the concept of interpersonal perception. Laing no longer sought to describe perceptions as simple, somehow direct, psychological phenomena that as if by themselves arise between a freestanding subject and the world of objects it confronts. Instead, he tried to conceive of them as constructions of a complex and, in the widest sense, social process.

Simply speaking, Laing relates the perceptions a self has of another person's behavior to the perception this other person has of the behavior of the self. Picking up on Bateson's studies on the circular causality of communication, Laing inserts the perception of the self in a feedback relation with the perception of the other.

In his book *Interpersonal Perception*, Laing explains his basic concept as follows: "I may not actually be able to see myself as others see me, but I am constantly supposing them to be seeing me in particular ways, and I am constantly acting in the light of the actual or supposed attitudes, opinions, needs, and so on the other has in respect of me."[55]

It is these feedback aspects of perception that Rebecca Horn explores in her performances with the instruments she has constructed. The fundamental principle of these experimental performances is that "each performance has a central figure, who functions as a starting point and the goal of all activities. The instrument the central figure wears provides a means of communication among the participants."[56] The process of perception is tied to this reciprocal medial communication.

Interperceptions

This principle is realized in exemplary fashion in what may well be the best known of her early works. The title of the twelve-minute Super 8 film from 1970 documenting the eponymous performance is *Einhorn* (*Unicorn*). This title, first, emphasizes the connection with the artist's individual mythology. It also suggests that the work is a variation on the old theme of the elusive mythical creature. The film's rudimentary plot indeed presents the sudden appearance of a unicorn on a forest path, its wandering about in a field of grain, and its equally sudden disappearance. Yet the suggestion does not last. It quickly turns out that the unicorn is staged here not as a fairy-tale figure but as a hybrid entity composed of human and nonhuman components (fig. 1.7)—half woman, half instrument, almost a mythological cyborg goddess in Haraway's sense.[57]

This characterization is warranted in that the actor entering into the movement-image becomes a unicorn thanks to a rod-shaped "extension" being fastened to her head with white bandages. This extension appears as an antenna in a double sense: technologically, as a device for sending and receiving signals; biologically, as a body part for scanning and feeling out one's surroundings. Accordingly, the entry of the unicorn no longer evokes the traditional ideas of the elusive, the good, or virginity. Rebecca Horn's unicorn instead stands for the concrete connection—which Rainer Maria

Rilke did much to introduce into the modern imaginary—between the mythical creature and the sense of touch. One is tempted to say that by joining body and technics, the hybrid entity at the center of this filmed performance condenses and updates the well-known medieval depiction in which the Dame à la licorne touches the unicorn's horn with her hand (fig. 1.8).[58]

In the accompanying text, the artist explains that the "instrument" in this performance consists of wood. The purpose of this instrument, she writes in terminology reminiscent of 1920s media art, is to "enhance" the actor's walk.[59] Her way of walking is characterized, it is suggested, by the knowledge "Angelika" seems to have of how in walking, one uses "exclusively the legs" while the rest of the body is "frozen."[60] This implicit knowledge is made perceptible by the feedback of the specially made instrument, in two respects.

On the one hand, the artist, by fitting and testing the instrument together with the actor, that is, by finding the "right proportions, body weights and object heights," makes the actor aware of the particularity of her walking movements. In this sense, the rod on her head, the artificial horn, changes the perception of its wearer. At the same time, the perceptions the other participants in the performance (the artist, the camera operator, etc.) have of "Angelika" are thereby transformed, and these perceptions in turn have an—interpersonal—effect on the actor.

On the other hand, the rod-shaped object in the film serves to guide the observer's attention toward the particularities of the walking movements. This happens especially in that on several occasions the white horn makes the body's up-and-down movements in the walking process, which usually are barely perceptible, visible against a black background, against the shadows on the forest path as well as against the dark forest on the edge of the field of grain (fig. 1.9).

The production of this effect can be compared to a procedure applied already in the classic studies of movement carried out by experimental physiologist Etienne-Jules Marey in the late nineteenth century. In Marey's work, too, test subjects wore light-colored hats or white rods attached to their backs such that, as they were walking along a black background, they left clear marks on the chronophotographic plates (fig. 1.10). On the basis of such recordings, other physiologists constructed models of human walking movements that brought out the up-and-down movements of the body by way of head rods (fig. 1.11). In a similar way, the head extension of Rebecca Horn's *Unicorn* "enhances" the perception of the observer.

The targeted deployment of feedback to intensify perception is evident in other works with body extensions as well. Thanks to the inversely curved double horn of *Cornucopia*, which links mouth and breasts, "one's perception expands triangularly," that is, it is subjected to an extension in order to experience one's own body in a new way (fig. 1.12).[61] The performance *Finger Gloves* concretely applies this procedure to the domain of the tactile. Long, lightweight wooden tubes are affixed to the fingers such that thanks to a "new modal practice," the flexibility of the hands can be perceived: "I feel me touching, I see me grasping, I control the distance between me and the objects."[62] Interpersonal perception here becomes a combination of a person's different sense modalities. It acquires a synesthetic quality.

In the exercise *Scratching Both Walls at Once* (fig. 1.13), finger extensions are used to scan a room from the inside. Here, the sense of touch enhanced by leverage is not only being *watched*, it is equally being *listened to*. As the sound film makes clear, the finger gloves moving along the walls produce an acoustic scratching that, together with the walking sounds produced by the actor's shoe heels (extensions of her feet) on the wooden floor, opens up the room in question on this additional register of sense perception. Here, too, interpersonal perception transitions to intermodal perception, to interperception.

This background explains why the artist, in the statements that accompany her early works, does not speak merely in a general way of sensations and representations or of wishes, projections, and identifications associated with the instruments she built.[63] Much more specifically, namely in terminology reminiscent of Laing (and Bateson), she addresses in this context "experiential fields," "new models of interaction rituals," and a sense of "initiation."[64] Indeed, Bateson spoke of "initiation ceremonies" even earlier than Laing to describe the appropriate therapeutic response to the psychotic experience.[65]

Laing's terminology can, however, shed light on some further aspects of Rebecca Horn's early works. The idea, for instance, that "personal experience transforms" one's surroundings "into a field of intention and action"[66] can serve to describe the particular form of experience to which Rebecca Horn's "personal art" is to give shape. Similarly, Laing's insistence that "the 'inner'" is nothing but "our personal idiom of experiencing our bodies, other people, the animate and inanimate world"[67] offers an explanation of the artist working with instruments of her own making. And, to give one last example, his assertion, "My experience is not inside my head.

My experience of this room is out there in the room,"[68] describes the particular attention Rebecca Horn devoted to her studio apartments in Berlin and New York or, in *La Ferdinanda* (1981), to a Medici villa.

A media theory perspective on this alignment can benefit from a closer look at another pioneer of interpersonal psychology cited repeatedly by Laing. In his comprehensive *Psychology of Interpersonal Relations*, Fritz Heider returns to the distinction between "thing" and "mediation" he had made in an influential article in the 1920s.[69]

In the 1958 book, Heider states once again that things are to be conceived of as "real solid objects with properties of shape and color, . . . placed in particular positions in real space."[70] Mediations, on the other hand, are the patterns of light or sound waves that we usually do not perceive as such but which make the perception of things possible for us in the first place.[71]

Transposed into this terminology, we might say that in her artistic work, Rebecca Horn employs *things* to make the experience of *mediations* (or *media*) possible. The wooden rod in *Unicorn*, for example, draws attention to light conditions and body movements; the *Körperfächer* (*White Body Fan*) depicts the wind accompanying the performance; and the tubular finger extensions of *Scratching Both Walls at Once* bring out the particular acoustics of the room in which the exercise takes place.

This also sheds additional light on the role of the sense of touch. Rebecca Horn takes this sense as her starting point because, like that of taste, the sense of touch, according to Heider, makes do with a minimum of mediation.[72] It is for that reason that it allows for opening up the other modalities of sense from the ground up.

Heider's perspective even yields a better understanding of the particular way this art works: as in the reversible figures of Gestalt psychology, the sudden "tipping over" of a focus plays a central role, from the level of things to the level of media. In this respect, Rebecca Horn's media art is concerned not only with enhancing perception by means of extensions of the body; it aims at *perceiving perception*.[73]

This, precisely, marks her art as eminently cybernetic, and it may not be an exaggeration to see it as an implementation of the kind of innovative open-ended practice of reciprocal performative adaptation of persons and things (and media) that, according to Andrew Pickering, Laing precisely did *not* achieve in his experimental treatment of schizophrenics at Kingsley Hall. For Pickering, Laing did indeed act more in tune with British cybernetics in that he—unlike, for example, Grey Walter and Ross Ashby—was fully devoted to the ideals of "symmetric, open-ended, and reciprocal interaction." Yet insofar as, for him, "interaction" referred almost exclusively to the cooperation of human actors, he remained far behind Walter and Ashby, whose work included technical objects as well.[74]

Productive Obstructions

In her cybernetic experiments, however, Rebecca Horn explores not only *movements* of the body, the head, the hands. As *Unicorn* intimates, these experiments also include the body's motionlessness, from fixed postures (the "frozen"-ness of the walking) via arbitrary obstruction to forced detention. The feedback strategies thus continue in a kind of dialectic: the sense of touch is now seen not only as active messenger of touching but also as passive subject of protection and isolation.

To be sure, the extensions lead from the body to art because they stand for an enlargement of expressive movements and an expansion of the process of perception. Yet at the same time, they allow for a practice of fixation and stopping that characterizes this art just as much.

This point is illustrated particularly well by *Arm Extensions* (fig. 1.14). The body, legs, and arms of the actor in this performance are tied up crosswise with red bandages. This already constitutes a first level of extension, on the one hand insofar as the bandages enlarge the actor's skin, on the other, and especially, insofar as the bandages, usually meant to stop bleeding, are as if soaked in blood. Their color is red, not white. They bring the inside of the body to the outside.

The particular form of this extension—the bandaging—immobilizes the actor "like a mummy." She is unable to walk, barely able to lean forward or back. Moreover, her arms, too, are stuck in "big wadded stumps" of red bandages reaching down to the floor.[75]

This is the second aspect of the extension. The wadded stumps extend the arms of the actor like crutches or canes. But instead of helping her regain movement, as crutches do for patients, they constitute a real obstacle for the actor: "all movements become impossible for her."[76]

The *Arm Extensions* thus reverse an essential achievement of walking upright, namely the free movement of the arms and hands. At most, the arms here can serve as "balance-pillars" for the tied-up body.[77] Yet, inversely, this is precisely where their tactile potential lies. Because the arms touch the floor, they can explore a surface that usually serves only to be stood on and as such is usually barely perceived. The obstruction, arbitrarily posited and accepted, opens up new experiences.

The *Overflowing Blood Machine* (fig. 1.15), too, uses an extension of the body to stage a figure of motionlessness. Here, however, it is not a circumscribed limb that is extended or enlarged, nor does the sense of touch play a decisive role. This "object machine" instead moves the entire system of blood circulation from the inside of the body to the outside.[78] It confines the actor in a cage formed by transparent tubes in which a red liquid is circulating.

Again, this is but the first aspect of the extension. Not unlike *Arm Extension*, what emerges here might literally be called a *Blutbild*, or hemogram. This is the second extending aspect: the "pulsating garment of veins" renders the circulation of the blood visible on the body.[79]

This new kind of image, however, is contingent once more on an arrest, a fixation. The *Overflowing Blood Machine* is at the same time an *overpowering* machine. It "forces . . . the motionless person" into its continual functioning, takes him captive, arrests him as in a cage.[80]

Incidentally, this work, too, goes back to the iconography of nineteenth-century biomedical science. In the 1880s, cooling bonnets and blankets made of rubber tubes were being sold as medical devices. They covered and fixated the head and the entire body in a way similar to *Overflowing Blood Machine* (fig. 1.16).

The third and, from today's perspective, most telling example from this early series is the *Measure Box* (fig. 1.17). It stages a situation of constraint similar to that of *Overflowing Blood Machine*. At the same time, the title suggests a kinship with the methods of nineteenth-century anthropometry, which scanned and measured the human body with a plethora of instruments.[81]

In *Measure Box*, the actress is locked into an upright, rectangular metal frame. Between its vertical braces, a larger number of silver metal rods have been mounted horizontally at regular intervals. These rods can be understood as, simultaneously, objectification and multiplication of groping fingers (first aspect of the extension). They have pistil-shaped, flattened ends and can be pushed back and forth within the frame with great precision.

Once the actress is standing inside the frame, the rods are used to fix the outlines of her body starting from the four corners. Whereas Pliny famously attributed the emergence of painting to the tracing of a shadow on the wall, *Measure Box* suggests another genealogy of art. It allows for *externalizing* the silhouette of the body in a particular position of the rods, which here, however, amounts to both depicting and measuring (second aspect of the extension). The presence of art is already the presence of science—and vice versa.

In the same movement, however, the counterside of media comes to the fore. The actress is arrested inside the frame. This renders the idea, as Laing once remarked, that what scientists usually call *data* ought to be called *capta*, perceptible in a particularly concise way.[82] The given, on this view, is also always the captured, the arrested. Measuring rods, to put it briefly, also always function as prison bars. Or: measurements are not reducible to the objective collection of "mere" data; they are always the result of a preceding capturing and arrest of phenomena.

Yet even here, another turn is possible. In Rebecca Horn, this locking in is not an ultimate dead end, not a detention without exit. It also marks an apex of concentration, a point of rest and protection for a renewed departure to new performances, new communications, new perceptions and interperceptions. This is what works like *White Body Fan* or *Die sanfte Gefangene* (*The Feathered Prison Fan*) suggest, and the *Kakadu-Maske* (*Cockatoo Mask*) shows it quite clearly (fig. 1.18).

This mask completely covers the artist's face with two interlocking, closed wings of white feathers. Someone standing before it, however, can separate the interlocking feathers, opening the mask, stick their own head in, and touch the artist's scalp: "The feather-enclosure isolates our heads from the surrounding environment, and forces us to remain intimately alone, together."[83] The extensions here appear no longer as a prison but as a protective space that makes a new commonality of touching, communication, and art possible.

Restraint and Liberation

Looking back at her works from the 1970s, Rebecca Horn has emphasized the aspect of insulation, of tactile protection. In conversation with Germano Clement, the artist explains, "Looking back at my first pieces, you always see a kind of cocoon, which I used to protect myself." By way of example, she goes back to the fans, in which she could isolate and lock herself but that could also be opened again to include other people in intimate rituals: "This intimacy of feeling and communication was a central part of the performances."[84]

This emphasis can be understood as a renewed return to Roussel, via the detour of cybernetics as it were, since almost all figures in his novels are captives at least for a while. This is true of the living dead housed in the cooled glass case of *Locus Solus*, and it is true of the shipwrecked in *Impressions of Africa* whom King Talou has in his power. It is true of Lucius who, gone mad, lives in Locus Solus, and it is true of Naïr who, fallen out of favor with Talou, is fettered to a pedestal as a living statue and condemned to fabricate fetters for others.

Even if not all these captives succeed in liberating themselves, they do create astonishing spaces of sensation and communication. Lucius succeeds in drawing grooves into a wax tablet by means of an awl and rays of light, grooves that an acoustic apparatus turns into healing song. Naïr obtains from fruit rinds, which look like insect cocoons, very fine threads from which on his loom he weaves mosquito nets, regulating his complicated work with voicelessly recited sentences. Looked at from this perspective, Roussel's machines, too, serve to insulate and protect.

Long before there were sensors, trackers, and tracers, Raymond Roussel and Rebecca Horn thus thematize what I have called media's sense of touch. Roussel thinks up a multitude of machinic arrangements that take over human activities of touching—from the mechanical tarot card in *Locus Solus*, whose cones of lights are burrowing into the skin, all the way to the remarkable painting machine in *Impressions of Africa* that turns light signals into splashes of color.

Rebecca Horn follows in his footsteps when in her early objects and performances she explores not only the activity but also the passivity of the sense of touch, the ambulatory openness of *Unicorn* as much as the closure and fixation of *Measure Box*. The kinetic sculptures she went on to build materialize a multitude of machinic touchings: spoons strike against one another, shoes step on the ground, and rhinoceros horns clash (*To Sleep as Little Spoons, American Waltz, Kiss of the Rhinoceroses*).

These literary and artistic depictions of tactile agency obviously do not aim to engage with the "(media-)technological a priori" of the present day. Raymond Roussel and Rebecca Horn, in fact, have no concept of such an a priori. Their engagement with media's sense of touch instead derives from a largely autonomous and open-ended process firmly anchored in the a posteriori, a process in which body and art, people and things, humans and machines reciprocally and performatively refer to each other to produce experiences of the new.

This is exactly the process to which Deleuze refers when he says that Roussel's machinic assemblages experience and authenticate difference. And it is on just this process that Rebecca Horn's "performance-experiments" are based, which present us with the vital use, the aesthetic benefit, and the downright therapeutic effect of dealing with technical objects. László Moholy-Nagy coined the formula, "Not against technics [*technik*] but with it."[85] Both, the writer as much as the artist, are devoted to this classical motto of a media art aiming at life.

From this perspective, today's media moving in on us does not appear as a hostile act per se. Rather, this closing in is, first of all, a reminder, however distorted, of the fact that media are nothing but literal extensions of the human body. Their genesis—as both Raymond Roussel and Rebecca Horn presuppose—is tied back to the skin. From this point of view, smartphones and tablets are not *essentially* different from wristwatches and glasses or clothes and makeup.

This shifts theory's focus of attention. The question of media becomes the question of their use. In fact, the use made of a specific machine or a specific instrument in a concrete situation is as central to the writer as it is to the artist. It is its use that decides whether a given activity acts to restrain or to liberate—or indeed whether the actors make their way to liberation through restraint.

Michel Foucault has said of Roussel's machines that they "are, in a way that is more or less clear, not only a repetition of hidden syllables . . . but also an image of the process itself."[86] A look at the labor of the captives and prisoners in *Locus Solus* and *Impressions of Africa* confirms this point. Like Roussel himself, Lucius, Naïr, and all the others do not simply follow their fancy or imagination. Rather, they subject themselves to a specific rule, and this obedience leads them to a different and possibly greater freedom. Indeed, in Roussel, ritualization and formalization most often signify an opening and a way out.

Yet Rebecca Horn in her early works can hardly be said to follow a different path. While she voicelessly recites the myth of her proper name, she interweaves the arbitrary encounter of an actor and an instrument, a person and a thing, to explore the perceptual effects that result from this encounter within a given group or with regard to a certain environment. By means of original machinic assemblages, in which horns, cones, and tips time and again encounter surfaces, both the writer and the artist restrain their creativity to proceed in an all the more autonomous way from the body to art. They capture the unicorn. But that, precisely, enhances their powers of imagination.

Both, we may conclude, follow the already-cited advice of the snake psychiatrist in *Buster's Bedroom*: "You probably think of restraint as a loss of freedom. But if you take that notion and turn it inside-out, upside-down, restraint can liberate you."[87] Accordingly, the way out of a sensor society can never be found against technology, only ever with it.

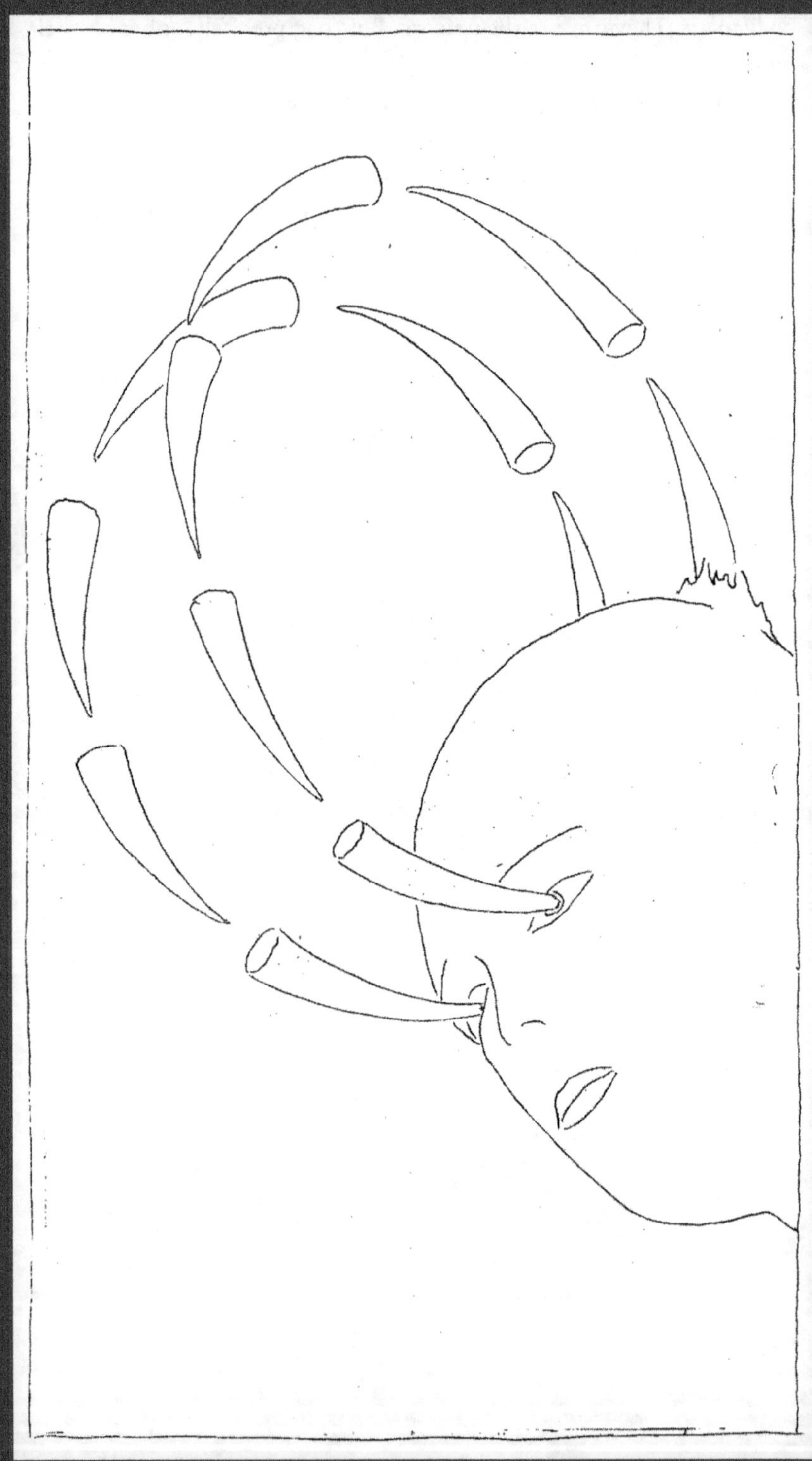

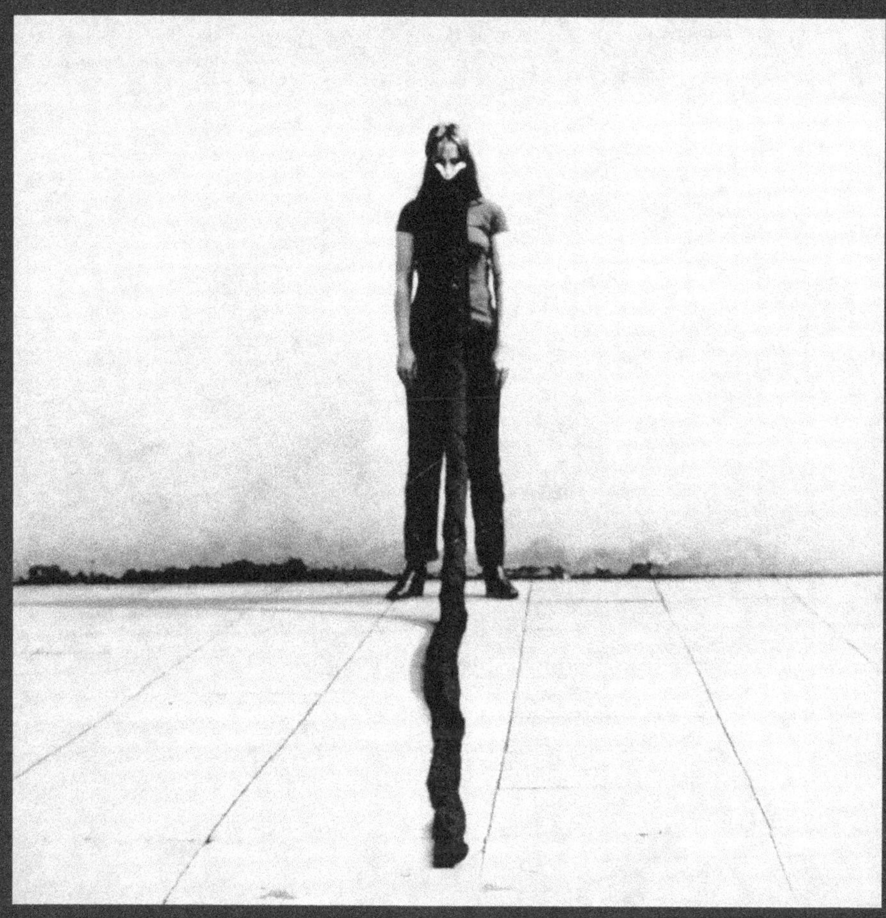

FIGURE 1.1
Markus Raetz, *Ohne Titel* (1980). Etching for Raymond Roussel, *Impressions of Africa*. © VG Bild-Kunst, Bonn 2020.

FIGURE 1.2
Rebecca Horn, *Rüssel* (1970). © VG Bild-Kunst, Bonn 2020.

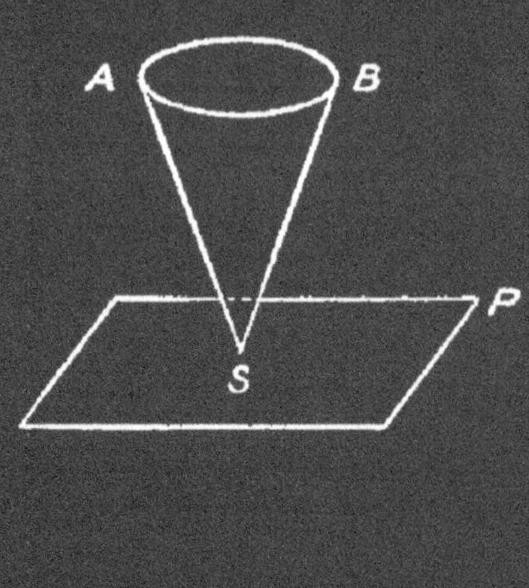

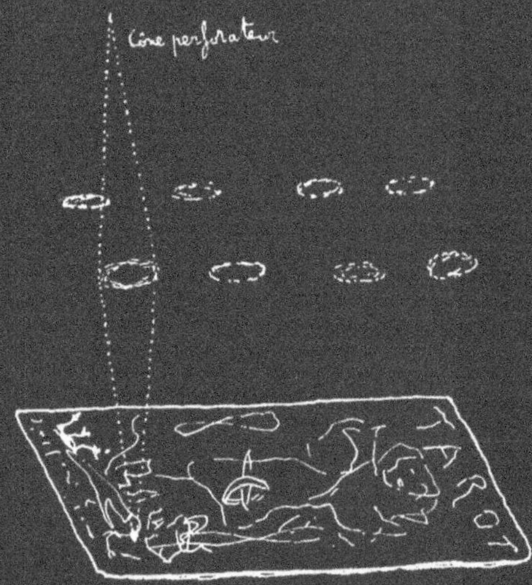

FIGURE 1.3

Jean Ferry, one of the double light cones above the tarot card (1960). Drawing for Raymond Roussel, *Locus Solus*.

FIGURE 1.4

Henri Bergson, the cone model from *Matter and Memory* (1896).

FIGURE 1.5

Rebecca Horn, *Handschuhfinger, ein Instrument zur Erweiterung der manuellen Sensibilität* (1972).

FIGURE 1.6

Rebecca Horn, *Kopf-Extension* (1972).

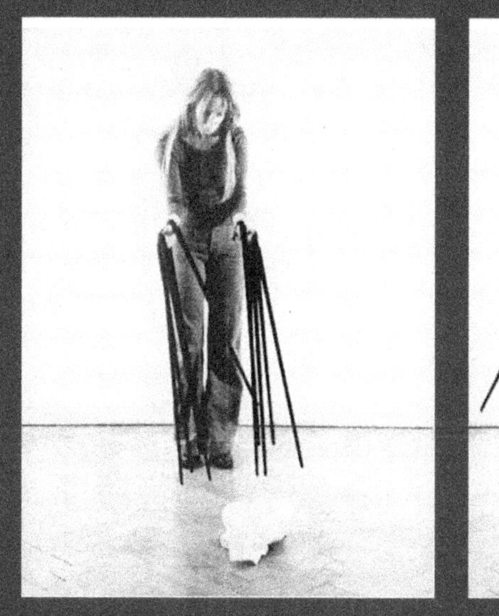

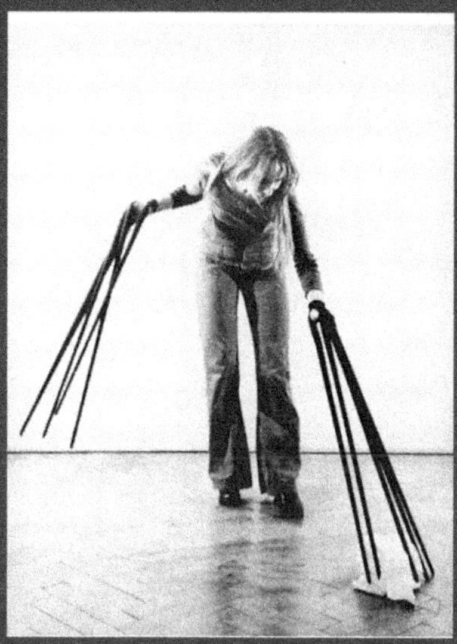

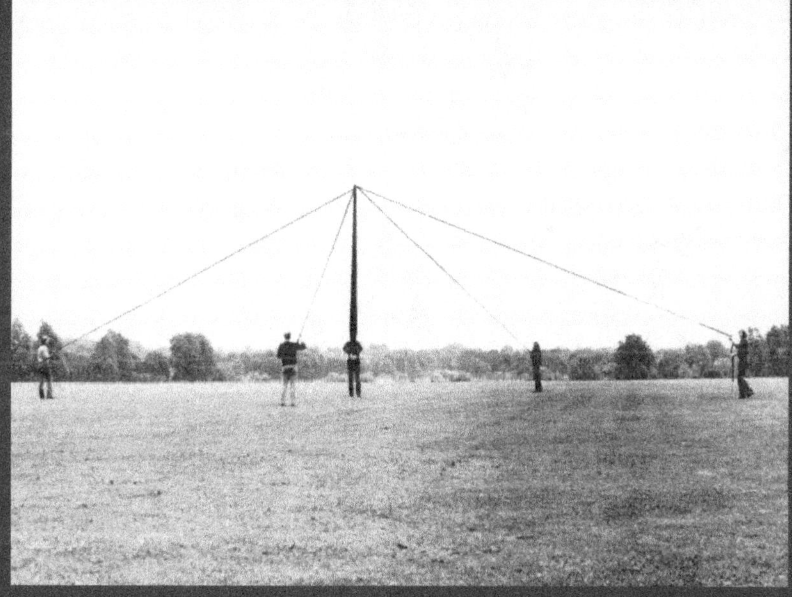

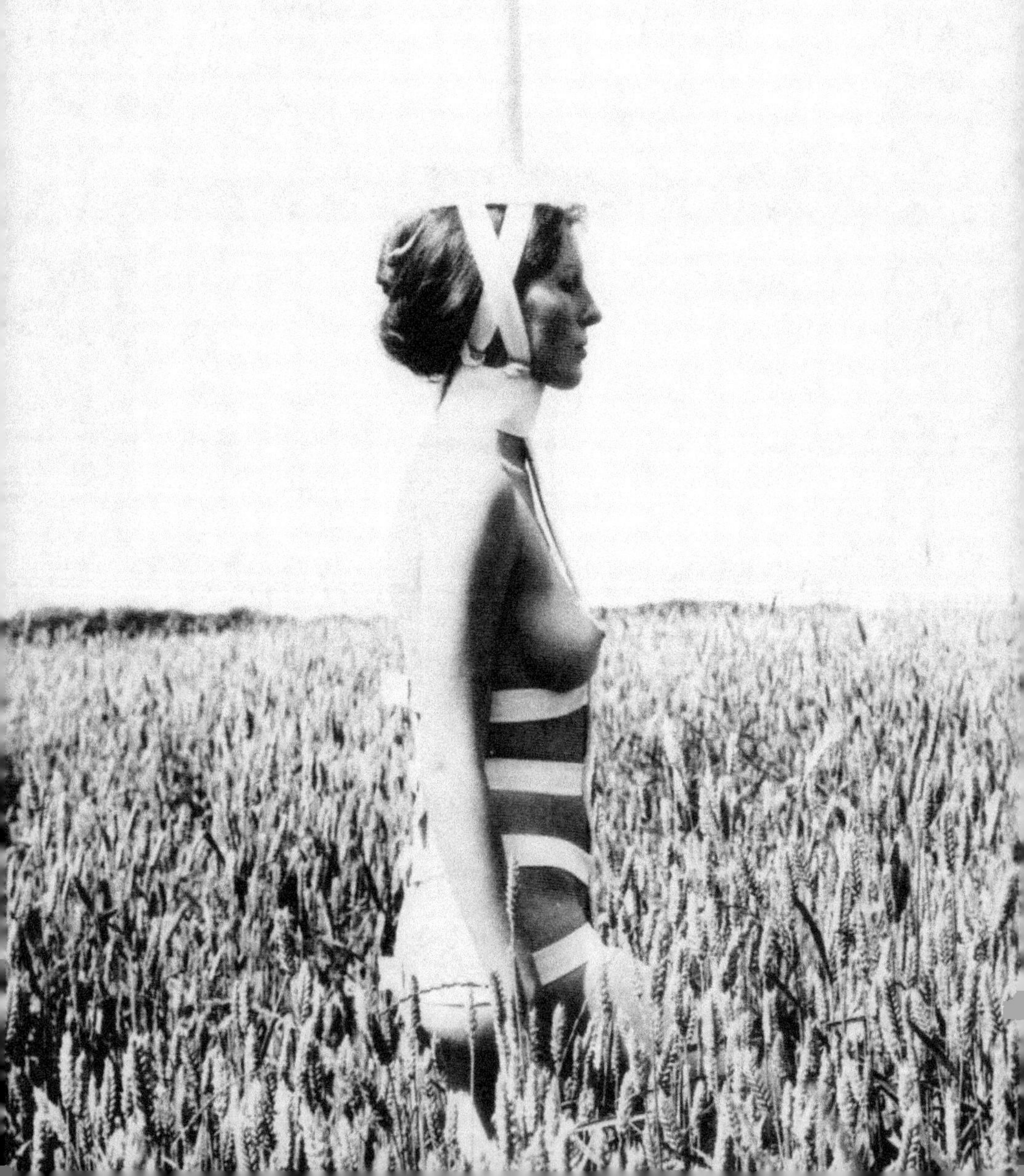

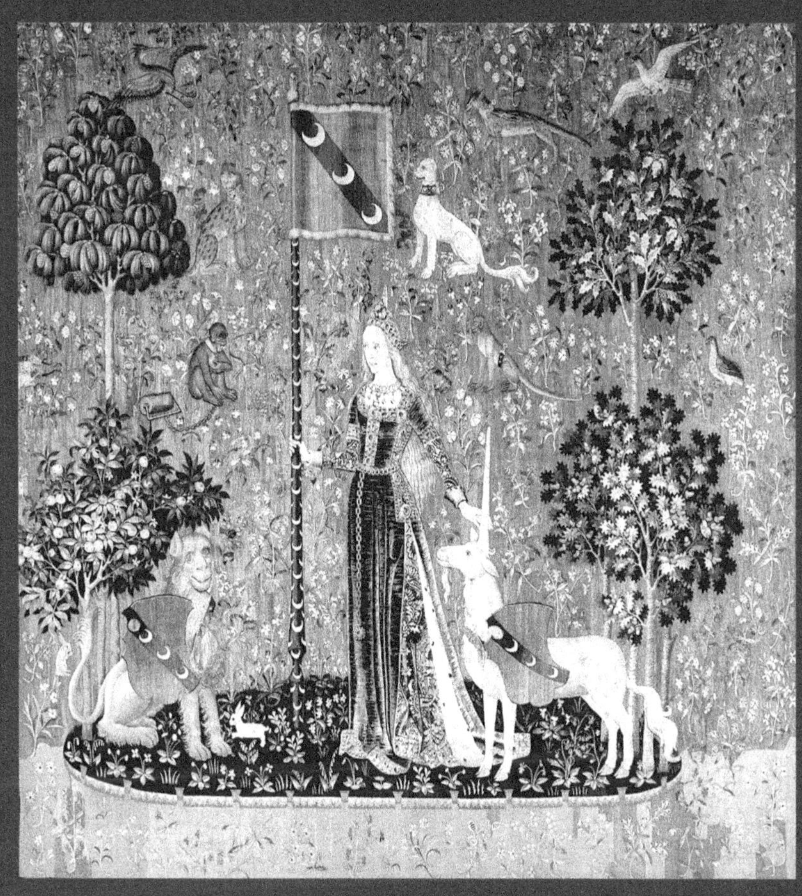

FIGURE 1.7
Rebecca Horn, *Einhorn* (1970–72).
© VG Bild-Kunst, Bonn 2020.

FIGURE 1.8
The Lady and the Unicorn: Touch
(between 1484 and 1538).

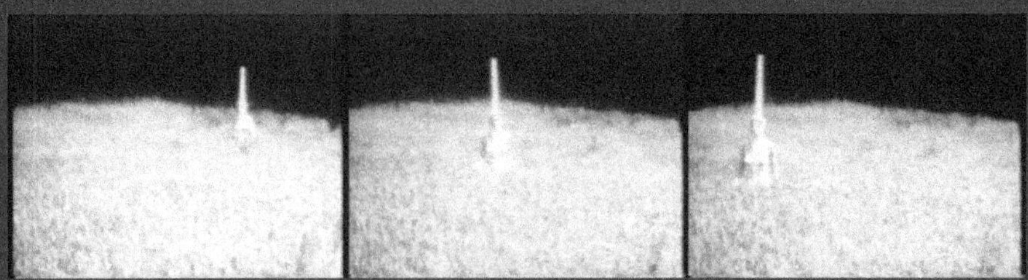

FIGURE 1.9
Film stills from Rebecca Horn, *Einhorn* (1970). © VG Bild-Kunst, Bonn 2020.

FIGURE 1.10
Etienne-Jules Marey, chronophotograph of a man running (ca. 1885).

FIGURE 1.11
Spatial model, following Otto Fischer, to illustrate the movements of the human walk (ca. 1895).

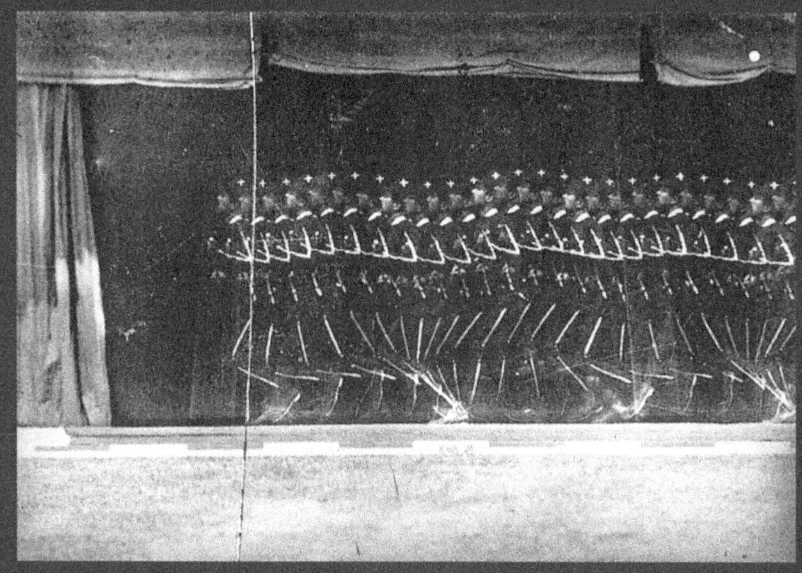

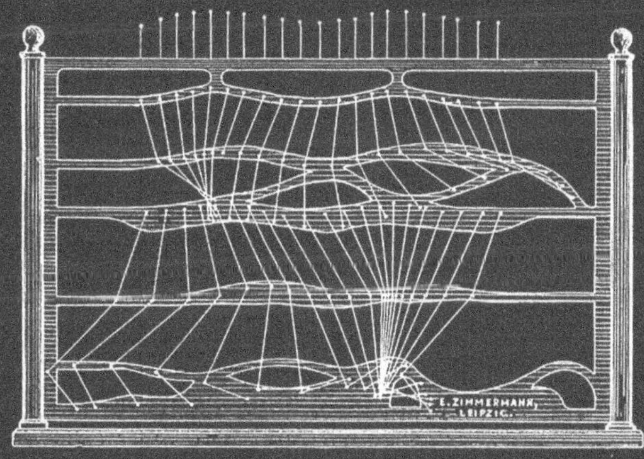
E. ZIMMERMANN,
LEIPZIG.

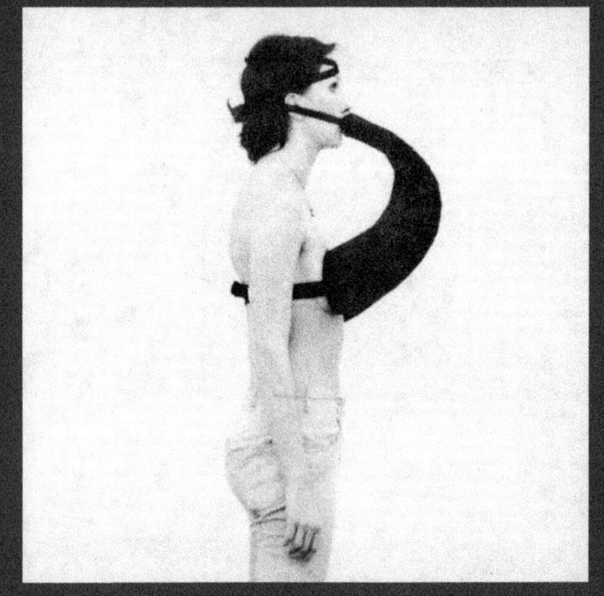

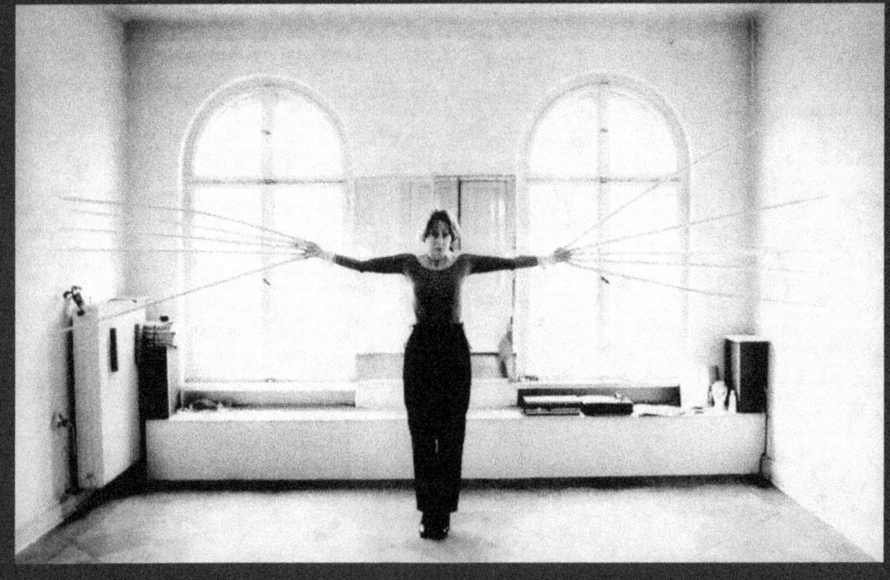

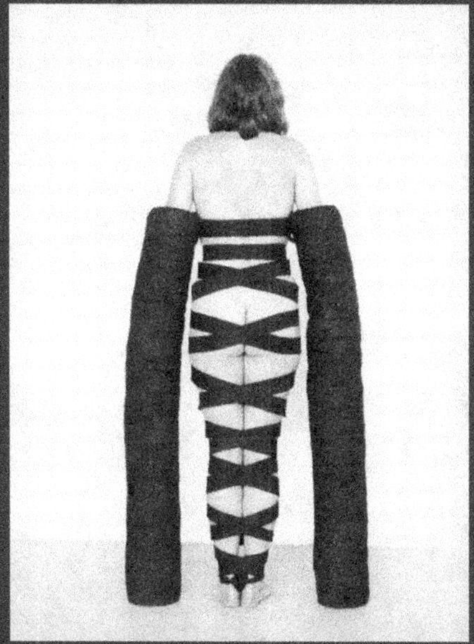

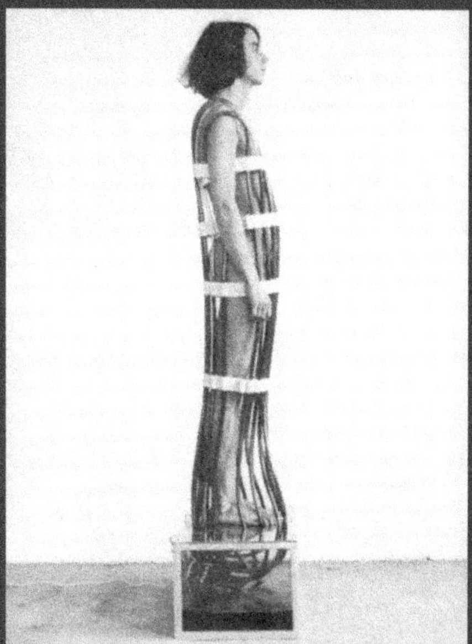

FIGURE 1.12

Rebecca Horn, *Cornucopia: Séance für zwei Brüste* (1970). © VG Bild-Kunst, Bonn 2020.

FIGURE 1.13

Rebecca Horn, *Mit beiden Händen gleichzeitig die Wände berühren* (1974–75). © VG Bild-Kunst, Bonn 2020.

FIGURE 1.14

Rebecca Horn, *Arm-Extensionen* (1968). © VG Bild-Kunst, Bonn 2020.

FIGURE 1.15

Rebecca Horn, *Überströmer* (1970). © VG Bild-Kunst, Bonn 2020.

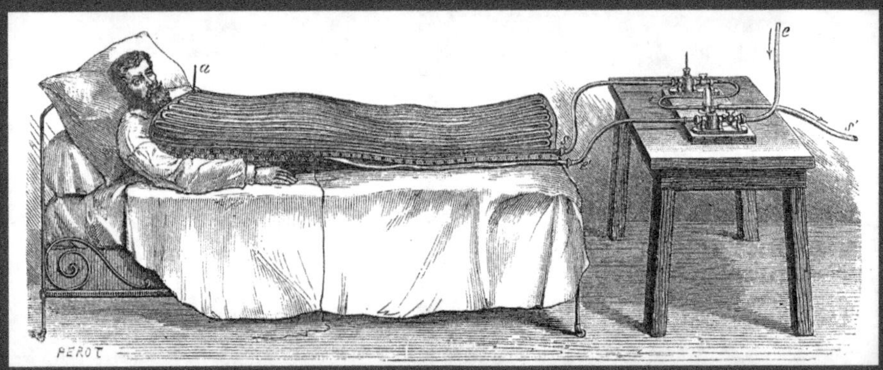

FIGURE 1.16

Dumontpallier and Galante's cooling blanket (1880).

FIGURE 1.17

Rebecca Horn, *Messkasten* (1970).

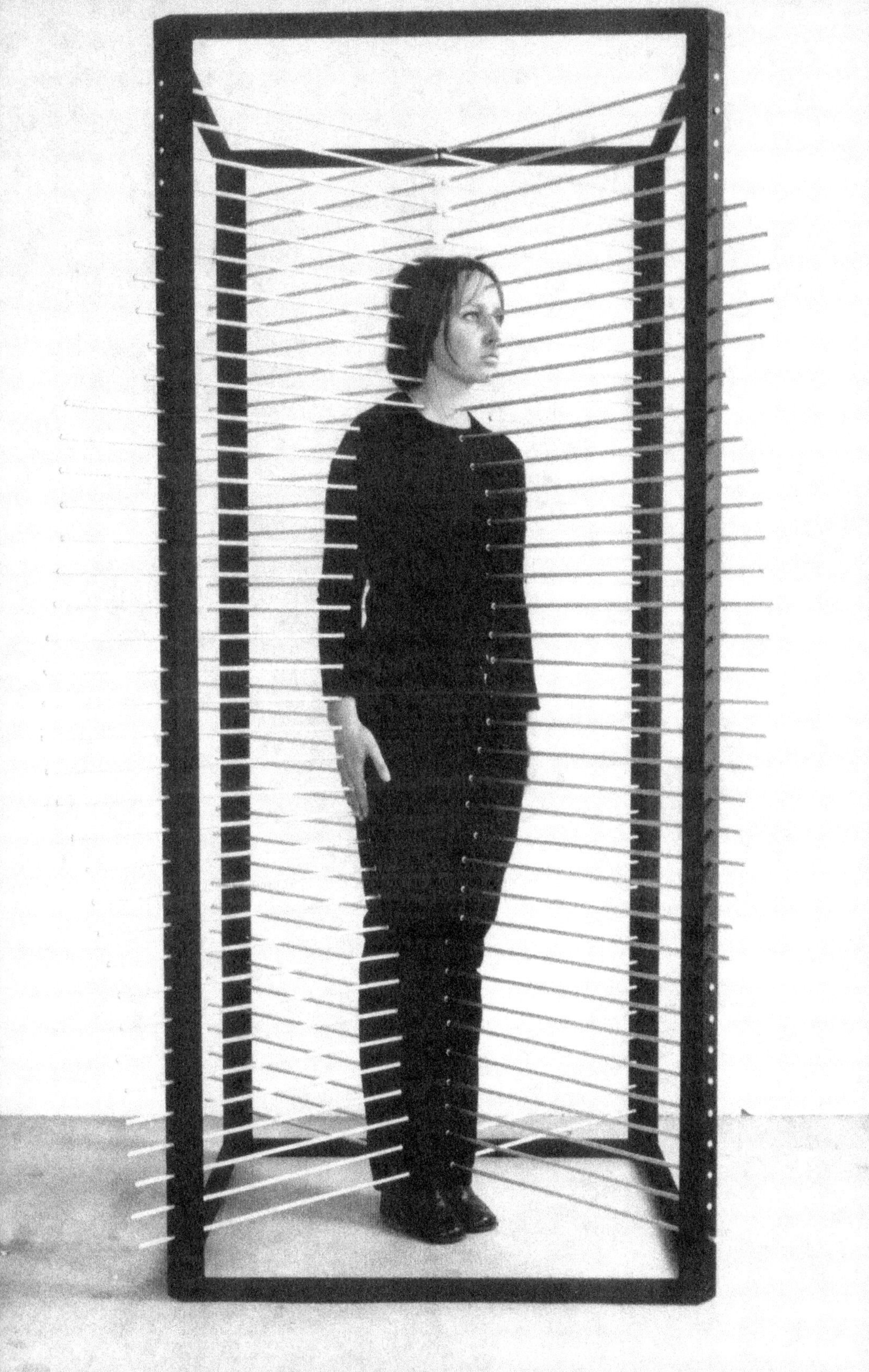

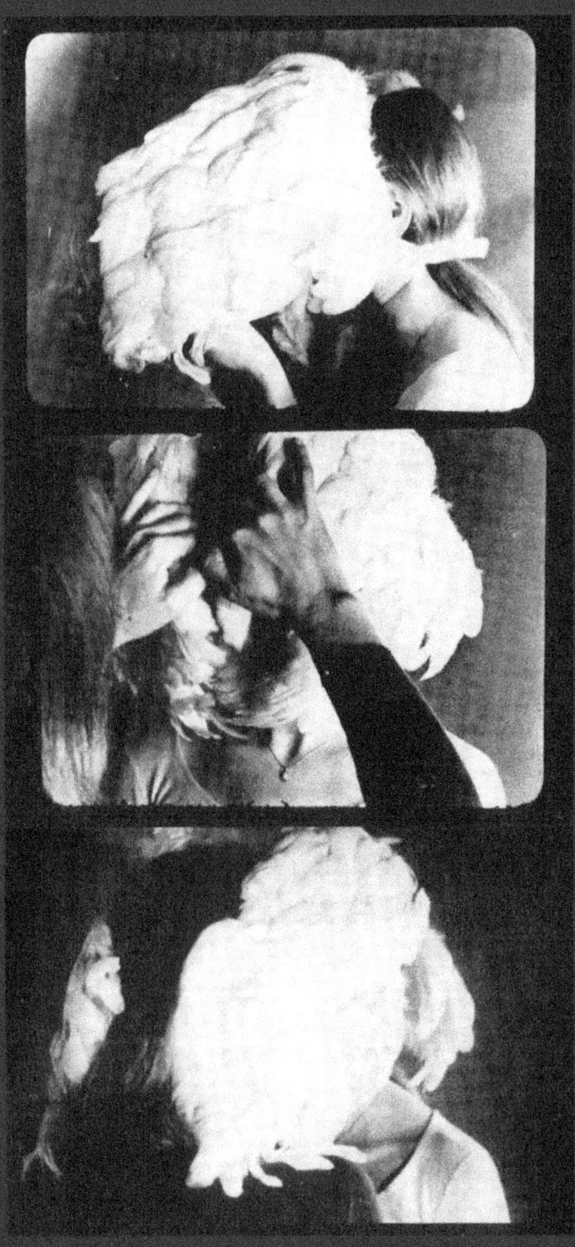

FIGURE 1.18

Rebecca Horn, *Kakadu-Maske* (1973).

TWO

Impressions of Modernity

In this room, Sigmund Freud and Walter Benjamin meet. Dominating the room is a plaster cast of Michelangelo's statue of Moses. The horned Moses is surrounded by the drawings, photographs, and books that Freud relied on in his engagement with the statue. Next to his manuscripts and letters are Benjamin's excerpts, notes, and sketches concerning the artwork essay. A postcard sent by Benjamin shows the rhinoceros sculpture at the Trocadéro with the Eiffel tower in the background. Hanging on the walls are photographs by Sigfried Giedion and László Moholy-Nagy. They show iron structures such as the Bibliothèque nationale in Paris and the Marseille transporter bridge. Lying in a glass showcase, there is Benjamin's letter to Giedion; next to it are excerpts from the correspondence between Giedion and Moholy. This room's motto was coined by the latter. It reads, "The printer's work is part of the foundation on which the new world will be built."[1]

The inventor of psychoanalysis chose not to take the first and best opportunity to study the horn. During a longer stay in Rome in September 1912, Freud almost daily visited the church San Pietro in Vincoli, which houses the tomb Michelangelo Buonarotti designed for Julius II. Freud's attention is entirely focused on the marble statue of Moses, a central component of the tomb built over a period of almost fifty years and completed in 1554. It shows a horned Moses (fig. 2.1).

Freud is already familiar with the statue from earlier visits to Rome. In the fall of 1912, his engagement with the sculpture that has long attracted as much as mystified him becomes more intense. He visits it not only to look at it again and again. He also makes drawings of it and even takes measurements.[2] This is the basis on which he writes, in the weeks and months that follow, the essay titled "Der Moses des Michelangelo [The Moses of Michelangelo]." This text of about twenty pages is printed in *Imago* in 1914—anonymously, at first. Only in 1924, in the first edition of the *Gesammelte Schriften*, does it appear under Freud's name as author.[3]

The text is remarkable for several reasons. First, it contains an analysis of the body movement that Freud was convinced explains the peculiar posture and gestures of the figure of Moses depicted by Michelangelo. With its three drawings that each illustrate one phase of this movement, this analysis recalls studies in experimental physiology (Eduard Weber, Étienne-Jules Marey, etc.) that divide body movements into sequences of "cinematographic" images as well.[4]

Second, it is in this essay that Freud explicitly refers to the art historical writings of Ivan Lermolieff, a.k.a. Giovanni Morelli, in whose particular method—which consists in focusing on apparently minor details (e.g., ears, eyes, or fingernails)—he recognizes a procedure related to the psychoanalytic effort of interpretation. In a famous essay, Carlo Ginzburg has shown how vast a perspective this reference opens up. According to Ginzburg, an entire epistemology of the individual case, of the example, of the detail connects the physician's and the art historian's gaze.[5]

The Moses essay, published the same year as Freud's programmatic "Zur Geschichte der psychoanalytischen Bewegung [On the History of the Psycho-Analytic Movement]" can moreover be read as a reaction to the conflict with Alfred Adler and C. G. Jung then simmering in the psychoanalytic movement. And finally, it prepares the detailed discussion of Moses in terms of a psychology of religion in Freud's late work.[6]

Our starting point for giving a new reading of this enormously dense and suggestive text is something else. It is the remarkable fact that while Michelangelo presents the figure of Moses with two clearly visible horns on the head, Freud at no point in his study mentions this fact. To be sure, he does cite other authors who speak of "Moses with the head of Pan" or the "animal cast of the head," and the drawings of the statue accompanying the text clearly show the horns on the head of Moses.[7] Yet although these head extensions quickly impress themselves on the viewer as phallic objects, Freud has not a single analytic word to say about them.

From the point of view of psychoanalysis, this lacuna is all the more remarkable for the fact that the motif of the horned Moses is generally held to go back to a mistranslation or copy error, that is, to a parapraxis (*Fehlleistung*). The biblical passage to which Michelangelo's depiction of Moses refers describes how, after Moses's conversations with God on Mount Sinai, "the skin of his face shone" (Exodus 34:29), as modern translations have it.[8]

In the Hebrew Bible, this passage reads *kî qāran ōwr pānāw*. A widely accepted explanation holds that the Latin version of the Bible composed by Saint Jerome, the Vulgate—which became the standard text starting in the eighth century and was likely familiar to Michelangelo as well—erroneously rendered the phrase as *cornuta esset facies sua* ("his face is horned") when it should have read *coronata esset facies sua* ("his face shone"). Michelangelo's horns would then be the result of a veritable slip: *coronata* became *cornuta*.

To this derivation of the horns, some—notably early psychoanalysts—have objected that the decisive Hebrew term, *qāran*, in fact means both, "being horned" as well as "shine." In this respect, to speak of the horned Moses would have to be regarded not as parapraxis, but as an emphatic intervention on Jerome's part in favor of one of the two possible meanings of the ambiguous term *qāran*.[9]

And indeed, Jerome's comments on other passages in the Bible show that the translator was familiar with both meanings of the word. Everything thus suggests that he consciously opted for *cornuta*. Yet he probably did not have bodily manifest horns on Moses's head in mind but, in keeping with metaphors of horns found throughout the Bible, saw it as a general expression of strength, power, and dignity.

If we follow this explanation, it becomes understandable why the first depictions of horned Moses heads do not appear in the visual arts until the eleventh century, two centuries, that is, after the Vulgate had spread. Art historians have shown that such depictions of Moses came up only once a connection was established between the reading of the Vulgate and traditional iconographies of the horn in Anglo-Saxon and Scandinavian areas (fig. 2.2). In the Middle Ages, these representations spread beyond the north of Europe and from there made their way to Italy in the fifteenth and sixteenth centuries. The Moses Freud visited repeatedly in the small Roman church was thus a figure with a heavy northern accent.[10]

Two Intense Media Scenes

Freud's omission of the horns, meanwhile, is remarkable not just from the psychoanalytic point of view. It is remarkable from a media studies perspective as well. Moses's horns are important elements of an archaic account that is almost entirely about communication. The fascination exercised by the idol cast in the image of a calf from the Israelites' jewelry is but one indication. As important as this idol is in the narrative for underscoring the divine interdiction of images—"but my face shall not be seen" (Exodus 33:23)—it does distract from a narrative structure that emphasizes the improbable aspect of all communication.[11]

For the episode recounted is fundamentally characterized by the phenomenon of repetition: Moses ascends Mount Sinai *twice*, and he descends *twice* with tablets of the Law. Indeed, the communication Moses as personified mediator between God and people tries to produce and at the same time regulate fails at the first attempt. Having destroyed the first set of "tablets of stone, written with the finger of God" on both sides (Exodus 31:18) out of anger about his people's misbehavior (as expressed in the dance around the golden calf), it is only with the second, more succinctly inscribed tablets of stone that he succeeds in concluding the alliance he seeks.

In the reprise, the horns or rays—like, incidentally, the blanket with which he covers them for a while (in Michelangelo's figure, it covers the knees of the seated Moses)—function as visual amplifiers of acts of oral and written communication. They emerge from the direct conversation with God and thus do not merely function as placeholders for an abstract glow: they stand for a kind of secondary luster (*Abglanz*). It is what we might call this reactive shining that on Moses's return places his role as powerful messenger literally before the eyes of his partly "stiff-necked" (Exodus 33:5), partly frightened people.

The prohibition of images is thus not universal. The face of God, to be sure, may not be seen and certainly may not be represented. But visual auxiliaries such as rays of light or pillars of cloud (Exodus 33:9) that intensify the medial contact with God on other channels are quite permitted.[12]

Freud now conceives of Michelangelo's statue as an artistic representation that straddles both parts of the biblical story. For him, the phenomenon of repetition contained in Moses's ascending Mount Sinai twice is, as it were, inscribed in the statue. The work for him combines elements of the first part (the angry gaze) with elements of the second (the horned head).[13] The psychoanalyst's reaction to being "powerfully affected," in turn, consists in outlining an intense media scene—and in doing so, initially, in a very practical sense.

Certainly, Freud time and again seeks to be close physically to the statue of Moses at San Pietro in Vincoli. In Benjaminian terms, we might say that in this regard, he begins with the statue's *cult value*, its "here and now," its "unique existence in the place" it finds itself in.[14] As he goes on, however, Freud embeds the artwork in an entire network of differently constituted reproductions: from the drawings that he partly makes himself, partly commissions an artist to produce via postcards featuring relevant motifs he sends to friends and colleagues (fig. 2.3) but also takes home with him, via the meticulously planned photographs of details he later has Ernest Jones take, to the journals and books about Michelangelo he consults at home in Vienna, which in turn contain reproductions of the statue, and, finally, to the plaster cast of the *Moses* statue in the Vienna Academy of Fine Arts, which Freud also studies in detail.[15]

The author of *The Interpretation of Dreams* thus relies not only on the "auratic mode of existence of the work of art" in Rome. As he continues to engage the statue, he also brings out its *exhibition value* in mobilizing the most various instances of its technical reproducibility. One almost gets the impression that Freud seeks to validate Benjamin's later insight that in going through a series of reproductions, it is "much easier" "to get hold of a painting, more particularly a sculpture, . . . in a photograph than in reality."[16]

Freud embeds the *Moses* statue in an intense media scene, not just on the level of procedure but on the level of content as well. The particularity of this scene as he projects it in his essay is that it is dominated no longer by the sense of sight but by the sense of touch. The absence of Moses's conspicuous head horns that are directed toward the gaze of the observer is compensated, as it were, by the presence of a capacity to perceive all of the body's periphery.

Not that Freud actually touched the statue with his own hands. He remains at a distance. He stands or sits in front of it, paces before it, steps toward it and back again, and again and again looks at it from the side opposite the direction of Moses's gaze. Nor does Freud posit an analogy between manual and visual scanning, as the sculptor Adolf von Hildebrand did a few years earlier in his influential treatise *Das Problem der Form in der bildenden Kunst* (*The Problem of Form in the Visual Arts*). Freud does *not* look at the *Moses* statue with a tactile gaze.[17] Rather, it is the *Moses* statue itself that, in his presentation, becomes a medium of tactility. It is the sculpture that touches and besieges the observer in manifold ways and precisely in doing so makes its unique impact.

This is manifest in a number of formulations in Freud's text. The author is not simply "powerfully affected" by the statue but feels "moved" and "gripped" as if the work of art had a downright violent effect on his body. In this sense, Freud also feels an "almost oppressive" effect emanating from the *Moses* statue. He feels "defeated" and finally even "overawed."[18]

These formulations not only convey the characteristics of the sublime in aesthetic sensation, which in the present case is attributable not least to the mighty materiality and sheer size of the statue. Nor does Freud's terminology simply manifest the heavy "preponderance [*Übergewicht*]" of the objective mind Georg Simmel described a few years earlier with regard to contemporary mental life.[19] Instead, the *Moses* statue for Freud *is* a pressure, and in a double sense. For him, on the one hand, it represents the "effective expression" of the intentions and emotions of the artist; on the other, it functions as a "script" the artist has "traced . . . in the stone."[20]

The *Moses* statue thus not only *contains* the motif of the tablets formed from stone, in which laws have been inscribed with the bare finger. In a certain way, the statue itself, as a whole, is a bearer of writing, a press-work (*Druck-Werk*) imprinted by hand with the artist's message—which must be deciphered and read accordingly.

A Living Archive

Freud underlines the *Moses* statue's tactile qualities by seeking out the mechanism of its fabrication and effect in the artwork itself. His interpretation precisely does not focus on the angry gaze Moses, his head turned to the left, hurls at his misguided people. Freud avoids this gaze by looking at the statue primarily from the other side, that is, from his own left, not his right.

What becomes salient in this perspective are the manifold (auto)contacts of the body depicted by Michelangelo—for example, the simple but fundamental fact that Moses is sitting; or that his left hand rests on his lap; or that the right foot rests entirely on the pedestal whereas only one toe of the left foot touches it.

And the motif that Freud moves to the center of his study, too, is a tactile motif. The right index finger becomes the protagonist of the study—which may not be all that surprising, given another prominent depiction of an index finger by Michelangelo, the *Creation of Adam* in the ceiling fresco of the Sistine Chapel.

Freud very much insists on Michelangelo showing how Moses with the index finger of the right hand is touching the left side of his beard. Many art historians, he adds by way of explanation, have held that Moses is "playing with his beard as an agitated man nowadays might play with his watch-chain." The psychoanalyst vehemently disagrees. For Freud, there can be no question of play here: in his view, one is dealing here with a "despotic finger" exercising immense pressure on the body.[21]

The aspect of overwhelming, which we saw in Freud's being "powerfully affected" by the statue, returns here in different form. According to Freud, the finger "is pressed so deeply against the soft masses of hair that they bulge out beyond it both above and below, that is, both towards the head and towards the abdomen."[22] The photograph accompanying the first publication of Freud's text (taken from one of the books on Michelangelo Freud had consulted)[23] vividly stages this bulging. It clearly shows how Moses's "inward pressing index finger" practically sinks into the billowing beard (fig. 2.4).[24]

This seems so important to Freud that his presentation at this point adopts the gestures of insistence. In a single passage, he speaks of the "pressure of the index finger," the "pressure of one finger," the "pressure of the right index finger," and, a little later, of the "pressure of one finger, the longest and uppermost one of the hand." But that is not all. According to Freud, the finger is not only "pressed," it also "clutches" at the beard; it not only "compresses" the beard, but "presses" it with an "iron grasp"—as if a mark were to be left in it.[25]

In fact, the beard as the counterpart of the index finger, which in the biblical account serves as a writing instrument, on Freud's reading becomes a kind of recording surface. Moses's finger does not leave a simple, closely circumscribed imprint on the beard. This is also where the thesis of the sequential movement comes in that for Freud explains the remarkable posture of Michelangelo's *Moses*. According to this thesis, the right index finger has pulled the left half of the beard over to the right side of the body. The beard thus becomes a "trace of the path taken by this [the right] hand." Freud even speaks of a "beard trace" (*Bartspur*) that for him is simultaneously a "wake" (*Wegspur*).[26]

At this point, the attention the bearded Freud had paid earlier to the symbolism of this kind of facial hair in a different text[27] suggests highlighting the phenomenon of a semioticity that is grounded in the body. In fact, the trace described with regard to Moses is an *imprint*, a sign produced by the physical contact of the designated and the designating. Given the enormous significance psychoanalytical theory attributes to the concepts of "trace" and "facilitation" (*Bahnung*, lit. preparing the ground or paving the way), Freud's choice of terms in the Moses essay resonates deeply and widely.[28]

Let's note for the moment that we are dealing with a kind of diversion, a displacement of the motif of tactility. The pressure exerted by the work of art on those observing it is shown to be a gesture within the work. As the essay continues, it is this construction, precisely, that allows Freud to newly explore Michelangelo's *Moses* in a surprising way. The pressure Moses exercises on his own body is the leitmotif of this exploration. Thanks to the finger pressing, the hand, Freud writes, "mediates" in a "very singular" way between the tablets and the beard.[29]

However, the hand serves as mediator between writing and body, in more than one respect. Moses presses the index finger into the beard while with his palm he is pressing down on the tablets that in turn contain the imprints of fingers writing—something that Michelangelo does not explicitly depict, as Jones reports in response to a query from Freud.[30]

The hand is not the only one to produce a tactile mediation between writing and the body. Moses's right arm, too, exerts pressure on his body, since this arm is to "squeeze" the tablets "against his side" and thereby prevent them from falling and shattering on the ground.[31]

This is the core of Freud's interpretation of Michelangelo's work of art. Moses will *not* jump up, he will *not* hurl the tablets to the ground: "In his first transport of fury, Moses desired to act, to spring up and take vengeance and forget the Tables; but he has overcome the temptation, and he will now remain seated and still, in his frozen wrath and in his pain mingled with contempt. Nor will he throw away the Tables so that they will break on the stones, for it is on their especial account that he has controlled his anger; it was to preserve them that he kept his passion in check."[32] This, of course, would constitute the opposite of a cinematographic image of affect depicting Moses—angry but still hesitating—just before jumping up and breaking the tablets. It is not *this* Moses whom Freud sees. Instead, he is confronting a work of art that is stable through and through, that is literally compressed in itself. Ultimately, it is not saying anything other than that this Moses will "remain sitting like this . . . for ever."[33]

Such persistent sitting, however, is not an end in itself. It serves to protect the tablets, to preserve writing. Michelangelo thus considerably modifies the motif of the broken tablets of the Law: "he does not let Moses break them in his wrath, but makes him be influenced by the threat that they will be broken and makes him calm that wrath."[34]

Freud at this point is not stingy with pathos. For him, the overcoming of wrath staged by Michelangelo, which also leads to the preservation of the tablets of the Law, expresses the "highest mental achievement," namely "that of struggling successfully against an inward passion for the sake of a cause to which he has devoted himself."[35] From this perspective Moses appears as a figure who preserves writing, a person who is a *corpus* in both senses, a body and an archive: a living archive.[36]

The Shifting of the Horns

The interpretation just sketched lends itself to being understood against the background of the polemics that characterized the psychoanalytic movement at the time. Is it not Freud himself who in the early 1910s was full of wrath toward Adler and Jung, trying meanwhile to preserve his tablets of the Law, as it were—the supposition of infantile sexuality, the principles of *The Interpretation of Dreams*, and so on—from being broken?[37]

That is why it is all the more remarkable that Freud's essay does not stop at elaborating the allegory. As if he were acutely aware of the mediality of his own writing, Freud turns to a detailed discussion of the tablets, which are part of Michelangelo's statue—and in this context, he does talk about horns.

At first, the tablets seem to be quite trivial: "And we can see that the two apposed, rectangular tablets stand on one corner." Then, the surprise: "If we look closer we shall notice that the lower edge is a different shape from the upper one, which is obliquely inclined forward. The upper edge is straight, whereas the lower one has a protuberance *like a horn* on the part nearest to us, and the Tables touch the stone seat precisely with this protuberance."[38]

This horn is the truly Morellian element of Freud's interpretation. The plaster cast of the *Moses* statue he repeatedly studies in the Vienna Academy of Fine Arts does not feature this detail, or at least not with sufficient clarity. There, the lower edge of the tablets "is quite incorrectly reproduced," as Freud notes, almost with indignation.[39] Judging by the condition of the cast in the Vienna collection today, the complaint is warranted at least insofar as the edge in question is much more rounded than in the original in Rome (fig. 2.5).[40]

Hence Freud is all the more fascinated when he discovers the "protuberance" on the statue. He does not find any explanations of *this* horn, nothing in the art historical literature that would help him. Still on site, he makes drawings of the horn. Back in Vienna, he instructs Jones, who is in Rome in December 1912, to take photographs of the conspicuous element. Jones does his best and sends two prints to Freud, yet at the same time he tells him that "the projecting pediment interferes inevitably with the view of the tables."[41]

And indeed Freud does not consider the two photos a success. In another letter, he sends Jones in Rome a copy of his own drawing of the horn on the tablets' lower edge and asks for new pictures: photos, additional drawings, too, if need be (fig. 2.6). Again, Jones does his best and announces that he will send a drawing. Unfortunately, though, it seems that neither the photographs nor the drawings by Jones have survived. All that can be said with some degree of probability is that "the hand of an artist" from which Freud received drawings he commissioned belonged to none other than his English friend and student.[42]

Whatever the case may be, in depicting the horn at the edge of the tablets, the technical reproducibility that Freud had thus far employed so intensely in his studies—from the plaster cast of the statue to the reproduction of photographs in books—seems to have reached its limits. The reason is clearly stated by Jones: because of its lateral position and the spatial constellation of the memorial englobing the statue, the spot in question is almost impossible to frame in a photograph.

Ironically, this difficulty in turn results from a structural modification of the Julius mausoleum that had been made as recently as the 1810s. The spot at issue only became visible to visitors as a consequence of the *Moses* sculpture being moved a short distance forward.[43]

This is the backdrop for Freud's including, in the version that is finally published, an additional drawing besides the three movement images. This "Figur D" is dedicated to the detail that becomes the decisive element in Freud's engagement with the *Moses* statue. In addition to the tablets with their lower edge, this drawing also shows Moses's right hand and beard, that is, the section precisely opposite to the wrathful gaze on which Freud's interpretation focuses (fig. 2.7).

Intriguingly, however, everything seems to indicate that this drawing was not made in front of the statue in Rome, nor from memory, but instead is based on yet another photograph.

For the first publication of his essay, Freud used a photograph of the Michelangelo statue that brings out the way Moses presses on his beard particularly well. This photograph was taken from Max Sauerlandt's 1911 book about Michelangelo (see fig. 2.4).

Opposite this figure in Sauerlandt's book, there is another photograph of Michelangelo's statue. It does not show, as was commonly done, the artwork from a perspective corresponding to the direction of the gaze of the depicted Moses. Like Freud himself, this photograph instead views the *Moses* statue from the opposite direction such that the horn on the lower edge of the tablets is at least partially visible (fig. 2.8).

The detail sketch "D" Freud includes in his essay, however, is nothing but a copy of the decisive section of this photograph, an enlargement of a

Morelli detail executed by hand (fig. 2.9). Since it was probably produced by tracing on paper, however, we might also call it an imprint.[44]

Undoubtedly, for Freud, the horn on the lower edge of the tablets was one of the "despised or unnoticed features" of Michelangelo's work of art from which something "secret and concealed" could be guessed. But what exactly can be guessed? Freud answers this question in a way that brings the horn on the tablets and the horns on Moses's head close together. First he notes, "It can hardly be doubted that this projection is meant to mark the actual top side of the Tables, as regards the writing." Only the top edge of such tablets is usually curved or notched. Then he adds, "Thus we see that the Tables *stand on their head*."[45]

In the calculated economy of the Moses essay, this passage prepares the discussion of the sequence of movements Freud supposes to be at the basis of Michelangelo's depiction: Moses at first carried the tablets the easiest way; he carried them upside down because his hand found an easier grip on the protuberance pointing forward.

The flip side of this transition, however, is a (re)surfacing of that element that, although salient, had been passed over by Freud with such aplomb. We reencounter the horns from Moses's head on the head of the tablets. Since there are two tablets, there are two horns here as well.

In this displacement of the horns from the head to the tablets, Freud once more underlines the significance of writing. In his interpretation, it is not decisive whether the person of Moses seems to shine or to be horned thanks to the conversation with God. In Freud's text, it is the tablets themselves, with the signs carved into them, it is writing in its materiality that appears as horned and is thereby also provided with a shine, a luster.

The Writing Pressure of the City

For Sigmund Freud, the literally impressive visits to Michelangelo's *Moses* statue were experiences in isolation. In 1910s Rome, he was glad when he could leave the "unlovely Corso Cavour" to make his way toward the "lonely piazza where the deserted church stands."[46]

For Walter Benjamin in 1930s Paris, such impressive experiences became an everyday phenomenon. The French metropolis generally confronted the allegoricist of capitalist society under the sign of pressure. On the one hand, there are the printed works collected for decades and centuries in the miniature city of the Bibliothèque nationale on rue de Richelieu, through which Benjamin explored the "capital of the nineteenth century." The bibliography of the *Arcades Project* gives an immediate sense of just how much Benjamin explored Paris with the help of printed works.[47] On the other hand, the rest of the city, too, turns out to be a library, a living archive, as writing pressed into stone or, in the words of Charles Péguy, whom Benjamin so admired, as an "inscription" that is at the same time an "incorporation," an embodiment.[48]

One of the guiding principles of the *Arcades Project* is indeed that "one can read the real like a text."[49] With this principle, Benjamin on the one hand takes up traditional discourse about the "book of nature" in order to be able to view the city—not unlike Louis Aragon in *Le paysan de Paris* (*The Paris Peasant*)—as a mythological landscape whose secrets, threatened by extinction, are to be tracked one last time. On the other hand, he at least implicitly refers to Marx, for whom the materiality of industry and of its history was the "*open* book of the *essential powers of man*."[50]

Benjamin's engagement with the French capital is concerned with books not just in a figurative sense. What Parisian reality turns into an expansive space of reading is not only the abstract essential powers of the human being that, in their production of commodities, record themselves. What turns the city into reading material is the specific form of capitalist commodity production: the manufacture of goods for an anonymous mass market comes with the necessity to advertise these goods, and this necessity leads to a remarkable disembedding of typographies: "Script—having found, in the book, a refuge in which it can lead an autonomous existence—is pitilessly dragged out into the street by advertisements."[51]

On billboards and building walls, writing moves from the horizontal of desks to the vertical of walls and thereby conquers a new place in the city's surface structure (fig. 2.10) between street signs, traffic signals, and movie theater screens displaying the intertitles of silent films. As if in return, however, the liberated printed texts find their way back to the book as well, in Mallarmé as well as in Aragon: in the type of postings, newspaper articles, and posters, liberated from lines and set in columns or put in frames, that conspicuously disrupt the previously common fabric of printed texts.

Benjamin paid a lot of attention to the printing techniques that allowed for and favored this redistribution of writing, especially in his artwork essay. At the very beginning, he describes their development from ancient techniques of casting and embossing via the classic procedures of woodcuts, engravings, and etchings to lithography (which has a special relationship with the printing of posters), and from there to the more advanced reproduction techniques of photography, phonography, and cinematography, which, as the suffix *-graphy* suggests, can still be considered implementations of writing.[52]

Whereas other contemporary commentators saw in the spreading of typography and images in public space an increasing "opticization" of the city,[53] Benjamin emphasizes the tactile aspects of this new perceptive world. Like the Michelangelo statue in Freud, newspapers, advertising, and film in Benjamin become effective media of impression. For the reader of the classified section of a newspaper, this reading becomes "a series of shocks and collisions." The switches between scenes and shots in films have the movement images "percussively" penetrate moviegoers, who are left with no other option than to employ their ocular muscles as "shock absorber[s]." Dada already had turned the work of art into a "projectile": "It jolted the viewer, taking on a tactile quality."[54]

This highlighting of the tactile aspects of modern culture explicitly picks up on the work of art historians like Alois Riegl who—thanks not least to Adolf von Hildebrand—had stressed the part the sense of touch played in visual perception.[55] Implicitly, however, Benjamin's exposition also takes up an avant-garde aesthetics of the tactile with which he was familiar from his personal contacts with the constructivist movement starting in the mid-1920s. It was, in particular, thanks to his meeting with László Moholy-Nagy and his exchanges with Sigfried Giedion that Benjamin came into contact with a conception of constructivist creativity that not only promised to operate the transition from new kinds of materials to a new kind of architecture via tactile exercises but simultaneously also sought fully to exhaust the potential of photography, phonography, and cinematography.

Indeed, those of Benjamin's writings that today are read as contributions to media theory are eminently indebted to Moholy's and Giedion's Bauhaus aesthetics.[56] This is true of the *Kleine Geschichte der Photographie* (*Little History of Photography*), a text in which Benjamin quotes from Moholy's writings twice (although omitting the name of the author and of the *Bauhaus* journal in one instance) and whose general historical outline follows the model of an exhibition on the history of photography Moholy had curated in 1929.[57] It is equally true of the theme, so salient in the artwork essay, of "reproduction," which already featured prominently in *Malerei—Fotografie—Film* (*Painting, Photography, Film*), where Moholy in fact also refers to book printing, lithography, and other reproduction techniques. Moreover, it is here already that Moholy raises the problem of what Benjamin would describe as the decay of the aura, declaring, for example, that thanks to the facts of reproducibility, contemporary culture can "free" itself "from the domination of the individual hand-made piece."[58]

Even the motif of the arcade already occupies a central place in Giedion's *Bauen in Frankreich* (*Building in France*), for which, incidentally, Moholy designed the cover (fig. 2.11).[59] Moreover, when Giedion remarks in this treatise that in Le Corbusier's architecture, "the shells fall away between interior and exterior," his tactile expression converges precisely with Benjamin's depiction of the decay of the aura as a "peeling [*Entschälung*] of the object from its envelope."[60]

Against this backdrop, Benjamin contextualizes the notion of "tactile vision" in a new way, referring it to the leveling of all distances in which he sees a decisive characteristic of a culture dominated by capitalism. Accordingly, modernity as a whole is defined by its attempts to bring things closer "spatially and humanly": "More difficult to repudiate every day, a need imposes itself to get hold, at close range, of the object in the image or rather, in the copy, the reproduction."[61]

To state the fact that the "tactical dominant asserts itself in optics itself" is to diagnose a present age whose ideal is realized in *getting hold* and *disposing of* people and things as immediately as possible.[62] Just as the universal medium, money, suggests that people and things are constantly available to be freely possessed, advertising and film stand for the insistent and obtrusive proximity of all objects in the commercialized space of the city. Benjamin thus describes the counterside of media: "the advertisement . . . tears down the stage upon which contemplation moved, and all but hits us between the eyes with things as a car, growing to gigantic proportions, careens at us out of a film screen."[63]

Besides films such as *L'arrivée d'un train en gare de La Ciotat* or *Berlin—Die Sinfonie der Großstadt*, Benjamin here is talking about actual movements in city traffic. For Benjamin, the busy goings-on in the streets of capital cities represent the "matrix" for the leveling of distances and the becoming dominant of the tactile. Urban traffic is a comprehensive expression of what advertisements, newspapers, and films convey only punctually. For, at the core, it is in the contact and percussions, in the "pokes" (*Püffe*) city dwellers give each other that the tactile culture of modernity manifests itself.[64]

These contacts are the vivid model for the experience of "shock" Benjamin considers to be so central. In French, *choc* simply means "collision" or "impact," that is, it names the effect of a physical contact. Such a conception of shock is particularly evident in his studies on Baudelaire, where he repeatedly refers to "the close connection in Baudelaire between the figure of shock and contact with the urban masses." Accordingly, it is not so much the temporal figure of suddenness but the spatialized form of a material contact that is decisive for the experience of modernity.[65]

Benjamin's observation of big-city tactility, however, is rather specific. His interest in the experiential figure of shock has other forms of physical contact and collision in urban space recede to the background. While he does mention fairground attractions like "dodgem cars and other similar amusements,"[66] the city traffic phenomena of vibration, humming, and roaring writers and artists had described time and again since the turn of the century go largely unnoticed.

"Naturally, a city always vibrates to some extent, but only supersensitive nerves can detect it" is August Strindberg's comparatively unimpressed observation concerning the traffic on Paris bridges in 1896.[67] But just a few years later, the Italian futurists enthused about the roaring of cars and planes and initiated, in addition to a new art of noise destined to harmonize the "irregular vibrations" of the city,[68] a "tactilism" meant to place the sensing hand at the center of the production and reception of art.[69]

In *The New Vision*, Moholy still approvingly referred to Marinetti's manifesto.[70] Just how skeptically Benjamin would view such references not much later is conveyed by the afterword to the last version of his artwork essay.

Tactile Modernity and Its Counterimage

In a way similar to Freud in his study of Michelangelo's *Moses*, Benjamin in the writings from the time he was working on the *Arcades Project* does not one-sidedly situate the activity of touching on the side of the subject but also and, in fact, more strongly on the side of the object. According to Benjamin, some reproduction techniques that really operate in the visual register are already by themselves subjected to the dominance of the sense of touch, such as the photo camera, which gives "the moment a posthumous shock, as it were," or the movie camera, which, not unlike the surgeon's lancet, "penetrates deeply into the tissue of the event." And thanks to technical reproductions, works of art, such as records or photographs, acquire the ability to make steps toward and/or "to accommodate [*entgegenkommen*] the receiver in his own situation."[71]

In such a constellation—described by Moholy-Nagy as "domestic pinacotheca"—it is no longer necessary to take the road to Rome to look at a statue in a church. Thanks to illustrated books readily at hand, the relationship is inverted: "The cathedral leaves its site to be received in the studio of an art lover."[72]

Benjamin describes the consequences of this object-oriented tactilization as a far-reaching transformation of what is commonly called culture. Viewed horizontally or synchronically, the culture of modernity is characterized essentially by the "fantastic form" of commodity production as Marx described it, by that "fraternization of impossibilities" which one school of sociology describes as the "symmetrization" of all human and nonhuman agents. Under capitalist modes of production, people—workers, prostitutes, but also writers and artists—turn into things, namely into commodities, whereas commodities become sensual-supersensual beings "abounding in metaphysical subtleties and theological niceties."[73]

Accordingly, writings become images, and images become things that literally move in on those who view them. Newspaper readers advance to being reporters apparently with great ease, and mere pedestrians just as easily become actors in a movie. Inversely, actors in motion pictures are demoted to mere props, whereas props—a clock, for example—are perceived in the cinema as authentic actors.[74]

Viewed vertically or diachronically, modern culture for Benjamin is first of all a means of emancipation and tool for domination for the bourgeois classes, especially insofar as they conceive of culture as a handing-down of experience, knowledge, and techniques. Tactile modernity transforms this kind of tradition into strategies of habituation: what is handed down are no longer *things* that—like the *Moses* statue in Freud—preserve narratives as much as the traces of the narrating artist, but *situations* or *spaces* in which stimuli and reactions, suggestions and associations prevail. In yet another image with tactile connotations, Benjamin in this connection speaks of an "immense concussion of what is handed down" and of how this shaking-up makes tradition "handy." The result is a "liquidation of the traditional value of the cultural heritage," which, however, has not only destructive but also progressive potential.[75]

While in such a situation the cultural values of the artwork's uniqueness and authenticity fade, reproducibility also allows new forms of appropriating culture to emerge. The contemplation and recollection that were common attitudes to take in front of a traditional painting and even early photographs are replaced by the experiential forms of the event (*Erlebnis*) and of distraction. The "rapt attention [*Aufmerken*]" demanded and made possible by the "total" image of painting is sidelined in favor of a "passing notice [*Bemerken*]" characteristic of the "fragmented" image of films and of architecture.[76]

Accordingly, what once was called cultural memory becomes a practice of using and getting used to. In tactile modernity, culture becomes a sort of testing continually subjected to the judgment of an audience. This is what Benjamin sums up in saying that in a tactilized culture, the "field of what can be tested" expands considerably.[77] We might also say, in such a culture, what can be touched (*Tastbare*) becomes what can be tested (*Testbare*).

Benjamin's description of the foundational facts of tactile modernity—the capitalist form of production and its concomitant leveling of traditional distances between people and things—is comparatively clear. Inversely, the suggestive counterimage he outlines remains unclear. In the artwork essay's well-known definition, "aura" is "the unique apparition of a distance, however near it may be." Need-driven tactility is thus confronted with a desiring gaze: the "distance" characteristic of the aura is particularly salient in the dreamy gaze of looking at a painting of "which our eyes will never have their fill," or it opens up in the fantasy-charged viewing of early photographs in which the faces of those portrayed appear as if they "could see *us*."[78]

As Benjamin's argument develops, this mirroring of the gaze back onto the viewer—which the Lacan of the mirror stage would undoubtedly have dismissed as imaginary but the Lacan of the Seminars would probably have seen as confirming his own theory of image and gaze[79]—becomes the core of the aura as a visual phenomenon. The contrast with physical touch is readily apparent in the formula "to experience the aura of an object we look at means to invest it with the ability to look back at us."[80]

For Benjamin, however, the fact that in this definition "a response characteristic of human relationships is transposed to the relationship between humans and inanimate or natural objects" does not signal a return to mysticism, superstition, or notions of omnipotence.[81] Animism, the "empathy with inorganic things" that occurs as if under the influence of drugs,[82] is nothing but the theoretically and historiographically appropriate attitude toward a culture in which humans become machines and technology, *en revanche*, turns out to be magic. That images can look at their viewers is, in that regard, a phenomenon deeply anchored in capitalist culture.

The Interior of the Aura

Aura is primarily a visual phenomenon. Nonetheless, it also has tactile dimensions, as a closer look at the successive conceptions Benjamin, stimulated by Baudelaire's prose piece *Perte de l'auréole*, develops starting in 1930 reveals.[83] In the notes from his experiments with hashish and mescaline, "aura" at first refers to the relationships people and things entertain with their surroundings. It is a relational concept whose basic intuition consists in not seeing this relationship as sharply defined by the respective physical surfaces. Benjamin rejects contemporary conceptions of aura, like those of Rudolf Steiner and Charles Webster Leadbeater, as "conventional and banal."[84] (These authors supposed that the human body is continued by a circle of light of a characteristic color.)

Nonetheless, he later occasionally picks up on related concepts, for example when, in reference to Baudelaire, he thematizes the "halo" of the poet (which, incidentally, the poet loses in the shoves and pushes of the urban masses) or when, as if on the contrary, he speaks of the "halo of the commodity" and "the luster surrounding it." And while the somewhat different conception of the aura as "breathy circle" or an atmosphere one can "breathe" is clearly distinct from Steiner's and Leadbeater's "magic rays," it nevertheless remains in the register of a fuzzy, as if immaterial, limitation of corporeal beings in their relationship with the outside world.[85]

"First, genuine aura appears in all things."[86] In Benjamin's hashish notes, this is the initial step to mark the distance vis-à-vis anthroposophical and theosophical aura conceptions, where aura indeed only occurs in human beings. For Benjamin, on the contrary, it can be found in people *and* things, in natural as well as artificial objects: mountains and tree branches on the one hand, photos and paintings on the other. And while Freud in displacing the horns from Moses's head to the head of the tablets of the Law ascribes a luster to these tablets as well, Benjamin for his part does not hesitate to grant a distance to printed writing, however close it may be: "Words, too, can have an aura of their own," he writes in the context of the Baudelaire studies. This means: words can look at the reader—and it is even possible to read in their "face" whether they recognize the reader or not.[87]

In the next step, the quality, as it were, of the limit of the body changes. It is no longer a matter of a circle of light, nor of a breath, but of an "ornament" or, more precisely, an "ornamental circumscription [*Umzirkung*]" of the body: an outer contour of the kind formed by folds, ruffles, or fringes on human clothing. Perhaps Benjamin's pronounced fascination with folds and edges, his *Saumseligkeit*, is not to be attributed to the effect of drugs alone: on the one hand, his description recalls not only the focusing of the art historical gaze on what may seem like negligible details propagated by Morelli, but also and above all, it evokes what Warburg called the "moving accessories [*bewegtes Beiwerk*]" of depicted entities (for human beings, hair or clothes, for example).[88]

On the other hand, Benjamin in this context makes reference to his rather sober viewing of "Van Gogh's late paintings, in which . . . the aura appears to have been painted together with the various objects."[89] Concretely, this refers to the background dissolving into a multitude of brushstrokes arranged in rays and curves that—as in the *Cypresses* or *The Church at Auvers*—attach to the forms presented in the foreground.

These are the decisive moves to prepare the tactile dimension of the aura. For, in a further step, the ornamental circumscription becomes a casing "in which the object or being is enclosed as in a case."[90] The aura thus appears as a cover or protective skin for a concrete body.

This encasing may serve the safekeeping of a precious object (a pocket watch, say, a thermometer, or cutlery),[91] but it can also serve as a case for people to protect against the tactility of modernity. Already in *Einbahnstraße* (*One-Way Street*), Benjamin had described a whole series of such accommodations. There, cupboards, sewing boxes, and pantries are presented as familiar protective devices from a time gone by. In the artwork essay, he only makes a general remark with a view to the history of architecture: "The human being's need for shelter . . . is a constant." In the context of the *Arcades Project*, however, he brings this to a head: "In the most extreme instance, the dwelling becomes a shell."[92]

At this point at the latest it becomes possible to read Benjamin's aura concept in conjunction with Giedion's tactile-based statements about the development of modern architecture. Thus Giedion in *Building in France* argued in favor of understanding "the exterior" of buildings based on steel construction "only as an encasement (*enveloppe*), or epidermis."[93] The fact that these statements are aimed at the architect Henri Labrouste, one of the pioneers of iron construction in France who was also responsible for the Bibliothèque nationale on rue de Richelieu (fig. 2.12), will have rendered them all the more convincing for the author of the artwork essay, who conducted much of his research in just this library. Starting from Giedion's plea, Benjamin, however, is interested not only in the envelope architecture of the arcades, exposition spaces, and train stations discussed at length in *Building in France* (fig. 2.13). His attention is just as arrested by the interior of these "cases" inhabited by the French bourgeoisie of the late nineteenth century. Benjamin also examines the aura's *intérieur*, as it were.

In his view, the interior of the period's bourgeois cases is characterized primarily by soft materials. Besides the use of "covers and cases" for storing valuable items, one was above all surrounded by "velvet and plush covers."[94] The "étui-man" dwelling in such surroundings belonged to the sort of people who handed things down "by making them untouchable and thus conserving them"[95]—which means nothing other than preserving their aura. In precisely this sense, the aura's contemplative visuality has a tactile counterpart: it consists in the traces the bourgeoisie leaves in the interiors of its architectural cases.

Only in his later treatise, *Mechanization Takes Command*, does Giedion analyze the activity of upholsters that thanks to curtains, drapes, carpets, and plush contributed to the "victory of the trimmings over the wood" in the bourgeois habitats of the mid- and late nineteenth century (fig. 2.14). These analyses should be seen as a supplement to, perhaps even a continuation of, Benjamin's investigations.[96] Nonetheless, the author of the *Arcades Project* already points to the social function of the production of imprints made possible by the triumph of the trimmings: "Since the days of Louis Philippe, the bourgeoisie has endeavored to compensate itself for the fact that private life leaves no traces in the big city. It seeks such compensation within its four walls—as if it were striving, as a matter of honor, to prevent the traces, if not of its days on earth then at least of its possessions and requisites of daily life, from disappearing forever" (fig. 2.15).[97]

The point of the passage is that it captures the phenomenon of the trace in its proper dialectic. For, according to Benjamin, it is not only the bourgeoisie that reacted to the new situation in the anonymous metropolis. The state, too, intervened by establishing "an extensive network of controls" that brought "bourgeois life ever more tightly into its meshes." Administration and police set out "to establish a multifarious web of registrations" and thereby to "compensat[e] for the elimination of traces that takes place when people disappear into the masses of the big cities."[98]

This observation is essential. It both historicizes and gives concrete expression to the capitalist regime of *getting hold* and *disposing of* people and things that manifests in the disembedding of writing Benjamin describes with regard to the 1920s. Benjamin goes on to cite the norming of urban space by installing house numbers and Alphonse Bertillon's police identification techniques as examples of the nineteenth-century "network of controls." What he outlines here are none other than early, analog manifestations of a society of control. These represent the flip side, as it were, of that tactile modernity whose culture has become "testable." Benjamin was fully aware of the contemporary relevance of his observation: "Since that time, there has been no end to the efforts to capture" the human in "speech and actions."[99] There is nothing to add from today's perspective.

Return to Freud

The notion of a tactile protective envelope in whose interior traces are left is central to psychoanalytical theorizing in the 1920s, and in his studies on Baudelaire, Benjamin discusses the screening from the tactility of modernity by directly picking up on this notion.

Citing research conducted in general biology since the 1880s on amoeba, ciliates, and other "elementary organisms," Freud in *Beyond the Pleasure Principle* describes the "living organism" as "an undifferentiated vesicle of a substance that is susceptible to stimulation" where "the surface turned towards the external world . . . will serve as an organ for receiving stimuli."[100] The question whose answer Benjamin, in referring to this description, seeks to get closer to is: how is a work of poetry constituted if—as in Baudelaire—it is grounded in urban experiences "for which exposure to shock [*Chockerlebnis*] has become the norm"?[101]

The answer he gives to this question is, put briefly: such poetry would "have a large measure of consciousness"; concretely, it would for example have a notion of a plan that "was at work in its composition."[102] And this, he says, is just what was the case for Baudelaire.

This answer is supported argumentatively with a view to the role Freud assigns to the system *Perception/Consciousness* (*Pcpt./Cs.*) within his model of the psychical apparatus. There, this system serves not only to *receive* stimuli, it is also tasked with *protecting* the organism from stimuli. Benjamin quotes Freud: "For a living organism, protection against stimuli is almost more important than the reception of stimuli. The protective shield is equipped with its own store of energy and must above all strive to preserve the special forms of conversion of energy operating in it against the effects of the excessive energies at work in the external world."[103]

Then he adds: "The threat posed by these energies is the threat of shocks. The more readily consciousness registers these shocks, the less likely they are to have a traumatic effect."[104] According to Benjamin, the organism, in habitually confronting itself with tactile shocks, undergoes a "training in coping with stimuli" that results in a more alert consciousness.

Benjamin in this context does not take up the motif of the protective envelope. This, however, seems to suggest itself since, not unlike Benjamin's conception of aura as "ornamental circumscription," Freud's notion of a "special envelope or membrane" surrounding the organism is profoundly relational. The position of the "system *Pcpt./Cs.*," which is linked to the "receptive cortical layer," is essentially defined as a position "between the outside and the inside."[105]

As Freud explains elsewhere, this surface organ separates and connects "what is unreal, merely a presentation and subjective" on the one hand with what is real and objective on the other.[106] In other words, it conveys both the connection and the difference between ego-libido and object-libido. We might say, in Benjamin's terms, that ideally, the enveloping surface allows the subject to be as solidly "enclosed" in its surroundings as a thing is in its case. And Freud indeed says that one characteristic of the system *Pcpt./Cs.* is to be "immediately abutting . . . on the external world."[107]

Remarkably, Freud's first reference to the biological model of elementary organisms occurs in a text written around the same time as the Moses essay. In "On Narcissism: An Introduction" of 1914, he explains that there is an "original libidinal cathexis of the ego" that "is related to the object-cathexes much as the body of an amoeba is related to the pseudopodia which it puts out."[108] This designates a tactile relationship because, following Ernst Haeckel, contemporary biological literature did indeed describe the pseudopodia or "false feet" at issue as "organs of touch" (fig. 2.16).[109] As protuberances of the organism that spontaneously formed and receded again, they were assigned an important role in the so-called trial movements by means of which single-cell organisms orient themselves in their environments. In other words, the affinity between touching and testing is explained biologically.

Against this background, Freud, in *Beyond the Pleasure Principle* as well as in other, shorter texts of the 1920s, describes the basic function of the psychical apparatus as "a motor palpating" and "an experimental action" in which "antennae" are first put out into the surroundings and then quickly retracted "to take small specimens of the external world, to sample it in small quantities."[110]

It does not seem that Benjamin takes up this notion when he describes how the dominance of the sense of touch leads to a new culture of the testable. For him, the subject's tactile *activity* remains tied primarily to the bourgeoisie's production of traces. He largely ignores it when, in referring to Freud, he focuses on the structural aspect of the "cortical layer" and the functional aspect of consciousness—which also leads him not to concern himself further with the peculiar, changing quality of this surface of the psychical apparatus. Freud, however, discusses this makeup in detail.

Although he does not use the term *cornification* in this context, the subject clearly indicates that this process is just what is meant. According to Freud, these tiny bits of living substance acquire their protection from stimuli when the "*outermost surface ceases to have the structure proper to living matter, becomes to some degree inorganic and thenceforward functions as a special envelope or membrane resistant to stimuli.* In consequence, the energies of the external world are able to pass into the next underlaying layers, which have remained living, with only a fragment of their original intensity."[111]

That this is indeed a description of a keratinization process is supported, first, by the imagery of membrane and cortex (*Rinde*, "bark" or "rind") Freud adopts in his presentation. The primitive surface of the living elementary organism is nothing but its outer skin, its "ectoderm" (fig. 2.17). Second, natural horn plays a protective role as well. This bodily function is just what Freud takes up in speaking of a "protective shield against stimuli," simultaneously giving it a psychological turn. Finally, and especially, the cogency of the reading suggested here is supported by the notion of a transition of a living outer layer to the anorganic, its "death," taking place on the body itself.[112] Natural horn, in human beings at least, is nothing but dead skin.

In the context of his studies of Baudelaire, Benjamin does not seem to be aware of *this* form of protection from stimuli. Besides a heightened form of consciousness, he only discusses there the parrying of "shocks" in battle or duels and the administration of shoves with which pedestrians make their way through the crowd as reactions to tactile modernity.[113] The hardening of the envelope Freud describes is echoed in Benjamin only in the description of the aura as *étui* or case, in whose interior traces can be left. And in fact, in Freud, too, it is only in the inner, "the deeper layers" of the vesicle susceptible to stimulation, that a "permanent trace" can be left.[114]

For Freud's theory, this results in a difficulty: with this hardened envelope, how are the little lumps of substance susceptible to stimulation supposed to form pseudopodia or antennae to explore the outer world by touch? Freud responds to this problem by shifting the activity of touching to the organism's interior. In the texts from the 1920s, the bodies of amoebas in any event no longer form false feet to operate object cathexes. Instead, it is now the layers of substance that lie below the protective vesicle layer that are susceptible to stimulation and feel it out from the inside. They send out, "in rapid periodic impulses," as the "Note on the 'Mystic Writing-Pad'" has it, "cathectic innervations" into the system *Pcpt./Cs.*, onto the inner wall, as it were, of the organic envelope or membrane, and just as rapidly withdraw them again.[115]

In his discussion of "Negation," Freud clarifies this conception: "The ego periodically sends out small amounts of cathexis into the perceptual system, by means of which it samples the external stimuli, and then after every such tentative advance it draws back again."[116] Although Freud does maintain the tactile conception, all that remains is an energetic, no longer physical contact between the protuberances of the living bodies and their external surroundings. Not unlike in Benjamin, the subject seems to be confined in a case whose interior tends its "traces as nature tends dead fauna embedded in granite."[117]

A Different History of Modernity

Since the publication of Freud's study "The Moses of Michelangelo," psychoanalysis has time and again engaged with the question of the horn. In an appendix to the chapter on the shofar, the ram's horn, in a 1919 book—a chapter that is partly a study in the psychology of religion, partly a music history—Theodor Reik directly addresses the horn on the head of Moses in Michelangelo's statue. According to Reik, these horns, in which he also sees rays of light, serve as a "symbol of divine power, especially in its sexual form."[118]

A few years later, shortly after having overseen the translation of Freud's Michelangelo essay into French, Marie Bonaparte also turned to the psychoanalysis of the horn. In her 1928 lecture "On the Symbolism of Head Trophies," she declares, not unlike Reik, that the "heroic horns on the forehead of gods, of kings" are "the insignia of power." She also explains that the horn, worn as an amulet or used as wall decoration, can be deployed as a "magical weapon" to defend against the evil eye and other demonic influences.[119]

Even later and in a different context, the Lacanian Serge Leclaire in a detailed analysis of a unicorn dream points first to the sexual meaning of the horn as phallus. He then goes on to show how in the case in question, this motif inserts itself into an entire phantasm in which the figures of the skin, of leather, of the epidermis, and of the envelope stand for the problematic ties with an overbearing mother.[120]

As we saw, it does not suffice to evoke such studies to try and fill the conspicuous lacuna in Freud's Michelangelo essay—the fact that he does not say one word about the horns on Moses's head. For, on the one hand, Freud does thematize the horns depicted by Michelangelo, albeit in a remarkably shifted manner. He is not interested in the luster on Moses's head but in the shining of the tablets of the law that on their top edge also bear horns.

On the other hand, making reference to other contributions to the psychoanalysis of the horn blocks the view onto the fact that Freud, elsewhere and in at least as subtle a manner, engages a second time with this object that is at the same time a material. In *Beyond the Pleasure Principle* and in other writings from the 1920s, he describes the emergence of the "cortical layer" that surrounds the elementary organism filled with a substance susceptible to stimulation as a hornification. The membrane or envelope that encloses the organism becomes a protection from stimuli for the psychical apparatus in that it loses the structure proper to life and becomes "anorganic." If we refer this finding back to the statue by Michelangelo, we see the horns on Moses's head not as antennae that amplify the perceptive capacities of this exemplary messenger. They appear instead as protective envelopes that are felt out from within.

This leaves fully intact the view held by both Freud and Benjamin that tactility is a primary characteristic of modernity. Both suppose that humans discover their environment above all by touching it and feeling it out, that they orient themselves in it by touching and grasping. Yet Freud and Benjamin equally demonstrate that the sense of touch is not a purely human faculty. The more or less urban surroundings in which organic individuals move, too, act on these individuals by means of pressing *movements* (pushing, shoving) and press *works* (written tablets, books, advertising panels). Taking a pun from Roussel, we might say that the *impressions* of modernity the subject receives are, for Freud and Benjamin, also always *impressions*, imprints, prints.

Against this background, Freud and Benjamin not only address the general problem of handing on experience and knowledge. Via the motifs of writing and the trace, they simultaneously transpose this problem into a, in the widest sense, theological register. As different as the subjects they discuss are, as different as their resulting studies are, both nonetheless agree in discussing, with the help of these motifs, the question of how the conversation with God can or does take place in modernity.

Freud and Benjamin suppose that it is no longer mediating persons who through their communication with God receive a luster. If there is anything in modernity that can acquire this special status, it is tablets, signs, and books. They can have aura.

It is Benjamin who provides this constellation with a precise historical and materialist marker that continues to be decisive for today's confrontation with the sensor society as well. For Benjamin, it is the social organization of capitalism that leads sacred works of art to appear as secular writings or prints and that inversely makes it possible for secular texts to attain the status of religious objects. What manifests itself in the writing of modernity, then, is not only the trace of the narrator or the imprint of a divine finger but first of all, and above all, the fantastic hand of capital.

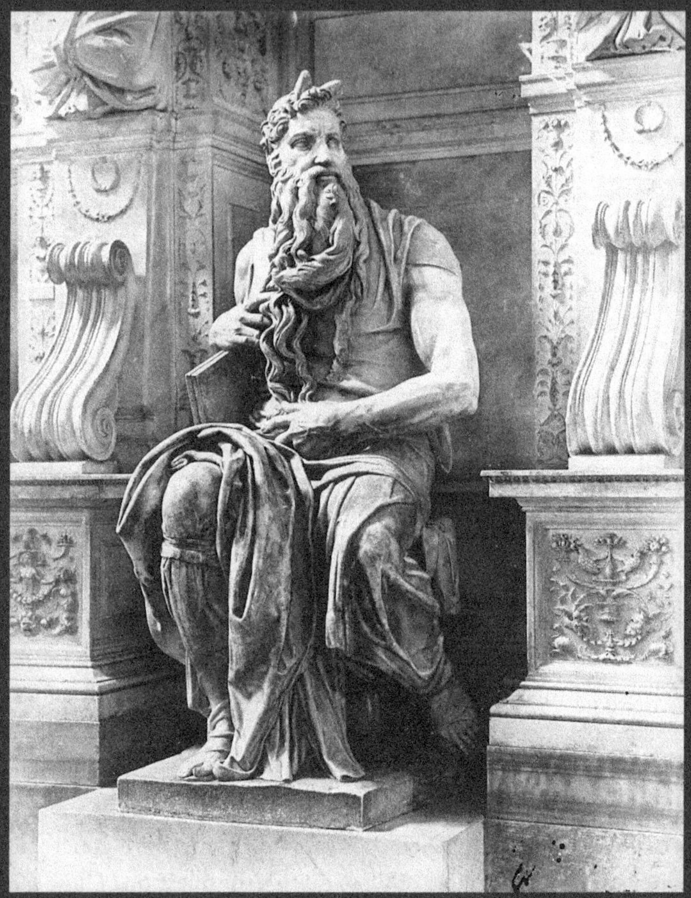

FIGURE 2.1
Michelangelo Buonarroti, *Moses*, statue, detail of the tomb for Julius II. Photograph by James Anderson (between 1845 and 1855). Courtesy the J. Paul Getty Museum, Los Angeles.

FIGURE 2.2
An early depiction of the horned Moses (Bury Bible, ca. 1135).

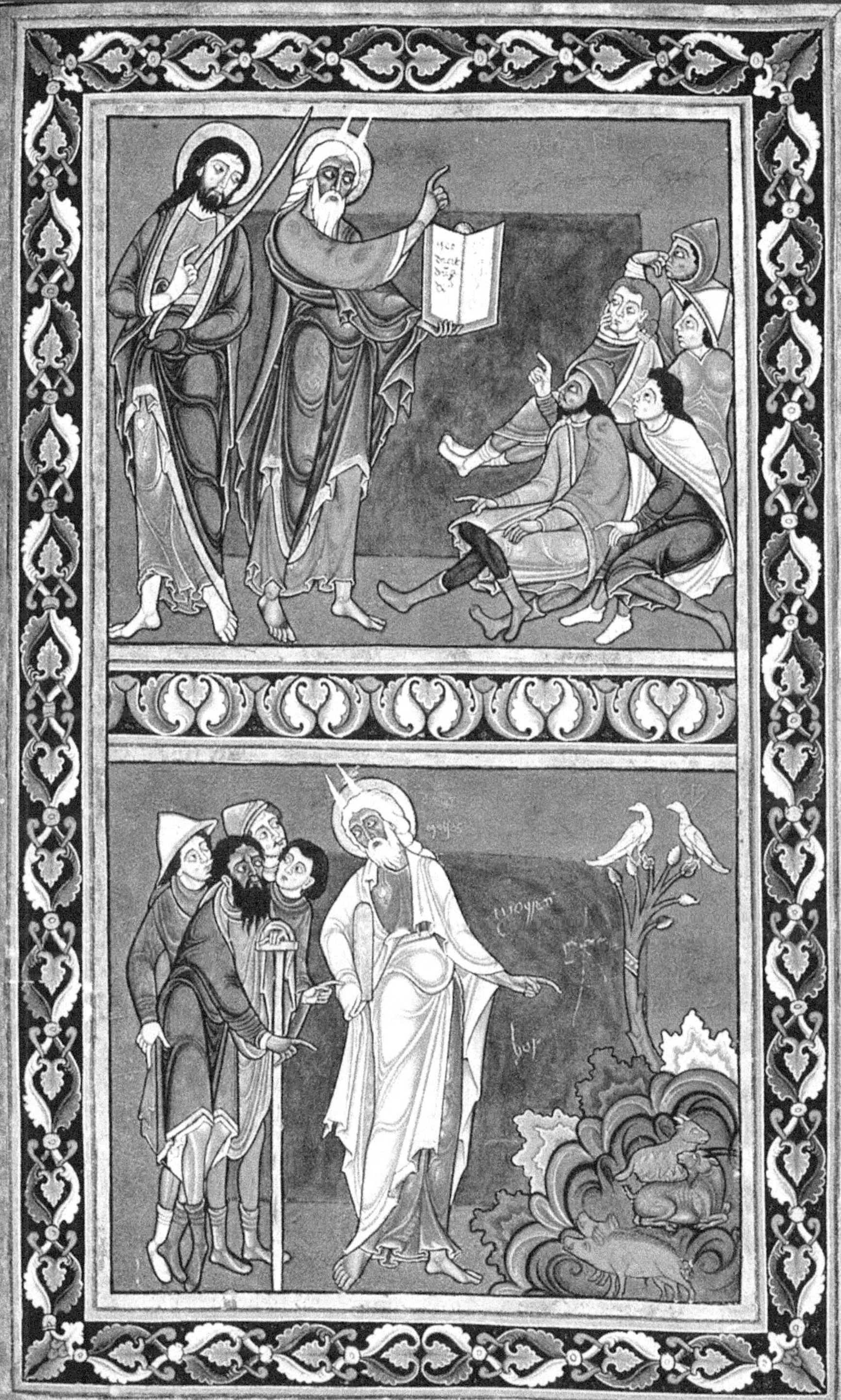

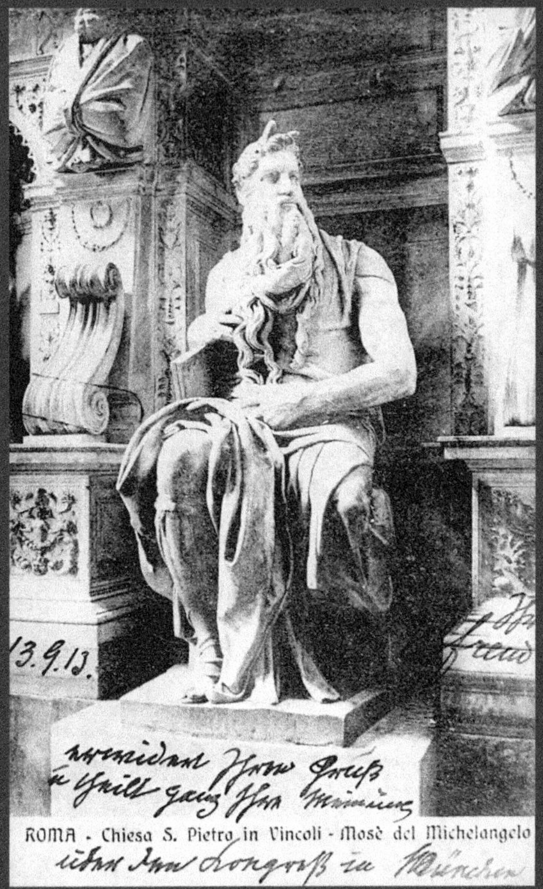

FIGURE 2.3

Postcard from Sigmund Freud to Sándor Ferenczi, September 13, 1913. "Your Freud returns your greetings a[nd] entirely shares your opinion about the Munich conference." © ÖNB Wien–NB 800.326 B.

FIGURE 2.4

Partial view of Michelangelo's *Moses*, used in the first publication of Freud's essay. Photograph by Domenico Anderson (ca. 1900).

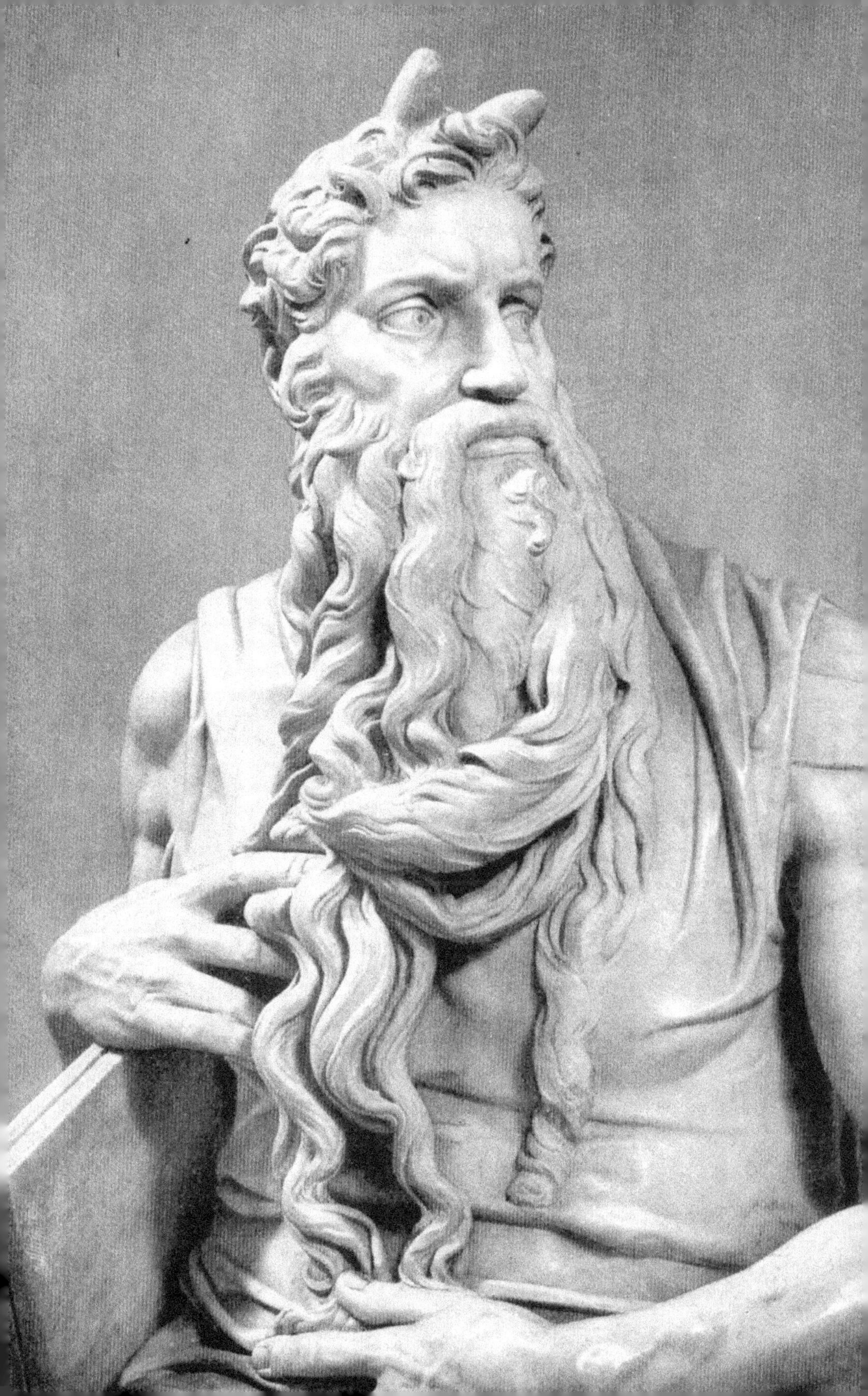

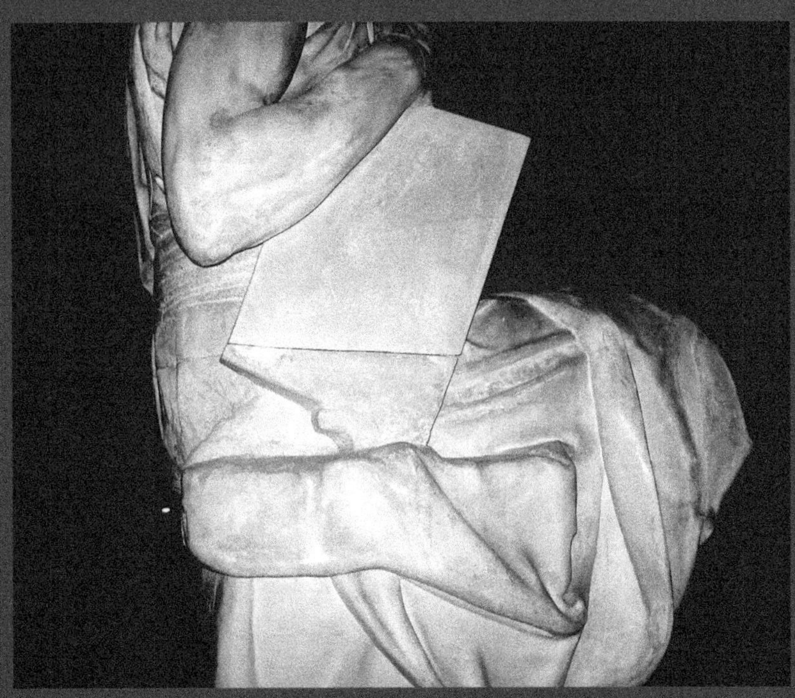

FIGURE 2.5
Side view of the plaster cast of the *Moses* statue by Michelangelo in the plaster cast collection of the Vienna Academy of Fine Arts. Photograph by Benjamin Prinz (taken in July 2016).

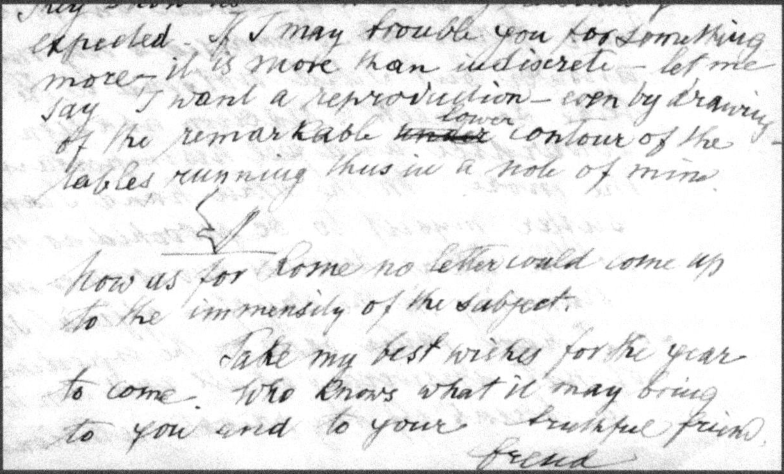

FIGURE 2.6

Sigmund Freud, sketch of the horn on the tablets' lower edge, excerpt from his letter to Ernest Jones of December 26, 1912.

"If I may trouble you for something more—it is more than indiscrete [*sic*]—let me say I want a reproduction—even by drawing—of the remarkable lower contour of the tables, running thus in a note of mine [sketch] / Now as for Rome no letter could come up to the immensity of the subject. / Take my best wishes for the year to come. Who knows what it may bring to you and to your truthful friend / Freud." Courtesy Library of Congress, Washington, DC, Manuscript Division, Sigmund Freud Papers.

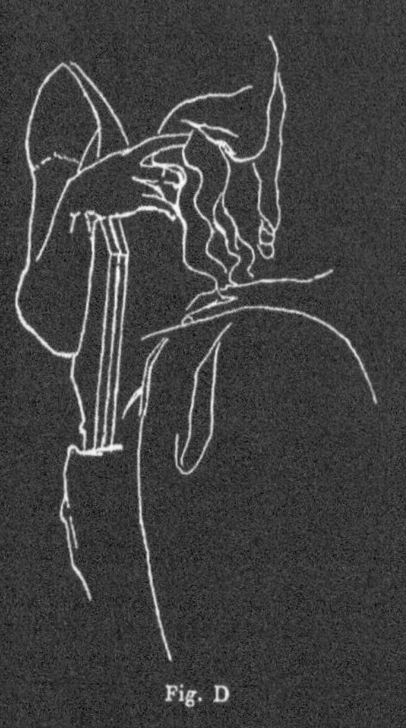

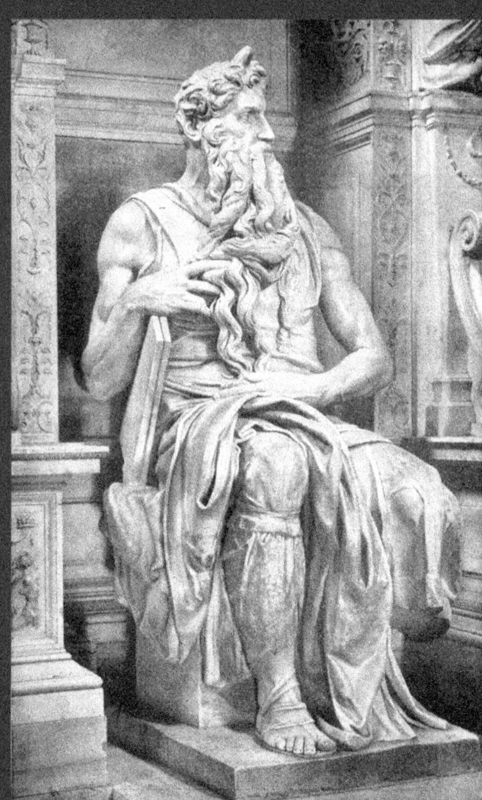

FIGURE 2.7

Sigmund Freud, sketch of a detail of the *Moses* statue ("Figur D"—"Figure 4" in the English translation).

FIGURE 2.8

General view of Michelangelo's *Moses*. Photograph by Domenico Anderson (ca. 1900).

FIGURE 2.9

Superimposition of Freud's "Figur D" on Domenico Anderson's photograph. Montage by Johannes Hess.

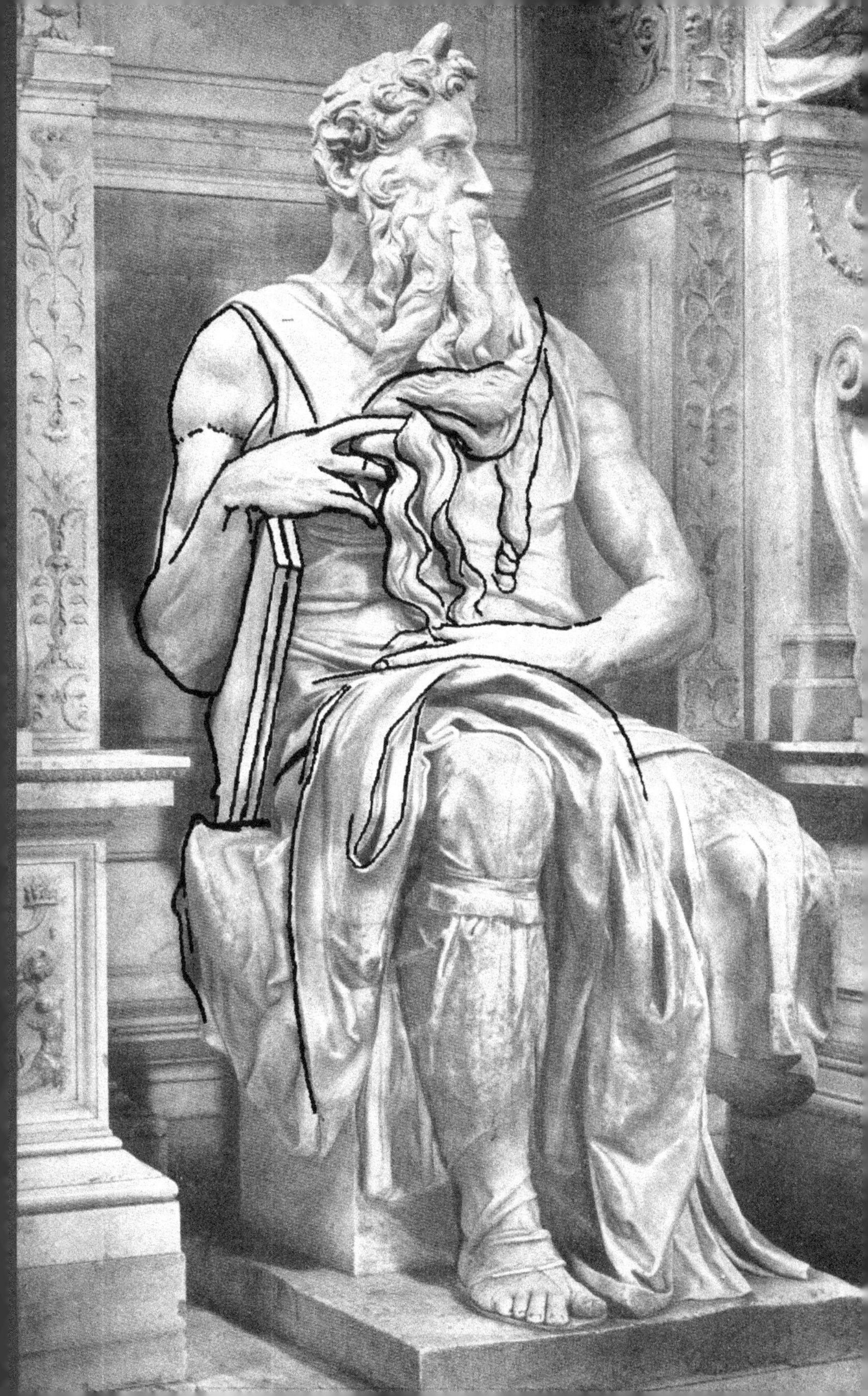

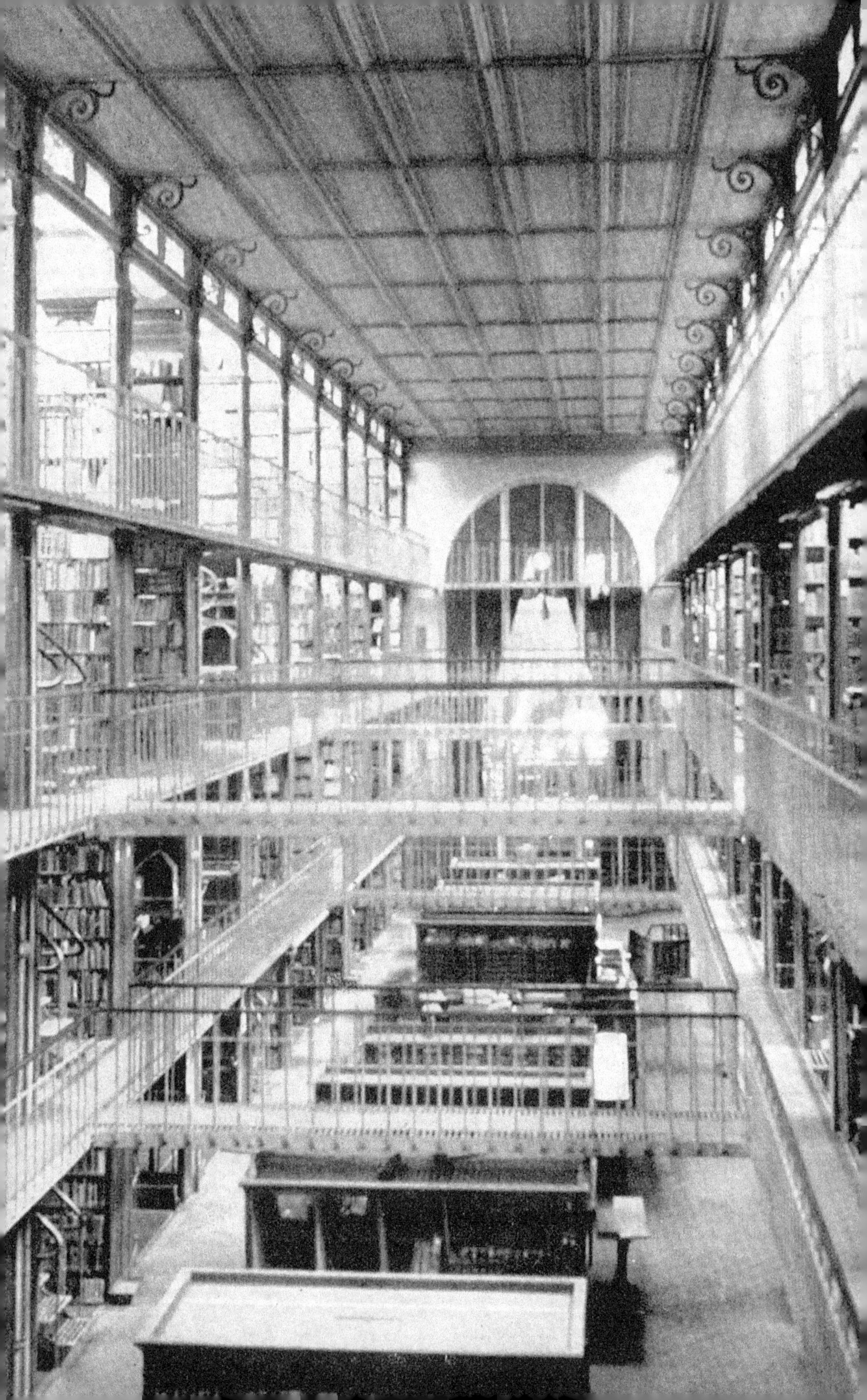

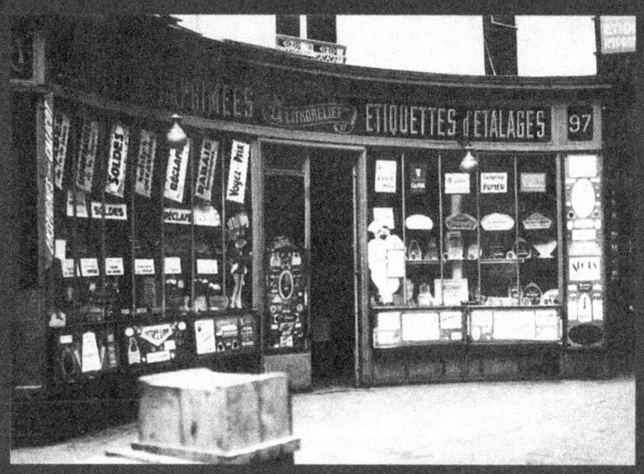

FIGURE 2.10
Germaine Krull, store in an arcade, Paris (ca. 1927–28).

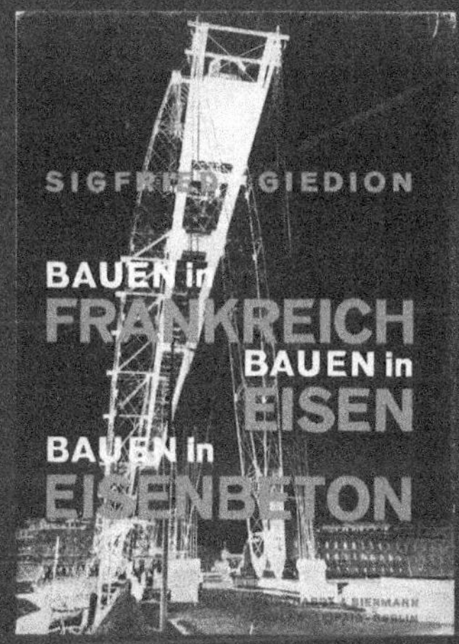

FIGURE 2.11
László Moholy-Nagy, cover for Sigfried Giedion's book *Bauen in Frankreich* (ca. 1928).

FIGURE 2.12
Sigfried Giedion, photograph of the stacks in the Bibliothèque nationale, Paris, designed by Henri Labrouste (from Sigfried Giedion, *Mechanization Takes Command*, 1948).

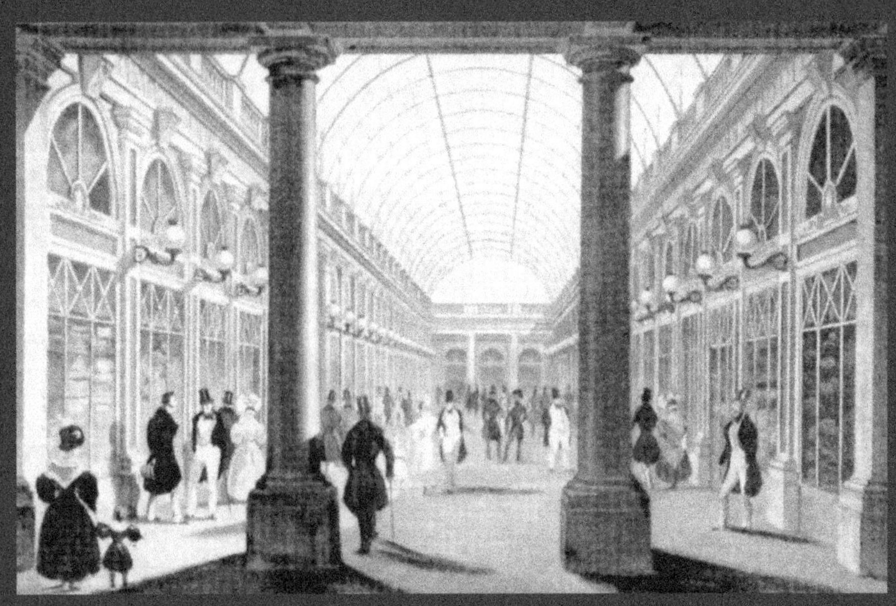

FIGURE 2.13

Pierre-François Fontaine, Galerie d'Orléans in the Palais Royal, Paris (1829–31; from Sigfried Giedion, *Mechanization Takes Command*, 1948).

FIGURE 2.14

Draperies and cushions for a smoking room in Oriental style (ca. 1879; from Sigfried Giedion, *Mechanization Takes Command*, 1948).

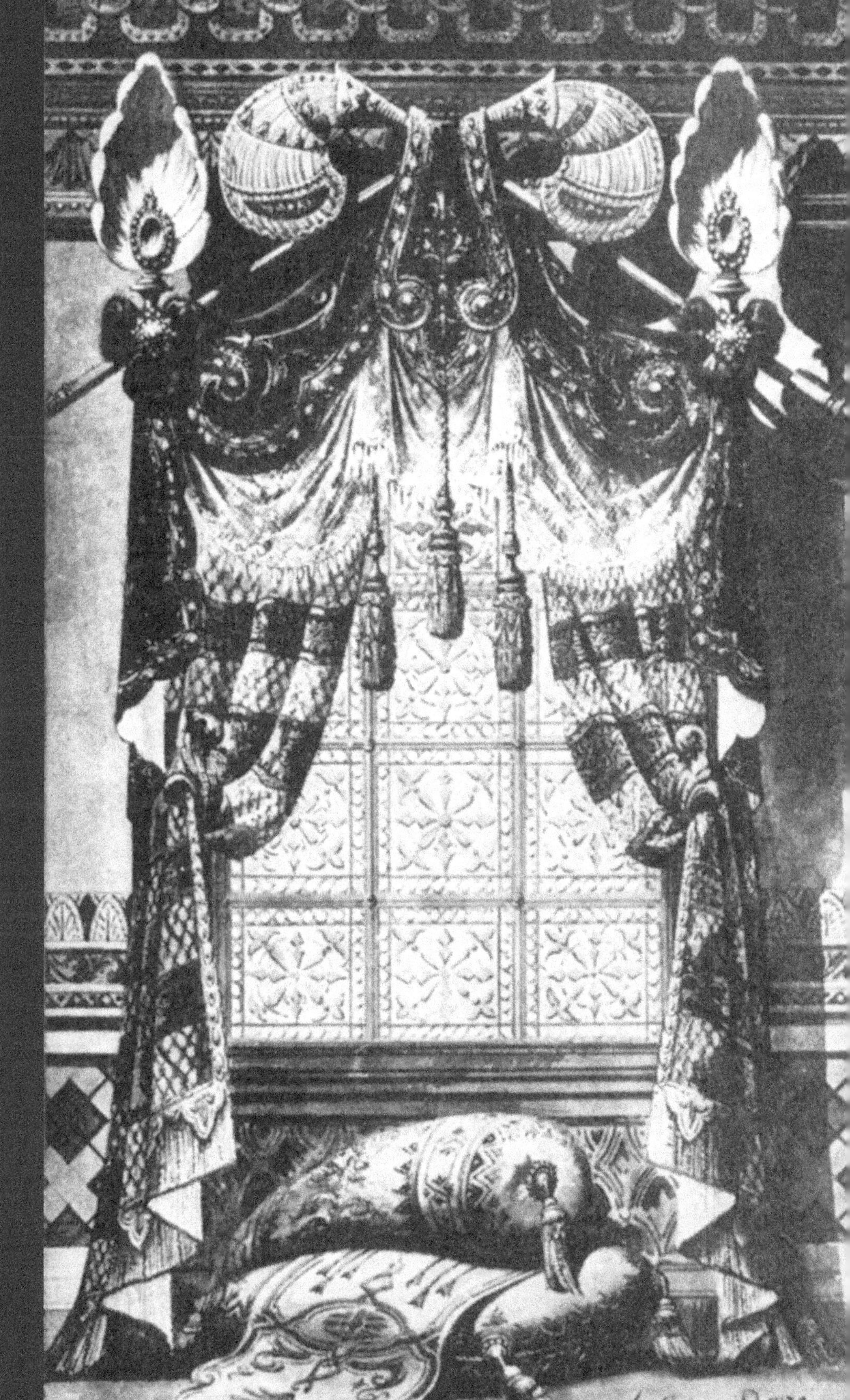

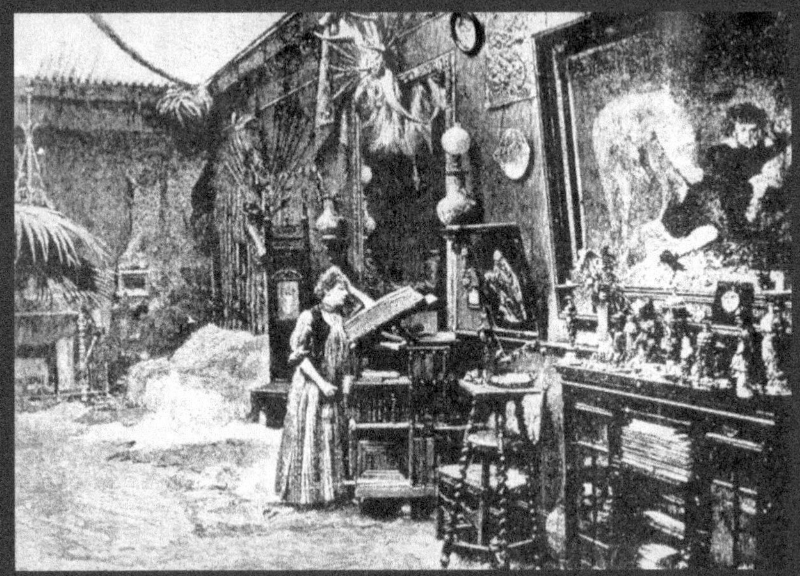

FIGURE 2.16

Haeckel's depiction of *Amoeba vulgaris*'s pseudopodia (1878). The amoeba is shown in two successive states. On the left, "several short," on the right, "several longer extensions [*Fortsätze*] and lobopodia are stretching out." In the protoplasm of the "naked cell" lie the nucleus (*n*) as well as "several foreign corpuscules ingested as food (*i*)."

FIGURE 2.17

Sigmund Freud, schema of the psychical apparatus (1923). The system perception–consciousness (*W–Bw.*) appears as a protective envelope that sits on top of the preconscious, the Ego, and the Id.

FIGURE 2.15

"Victory of the trimmings over the wood." Sarah Bernhardt's *salon* (ca. 1891; from Sigfried Giedion, *Mechanization Takes Command*, 1948).

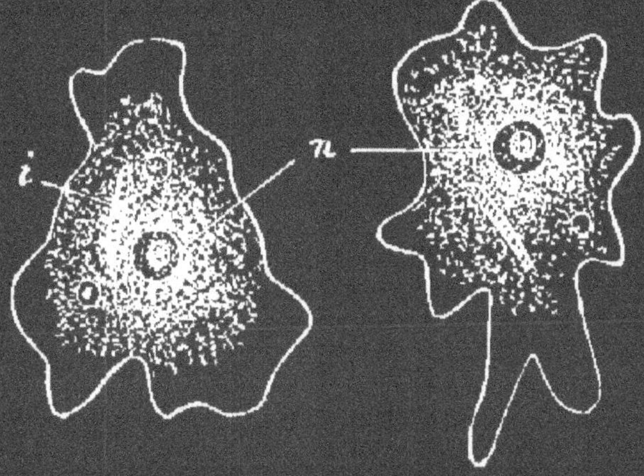
i
n

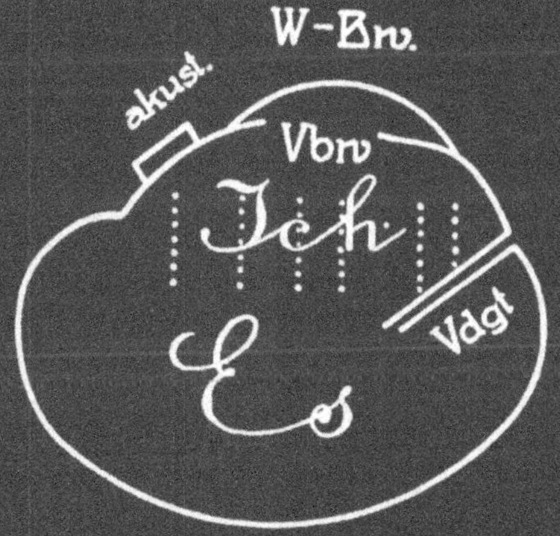
W-Bw.
akust.
Vbw
Ich
Es
Vdgt

THREE

Rhinoceros Cybernetics

Facing each other in this room are the Catalan artist Salvador Dalí and the Romanian diplomat and philosopher Matila Ghyka. Exhibited in the room are several Dalí paintings from the 1940s and 1950s: *Leda Atomica, Madonna of Port Lligat*, and *Paranoiac-Critical Study of Vermeer's "Lacemaker."* Lying next to a model of the DNA double helix are spiral-shaped horns of sheep, antelopes, and wild goats. The paintings are confronted with those illustrations from Ghyka's works about mathematics and art on which Dalí evidently relied as he painted them. Next to the letters Ghyka sent to the artist are some volumes on biology from Dalí's library: books by Francis Crick and James Watson, issues of *Scientific American*, but above all D'Arcy Thompson's treatise *On Growth and Form*. This room's motto comes from sociologist Heinrich Popitz: "Flintstone allows for shaping horn, horn allows for shaping wood. It is this exploitation of differences in hardness that must have given humans the idea of using one material as a means for working on another material and to perfect this means by working on it in turn."[1]

In 1962, Salvador Dalí appears in twofold form, as horned Moses and as cyborg. In *Dali de Gala*, the book by his friend, the photographer and filmmaker Robert Descharnes, we first see the artist in a detail from an old photograph, with two strands of his hair being held up (fig. 3.1). The original from the 1920s shows Dalí among his fellow students at the Madrid art academy. While his colleagues, palette in hand, are standing in a semicircle, he is sitting on the floor in front of them, slightly off center. Behind him, left and right, two fellow students are holding one strand each of his long hair up into the air—perhaps to draw attention to him, perhaps to tease him, perhaps also to point to a connection between brushes, hair, and painting. This latter interpretation is suggested by an abstract pastel painting of Dalí's from 1927. *Hair* shows nothing but wavy strands of hair that form patterns as complex as they are interesting.

Descharnes's book ignores such contexts by limiting itself to a section that shows only the torso, the face, and the hair held up in the air. But then, Dalí's commentary on this image opens up a further dimension: "I always make phantasms of deification spring from my head. Here it is Moses's horns."[2] The remark addresses a motif that Dalí was familiar with not only from cultural and art history but also from his intensive reading of Freud. Moreover, his famous visit to Freud in London at the end of the 1930s took place at the time that the psychoanalyst was finishing his great study *Moses and Monotheism*.

It therefore does not come as a surprise to see Dalí in the 1970s having a copy of Michelangelo's *Moses* installed in a niche of the glass-domed room of his theater museum in Figueres.[3] A little later, he creates a painting inspired by the sculpture. It shows a Moses head, surrounded by clouds and rock fragments, whose penetrating gaze returns to him like an electric flash and thereby begins to destroy his own figure.[4] Whereas at this point, then, the image of Moses literally begins to crack, the short remark in Descharnes's 1962 book indicates a less fractured and at the same time more contemporaneous context—among other things, Dalí's equally horn-shaped mustache, which by that time had not only become a kind of trademark of the artist but, in the collaboration with the photographer Philippe Halsman, had become a work of art in its own right.[5]

The photograph and commentary in Descharnes's book, moreover, allude to one of the main themes that occupied Dalí intensely in the postwar years. After the break with the surrealist movement and the turn to the classics of painting (Vermeer, Raphael, Leonardo, etc.) that followed it, the artist moved with great interest toward religion, mysticism, and magic. "Divine Dalí," as he started referring to himself around this time, began more and more to paint Madonnas, crucifixions, ascensions, and other biblical motifs, and in his writings, as references to psychoanalysis receded to the background, he increasingly cited philosophical and theological authors from the Middle Ages and early modernity. These especially included authors who had a connection with Catalonia, above all the theologian, philosopher, and poet Raimundus Lullus, the theoretician of the tree of the sciences, inventor of a logical machine, and founder of Catalan literature; the theologian of nature, Raimundus Sabundus, a student of Lullus and the author of the *Book of Creatures*; and Sabundus's admirer and translator, Michel de Montaigne, from whose *Essais* Dalí made a selection he illustrated and published in 1947.[6]

In the book by Descharnes, however, Dalí then also appears as a cyborg. A color photograph, a contemporary portrait of Dalí, serves as the volume's frontispiece. In the picture, Dalí is wearing a Catalan *barretina* on his head and glasses on his nose as he is focused on work on the easel or on reading. Once again, Dalí's comment drastically changes the context of the image: "The painter must be intelligent. Like a cook, he must officiate with a headgear. His headgear should be a soft substitute for Pallas Athena's hard helmet. The headgear should contain and conceal an electronic and cybernetic apparatus by means of which televised information could be communicated through the spectacles."[7]

The comparison between artists and cooks still recalls the statement from the 1930s, aimed at André Breton, that beauty would not be "convulsive" but rather "will be edible or will cease to be."[8] The evocation of Athena opposes the regime of the hard to the order of the soft that is so fundamental for Dalí's artistic work. In the same breath, the motif of protection and defense originally associated with Athena's helmet is transformed into an image of reception and communication.

It remains unclear, however, where the information comes from that the cybernetic apparatus on the head is to receive and project into the artist's glasses. Does it consist once more in phantasms that "spring from [the artist's] head" or is it in fact television images that are to be transmitted in order to link up with, overlay, and blend with perceptions of the real world, similar to today's head-mounted displays?

It seems, in fact, that Dalí imagined something like the latter. Descharnes at least claims that just prior to the taking of the portrait, the artist had acquired a glasses-like apparatus that allowed for projecting television images into the wearer's field of vision. There indeed existed at least a prototype of this apparatus. In the early 1960s, the Hughes Aircraft Company had developed the "electrocular," and like the owner of the company, the legendary Howard Hughes, it stood for a remarkable compromise between optical machines and airplane technologies: the purpose of the device was to transmit to pilots during flight television images of meteorological conditions on the ground or information on air traffic (fig. 3.2).

The basic idea was simple. At the end of a tube, into which a small television screen had been inserted and which was to be attached to the side of the head, there was a small mirror that could transmit the TV images to an eyepiece mounted at an angle in front of the right eye. And "since the monocle-type eye-piece is a transparent mirror, the wearer can look through the image, when necessary, to concentrate on what is actually in front of him."[9]

It is unclear how Dalí obtained the electrocular, and there are no photographs or other documents to show how and on what occasions he employed it. According to Descharnes, however, the artist was convinced that this device could be used to train that "second type of vision" that the inventor of the "paranoiac-critical method" had staged time and again since his surrealist phase.[10] What in his paintings, through painstaking labor, led to double views, optical illusions, and gestalt effects, it seemed, could also be achieved technically through the superimposition of images of reality and television images.

According to Descharnes, Dalí's enthusiasm for the connection between optical machines, aircraft, and cybernetics went so far that he—the Greek origin of the term "cybernetics" in mind—conceived of the artist as such as "the pilot of his own life."[11] "We already have prodigious cybernetic machines far superior to the people using them," Dalí said at the time in an interview, and he did not hold back with his expectation that painting would be "rescued by this new technique."[12] For that very reason, in the postwar years he increasingly sought to remain in touch with contemporary science and technology. He referred to Heisenberg as his "father," conversed with James Watson about the double helix of DNA, experimented with video technology as early as the 1960s, later worked with the inventor of holography, Dennis Gabor, and studied René Thom's work on the mathematics of morphogenesis as well as, for example, Ilya Progogine's theory of dissipative structures.[13]

Horned Moses and cyborg: the academic literature leaves no doubt that bringing together the Middle Ages and modernity, magic and technology, religion and science is one major characteristic of Dalí's postsurrealist œuvre. Nor is there any doubt that the horn, especially the rhinoceros horn, is the symbol par excellence of the period, stretching roughly from 1950 to 1965, that is commonly called the "nuclear phase" or phase of "nuclear mysticism" but to which Dalí himself referred as his "rhinocerontic period."[14]

The judgments of Dalí experts about this part of the oeuvre, however, diverge dramatically. Whereas some speak almost condescendingly of a "rhinomania" and see in these works just another whim of an "eccentric genius," others restrict the importance of this phase by assigning significance exclusively to the film project *L'histoire prodigieuse de la dentellière et le rhinocéros* (*The Prodigious Story of the Lacemaker and the Rhinoceros*), on which the artist was working with Descharnes from 1954 to 1962 and which has remained unfinished to this day.[15]

In what follows, by contrast, I set out to show that Dalí's turn toward the horn implies a profound revision of his conception of the relationship between body, image, and technology that remains relevant for media theory to this day—also and especially in discussions of media of the tactile. Dalí's interest in the newest achievements of science and technology can certainly be traced back all the way to his early work. Already in the 1920s, impressed with futurism, he praised "the simple and moving beauty of the miraculous mechanical and industrial world" and gushed about the "aesthetics of objectivity" that, thanks to microscopy and telescopy on the one hand and photography on the other, had found its way into both the sciences and the arts.[16]

Already in the 1920s, too, he "propagate[d] the idea that we truly live already in a post-machinist age," an age that was not characterized "by machinism and by an architecture of self-punishment"—as it was in Le Corbusier, at whom the charge of "machinism" is directed—but instead by the life-affirming architecture of Antoni Gaudí, which Dalí continued in the nourishing softness of motors, clocks, cars, and TVs.[17]

Nor is there any doubt that this postmachinist agenda had already been specified in the "laboratory" of surrealism by way of multiple references to contemporary science and Gaston Bachelard's "surrationalist" philosophy of science.[18] Besides modern physics with its curved spaces and non-Euclidean geometries, Dalí was above all interested, in this context, in the disciplines concerned with soft materials and living forms. His references here are quite detailed. In an explanatory remark on the melting clocks represented in *The Persistence of Memory* (1931), for instance, he cites the contributions to colloid research Jacques Loeb, Jacques Duclaux, and Charles Honoré Maurain made in the 1910s and 1920s. At the end of the 1930s, Dalí draws on the work of the biochemist Stéphane Leduc, a pioneer of "synthetic biology," to find a scientific explanation for the shine of the pearls depicted in Vermeer's paintings. And like other surrealists at the time, he engaged with attempts, partly mathematically oriented, partly biologically, to provide the field of aesthetics with a scientific basis, above all Édouard Monod-Herzen's project of a "general morphology."[19]

Around 1940, after the break with the surrealist movement, however, the artist's turn to the tradition of painting comes with a shift in his aesthetics of objectivity. What Dalí now seeks to study, grasp, and put to practical use are the concrete conditions and historical particularities of the "magic craftsmanship," that is, the technique of painting itself. This concerns not just specific colors, brushes, and surfaces but also and perhaps primarily specific machines for seeing, as he explains in a 1948 pamphlet, *50 Secrets of Magic Craftsmanship*.[20] In this treatise, set up partly as practical guide for aspiring painters, and partly as a variation on da Vinci's writings on painting, he evokes classical devices for producing central perspective views such as the camera obscura and the perspective grid but supplements them with constructions of his own that are meant to support the artistic observation of nature or of one's own pictures.

When compared to the electrocular, these constructs are emphatically low tech; nonetheless, they are intriguing in the idiosyncratic combination of the technological and biological that Dalí, an admirer of Roussel's, stages with their help.[21] His "aranarium," for example, consists of four round wooden frames whose supports are inhabited by spiders meant to cover the frames with their webs. Once that has happened, the artist, through these frames and webs, is able to study in unprecedented fashion the play of colors of a landscape mirrored in a crystal ball or glass bottle (fig. 3.3).

Although such hybrid constructs certainly contrast with Dalí's pronounced interest in contemporary technologies of image production, there is a shared point of reference: it is the "miracle" that, since Vermeer, has consisted, according to Dalí, in "using products of the earth and a simple brush to obtain the illusion of space." Vermeer's innovative achievement "was to superimpose successive and very fine layers of paint to create an illusion of atmospheric space. . . . Structures almost invisible to the naked eye produced spatial images." Accordingly, Dalí does not want to enter history as a surrealist or a former surrealist but as "the first after Vermeer to renew a technique," the technique of painting.[22]

This explains why Dalí's "post-machinist" agenda aims at overcoming the intellectualist subordination of the human to the machine by means of a fruitful adaptation of technology to life. The following pages seek to illustrate that in the rhinoceros phase this agenda undergoes a marked change: it sheds its anthropological connotations and begins to be guided by biology. In the years before 1950, the artist's work usually follows a prosthesis paradigm. Individual technical objects appear as extensions and deformations of the human body: tongues become spoons, the female breast turns into a drawer, a bent leg mutates into a table, et cetera et cetera.

Yet the moment Dalí turns to the apparently archaic organism of the rhinoceros, he goes beyond the anthropological horizon of this postmachinist vision and adopts the biological perspective of morphology. Human and machine no longer appear as complete forms that are first juxtaposed and then amalgamated. The comparative gaze on the armored rhinoceros suggests instead a more abstract relationship. Life and technics now appear as tied in and connected with one another in multiple ways.

The prosthetic paradigm is replaced by a contemplation of "nuclear" phenomena and processes on whose shared basis organism on the one hand and machine on the other differentiate in the first place. The idea of extending the human body is superseded by the superimposition and penetration of biological and technological components. At the same time, superimposition and penetration are understood in terms of phenomena and processes of morphogenesis that characterize life as a whole. This, precisely, is what makes Dalí relevant today: what he sketches is nothing short of a biology of media.

Inspired by the work of Matila Ghyka, whose significance for the Dalí of the postwar years has been noted repeatedly,[23] the artist picks up in particular on a treatise by the anatomist and zoologist D'Arcy Wentworth Thompson. In *On Growth and Form*, Thompson outlines a dynamic morphology of biological entities (cells, tissue, skeletons, etc.) and devotes an entire chapter to "The Shapes of Horns," which Dalí, fascinated with rhinoceroses, reads attentively. Following Thompson, Dalí begins no longer with an isolated technical object that would confront the human as a tool or machine but, via shells, carapaces, and the like, takes architecture, as a fundamental phenomenon of everything technical, as his guide.

Against this background, the question of tactility becomes relevant as well. It does so in a contradictory manner: while Dalí's enthusiasm for the Lullist ideal of chivalrous-courtly love and his interest in contemporary particle physics lead to pictorial representations in which everything is suspended and every contact between bodies, objects, and landscapes is avoided, the painting itself becomes a phenomenon of intensive layering that emerges thanks to the successive application, by the hand of the painter, of strata of materials. Instead of being subjected any longer to the primacy of photography, painting thus advances to become a phenomenon of sedimentation. It no longer appears as the automatic fixation of an objectivity but becomes a highly complex formation of shells and carapaces, a manually constructed expression of "a dermo-skeletal soul—bones on the outside, superfine flesh within."[24]

A Lecture at the Sorbonne . . .

The lecture Dalí gave at the Sorbonne in the mid-1950s is one of his most succinct statements of the interlocking themes and motifs of the rhinoceros period. On December 17, 1955, Dalí, accompanied by his friend, the painter Georges Mathieu, drove up to the "temple of knowledge" in a Rolls-Royce—the backseat filled with a heap of cauliflower. Greeted by a flurry of photographers' flashes, he began to speak in the university's large lecture hall to convey "the craziest communication of his life."[25]

Although he had long turned his back on surrealism, the very title of his lecture, "Phenomenological Aspects of the Paranoiac-Critical Method," picks up on Dalí's discourses of the 1920s and 1930s, and its content affirms this connection in that it refers to phantasms, dreams and fears, and the category of "objective randomness." Nor have the discourses of psychoanalysis and psychiatry been dismissed; quite the contrary. Already at the beginning of his lecture, Dalí declares that for him, the question to what extent his craziness (*délire*) is "creative and valid" remains central. And the fact, too, that the decisive part of the announced "communication" is a childhood memory evokes the psychoanalytically inspired prewar Dalí more than the postwar Dalí interested in nuclear physics and Catholicism. Nonetheless, the speaker does not explicitly address phenomenologists, psychoanalysts, or psychiatrists, but "scientists [*savants*], and above all morphologists."[26]

The childhood memory in question shows nine-year-old Dalí in his parents' home in Figueres, where the song of a nightingale "deeply move[s]" him "to tears" and puts him in a state of "lyrical ecstasy." He then sits in the dining room, "practically naked," pretending to be asleep in order to attract the attention of "a young servant girl." Then a tactile sensation asserts itself: "On the tablecloth, there were dry bread crusts that produced a very sharp pain in my elbow."[27]

He then feels how he is gripped and "absolutely obsessed" by the picture *De kantwerkster* (*The Lacemaker*), a reproduction of which hung on a wall in his father's office and was visible through the open door—and by rhinoceros horns. The "illusion" of the horns prompted by Vermeer's painting, he says, emphatically imposed itself. Although—or precisely because—his friends thought him "clearly crazy" because of it, he has remained faithful to the rhinoceros illusion in the years since and, ultimately, to this day.[28]

In keeping with an agenda he had outlined in the 1930s with regard to another "obsessive image," namely Millet's *Angelus*, however, Dalí now does not proceed to an interpretation of the evidently sexual contents of his memory (lacemaker = servant girl, rhinoceros = phallus, etc.). Rather, he tries "precisely *to make the most of*" the passive character of this memory "on the very plane of 'action,'" that is, to have it "intervene," as in an experiment, "in reality, in life."[29]

To this end, he first enriches the account of his childhood memory. This is of interest to us here because Dalí goes even further in transposing the scene of the viewing of the image onto a tactile register. What is foregrounded, though, is not touching or gripping but stinging or pricking—a motive obviously stimulated by the fact that the young woman in Vermeer's painting, with needles, threads, and bobbins, is engaged in a work whose product, lace, is referred to in French as *dentelle*, "little tooth," in Dutch *kant*, from Middle Dutch *cant*, "point." Dalí claims that the center of Vermeer's picture is empty in a remarkable way: "What moved me the most in this painting is that everything converged precisely in a needle, a pin, that is not painted but only suggested."[30]

In this staging of emptiness, however, Dalí sees an essential trait of Vermeer's art. This anticipates the later assessment cited above that Vermeer was so pathbreaking a painter because he succeeded in evoking a spatial image with "structures almost invisible."[31] In the Sorbonne amphitheater, Dalí declares Vermeer's strength to be that he "does not touch the object." In contrast, a modern painter like Matisse "assaults [*violente*] reality, transforms it," and makes it shrink down to "bacchic proximity."[32] The aesthetic concept of not touching is thus not based exclusively on the discourse of particle physics.

Dalí stresses this point: precisely by not touching his object, Vermeer grips the viewers of his painting. More than that: the effects of the suggested needle are eminently real for the viewer. This is true not only of young Dalí resting his elbow on the crumb-strewn table but of adult Dalí as well: "Very often I felt the sharpness of this needle with such reality in my own flesh, in my elbow, that I woke up with a start in the middle of the most heavenly nap."[33] A reproduction of Vermeer's painting takes on the job of stinging. Its empty center becomes an element that—similar to Benjamin's Dada painting or, later, Barthes's photographic *punctum*, "shoots out of" its context to "pierce" the viewer.[34]

What Dalí describes here is the counterside of (pictorial) media. The result of this description is an image charged with tactile energy, an image with immense expansive potential. He continues, "This painting [*The Lacemaker*] has always been considered very peaceful and excessively calm. For me it possessed one of the most violent forces in the field of aesthetics, which can be compared only with the recently discovered antiproton."[35] Just as for every particle, there is an antiparticle with the opposite charge, so the calm conveyed by *The Lacemaker* is only the positive charge, as it were, of a profound unrest of negativity. In that sense the pictorial image, one might say, does not exist without its tactilely effective antipictoriality, the stinging emptiness of its center.

The report thus enriched then transitions to a further engagement with the two elements that—putting aside another "obsessional image," namely Dürer's *Rhinocerus* drawing—encounter each other in the childhood memory as randomly as the sewing machine and the umbrella on Lautréamont's dissecting table.[36] The first step of this engagement consists in producing a copy, as precise as possible, of Vermeer's painting. Having made a request to this end, Dalí in November 1954 obtained permission from the Louvre to paint a copy of *The Lacemaker* in front of the original (fig. 3.4). In his lecture, he presents the result as a kind of confirmation of his delusional childhood memory: "I arrived at the Louvre not knowing what my copy would be like. And to the great surprise of my friends and of the Louvre conservator, what appeared on the canvas in place of the Lacemaker were rhinoceros horns. I must say I kind of expected it."[37]

On his own account, however, Dalí realized the deeper meaning of this defamiliarizing copy only later (fig. 3.5). In Port Lligat in the summer of the following year, he says, he understood the formal aspects of his copy. Surrounded by numerous large-scale reproductions of *The Lacemaker* he had hung in his house and garden, he recognized that on his own copy-painting, he had drawn none other but "strictly logarithmic curves" (fig. 3.6).[38]

At this point, he claims, the engagement with Vermeer linked up with the "study . . . of the morphology of the sunflower" he had begun two years earlier in a different context. Dalí points to a prominent predecessor: "Leonardo da Vinci already drew exceedingly interesting conclusions from it [the morphology of the sunflower]."[39] Da Vinci indeed, in his notebooks, remarks on the spiral arrangement of leaves of plants. Dalí goes on to explain that to this day, experts debate whether the arrangement of sunflowers' brown disk florets does indeed follow a logarithmic spiral. He, at least, had recognized in sunflower disks some elements of the Vermeer painting (silhouette, millinery, cushion, etc.).

Because of the similarity between the sunflower spiral and the curve of the rhinoceros horn, he "immediately . . . made inquiries about the rhinoceros horn itself," which left no doubt that "never has there been in nature a more perfect example of the logarithmic curve than in the curve of the rhinoceros horn." At this point, the conclusion he draws from this practical work on and with Vermeer is that "morphologically speaking, the *Lacemaker* is a rhinoceros horn."[40] Simultaneously, this seems to prove Dalí's craziness to indeed be "creative and valid."

. . . And a Visit to the Zoo

Dalí, however, does not content himself with noting a formal commonality between Vermeer's painting, the curvature of the rhinoceros horn, and the arrangement of sunflower florets. He rather understands the concordance he observed as a hypothesis to be tested. This pushes the encounter of the heterogeneous even further. Dalí in fact directly confronts Vermeer's masterpiece, which is both his smallest and in some parts his most abstract painting, with the huge and immensely impressive organism of the rhinoceros. He is actually concerned with an experimental scenario, a concrete interaction between painting and animal, between work of art and organism, between culture and nature. He continues, "The moment I saw for the first time the *Lacemaker* in a photograph, in an image, placed before a living rhinoceros, I realized that if there were to be a fight, the *Lacemaker* would win."[41]

This alludes to a public appearance of his some months earlier at the Vincennes zoo. In May 1955, he had posed there for a group of journalists as he was working on his version of the Vermeer painting by a rhinoceros enclosure (fig. 3.7). In the films made on that occasion, we see Dalí, surrounded by his companions, hurrying toward the rhinoceros enclosure, an easel under his arm. A large-scale reproduction of *The Lacemaker* is being hung inside this enclosure, from which the rhinoceros present does in fact retreat a few steps. Then we see Dalí, sitting on a wheelbarrow, working on his copy, time and again looking into the enclosure, a crust of bread—apparently an allusion to the childhood memory—being held to his head. Another scene shows Dalí, with *The Lacemaker* and the rhinoceros in the background, holding the almost completed copy of the Vermeer painting next to his mustache-armored face to give those present an even better view of the work (and himself).

The performance concludes with a remarkable sequence in which Dalí runs toward the back side of a large-scale paper copy of *The Lacemaker* held up by two of his companions in a wooden frame and pierces it with a lance (fig. 3.8). One might see this as alluding to Don Quixote, who in this case rebels not against the power of new kinds of machines but against the fascination exerted by traditional painting.[42] One can also, however, see in it a reflex reaction to the fact Dalí emphasized, namely that in Vermeer's painting everything is oriented toward a needle that is "not painted but only suggested." Dalí's attack on the image would then have to be conceived as a violent filling-in of this empty spot by means of a giant needle, a counterattack against the stinging qualities of the image, which, however, is thereby destroyed.

In a certain sense, the painter here is himself becoming a rhinoceros getting involved in a tactile struggle with *The Lacemaker* whom, in the end, it defeats thanks to a ruse, the attack from behind. Such an interpretation is strengthened by the fact that Dalí's lance is a narwhal "horn." Be that as it may, the press saw the performance at the zoo as an example of a "surrealist cure," as Dalí is said to have stated at the end: "I am cured, thanks to my paranoiac-critical method."[43] As in the Sorbonne lecture, this goes back to the Dalí of the prewar years.

The lecture does not mention the details of the zoo operation. Dalí leaves it at his assessment that in the event of a fight with the rhinoceros, *The Lacemaker* would emerge victorious. Speaking before the university audience, Dalí, it seems, considers the hypothesis that the Vermeer painting and the horn of the rhinoceros share a formal structure—the logarithmic spiral—to be confirmed by the experiment only preliminarily, for he goes on to verify it in other ways. Thus he tries to demonstrate that the horn is a basic visual component in other paintings as well. He first refers to some of his own paintings, *Corpus Hypercubus*, *Metamorphosis of Narcissus*, and *The Persistence of Memory*, and then to some works by Raphael that, with the help of copies and not unlike *The Lacemaker*, he has dissolved into arrangements of tiny horns.

In a last turn of his allocution, Dalí returns to the sunflower and explains why the comparison between this plant and Vermeer's painting does not really fit. The curves of the sunflower are too "melancholic" and lack dynamism. The expansive momentum of *The Lacemaker*, he says, is much better expressed in the form of the cauliflower, which "is constituted . . . by real logarithmic curves" and which, we may add, has been used as a metaphor for the clouds of smoke produced by atomic explosions.[44]

This reference to the cauliflower, however, was a real cliffhanger. As Dalí had to admit, the cauliflower heads he had piled up in the back of this Rolls-Royce were not large enough to allow for recognizing in them the structures of *The Lacemaker*. Nevertheless, he was utterly convinced that in the coming spring, he would be able to provide "huge cauliflowers" on which, viewing them from a certain angle, "everyone will see Vermeer's *Lacemaker* with its particular technique."[45]

Dalí follows up with two anecdotes on objective randomness that serve above all to make mention of people like Jean Cocteau and institutions like the Centre international d'études esthétiques, then evokes once more the much admired Raimundus Lullus, and sums up his remarks by voicing his conviction that "to have been able to go from the Lacemaker to the Sunflower, from the Sunflower to the Rhinoceros, and from the Rhinoceros to the Cauliflower, one must really be or have something between the ears [*dans le crâne*]"[46]—which may count as a final, positive answer to the question raised at the beginning of the lecture.

Whether this answer convinced the audience in the lecture hall of the Sorbonne remains open. While the reactions of listeners are recorded in the transcript of the tape recording, their spectrum—from "applause" to "stirs" and "laughter"—is too ambiguous for any meaningful conclusions to be drawn.

Among those in attendance was the psychoanalyst Jacques Lacan, who had known Dalí since the early 1930s. It seems that Lacan went to the lecture accompanied by some of the participants in his seminar. In the next meeting on December 21, 1955, in any case, he briefly mentions the lecture "we heard recently from one of my old friends at the Sorbonne, who recounted some astonishing things to us last Saturday, namely the metamorphosis of the lacemaker into rhinoceros horns and finally into cauliflowers."[47] The question of the plausibility of these "astonishing things," at least for the psychoanalyst, too, remains suspended. Nor was Lacan able, or willing, to make a connection between the rhinoceros and the elephant, to whom he had devoted some reflections in an earlier seminar.[48]

Some years later, however, a former student of Lacan's, Félix Guattari, returns to Dalí's rhinoceros period. Prompted by the big Dalí retrospective at the Centre Pompidou in 1979, Guattari and Deleuze in *A Thousand Plateaus* bring out the difference that exists between the psychoanalytic interpretation of animals—of which Freud's case study of Wolf Man is emblematic—

and the artistic experimentalization of nonhuman organisms: "For example, Salvador Dali, in attempting to reproduce his delusions, may go on at length about THE rhinoceros horn; he has not for all of that left neurotic discourse behind. But when he starts comparing goosebumps to a field of tiny rhinoceros horns, we get the feeling that the atmosphere has changed and that we are now in the presence of madness. Is it still a question of a comparison at all? It is, rather, a pure multiplicity that changes elements, or *becomes*."[49] In that he does not remain on the level of the "whole" rhinoceros but switches onto the molecular level of elementary components, Dalí's rhinoceros discourse here appears as a model for the processes of becoming-animal described in another chapter of *A Thousand Plateaus*. That would indeed be a clear verdict: Dalí was convincing; his madness is indeed "creative and valid."

The Spectacle of the Rhinoceros Period

In Dalí's Sorbonne lecture, the morphological comparison between the distribution of tiny rhinoceros horns and the phenomenon of goose bumps did not yet play a role. This comparison, which takes up the theme of an early painting (*Inaugural Gooseflesh*, 1928) and at the same time amplifies the tactile aspects that characterize Dalí's childhood memory of *The Lacemaker*, is progressively enriched in the course of the various projects and performances that mark the rhinoceros phase.

In his 1957 monograph about the artist, Michel Tapié quotes some of the remarks that, in one breath, speak of the painting of "rhinocerontic and dynamic corpuscules" and of painting as "cosmic goose bumps," and according to Descharnes, Dalí around the same time staged several performances that employed screeching sounds with the aim of producing goose bumps on female test subjects.[50]

Although Dalí himself dates the beginning of the rhinoceros period to 1952,[51] the motif of the rhinoceros makes its entry into his pictorial cosmos even earlier. Paintings, watercolors, and drawings such as *Rhinoceros Disintegrating* (1950), *Madonna of Port Lligat* (also 1950), and *Celestial Ride* (1957) show full views of the large animal, either dominating the space of the picture (fig. 3.9) or appearing at the picture's edge as a kind of heraldic animal (fig. 3.22). Further depictions are occasionally found in the 1960s and 1970s (*Op Rhinoceros*, 1970) but, as has already been the case earlier, come in to accentuate the phallic connotations of the rhinoceros only exceptionally, for example in the prints illustrating Casanova's memoirs (1967). Also dating from the early 1950s is the sculpture *Rhinoceros Dressed in Lace* (1954), which clearly takes up Dürer's classic depiction but also, via the lace motif, establishes a connection with Vermeer and, with the goose bump–like shell of a sea urchin, introduces a further motif in the overarching theme.[52]

In parallel with these representations of rhinoceroses, hornlike elements—more or less curved or more or less rounded cones, tetrahedra, and pyramids—make their way into Dalí's work. In paintings such as *Assumpta corpuscularia lapislazulina* (1952), *Portrait of Gala with Rhinocerotic Symptoms* (1954), *The Disintegration of the Persistence of Memory* (1952–54), and *Young Virgin Auto-sodomized by the Horns of Her Own Chastity* (1954), one of the most explicit representations of the horn as phallus, horn elements of various sizes function as "nuclear" components from which complex figures and motifs (faces, bodies, landscapes, etc.) are assembled.

Beyond that, these image corpuscules are used as quasi-analytic tools in the creative engagement with other artists. Dalí operates dismantlings similar to that of Vermeer's *Lacemaker* on the *Madonna Colonna* as well as other depictions of Mary by Raphael, on Leonardo da Vinci's *Leda and the Swan*, but also on a sculpture, attributed to Phidias, depicting the torso of the river god Ilisos on the Parthenon frieze.

Besides these artistic engagements with traditional art, Dalí also brings his work with and on the rhinoceros horn to bear in a series of other media. The most important project in this context is undoubtedly the film *The Prodigious Story of the Lacemaker and the Rhinoceros* (1954–62). The goal of the movie was to give a filmic representation of Dalí's critical-paranoiac activity: "Robert Descharnes attempts to show its development in Dali's life and to explain the application of this method both in his painting and in parallel investigations, like those that lead from Vermeer's *Lacemaker* to gooseflesh, via the rhinoceros and the cauliflower."[53]

In addition to documenting Dalí's execution of the Vermeer copy in the Louvre and the Vincennes zoo, *The Prodigious Story* was to contain a wealth of new sequences, of which, however, only a part were shot and whose subject changed as time went on. Dalí, moreover, put some of his visual ideas in practice on American television when, in 1956, he received an offer to have some scenes shot for *The Morning Show* on CBS. Among other things, they "included the head of a rhinoceros, twelve cauliflowers, a film clip of an atomic explosion, a reproduction of *The Lacemaker* and a photograph of a rhinoceros horn."[54]

Both the movie recordings by Descharnes and the CBS television program served as occasions for photographically documenting Dalí's activities, and it is these photographs that have played a decisive role in defining Dalí's rhinoceros period. They show the artist in action: in the Louvre, in the Vincennes zoo, and at home in Port Lligat. We see him swimming in the sea together with Gala and yet another large-scale reproduction of *The Lacemaker*, which he "baptizes." We see a copy of the Phidias sculpture installed in his studio, and standing on top of it, a row of natural horns. And we meet Dalí, a soft hat on his head, standing eye to eye with a mounted rhinoceros (fig. 3.10).

Probably the most forceful image in this series is the photograph published in Descharnes's book in which Vermeer's painting *The Art of Painting* is being reenacted. It shows Dalí in the role of the painter and Gala in the role of the model, holding in her hand not a book and a trumpet but a rhinoceros horn. She is surrounded by antlers mounted on the wall, and the painter's reading desk is furnished with reproductions of *The Lacemaker* and the photograph of a sunflower (fig. 3.11).

The books and essays Dalí publishes in the 1950s and 1960s further contribute to propagating the rhinoceros phase. In the 1951 "Mystical Manifesto," the rhinoceros features not only as the heraldic animal of "positivist and progressive science" (fig. 3.12), it is also at the basis of an entire intellectual construct that leads from Pythagoras and Euclid to Lullus and Sabundus and makes its way from there to Raphael and Vermeer to finally reach Gaudí and Dalí. In 1956, the Sorbonne lecture is published in a special issue of the journal *La vie médicale* on the relationship between art and psychopathology, side by side with articles on "The Sculpture of the Mentally Ill," children's drawings, and a study on the work of Odilon Redon.

The year 1956 also sees the publication of Dalí's book *Les cocus du vieil art moderne* (*The Cuckolds of Antiquated Modern Art*), in which, citing Gaudí, he reaffirms his rejection of Le Corbusier's "machinist" architecture and launches an all-out attack on abstract painting. The book begins with a reminder of the "already excessively famous lecture at the Sorbonne" and ends with a short description of the film project he is pursuing with Descharnes. In 1959, he and the publisher Albert Skira make plans for an English-language journal. Its title was to be *Rhinoceros* and the subtitle, *A Most Unique International Magazine Devoted to Maximum Spiritual Potential for Thinking Readers* (fig. 3.13).

Following the vivid depiction of the rhinoceros period in Descharnes's illustrated *Dalí de Gala*, Dalí in 1964 publishes his *Diary of a Genius*. It covers the years from 1952 to 1963 and contains a number of anecdotes pertaining to the rhinoceros period. The Sorbonne lecture, too, is documented and commented on once more. And as late as 1966, in his conversations with

Alain Bosquet, Dalí speaks of the rhinoceros as the "animal that carries an incredible sum of cosmic knowledge inside its armor" and dreams of the city of Paris one day devoting a statue to him in the form of a rhinoceros.[55]

The Geometry of Art and Life

As varied and suggestive as Dalí's activities during his rhinoceros phase presented themselves, they were not disconnected or unfounded. The foundation that linked them was not objective randomness, even if Dalí suggests as much when he writes in his diary that, out of nowhere, "the good poet Loten" (a reference to Emmanuel Looten) had given him a "rhinoceros horn" as a present in 1952, which prompted him, Dalí, to exclaim to Gala, "This horn is going to save my life!" This, he claims, was soon confirmed by the insight into the function of the horn as an "elementary geometric volume."[56]

The starting point and guiding thread of the works and performances was not simply the "creative" madness of the artist who, thanks to his paranoiac-critical method, connected apparently arbitrarily chosen motifs like the rhinoceros horn, the sunflower, and the cauliflower. The themes of this period, rather, were sustained by Dalí's engagement with scientific questions concerning morphogenesis and design that, as we saw with Leduc, Monod-Herzen, and others, had already occupied him in the 1930s.

In that sense, it was quite a rhetorical move to stress that he was turning to the scientists and especially the morphologists in the audience with "the craziest communication of his life." In fact, he had long turned to them, and one of the central claims of his lecture, namely that the logarithmic spiral is manifest in the rhinoceros horn as much as in the arrangement of sunflower florets, had been supported by scientific evidence for quite some time.

The decisive middle man for Dalí in this context was the Romanian author and philosopher Matila Ghyka. Born in 1881, the scion of an old Romanian aristocratic family, Prince Matila Costiesco Ghyka (his full name) began a career as a naval officer in France and during that time also obtained degrees in electrical engineering and law. He entered the diplomatic service in 1909 and subsequently worked in the Romanian embassies in Berlin, Rome, Paris, and London. An enthusiastic lover of art and literature, he met Marcel Proust, Léon-Paul Fargue, Paul Valéry, and others in Paris and became increasingly interested in the connection between literature, art, and mathematics. In 1927—about the same time, that is, as Monod-Herzen's treatise about science and aesthetics the surrealists so appreciated—Ghyka published a study about the aesthetics of proportions in nature and in the arts.[57]

This publication laid the foundations for a project that was to occupy him in the years and decades to come. It consisted in establishing a shared evolutionary context for the forms of nature and the forms of art—plants, organisms, landscapes on the one hand, artistic, architectural, and technical objects on the other—with regard to their geometric foundations and mathematical laws.

The enterprise drew from several different sources. There was, for one, Ghyka's keen interest in early modern mathematical and geometrical manuals that simultaneously were manuals of (perspectival) painting and architecture such as Piero della Francesca's *De prospectiva pingendi* (*On the Perspective of Painting*, c. 1470), Luca Pacioli's *De divina proportione* (*On the Divine Proportion*, 1509), and Albrecht Dürer's *Underweysung der Messung* (*Four Books on Measurement*, 1525). Then there were several publications by modern biologists that treated of the problem of form, especially the plates of Ernst Haeckel's *Kunstformen der Natur* (*Art Forms in Nature*, 1899–1904) and D'Arcy Thompson's richly illustrated opus, *On Growth and Form* (1917), which Ghyka repeatedly praises as an excellent treatise not least because it has an aesthetics of its own. And finally, there were contemporary art historical and art theoretical endeavors comparable to Ghyka's project, especially Theodore Cook's *The Curves of Life* (1914) and Jay Hambidge's *Dynamic Symmetry* (1920).

Ghyka summed up his enterprise in the succinct formula of a "vitalist Neo-Pythagorism."[58] He first spelled out its agenda in the *Esthétique des proportions*. There, he begins by explaining the proportions of the golden ratio, known since Euclid and Pythagoras, and the geometry of the five Platonic solids, and then demonstrates that a wealth of works of art and architecture are based on the forms thus described—from the Great Pyramid via Greek statues to the Hagia Sophia, from Cologne cathedral to American high-rises and modern industrial buildings.

In a separate chapter, he discusses the extent to which the principles of the "science of space" thus outlined can also be applied to natural phenomena such as snowflakes and crystals and whether they are also manifest in biological formation processes. Like D'Arcy Thompson, Ghyka pays special attention to the logarithmic spiral. Employing the examples of seashells in particular, but also with respect to plants like the sunflower, he discusses instances of spiral structures in nature, as Cook in particular had done before him.[59]

Dalí met Ghyka in the United States in 1946. In the fall of 1945, Ghyka had been offered a visiting professorship in aesthetics in the philosophy department at the University of Southern California. Shortly afterward, the book he is still best known for, *The Geometry of Art and Life*, came out, a condensed and updated version of the *Esthétique des proportions*. It seems that Dalí, who at the time was living and working in Pebble Beach near Monterey, met Ghyka, who had ended up in Hollywood, by chance at a dinner in Beverly Hills. An intense dialogue about problems of form and composition began that would continue until the mid-1950s, first in conversations, then in letters.

In his autobiography, Ghyka sums up the impression Dalí made on him at the time as follows: "I discovered that far from being the publicity-hunting practical joker whose mask he often borrows, Dali is a very great artist and deeply and respectfully in love with the painter's craft. He has meditated its secrets and techniques for many years."[60] But there were disagreements as well. Dalí could not but be displeased with Ghyka's assessment in *The Geometry of Art and Life* that—of all things—Le Corbusier's machine aesthetics took up the lost tradition of an architecture on Pythagorean foundations. They also had completely different judgments of the landscape that surrounded them in California. While Ghyka felt as if in paradise on earth on the West Coast, Dalí dismissed the open view onto the Pacific in Pebble Beach with the words: "This obvious postcard loveliness . . . bores me immensely."[61]

Be that as it may, after their first meeting, Ghyka sent Dalí a dedicated copy of his just-published book. He was surprised by the reaction. He recounts that *The Geometry of Art and Life* "unleashed" in the artist "an aesthetic reaction of unexpected strength and inspired him with new conceptions of mathematically controlled compositions."[62] As the copy of the *Geometry* preserved in the Dalí archives shows, Dalí did indeed work with and in Ghyka's book quite intensively. He carefully copied the errata listed at the beginning into the text, underlined passages, wrote and drew into the text and the illustrations, and neatly cut individual pages out of the book to use them elsewhere.[63]

The consequences are well known: Ghyka's explanations had a considerable effect on the creation of one of Dalí's most important paintings in the postwar period (fig. 3.14).[64] *Leda Atomica*, begun in 1946 and completed in 1949, started with sketches Dalí drew directly onto a page from Ghyka's book. He inserted Leda and the swan into a circle into which a pentagon and a five-pointed star have been drawn (fig. 3.15). While, as Ghyka explains, the ratios of the lengths of the lines intersecting in the star are characterized by multiples of the golden ratio, the star figure as a whole can be inscribed time and again in smaller form in the pentagon inside the star—or vice versa: it can "grow" from the inside to the outside.

For Ghyka, in fact, the five-pointed star is a prime example of the geometry of life in two respects. On the one hand, the pentagon contained in the star (as well as the Platonic solid corresponding to it, the dodecahedron) can be found again and again in the world of the living—especially in plants and marine organisms, among them the sea urchins so beloved by Dalí—whereas it is not to be found in the inorganic world of crystals. A plate from Haeckel's *Art Forms in Nature* showing the pentagonal structure of various marine organisms illustrates this observation (fig. 3.16).

On the other hand, the possibility of reinscribing the five-pointed star within itself again and again represents a pattern of development that, following D'Arcy Thompson, Ghyka calls "gnomonic growth." Since Aristotle, this has been conceived as a form of development in which the growing entity undergoes no change other than in size. It therefore does not grow thanks to a linear gain of arbitrary parts but, rather, by multiplying its own form.

As Ghyka goes on to elaborate, the logarithmic spiral, too, is an example of this kind of growth because it "is the only plane curve in which two arcs are always 'similar' to each other, varying in dimensions but not in shape." The "growth of shells and horns (antelopes, wild goat and sheep, et cetera)" furnishes concrete examples.[65] Similar examples for the occurrence of spiral forms in nature can already be found in Cook, who provides numerous illustrations of such horns (fig. 3.17).

When Dalí, then, bases the construction of his painting *Leda Atomica* on the form of the pentagon (fig. 3.18), he superimposes on the motif of erotic encounter and fertilization a geometric structure that, at least in Ghyka, stands for life. The reference to spiral forms, which were very much to occupy Dalí as well, in the volutes on the pedestal above which Leda is floating only serves to highlight the connection with Ghyka. This link is the background against which Dalí in *50 Secrets of Magic Craftsmanship* exhorts aspiring painters: "You must learn, in addition to the curves of sea urchins, those of spirals and volutes."[66]

It is even possible that Dalí adopted the very motif of the painting from Ghyka: on the last pages of *The Geometry of Art and Life*, there is an illustration featuring Cesare da Sesto's copy of a lost da Vinci painting, *Leda and the Swan*, whose "harmonic composition" is briefly discussed. If Dalí was indeed inspired by it, however, it would change the entire character of his painting. *Leda Atomica* would then no longer be the masterpiece of his "nuclear period" so much as, similar to the studies of *The Lacemaker* and of the works of Raphael, an artistic engagement with a painter who stands exemplarily for the synthesis of art and science and whom Dalí appreciated the most, besides the two just mentioned: Leonardo da Vinci.[67]

Growth and Form

Ghyka was well aware that Dalí let himself be inspired by him. The artist kept Ghyka updated on the progress of the work on his *Leda Atomica*, and Ghyka reacted to it. Thus he writes to Dalí on August 13, 1947, that he is "delighted to learn" that he would have a "spiritual part in the godfathership of your Leda." In January the following year, he thanks Dalí for sending "photos of the Pythagorean and stellar Leda."[68] At that point, Dalí had exhibited the as yet unfinished painting at the Bignou Gallery in New York with the aim, as he explained in the catalog published on the occasion, of familiarizing the public with his painting technique.[69]

What Ghyka could not expect was the fact that in his next publication, *50 Secrets of Magic Craftsmanship*, Dalí would make use of *The Geometry of Art and Life* both very extensively and very loosely. In fact, *50 Secrets* already is as spectacular a staging on a miniature scale as the rhinoceros period was to be on a grand scale. Dalí is not just offering a blend of his own texts, drawings, and paintings, he also uses the book like a stage to present long quotations and illustrations from books by other authors—from Luca Pacioli and Leonardo da Vinci via Giambattista della Porta all the way to Ghyka und Thompson.

Thus Dalí in *50 Secrets of Magic Craftsmanship* reproduces the page 15 he had cut from Ghyka's book on which he had made the first sketches for *Leda Atomica* and adds, by way of explanation, "Annotation on a page of Prince Matila Ghyka's book." However, he places this reproduction on the last pages of his book, whereas he presents the sketches and drafts that immediately preceded the *Leda* painting, as well as the painting itself ("In Course of Execution"), much earlier in the book.[70] Ghyka's "spiritual part" in the planning of *Leda Atomica* thus does not really become clear.

Dalí, moreover, takes a series of other illustrations from Ghyka's book without explicitly mentioning it. He dissolves table VI of the *Geometry*, which brings together eight "variations on the pentagon," into its components and places several of the pentagons represented in the margins of his text. At one of these points, he stresses the formal similarities to the pentagonal mouth apparatus on the sea urchin's lower surface, known as "Aristotle's lantern," by making a comment to that effect on one of Ghyka's pentagon variations. And at another point of the text he emphasizes, entirely in keeping with his source, that the pentagon is the "archetypical figure" of life because it is not found in the realm of minerals. Without further comment, he also takes the depiction of a logarithmic spiral from another table where Ghyka returns to the pentagon to illustrate the "Spiral of Harmonious Growth."[71]

The borrowings from Ghyka go even further. Indeed, it is Dalí's active reading and appropriation of *The Geometry of Art and Life* that leads him to establish a systematic connection between the spheres of art and painting technique on the one hand and of nature and life on the other. In Dalí, Ghyka's keen interest in early modern manuals on mathematics, painting, and architecture falls on very fertile ground. Where Ghyka insists on the decisive role of Pacioli's treatise *De divina proportione* in the early modern rediscovery of ancient conceptions of symmetry and proportion, Dalí quite simply adopts the setup of that treatise as a model for the layout of his own book. Both the arrangement of the running text on the page and the placing of the illustrations in the margins of *50 Secrets* follow the example of Pacioli.

In addition, Dalí adopts from Pacioli (and Ghyka) a large number of illustrations of geometric solids contributed to *De divina proportione* by none other than Leonardo da Vinci. Especially toward the end of Dalí's book, they are mounted in the margins along with their captions, whereas the name "Dalí" appears both on the title page and on the front cover in the letters designed by Pacioli. The artist further supplements these references to one of the classic works in the history of mathematics and art with images from studies in the history of science that depict the early modern deployment of the camera obscura and of grids in perspectival paintings.

In a similar fashion, Dalí takes up, independently amplifies, and further develops Ghyka's reference to D'Arcy Thompson. A second, enlarged edition of *On Growth and Form*, the British anatomist and zoologist's capital work, was published in 1945. Ghyka had already praised the "suggestive" tables and diagrams of the first edition of Thompson's book from 1917, on which his *Esthétique des proportions* had chiefly relied.[72] The second edition not only features more text (the length of the book increased from 793 to 1,116 pages) but also includes a wealth of new illustrations, especially photographs, on which Dalí greedily pounced. In *50 Secrets of Magic Craftsmanship*, he not only included the famous frontispiece of Thompson's book, Harold Edgerton's high-speed photograph of a splash of milk, he also copied other forms of drops and, by way of supplementary sketches, suggested a parallel between splashes, crowns, and domes—a sequence of motifs he was to explore further in some of the paintings from the rhinoceros period, the *Madonna of Port Lligat*, for example.

In addition, Dalí provides in the appendix of his book, titled "Notes," several long excerpts from the text of *On Growth and Form*. Besides the "splashes," which Thompson, however, describes less as domes than as "cup[s]" or "crater[s]," these excerpts are concerned with the "Form of Sea Urchins," "Spider Webs," and "Gnomonic Forms."[73] Dalí uses these texts to delve further into some of the motifs and themes discussed in *50 Secrets*. Thus, for example, he also refers the figure of the sea urchin, evoked time and again both textually and pictorially, to the form of the drop. Thompson likens the shape of the sea urchin's shell to a "drop of liquid lying on a plate" drawn out horizontally by gravity[74]—a motif presented in free-floating fashion in *Leda Atomica*.

Drops play a role in Thompson's discussion of spiderwebs as well, which, as we saw, perform an important function in Dalí's aranarium, too. Especially when dew condenses at the thicker points that certain types of spiders incorporate into the threads of their webs at regular intervals, Thompson explains, "these regularly arranged and beautifully formed globules on the spider's web were a frequent source of wonderment" for many naturalists.[75] And according to Dalí, such wonder will also seize the artist seeing, through his aranarium, scintillating rainbow colors.[76]

And when Dalí, once again addressing the aspiring painter, notes that the "archetype of the painter's spiral is given you by the logarithmic spiral which, in nature, can be admired in a great number of shells, and with the most astonishing perfection in the 'nautilus' because of its mathematical 'gnomonic' growth,"[77] he not only appropriates the terminology of *On Growth and Form*, he also explains this claim by way of the excerpt he has chosen from Thompson, asserting that it exemplifies the "gnomonic formation" of the pentagon through the multiplication of triangles. He thereby aligns, once again, the motif of the pentagon and that of the spiral.

Like the references to Pacioli, those to Thompson, too, are independently enriched by Dalí, among other things by bringing in the popular natural history of another British nineteenth-century author. From John George Wood's richly illustrated *Animate Creation*, he takes the depiction of a young and of an adult sea urchin, over which he draws crutches and knight's armor, reproducing the whole in the margin of *50 Secrets of Magic Craftsmanship* (fig. 3.19).[78]

What this twofold adoption, of Pacioli on the one hand and of Thompson on the other, ultimately leads to is a conjunction of nature and art, of life and technics. Toward the end of the book Dalí states quite explicitly that on the preceding pages, "morphology, which is the youngest, the most modern science, which has the greatest future, has . . . married with royal pomp the most lucid aesthetic geometry of the Renaissance." The imperative for all aspiring painters Dalí derives from this is that in their painting, they "must express . . . only the quintessence of the organic."[79] One could also say that the painter's task does not consist in construction, supported only by mathematics and geometry, but in the concrete recreation and refashioning of forms present in nature.

This agenda is enacted artistically in a painting produced in two versions in 1949 and 1950. To begin with, the *Madonna of Port Lligat* may be seen, in a number of ways, as a supplement but also as the counterpart to *Leda Atomica*. Both paintings are free variations on a classic painting. In the case of the *Leda Atomica*, it was Leonardo's *Leda and the Swan*; in that of the *Madonna of Port Lligat*, it is the *Brera Madonna* by Piero della Francesca, whom Ghyka, incidentally, also counts among the early modern renovators of mathematics and geometry-based perspectival painting. Like Dalí's *Leda Atomica*, the *Madonna of Port Lligat* depicts the motif of fertilization without contact, albeit transposed here from the world of Greek mythology into that of Catholic religion. And like the structure of *Leda Atomica*, the composition of the *Madonna of Port Lligat* is defined by a pentagon that, as we know by now, consists of "gnomonically" growing triangles (fig. 3.20).

What is remarkably different, however, are the floating elements surrounding the central figure. *Leda Atomica* contains on the right two large water drops and a ruler. The first version of the *Madonna of Port Lligat*, in contrast, shows on the left a fish, a spiral-shaped shell, and the shell of a sea urchin. On the one hand, the sea urchin is to be understood, following Thompson, as the formal equivalent of a drop of liquid. As Dalí's sketches in the *50 Secrets* suggest, however, this sea urchin shell is intended, on the other hand, as an optical device for the production and scrutinizing observation of images, a natural alternative as it were to the camera obscura. The "eye glass of the painter" in fact consists of the hollow shell of a sea urchin, on the back of whose pentagonal opening a lens is mounted. Through a magnifying lens attached to the front of the shell, the composition of images is then to be scrutinized through the "dome" of the sea urchin. In this optical machine, nature and technics do indeed seem to be intimately "married" (fig. 3.21).

The second version of the *Madonna of Port Lligat* takes a further small but decisive step. It leaves the free-floating perspective of the individual painter and observer behind and instead stages a kind of natural history of morphogenesis. The sea urchin, to be sure, is present here as well (it lies on the pedestal, opened up), as are the spiral shells and the volutes already seen in *Leda Atomica*. But what acts as the basis of both these forms, as of the painting as such, is a pedestal that contains on one side a splash of milk and on the other a rhinoceros (fig. 3.22).

This foundation makes the point that it is not the painter who creates incomparable perspectival works of art with the help of a grid and a camera obscura. Rather, nature, that is, life itself, already produces art and expresses it in the most varied of existences—in drops and splashes as much as in sea urchins and rhinoceroses—before these in turn come to be depicted, via the organism that is the human being, in drawings, paintings, and architectures.

An observation by Georges Canguilhem originally aimed at the work of the philosopher Alain may serve to sum up the basic insight of the aesthetics that is beginning to develop here: "Because matter and life are always already formed, the artist finds, in matter or in life, forms to extend [*prolonger*], be it by bringing them to an end [*achever*], be it by distorting [*déformer*] them."[80] We might also say that Dalí shifts Bachelard's "surrationalism" from the terrain of physics to that of biology.

And indeed, at this point it is no longer Ghyka but Thompson who provides the decisive background for Dalí's work. This can be demonstrated philologically, as it were. Ghyka spoke of the horn's logarithmic spiral only with reference to antelopes, goats, and sheep. But Thompson in this context elaborates on the rhinoceros as well. In his chapter on "The Shapes of Horns, and of Teeth or Tusks," he writes, for example, "The horn of the rhinoceros presents no difficulty. It is physiologically equivalent to a mass of consolidated hairs, and, like ordinary hair, it consists of non-living or 'formed' material, continually added to by the living tissues at its base. . . . Its longitudinal growth proceeds with a maximum velocity anteriorly, and a minimum posteriorly; and the ratio of these velocities being constant, the horn curves into the form of a logarithmic spiral."[81] Thompson proves the occurrence of this spiral in a series of other horns (among others, those of Highland rams, argali sheep, and wild goats) but also discusses it with regard to nails, claws, beaks, and teeth, dedicating an entire subsection to that remarkable tusk with which Dalí had attacked Vermeer's *Lacemaker* in the Vincennes zoo: the "horn" of the narwhal.

The prominence in Dalí of the reference to *On Growth and Form* is apparent in another way as well. For it is Thompson who in his chapter on phyllotaxis, that is, the regular arrangement of the leaves of plants, points to the spiral pattern of the sunflower (fig. 3.23). Like Dalí in his Sorbonne lecture, Thompson mentions da Vinci's interest in the question (without, however, imputing to da Vinci a concrete study of sunflowers, as Dalí does), and he, too, leaves open the question whether the spirals in this case are in fact logarithmic. Moreover, on the very next page, Thompson provides another motif that Dalí was to take up in his rhinoceros period, the cauliflower (fig. 3.24). It seems, in fact, that the photograph of the cauliflower included in *On Growth and Form* is the very image that Dalí used in his lecture as well as on other occasions—in his painting *Living Still Life* (1956), for example.

A Moderator and Assembler of Forms

Though Dalí's appearances during the rhinoceros period were spectacular, his references to and engagement with morphology in the 1950s were not that surprising. In the French context, his elaborations on the matter picked up on the publications by Monod-Herzen and Ghyka who, in the name of morphology, had advocated making aesthetics more scientific since the 1920s. Via these authors, on whose work Dalí and the surrealists had partly picked up in the 1930s, Dalí's lecture also linked up with a tradition of morphological thinking in the philosophy and academic study of art, which in France goes back at least to Félix Ravaisson and continues via Alain to Henri Focillon. Even Bachelard in his 1957 *Poetics of Space* refers to the "logarithmic spiral" of certain types of seashells and approvingly cites Monod-Herzen.

Nor was the connection between Dalí's artistic practice and the subject matter of morphological research any longer a novelty around 1955. Besides art nouveau, the most varied of currents in modern art and architecture had long been citing the "art forms of nature"—some in the name of an angular functionalism, that is, of reduction and abstraction, some in the name of a more natural, more organic, more holistic design. Within surrealism itself, there is a certain turn toward the iconography of natural history and evolutionary biology, especially in Max Ernst, who as early as the 1920s outlined a *histoire naturelle* of his own (which incidentally also featured a rhinoceros) and since the early 1940s had found inspiration in a three-volume work by another British naturalist, James Bell Pettigrew's *Design in Nature*.

Independently of these developments, the younger art scene of the postwar years, too, turned to morphological problems and to D'Arcy Thompson in particular. In 1951, Richard Hamilton and the Independent Group organized an exhibition at the London Institute of Contemporary Arts with the telling title *Growth and Form: The Development of Natural Shapes and Structures*. It featured illustrations from Thompson's book and Haeckel's *Art Forms in Nature* side by side with X-ray images of the human body. In parallel, a volume came out that contained the contributions to a symposium, organized in conjunction with the exhibition, about the problem of form in nature and in art. Contributors included not only art historians such as Ernst Gombrich and Rudolf Arnheim but also biologists such as Conrad Waddington and Albert Dalcq, whose work had been praised by Thompson.[82]

The truly spectacular aspect of Dalí's Sorbonne lecture and the performance at the Vincennes zoo was something else. One might think that it consisted in the palpability with which he attempted to reinscribe art in nature: Dalí *really* showed up at his lecture with a pile of cauliflower, he *really* went to the zoo to make *The Lacemaker* meet a rhinoceros. In a certain way, however, this very palpability worked against what Dalí was actually trying to do. For, just as it was not Vermeer's painting but only a reproduction of *The Lacemaker* that was being held in front of a rhinoceros in the extremely artificial setting of a zoo, so in the Sorbonne lecture hall it was only a photograph of a cauliflower that showed the sought-after spiral pattern. What was confronted in both cases, then, was not really nature and art but, in the end, art and artificiality.

Nonetheless, Dalí's reference to Thompson intervened fundamentally in the conception of what an artist is and does. As biologically inspired as it presented itself, Ghyka's "vitalist Neo-Pythagorism" was also, as its author himself freely admitted, a Neoplatonism that submitted art and nature to the rule of certain numbers, proportions, and geometries. In this conception, the task of the artist ultimately could only consist in imposing on reality these numbers, proportions, and geometries in ever new constructions, thereby asserting them in the present and at the same time confirming them in their eternal validity.

Dalí certainly, as we saw, appropriated individual aspects of this theory in a series of paintings, from *Leda Atomica* (1946–49) to at least *The Last*

Supper (1955). But he did not want to have anything to do with a thoroughly rationalized and abstract conception of space of the kind Ghyka propagated with reference to Le Corbusier.

In referring to Thompson, Dalí was able to assume an opposite standpoint, as it were, which comes to bear in his engagement with Vermeer in particular. In the attempt to understand the compositional principles of *The Lacemaker* in the context of the morphology of *On Growth and Form*, Dalí relied on a kind of Aristotelianism in which forms no longer appear as eternal ideas and primarily mathematical constructs but as products of nature that are imitated, continued, and perfected in art as well as in architecture and technology. This, however, has significant consequences for the self-conception of the artist.

For, if the shell of the sea urchin already forms a pentagon on its lower surface, if spiders already design highly complex webs, and if even horns like that of the rhinoceros correspond to the form of a spiral, then the painter can no longer be an absolute figure who creates supratemporal works of art almost from nothing, thanks solely to insight into formal principles and craftsmanship. Nature itself already produces art expressed in the most varied entities and across all times—in sea urchins, spiderwebs, or rhinoceros horns, for example—before these can then also be expressed thanks to the human being—in paintings by Vermeer and Dalí, for example. The *Natura naturans* thus comes to meet the artistic process of creation halfway, and by taking up and continuing this preparation, the artist acts not so much as a creator but as moderator and assembler of forms. We might indeed say that in this sense, the artist becomes a cybernetician, a helmsman and "pilot" of living forms.

Dalí was quite aware that his referring to Thompson would lead to such a redefinition of the role of the artist. Yet he did not see this as a limitation or a danger but rather as an enrichment and welcome invitation to bring out the multiple facets of artistic creativity. As smoothly as Thompson switched between the form of a water drop and that of a sea urchin or the form of a human femur and a crane head, so Dalí effortlessly switched between different forms of images, independently of whether they had been fashioned by art, nature, or technology.

Already in his surrealist days, Dalí had called himself "the father of painted dream photographs."[83] He reaffirms this alignment of painting and photography with new vigor in *50 Secrets of Magic Craftsmanship* when he equates the manual production of a painting with the chemical development of a photograph—even if or precisely because this equation can be conveyed only by way of another technical image, namely film. He declares, again addressing the aspiring painter: "Thus if the successive layers of your picture were to be filmed, from your imprimatura, your underpainting, your successive overpaintings and glazings, up to the last touches and the last varnishes, one would see in the film of your picture something like a vision which, beginning as an almost impalpable mist, would gradually materialize without discontinuity and in a progressively visible manner, like a photograph that was being very slowly developed."[84] Within the perspective thus sketched, however, the production of images could also leave the traditional domain of art entirely and acquire a scientific-experimental character. Descharnes thus reports that in the 1950s, Dalí entered into a dialogue with the ophthalmologist Gaétan Jayle about whether it would be possible "to have a kind of contact lens filled with fluid introduced into the eye—so that images controlled from outside could even be registered during sleep."[85]

In the background of this dialogue, evidently, there is the "electrocular," the television monocle with which TV images and images of reality could be superimposed. Just how enduringly Dalí was impressed with this technological realization of the "second kind of vision" is also apparent in that as late as 1975, he included (or had included) such an object, *Spectacles with Holograms and Computers for Seeing Imagined Objects*, in the series of prints called *Imaginations and Objects of the Future* (fig. 3.25).

Horn Images

Given such a generalization of the concept of the image, it seems paradoxical that Dalí should have continued to expand his conception of morphology. But already in *50 Secrets*, he is quite aware that the problem of form does not concern plants, animals, and human beings alone but all of their natural surroundings. It is in this sense that he notes, "the phenomenon of painting is consubstantially linked to geography, to geology, to botany, etc."[86] And even if he did not go through with the project announced in the same breath to produce a book developing this notion, to be titled *The Geomorphology of Painting*, he insisted in the years that followed on the contributions the particularities of the Catalan coastline made to the artistic activities located or starting from there. In his paintings as in his writings, he repeatedly points out that the peculiar form of the rocks at Cap de Creus was not only a decisive inspiration for Gaudí but also largely explained the distorted faces and bodies in some of his own paintings.[87] In the guise of a pronounced local patriotism, Dalí's Thompsonian morphology thus transitions to what can only be described as an ecology of (media) art.

This also allows for a more precise description of the specificity of the activity called "painting." Indeed, it is possible to claim that Dalí's increasing interest in the techniques of painting was the counterpart to the generalizations of the pictorial naturalism inspired by Thompson. The generalization of the concept of the image entailed the necessity to specify what a painting is. In *50 Secrets of Magic Craftsmanship*, painted images become geological-biological facts. Dalí stresses time and again that a painting consists of successive "layers" and accordingly pays much attention to the temporal succession of applying these layers, to varying "coefficients of viscosity" of the materials used, and especially to the properties of the binders or "media."

The exemplary engagement with Vermeer's *Lacemaker*, too, points in the direction of such a specification. It does not tend toward geometrizing and mathematizing what is *represented* but toward naturalizing *representation*. The staged proof that *The Lacemaker* is determined by the form of the logarithmic spiral serves to associate the surface of this painting with the natural surfaces of the rhinoceros horn, the sunflower, and the cauliflower.

It is for this very reason, we might say, that the tactile aspects play such a prominent role in Dalí's account. Vermeer might not touch the object he represents in any way, but the canvas on which he paints becomes the object of the most intense brushing and dabbing—exactly as described in the minutest detail in *50 Secrets*.

This is where the rhinoceros period opens onto an experimental ontology of the image that pays particular attention to the properties of what Moholy, for example, calls the painting's "texture" or "facture" and what Flusser, speaking of photography, calls "the surface of the image [*Bildfläche*]."[88] Following Dalí, in the viewing of such surfaces the geological adjoins the biological and the biological the technological. This simultaneously outlines the foundation of a media theory centrally concerned with the encounter between the "opposite skins" of bodies and machines.

Dalí presents the considerable scope of this project in a 1957 painting, one of the last to prominently feature the rhinoceros motif. *Celestial Ride* shows a rhinoceros striding on long, spindly legs across a barren civilizational landscape. While a female figure, her face shrouded, rides on the animal, TV images of a baseball game are shown on the rhinoceros's armor (fig. 3.9). The motif not only takes up the mounted rhinoceros from the

"Mystical Manifesto" (fig. 3.12) and the spindly-legged elephants from *The Temptation of Saint Anthony* (1946). In superimposing archaic animal and modern media technology, it equates the outer skin of an organism with the surface of a technical image—and vice versa. From Dalí's perspective, there is no longer any essential difference between these two layers: despite their very different consistency, both appear to him as images.

Dalí insists on this idea when at the end of the 1960s he designs a cover for TV *Guide* on which he places in an empty landscape two lonely thumbs on whose nails TV images appear (fig. 3.26). In the 1920s, the "liberation of the fingers" had literally given wings to Dalí's imagination,[89] and he had already explored the motif of freestanding thumbs in an illustration for Montaigne's *Essais* in 1947 (fig. 3.27).

On the cover for TV *Guide*, Dalí develops the motif of isolated thumbs morphologically. Via the thumbnail, he puts the organic material horn on the same level as the glass surface of the TV screen. Optical media, then, are constituted both biologically and technologically. In the accompanying interview, he emphasizes the postmachinist perspective thus manifest. In the past, he says, he created soft watches and soft violins: "Now I create soft television set!"[90]

Against this background it becomes clear just how consequential Dalí's remarks on cybernetics quoted at the beginning of this chapter are. They manifest not just the final version of his vision of a "post-machinist age" but also his nuanced understanding of the counterside of media. At the end of his conversations with Alain Bosquet, he returns to this vision: "People usually think of cybernetics as something abominable, they imagine that the world is being guided more and more by mechanical brains. They're afraid that the intervention of human genius is decreasing. But in point of fact, the opposite is true. Cybernetic machines are getting rid of the things that encumber us."[91] For Dalí, the liberating, productive aspect of cybernetic machines is apparent, on the one hand, in contemporary image recognition and processing procedures. He explains that cybernetic image machines can "supply dots and dashes" and will, on that basis, be able to produce images that float in space, as it were: "We'll soon be able to form images that seem to be a yard away from the basic surface. With the help of all the points, and of all the images thus formed, we'll attain a divisionist painting seconding that of Seurat at the beginning of the century."[92]

As we will see in the next chapter, he thereby links up with McLuhan's thesis that television is not a visual but a tactile medium. For now, let's note that in Dalí's performative perspective, cybernetic image machines do nothing that differs from what painters do, painters who since Vermeer have been creating spatial illusions by brushing and dabbing paint onto a plane surface. That is why he is convinced that machine paintings will contribute to the rescue of painting.[93]

On the other hand, the machines of cybernetics in Dalí's view are not only tools, they also have a "magical dimension." They belong to nature, since they have a life, not to say a mind, of their own. As a faithful student of Lullus, the artist notes with fascination that cybernetic machines "are already starting to act like human beings and with their own psychology." The problem is just that so far, they have not been fed "sublime" programs: "they even get away with serious pranks on the scientists employing them for their questionable programing, for sometimes the computers act like cretins, which is a marvelous retort to the insufferable logic of human beings."[94]

Dalí's rhinoceros phase as a whole can thus be understood as a period of transition, a transition in which the synthesis operated by painting between magic and technics, Moses and cyborg, translates itself into a performative way of dealing with the most varied of media technologies. This translation achievement can still be taken up constructively by media studies today, especially when media theory seeks to understand the cooperation and the conflict between human and nonhuman surfaces.

FIGURE 3.1
Dalí at the Madrid art academy (ca. 1925).

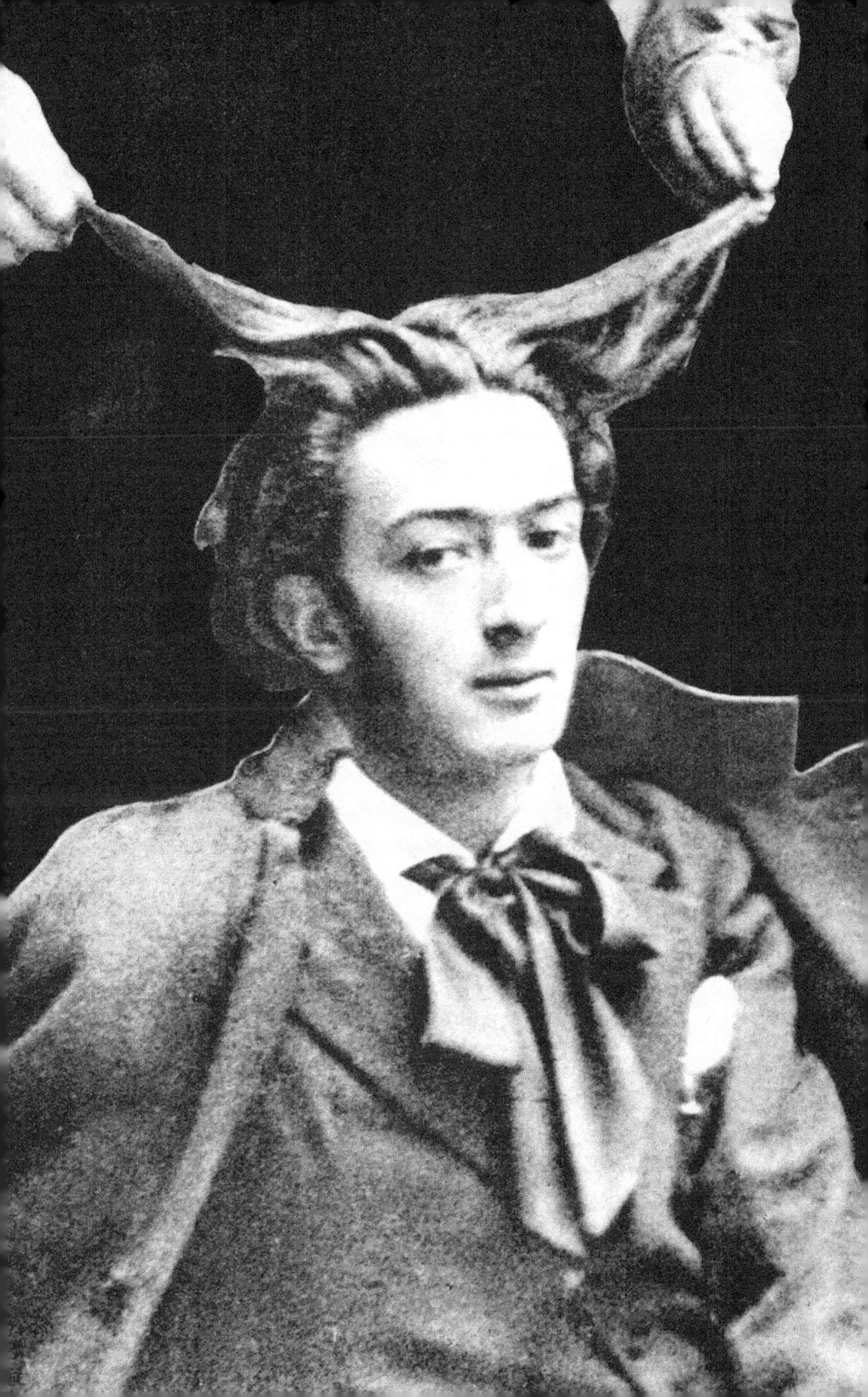

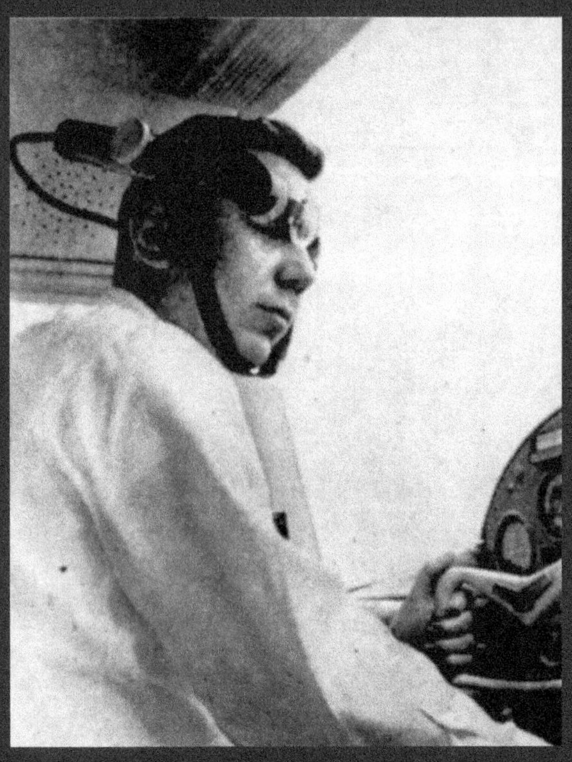

FIGURE 3.2
The Hughes Aircraft Company's "electrocular" (1962).

FIGURE 3.3
Salvador Dalí, "Retrospective utilisation of aranarium" (1948).

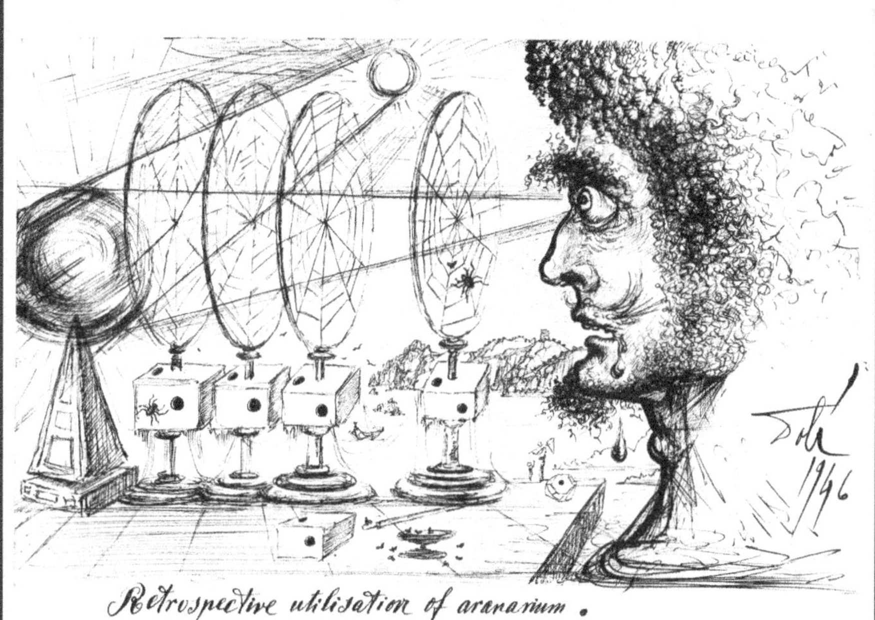

Retrospective utilisation of aranarium.

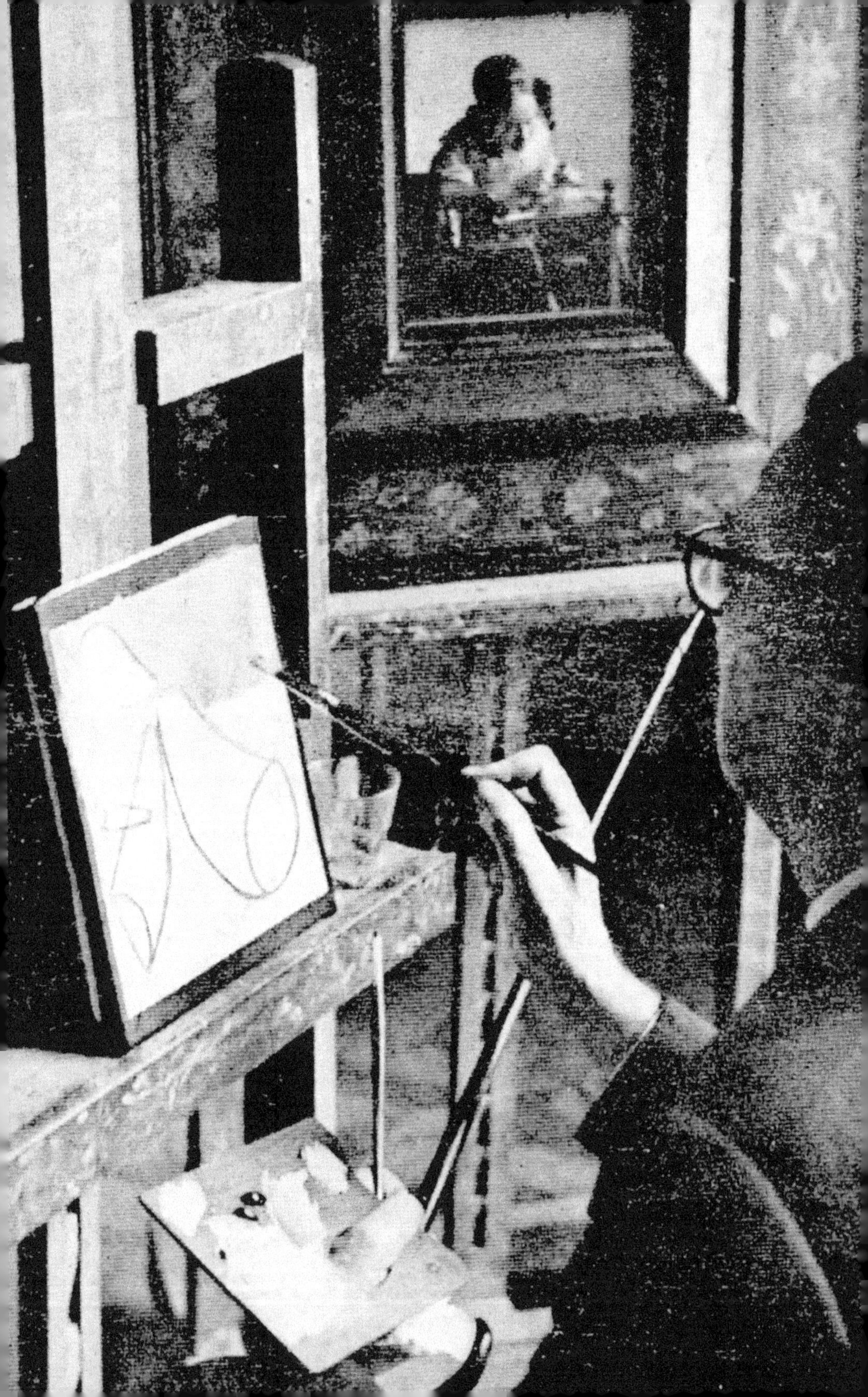

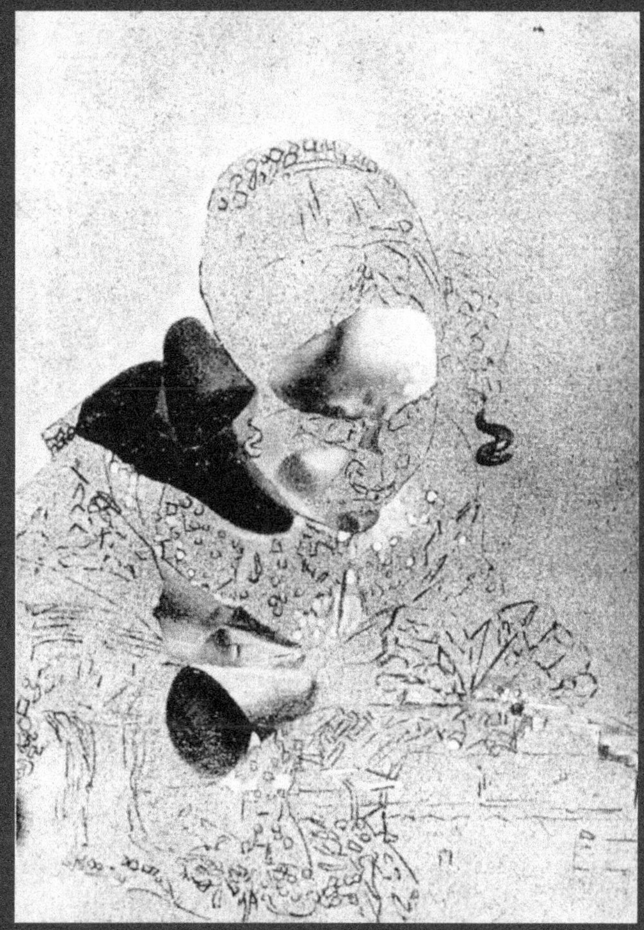

FIGURE 3.4
"Dalí executes a critical-paranoiac copy of Vermeer's *Lacemaker* in the Louvre." Photograph by Robert Descharnes (1954).

FIGURE 3.5
Salvador Dalí, sketch for *Paranoiac-Critical Study of Vermeer's "Lacemaker"* (1955). © Salvador Dalí, Fundació Gala–Salvador Dalí/VG Bild-Kunst, Bonn 2020.

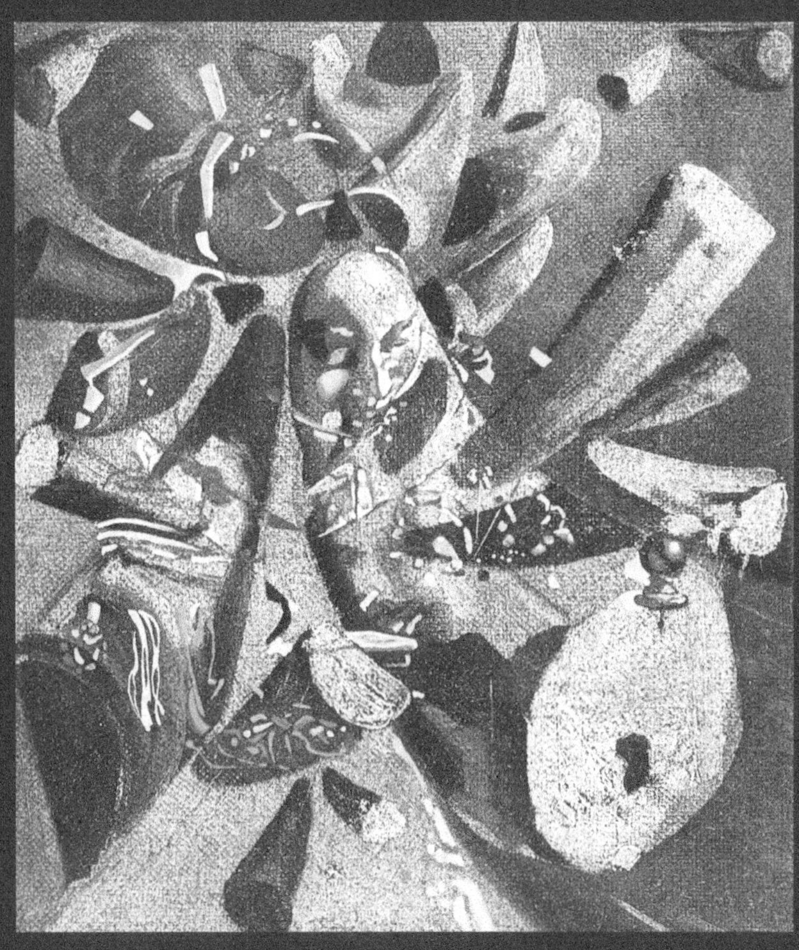

FIGURE 3.6

Salvador Dalí, *Paranoiac-Critical Study of Vermeer's "Lacemaker"* (1955). © Salvador Dalí, Fundació Gala–Salvador Dalí/VG Bild-Kunst, Bonn 2020.

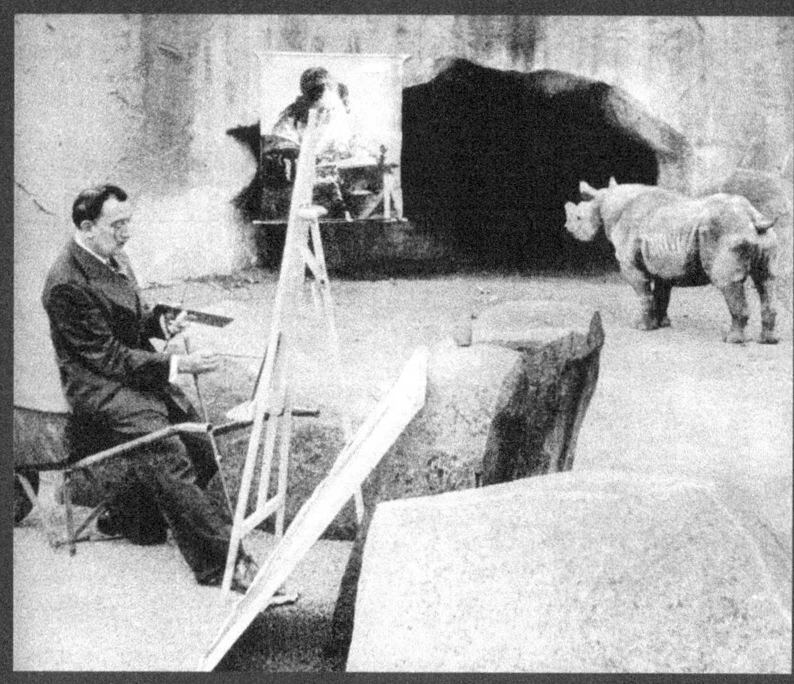

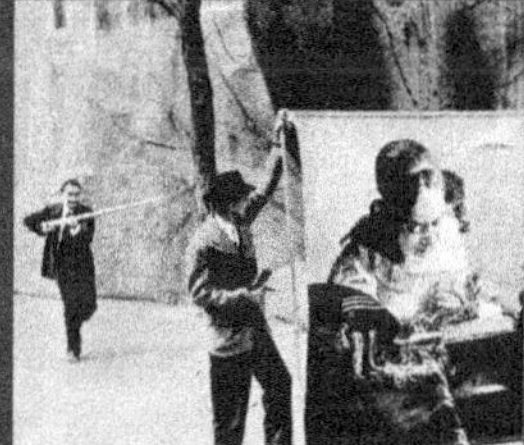

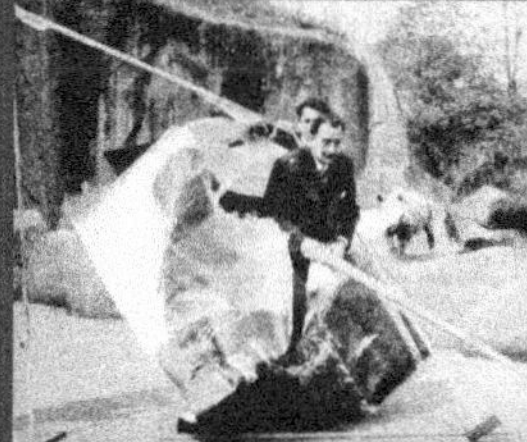

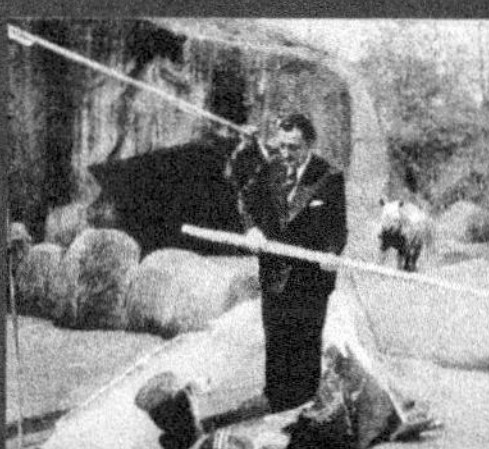

FIGURE 3.7

Dalí continues working on his version of *The Lacemaker* at the rhinoceros enclosure in the Vincennes zoo (1955).

FIGURE 3.8

At the zoo in Vincennes, Dalí also pierces through a large-scale reproduction of *The Lacemaker* with a lance (1955).

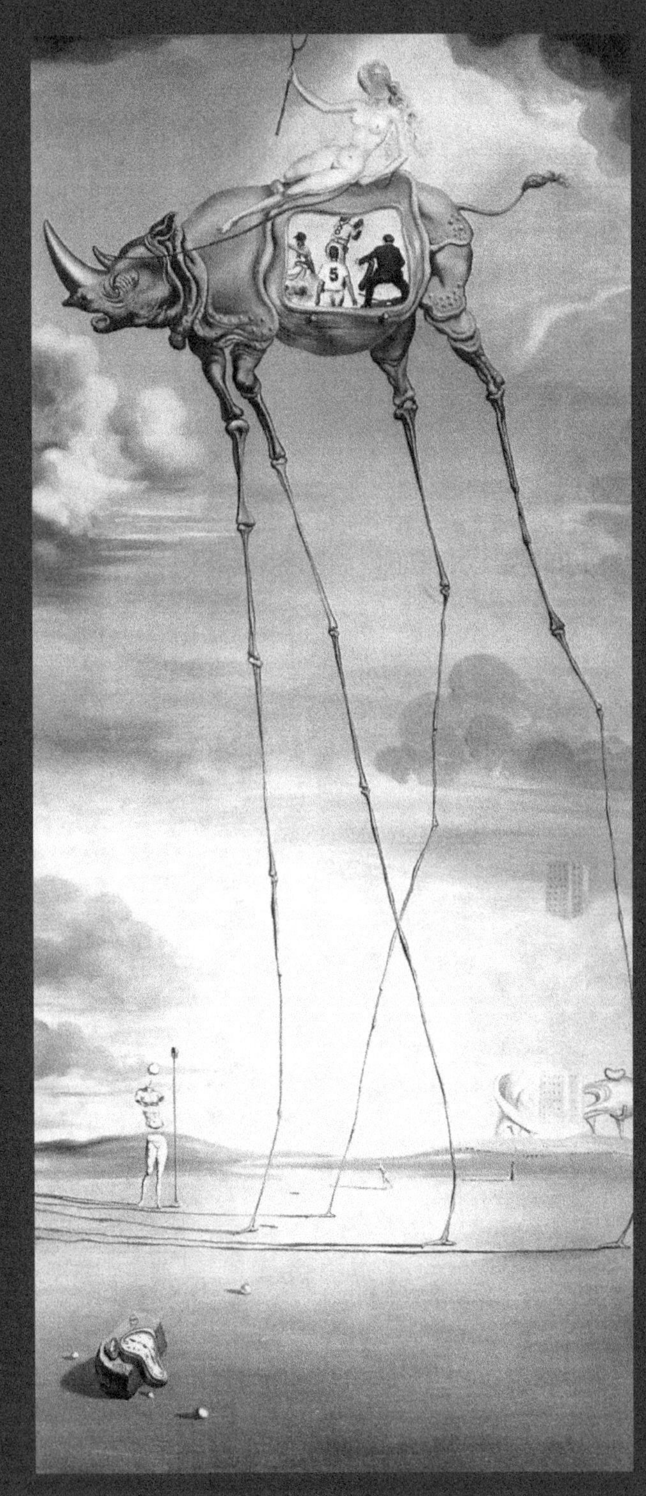

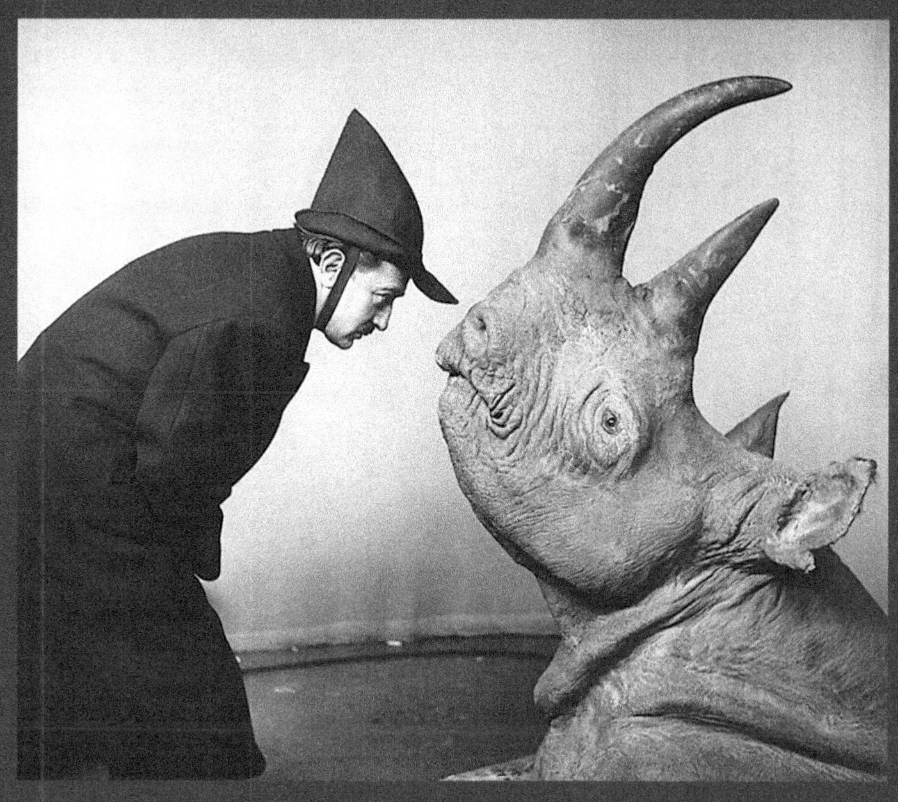

FIGURE 3.9
Salvador Dalí, *Celestial Ride* (1957). © Salvador Dalí, Fundació Gala-Salvador Dalí/VG Bild-Kunst, Bonn 2020.

FIGURE 3.10
Dalí poses with a rhinoceros. Photograph by Philippe Halsman (ca. 1960).

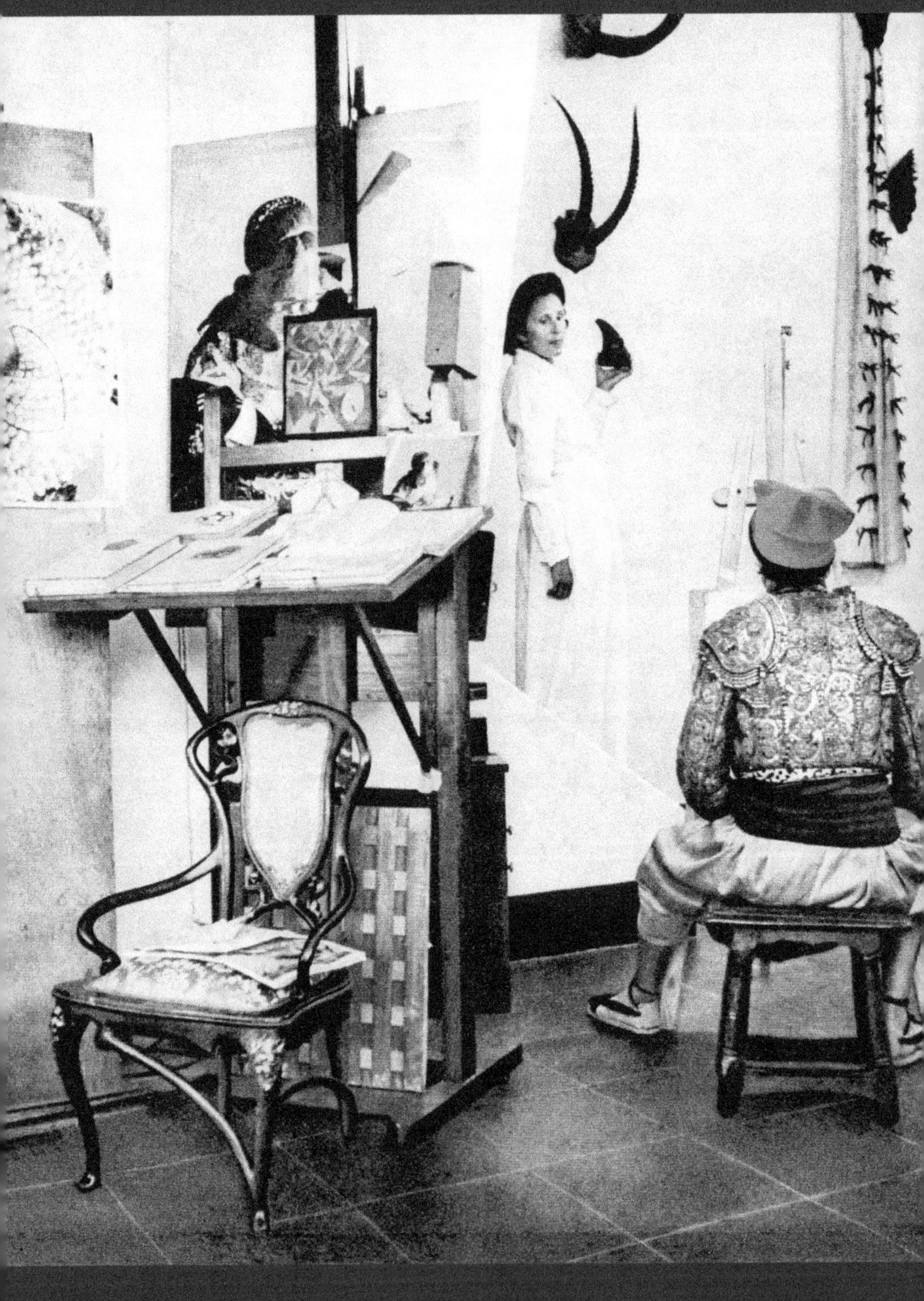

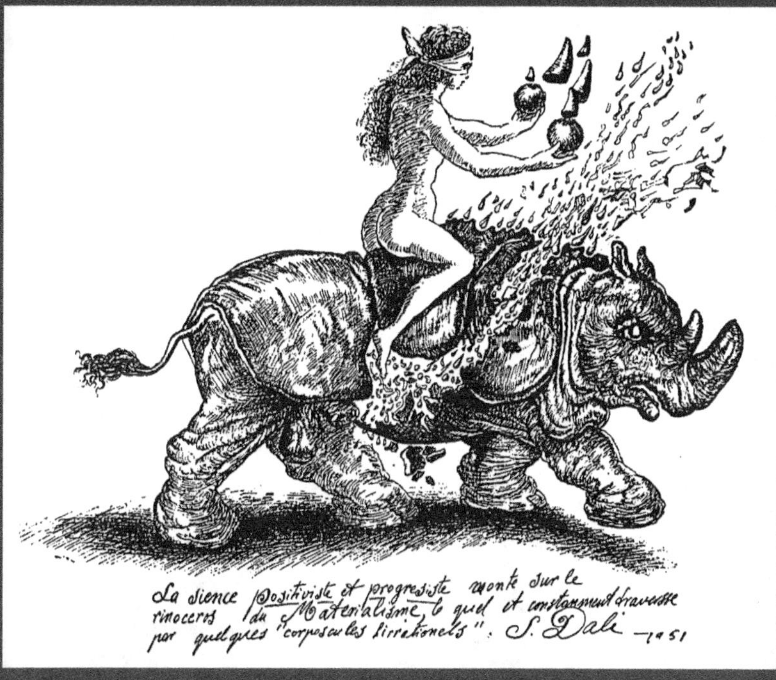

FIGURE 3.11
"Dalí and Gala in Vermeer's studio." Photograph by Robert Descharnes (ca. 1960).

FIGURE 3.12
Salvador Dalí, "La science *positiviste et progresiste* monte sur le rinoceros du Materialisme, le quel et constamment traversse par quelques 'corpuscules lirrationels'" (1951).

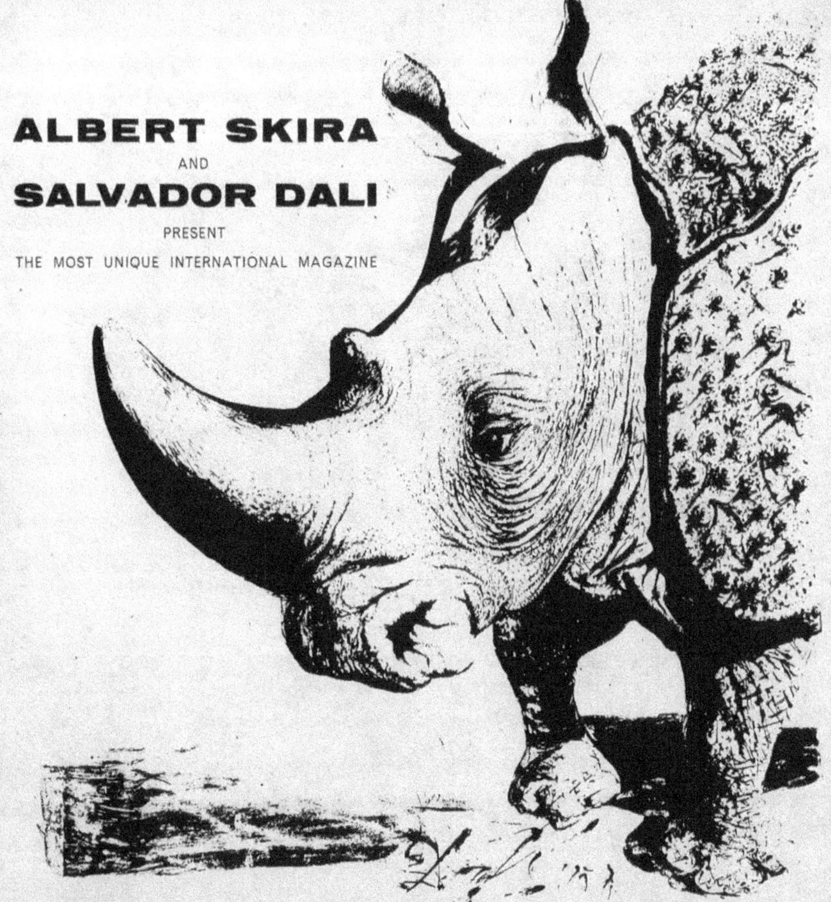

RHINOCEROS

A most unique international magazine devoted to maximum spiritual potential for thinking readers concerned with: The Cosmogonic Unity of Our Century • The future Ecumenical Congress of Pope John XXIII • The New Moral and Scientific Values of Soviet Russia • The Imminent "REALIST-QUANTIST PAINTING" Emerging from Abstract Art • "CLEDALISM"—New Gothic Concept of Love • Electronic Silverwork • Dynamic Traction Architecture • The Antigravitational "ANTI-MATTER" Possibilities in the United States

First Limited Edition Issue to be published in [illegible] languages, October, [illegible]. Mr. Dali will invite a select number of persons throughout the world to subscribe this year. For further information about RHINOCEROS, return this coupon.

SKIRA, Inc., Publishers [illegible] Fourth Ave., New York 16

NAME ______

______

ADDRESS ______

CITY ______ ZONE ______ STATE ______

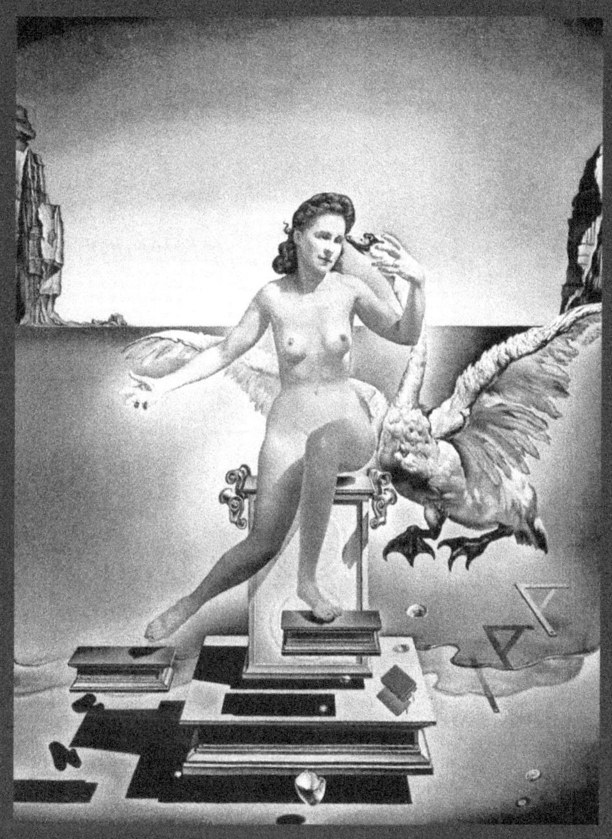

FIGURE 3.13

Cover of the journal *Rhinoceros* planned by Dalí and Albert Skira (ca. 1960). © Salvador Dalí, Fundació Gala–Salvador Dalí/VG Bild-Kunst, Bonn 2020.

FIGURE 3.14

Salvador Dalí, *Leda Atomica* (1949). © Salvador Dalí, Fundació Gala–Salvador Dalí/VG Bild-Kunst, Bonn 2020.

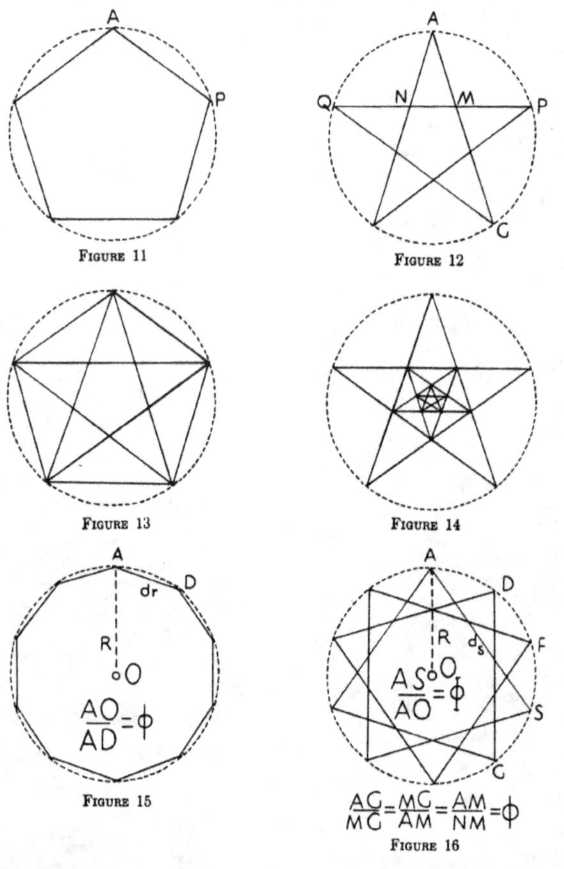
THE GOLDEN SECTION 15

FIGURE 3.15

Left: a page from Ghyka's *Geometry of Art and Life*; *right*: one of Dalí's sketches for *Leda Atomica*.

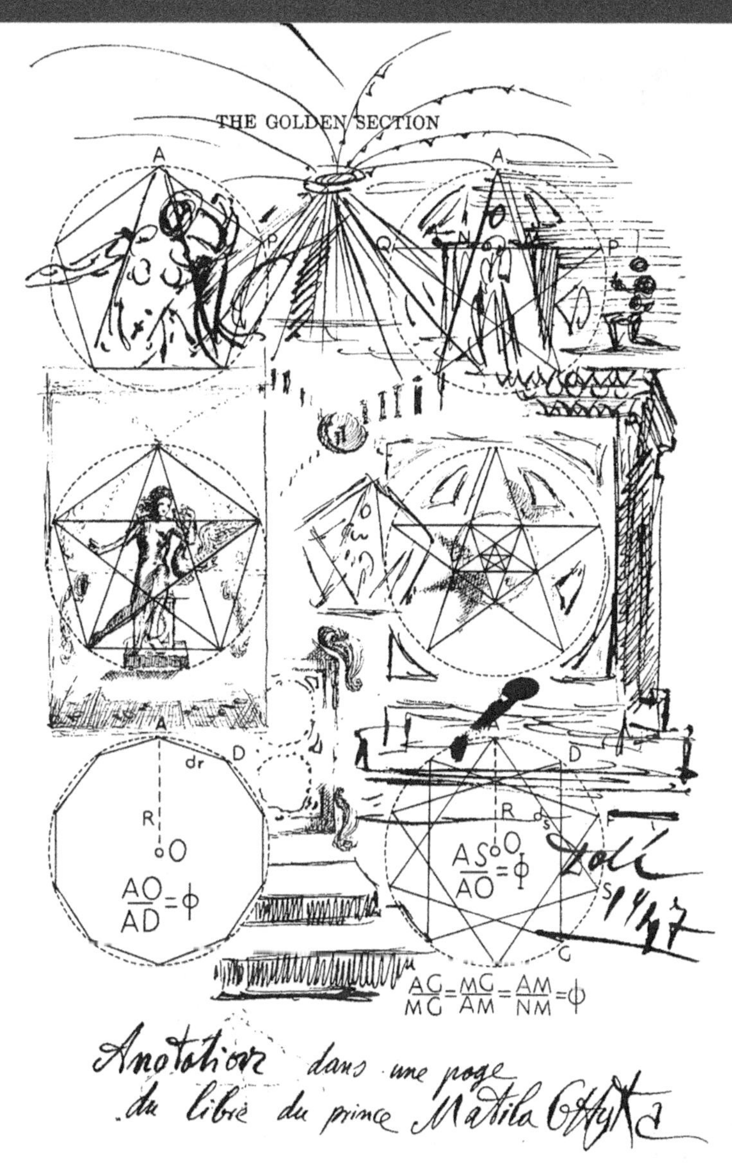

Anotation dans une page
du libre du prince Matila Ghyka

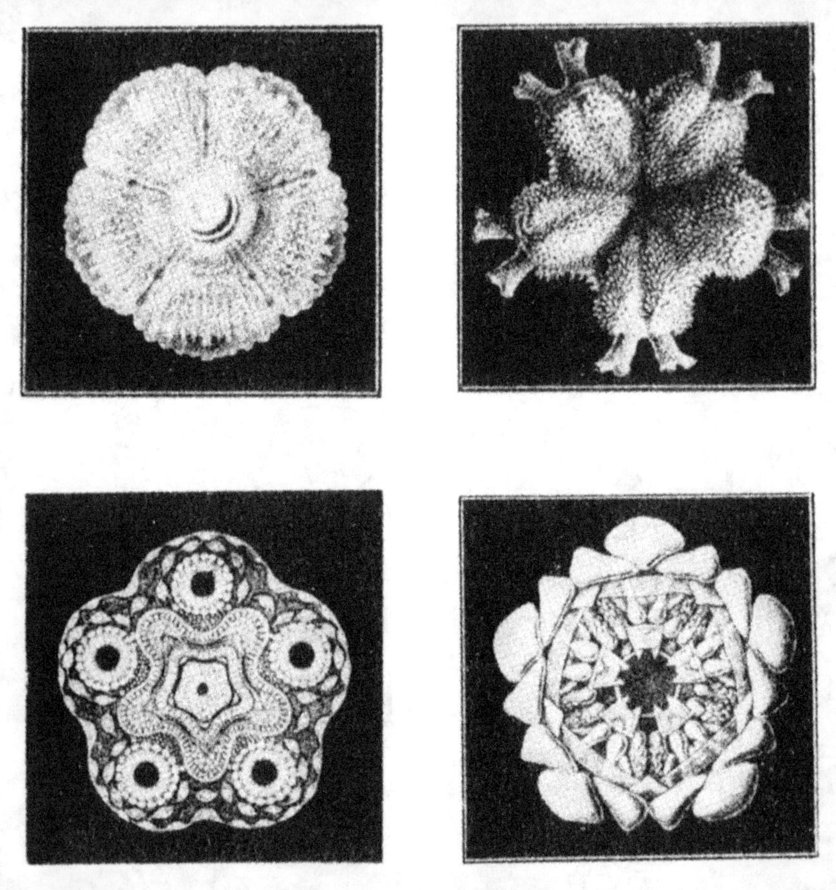

FIGURE 3.16
Illustration in Ghyka's *Geometry* of the pentagonal symmetry of marine organisms (following Haeckel's *Kunstformen der Natur*).

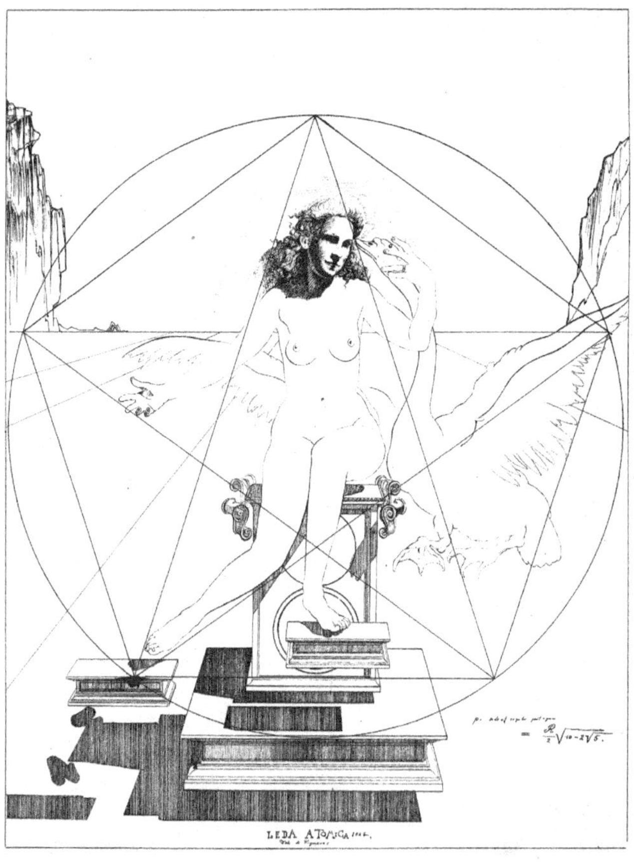

FIGURE 3.17
See over.

FIGURE 3.18
Salvador Dalí, sketch for *Leda Atomica*.

are as clearly fighting weapons as those of the common (Fig. 247) or the Jamnapuri goat (Fig. 246) are peaceful ornaments. Whether the horns of the Sind ibex would be useful as scimitars or not (Fig. 244), they would certainly help to break a fall if the animal kept his head in and broke the shock upon their massive curves. Much the same use might be predicted for the firm spirals of Pallas's Tur (Fig. 230) or the Tibetan Argali sheep (Fig. 233). But I cannot agree with the theory (brought forward in the *British Medical Journal* for September 27th, 1902), that such an open

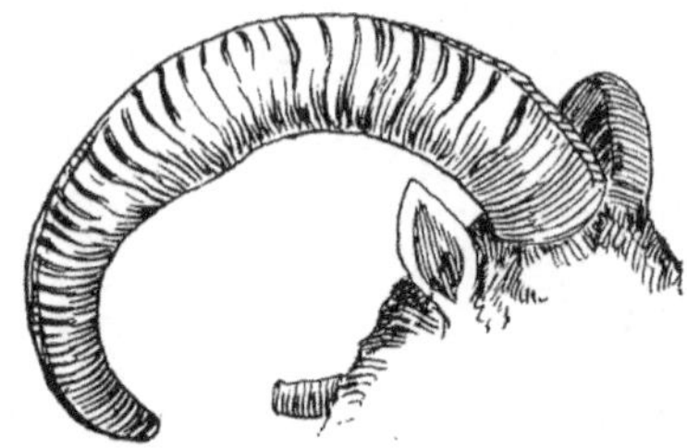

FIG. 242.—(PERVERSION). CYPRIAN RED SHEEP (OVIS ORIENTALIS).
(From Biddulph, *Proceedings of the Zoological Society*, 1884.)

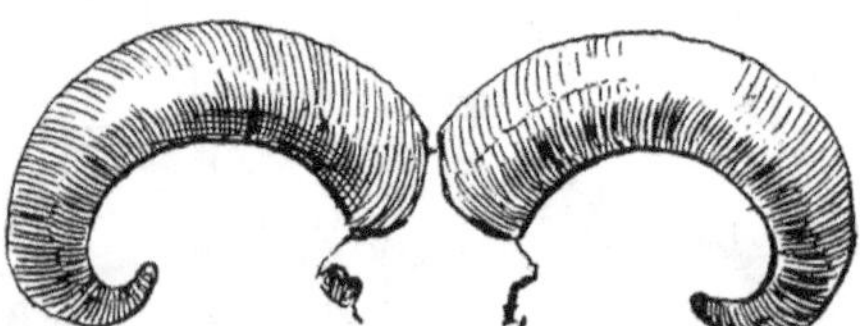

FIG. 243.—(PERVERSION). BHARAL (PSEUDOIS NAHURA).
(Drawn from figure on p. 387 of Rowland Ward's "Records of Big Game." Sixth edition, 1910.)

conical helix as that of a Highland ram's horn could in any way serve the purposes of a megaphone.

It is only right to quote Dr. Wherry's exact words in mentioning the theory of horn spirals which he originated. In the *British Medical Journal*, of September 27th, 1902, he announced "*that in the antelopes the right-hand spiral is on the left side of the head and the left-hand spiral on the right of the head*" (heteronymous), and "*that in sheep the right-hand spiral is on the right of the head and the left-hand spiral on the left*" (homonymous). "*The wild goats agree with the antelopes in regard to the spiral direction of*

FIGURE 3.17

Theodore Andrea Cook, "The Spirals of Horns" (1914).

their horns, and the oxen agree with the sheep in cases where the spiral can be noted."

Now it is often by apparent " exceptions " that a " rule," or theory such as this can be corrected or enlarged ; and Mr.

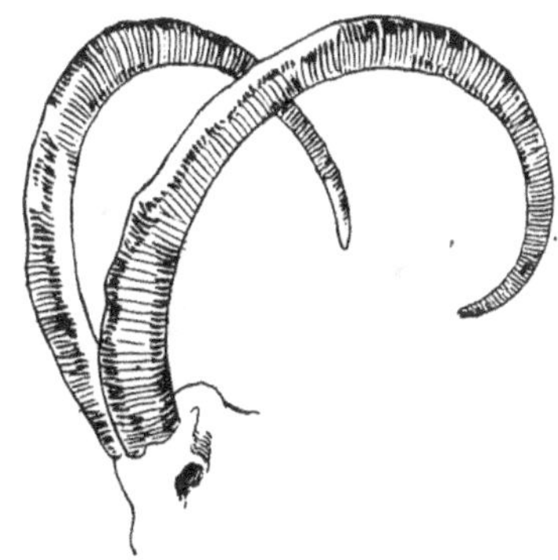

Fig. 244.—(Perversion). Mr. A. O. Hume's Sind Wild Goat.

Shot by Col. F. Marston. (Drawn from p. 378 of Rowland Ward's " Records of Big Game." Sixth edition, 1910.)

Lydekker has pointed out two serious exceptions to Dr. Wherry's statement which was evidently based on what he had observed. Did Dr. Wherry refer to the markhor (Figs. 228 and 229) when he used the words " wild goats " above ? If so, how is it that

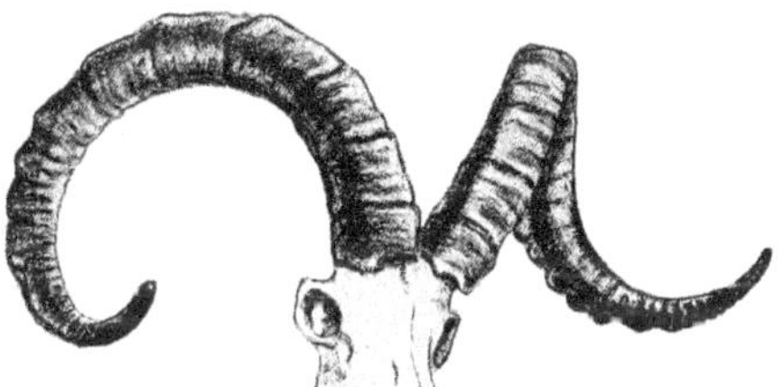

Fig. 245.—Dauvergne's Ibex (Capra sibirica dauvergnei). (Sterndale.)

all tame goats save one are homonymous, whereas the markhor is heteronymous. Is domestication a sufficient reason to assign for the change in spiral arrangement ? Surely an easier explanation may be drawn from the fact that the true ancestor of tame goats is not the markhor but the so-called " Persian ibex " of

The shell is composed of a vast number of separate pieces, whose junction is evident when the interior of the shell is examined, but is almost entirely hidden by the projections upon the outer surface. These pieces are of a hexagonal or pentagonal shape, with a slight curve, and having mostly two opposite sides much longer than the others. As the animal grows, fresh deposits of chalky matter are made upon the edges of each plate, so that the plates increase regularly in size, still keeping their shape, and in consequence the dimensions of the whole shell increase, while the globular shape is preserved.

If a fresh and perfect specimen be examined, the surface is seen to be covered with short sharp spines set so thickly that the substance of the shell can hardly be seen through them. The structure of these spines is very remarkable, and under the microscope they present some most interesting details. Moreover, each spine is movable at the will of the owner, and works upon a true ball-and-socket joint, the ball being a round globular projection on the surface of the shell, and the socket sunk into the base of the spine. When the creature is dead and dried, the membrane which binds together the ball-and-socket joint becomes very fragile, so that at a slight touch the membrane is broken and the spines fall off.

Other peculiarities of structure will be noted in connection with the different species.

The common Sea-urchin is edible, and in some places is extensively consumed, fully earning its title of Sea-egg, by being boiled and eaten in the same manner as the eggs of poultry.

The fishing for these creatures in the Bay of Naples is graphically and quaintly described by Mr. R. Jones:—"I had not swum very far from the beach before I found myself surrounded by some fifty or sixty human heads, the bodies belonging to which were invisible, and interspersed among these, perhaps, an equal number of pairs of feet sticking out of the water. As I approached the spot, the entire scene became sufficiently ludicrous and bewildering. . . . . Down went a head, up came a pair of heels—down went a pair of heels, up came a head; and as something like a hundred people were all diligently practising the same manœuvre, the strange vicissitude from heels to head and head to heels, going on simultaneously, was rather a puzzling spectacle."

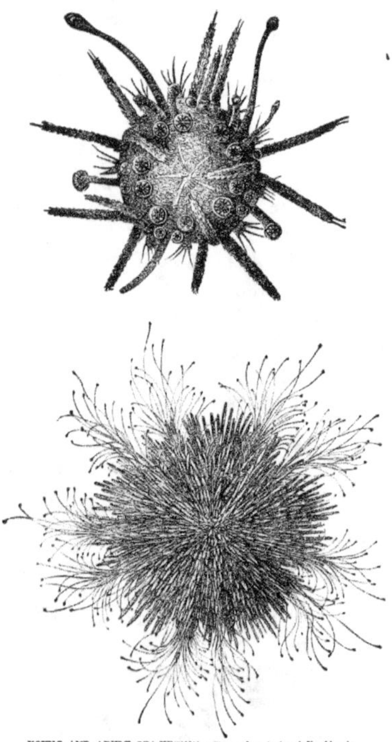

YOUNG AND ADULT SEA-URCHIN.—*Strongylocentrotus dröbachiensis.*

After inquiry, it proved that these divers were engaged in fishing for Sea-urchins, which

FIGURE 3.19

Salvador Dalí, drawing of knight's armor (*right*) over an illustration of sea urchins from John George Wood's natural history (*left*).

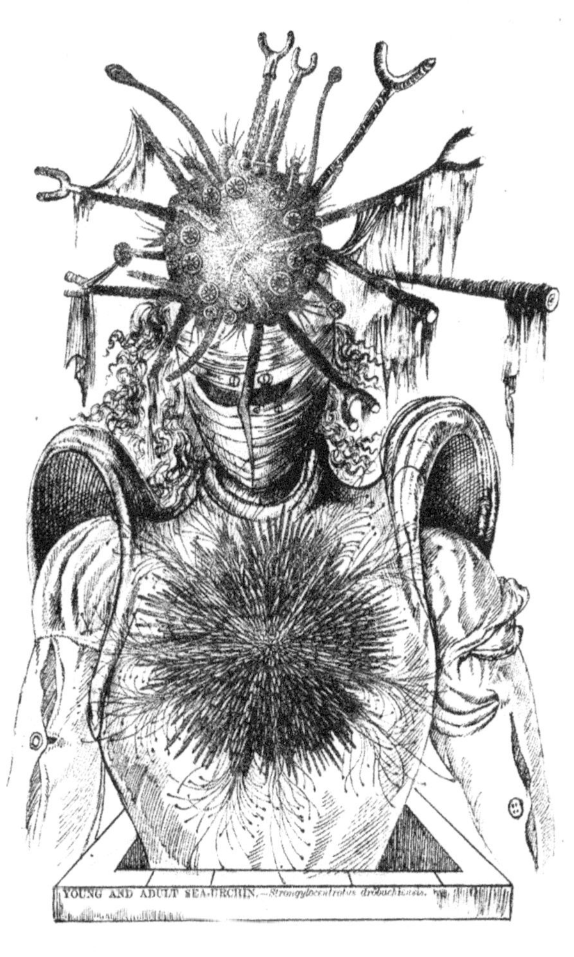
YOUNG AND ADULT SEA-URCHIN.—*Strongylocentrotus dröbachiensis.*

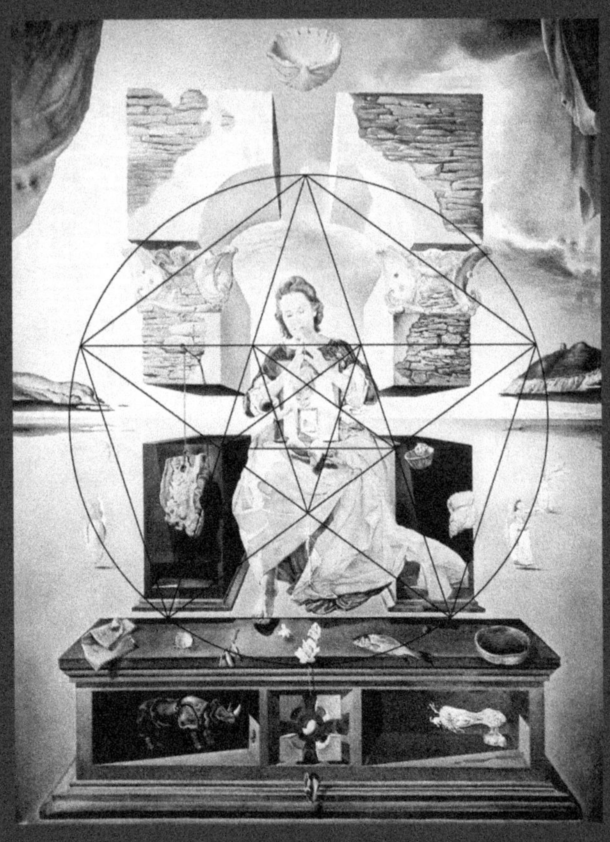

FIGURE 3.21
Salvador Dalí, "The eye glass of the painter" (1948). © Salvador Dalí, Fundació Gala-Salvador Dalí/VG Bild-Kunst, Bonn 2020.

FIGURE 3.20
Salvador Dalí, structural schema of the *Madonna of Port Lligat* (1950). © Salvador Dalí, Fundació Gala-Salvador Dalí/VG Bild-Kunst, Bonn 2020. Montage by Johannes Hess.

FIGURE 3.22
Salvador Dalí, *Madonna of Port Lligat*, detail (1950). © Salvador Dalí, Fundació Gala-Salvador Dalí/VG Bild-Kunst, Bonn 2020.

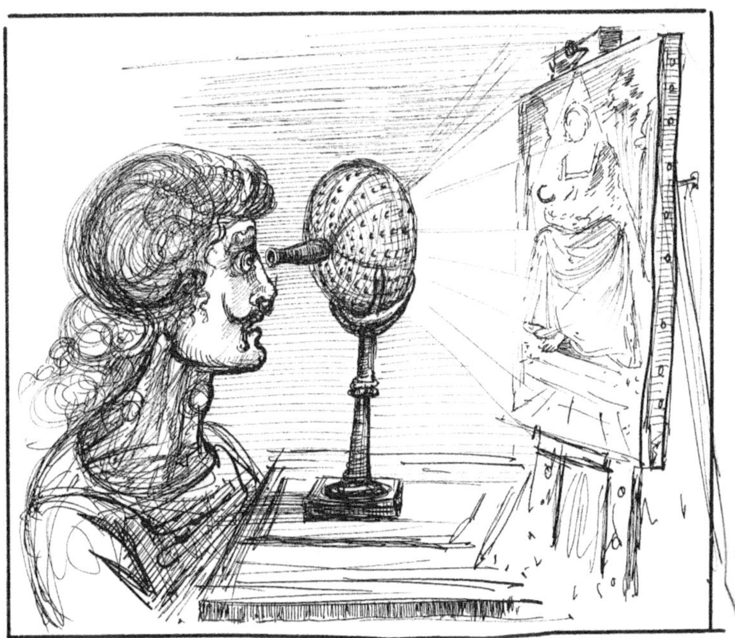

The eye glass of the painter.

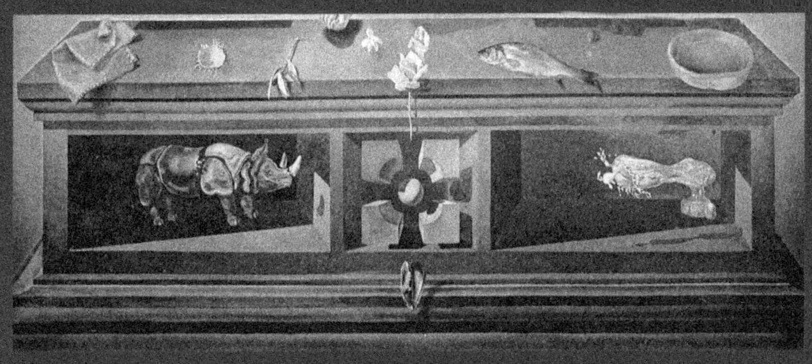

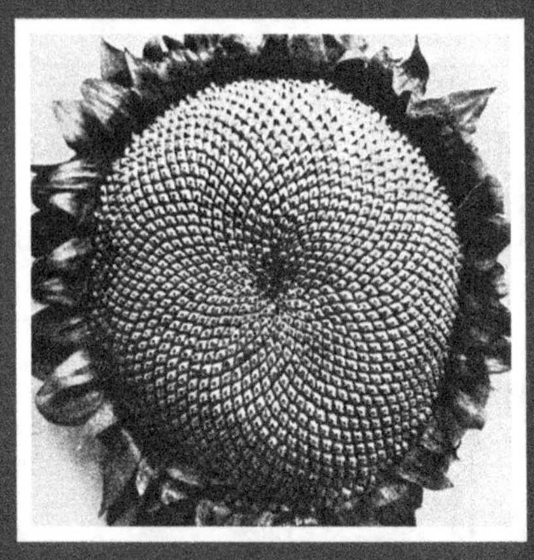

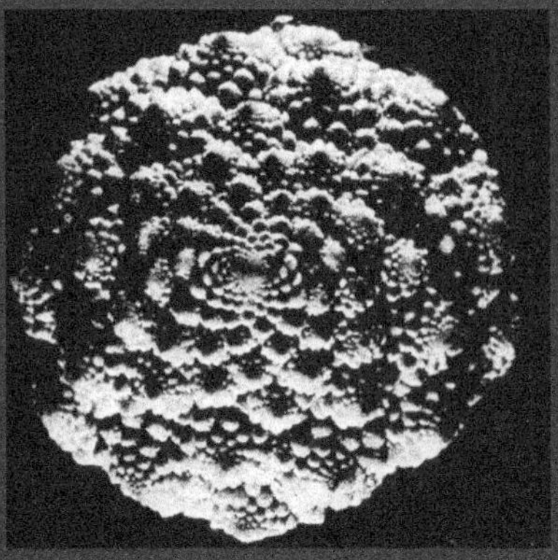

FIGURE 3.23
D'Arcy Wentworth Thompson, "A giant sunflower, *Helianthus maximus*."

FIGURE 3.24
D'Arcy Wentworth Thompson, "A cauliflower, its composite inflorescence shewing spiral patterns of the first and second order."

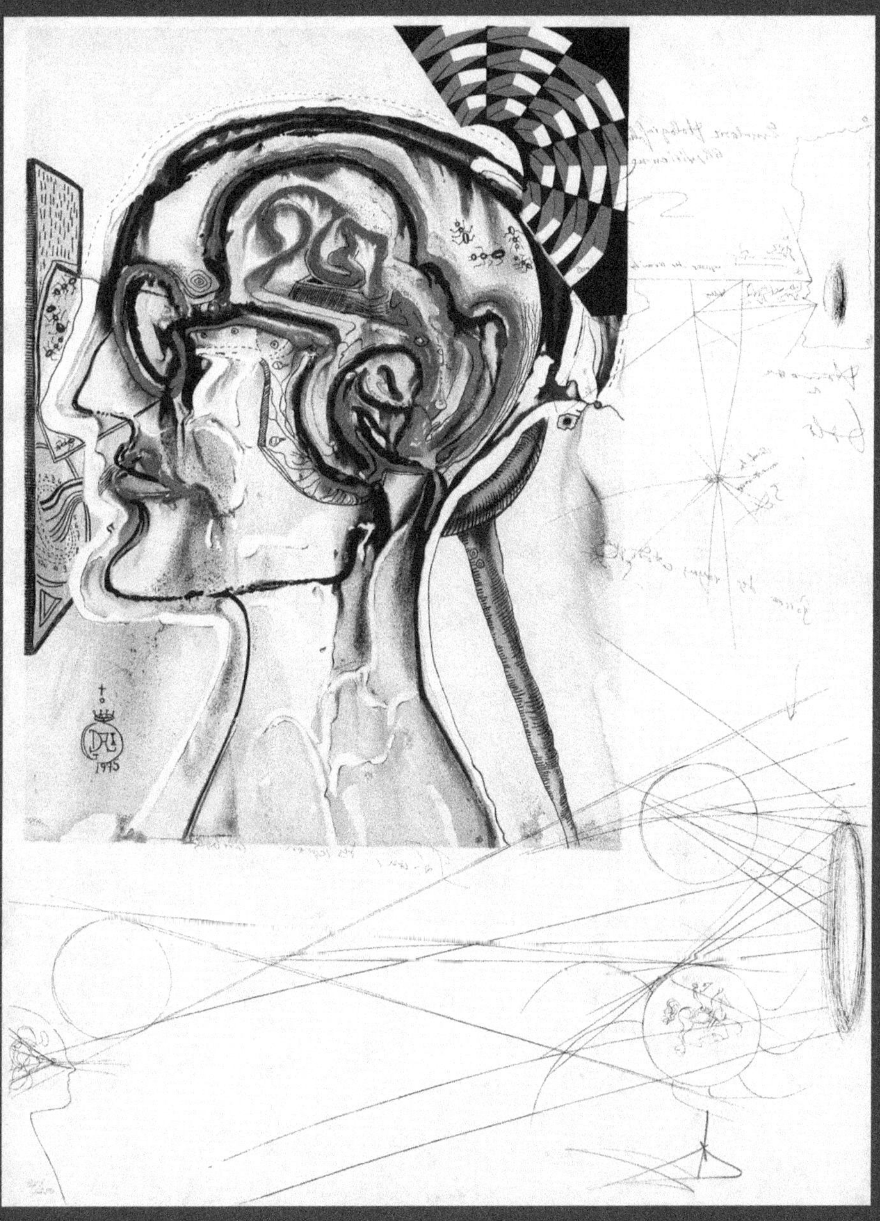

FIGURE 3.25

Salvador Dalí, *Spectacles with Holograms and Computers for Seeing Imagined Objects* (1976). © Salvador Dalí, Fundació Gala-Salvador Dalí/VG Bild-Kunst, Bonn 2020.

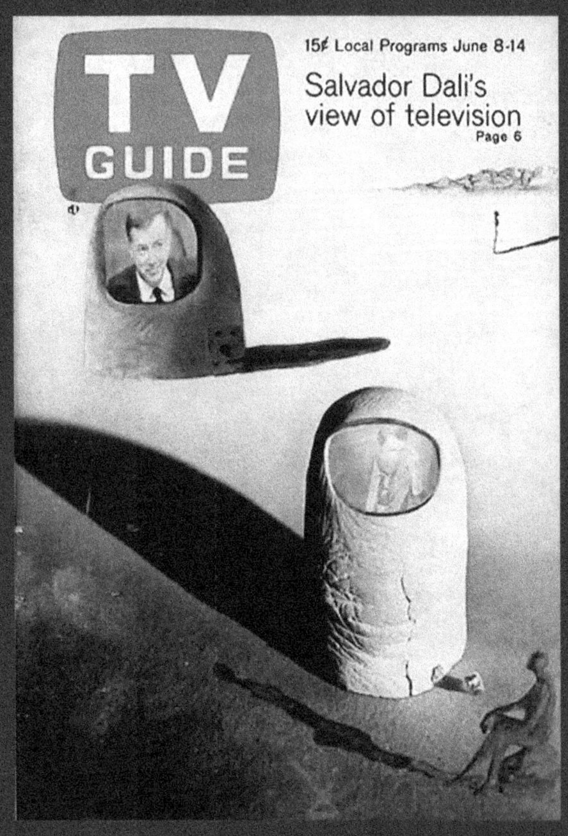

FIGURE 3.26
Salvador Dalí, cover for *TV Guide* (1968). © Salvador Dalí, Fundació Gala-Salvador Dalí/VG Bild-Kunst, Bonn 2020.

FIGURE 3.27
Salvador Dalí, illustration for Montaigne's essay on thumbs (1947). © Salvador Dalí, Fundació Gala-Salvador Dalí/VG Bild-Kunst, Bonn 2020.

XII

OF THUMBS

TACITUS reports, that among certain barbarian kings their manner was, when they would make a firm obligation, to join their right hands close to one another, and intertwist their thumbs; and when, by force of straining, the blood it appeared in the ends, they lightly pricked them with some sharp instrument, and mutually sucked them.

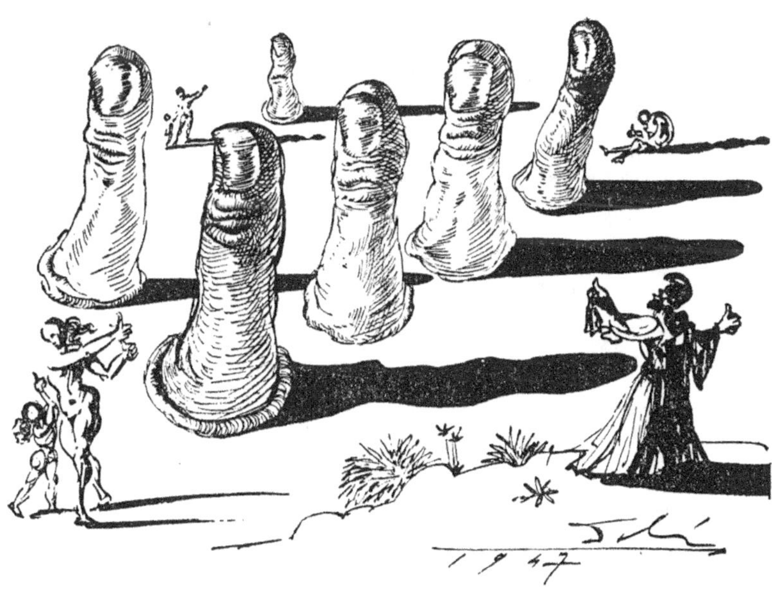

FOUR

A Surface Medium Par Excellence

In this room, Marshall McLuhan enters the Bauhaus in Weimar. Inside, a wax figure of McLuhan is seated in front of the Stone Age relief that is commonly called *Venus of Laussel* or *Woman with the Horn*. Next to him is a wax figure of Sigfried Giedion, sitting in front of a big-bellied TV from 1964. On the walls, photographs and films by László Moholy-Nagy show structures, textures, and factures of different materials: water, soil, wood, skin, asphalt, and silk. There are exhibits of letters exchanged between McLuhan and Giedion as well as excerpts from the correspondence between Moholy, Giedion, and Carola Giedion-Welcker. Screens display the "reflecting light games" Ludwig Hirschfeld-Mack and Kurt Schwerdtfeger developed at the Bauhaus as well as the religious experimental films of Rouault's student, André Girard. The motto of this room is taken from Friedrich Kittler: "All that remains of the real is a contact surface or skin, where something writes on something else."[1]

Marshall McLuhan is famous for considering television not as an optical but as a haptic medium. In his principal work on media theory, *Understanding Media* of 1964, he notes: "With television came the extension of the sense of touch or of sense interplay that even more intimately involves the entire sensorium." Two years earlier, he had already remarked that "TV is two-dimensional and sculptural in its tactile contours." Unlike cinema, "TV is not a narrative medium, is not so much visual as audile-tactile," he writes in *The Gutenberg Galaxy*, which is a more historical work and has a narrower thematic focus.[2]

Television is a tactile medium. It is not an extension of the sense of sight but an extension of the sense of touch. This thesis contradicts all everyday experience and all common conceptions of television in the kind of emphatic way that probably only "media theory" is capable of—that discourse, that is, whose rules McLuhan decisively defined. Isn't the very name of the medium, television, a clear indication of its connection with the sense of sight? Isn't it precisely, from a historical perspective, the endeavor "*to render* an object located at point A *visible* at any other point B" that stands at the beginning of the developments that crucially contributed to TV technology?[3] McLuhan was fully aware of such objections—and stuck to his thesis.

In the years following the publication of the two books just mentioned, McLuhan sought further proof to support his thesis, and in 1968 he came across the cover Dalí had designed for *TV Guide*. Almost alarmed, he writes to his assistant at the time, Sheila Watson, "Obtain cover of TV Guide for June 8–14. It is a Dali explanation of the tactile nature of the TV image. Wonderful interview inside, too."[4]

That same day, he comments on the cover image in one of his letters to Pierre Trudeau, who had just been elected prime minister of Canada. After a few observations on a recent TV appearance by Trudeau, McLuhan adds enthusiastically and as if by way of explanation, "The cover of the June 8–14 *TV Guide* is a Dali masterpiece. It manifests in detail the tactile quality of the TV image. . . . The two thumbs with the TV images on the nails are carefully separated to indicate the 'gap' or interval instituted by touch."[5]

The cover by Dalí was so important to McLuhan that he returned to it in his next book as well. In the foreword to *The Interior Landscape*, a collection of literary criticism, he notes, "Two thumbs exhibit two TV screens as thumbnails. That is pure poetry, acute new perception. Dali immediately presents the fact that TV is a tactile mode of perception. Touch is the space of the *interval*, not of visual connection." And with regard to those who still could not or did not want to follow such a conception of television, he adds, "I have been trying to elucidate this fact for years. In vain. The somnambulist knows better. Can't he *see* TV with his eyes? How could it be *tactile*?"[6]

The provocation of McLuhan's media theory here is twofold. It is not solely concerned with defining television, against all intuition, as a tactile and not as a visual medium. At the same time and no less counterintuitively, it aims at dissociating the concept of the sense of touch from the notion of physical contact or connection. Instead, it defines the tactile as a function of inserting gaps, of taking a distance, that is, paradoxically, as an agent of distancing. In a 1969 interview, McLuhan puts this conception of the sense of touch in succinct terms: "Touch is actually not connection but interval. When you touch an object there is a little space between you and the object, a space which resonates."[7]

But that is not all. McLuhan's doubly contradicting theory of television also comes with a symmetricization of the sense of touch. Despite his counterintuitive conception of the sense of touch, he is very much interested in the human experience of bodily touch. But unlike Benjamin, he does not focus on the "pokes" pedestrians administer to each other in the crowds of the metropolis. He directs his attention to phenomena such as the handshake or the "propensity to pat," which he, citing a travel guide for Greece, considers to be a particularity of southern and old Europe.[8]

He also addresses other aspects of bodily touch, and frequently so. In *Understanding Media*, for example, he discusses the surface conceptions of "the skin-diver, the water-skier, and the dinghy sailor," and he also notes that Brigitte Bardot "liked to drive barefoot in order to get the maximal vibration."[9] The impressions of modernity are thus an important theme for McLuhan.

This is also true insofar as he is interested not only in the human sense of touch but also in the tactility of technics. In fact, he does not hesitate to ascribe to media, too, a tactile faculty. As we saw earlier, Benjamin already had described Dada artworks as "projectiles" fired at the viewer.[10] Similarly, McLuhan describes the counterside of media. For example, he depicts TV viewers being "bombarded with light impulses" and explicitly draws a parallel between the "TV tube" and "firearms." In the same breath, he quotes James Joyce, who in *Finnegans Wake* speaks of "the 'Charge of the Light Brigade' that imbues his 'soulskin with sobconscious inklings.'"[11]

Moreover, not only the TV screen but the TV camera, too, is described as an agent of touch. According to McLuhan, this kind of camera is "ceaselessly forming" a "contour of things limned by the scanning-finger."[12] The tactile agency of television is thus manifest not just when it is broadcast into the living room but already in the recording of the image in the TV studio.

The preconditions for the symmetricization of the tactile can be found, first of all, in an early twentieth-century movement to which McLuhan is indebted, represented by Charles Péguy, Léon Bloy, Gilbert K. Chesterton, T. S. Eliot, Georges Rouault, Jacques Maritain, and others. The so-called *Renouveau catholique* ("Catholic Renewal") sought to contribute to a renewal of Catholicism through a pronounced engagement with artistic and literary modernism.[13] In the 1950s, this movement received an additional boost from the success of the posthumous publication of the works of Pierre Teilhard de Chardin, the paleontologist and Jesuit priest. In keeping with Teilhard's fascination with the "etherized" togetherness created around the globe by radio and television, McLuhan mobilizes Thomist philosophy and psychology to make the point that tactility is "sense interplay."

McLuhan thus misses out on the remarkable fact that Teilhard considered an exploring, tentative "groping" (*tâtonner*) to be a fundamental principle of biological evolution.[14] Instead, he goes back to Aquinas's theory of perception to turn the sense of touch into something more than a mere synonym for the contact between skin and matter, ultimately, to make it synonymous with "the very life of things in the *mind*."[15]

Subsequently, this psychologized theory of the sense of touch is joined with a conception of the medium of light that is largely defined artistically and art historically. This conception allows McLuhan, on the one hand, to ascribe tactile qualities to human seeing. Following Ernst Gombrich, for example, he repeatedly cites notions of "tactile vision" to be found since the late nineteenth century in authors such as Adolf von Hildebrand, Bernard Berenson, and Heinrich Wölfflin, among others, where they result, not least importantly, from a criticism of the allegedly false depth these authors saw as characteristic of mass media like the photograph, the stereoscope, or the panorama.[16]

On the other hand, however, the notion of "touching seeing" also makes it possible to conceive of technical pictorial media, such as television, and ultimately of all images as touching agents. It is in precisely this sense that McLuhan evokes artists and writers like Dalí and Joyce to describe television's sense of touch. As we will see, he also relies in this context on older and less prominent artists such as, for example, Georges Seurat, Georges Rouault, and Rouault's student, André Girard, a stained glass artist and experimental filmmaker who was part of the Renouveau catholique as well.

Yet above all, McLuhan here takes up an avant-garde aesthetics of the tactile that came to prominence in the German context around 1920. To specify the tactile characteristics of the TV image, he repeatedly cites the Bauhaus, founded by Walter Gropius in 1919. One essential element of instruction, famously, comprised touching exercises and studies of materials in the *Vorkurs*, or preliminary course. Yet in McLuhan, "Bauhaus" is not a label of functionality, standardization, or industrial design; rather, it is synonymous with holism and synesthesia. As the author of *Understanding Media* explains, this art and architecture school is to be conceived of as an institution whose "effort tend[ed] toward inclusive human awareness" and sought to promote "the nonliterate and even antiliterate values of tribal man."[17] Schematically, one might say that what McLuhan had in mind was not the now-classic modernism of the Dessau Bauhaus but the early, expressionist form of the Bauhaus in Weimar.[18]

In an astonishing parallel with Benjamin, László Moholy-Nagy and Sigfried Giedion act as decisive intermediaries. In 1949, McLuhan reviewed *Vision in Motion* and *Mechanization Takes Command*, the main works of these two authors closely associated with the Bauhaus.[19] Since 1943, moreover, McLuhan had been exchanging letters with Giedion, and he subsequently met him in person on several occasions.[20] Whereas he repeatedly and approvingly cites this theorist of architecture and technics in *The Gutenberg Galaxy* and *Understanding Media*, he mentions Moholy only occasionally. The engagement with Bauhaus aesthetics, however, permeates both the publications of the *Explorations* group in Toronto, which was of major importance for McLuhan, and the development of his own theory of media.[21]

This applies also and perhaps especially to his theory of television, as an article published in the early 1960s shows. In "Inside the Five Sense Sensorium," McLuhan makes the following suggestion: "Let us consider the hypothesis that TV offers a massive Bauhaus program of re-education for North American sense life. That is to query whether the TV image is, in effect, a haptic, tactile, or synesthetic mode of interplay among the senses."[22] With the publication of *The Gutenberg Galaxy* and *Understanding Media*, the hypothesis has become a certainty and the query has been answered in the affirmative. Television technology and Bauhaus art are thus being closely associated.

The connection between McLuhan, Moholy, and Giedion, however, exists not only on the level of content.[23] It also, and at least just as importantly, has a formal or, if you like, medial component. McLuhan's reference to the two authors associated with the Bauhaus leads him to view the medium of television not as such but through the lens of another, older medium. It appears, to use one of McLuhan's own succinct formulas, in the "rear-view mirror" of photography, more precisely, of photographed paintings and sculptures.[24]

As I will show in what follows, the photographs of works of art contained in books such as *Vision in Motion* and *The Eternal Present* play an important, perhaps even decisive role in McLuhan's reading of Moholy and Giedion. While he does not mention these photos explicitly, the relevance of the tactile aspects of visual phenomena and processes was clearly presented to him by the extremely crisp black-and-white photographs featured in both

Moholy's and Giedion's book publications. Especially the photomicrographs of the surface structures of paintings by Seurat and Cézanne, whose tactile qualities Moholy extensively comments on, led McLuhan to study the "texture" of the TV image. The photos Giedion published of prehistoric cave paintings and reliefs further stimulated these studies.

The result is a media theory that seeks to summarize its principles by subjecting its recipients to a "massage" by photographs. At the same time, this media theory outlines a conception of history in which, thanks to the mediation of the Bauhaus, the curved screen of the television stands next to the curved surface of the primeval *Woman with the Horn*.

Touched by the Bauhaus

From a Jesuit and Thomist perspective, the tactile tends to vanish into the ethereal and the psychological. Thomism closely associates the sense of touch with the *sensus communis*, a mental faculty that makes a selection among the stimuli received by the outer senses, forms them into a coherent whole, and thereby simultaneously creates the foundations for the constitution of the subject.[25] Teilhard further reinforces this psychologization by tracing "the envelope of thinking substance" produced, in his view, by "the extraordinary network of radio and television communications" back to the experience of an "'etherized' universal consciousness," to the (ultimately subjective) impression of being "simultaneously present, over land and sea, in every comer of the earth."[26]

McLuhan seeks to counterbalance this double vanishing of the tactile by citing several examples of bodily touch: observations on handshakes, reflections on handwriting, descriptions of grasping and releasing commodities. The reference to the Bauhaus, too, comes in here. In 1961, this reference was only an unproven, albeit stimulating hypothesis. Three years later, in *Understanding Media*, it has become an argument: "TV," we are now told, "is the Bauhaus program of design and living, or the Montessori educational strategy, given total technological extension and commercial sponsorship."[27]

In the early days of the Bauhaus, the touching exercises and the study of materials were primarily explorative and aimed at shaping individual artistic personalities. Given the increasing use of new kinds of construction materials in the second half of the nineteenth century (steel, concrete, etc.), the attention of the architects, sculptors, and painters active at the Bauhaus had shifted to the "material in itself." At the same time, their reform-pedagogical claim was that education at the Weimar institution was not only to consist of appropriating theoretical knowledge but also to include the concrete experience of different materials. Accordingly, Johannes Itten's exercises, for example by representing the characteristic properties of a material such as wood in drawings, were to train the development of the eye as a receptive sense and of the sense of touch as a productive sense (fig. 4.1). Other exercises were to make use of combinations of the simplest of materials (wood, wire, cardboard, wicker, etc.) for observing one's subjective feeling for materials (fig. 4.2).

When, in 1923, Moholy-Nagy became responsible for the Vorkurs, the character of these introductory studies changed.[28] The touching exercises then served instead to make the education of aspiring artists, designers, and architects more scientific, a goal pursued in the Soviet Union in the 1920s as well.[29] With custom-made "tactile tables" (fig. 4.3), Moholy in fact combined the touching exercises with an effort to develop and employ aptitude assessment procedures of the kind that contemporary applied psychology (*Psychotechnik*) used to explore and document the tactile capacities of job candidates with greater precision. Once again, touch served as a touchstone.

Moholy nonetheless maintained the explorative touching exercises in the curriculum. Like his predecessor Itten, Moholy considered study of the "tactile values" of different materials and surfaces a pedagogical device "to arouse and enrich the desire for sensation and expression." Invoking Marinetti's futurist tactilism manifesto, however, Moholy no longer sought to exclude the possibility that a new form of art might emerge from the touching exercises.[30]

Yet paradoxically, the studies students undertook under Moholy were not limited to directly touching and concretely dealing with wood, metal, paper, and other materials. Photography, too, was considered a contribution to the culture of touch.[31] Thus Moholy declares in his 1929 treatise *von material zu architektur*, partially translated as *The New Vision* in 1932, that "the documentarily exact photos of material (touch) values, their magnified, previously hardly perceived forms of appearance motivate almost everyone . . . to test and train their touch function [*tastfunktion*]"[32]—an observation clearly echoed by Benjamin when he writes in the artwork essay that photographic closeups "make completely new structural formations of matter [*Strukturbildungen der Materie*] appear."[33]

It is only coherent, then, that Moholy's treatise counters the pencil drawing, which Itten, in the catalog for the Weimar Bauhaus exhibition of 1923, had used to illustrate the exploration of the outer structure of a tree trunk, with the photograph of a sawed-off piece of wood on which the inner structure of the tree becomes visible (fig. 4.4). Photography thus functions as a propaedeutic for developing a new culture of materials "since its concentration of emphasis offers a quick [*verkürzt*], though an indirect [*gedämpft*], approach to actual experience with the material."[34] Other illustrations in Moholy's book, which show, among other things, surfaces of water, sand, and asphalt, are also meant to foster such a visual experience of materiality.

In many respects, Moholy's obvious fascination with the "precise magic of the finest tissue" recalls the *Micrographia* by Robert Hooke, in whom the early modern microscope had triggered a similar enthusiasm about the surfaces and textures of the most varied of materials.[35] Unlike Hooke, however, Moholy converts this fascination into conceptual distinctions meant to facilitate the aesthetic experience and description of differently structured "materials [*materialgefüge*]." Stimulated by the theory and practice of Russian constructivism, he distinguishes the "structure" of a material from its "texture" and "facture" and further supplements this triad with the property of "massing."[36] Although not always clear-cut, these categories, as we will see, are an important starting point for McLuhan's analysis of the TV image.

Moholy defines "structure" as "the unalterable manner in which the material is built up," the geological layers of a mountain range, for example, or the fibrous consistency of paper. "Texture," in turn, refers to the "organically resulting outward surface," its setting or envelope. Moholy adds an explanatory keyword, "epidermis, organic," illustrated by photographs of an old man's wrinkled facial skin, the shriveled skin of a rotten apple, and the fur of a tabby cat (fig. 4.5).[37]

"Facture," finally, is defined as "the sensorily perceptible result (the effect) of a working process" on the material. In his work on literature, Viktor Shklovsky defined facture as the "pedaling" of artworks' being-made. Analogically, Moholy's facture concept aims at a knowledge and experience of "the upper surface of material which has undergone change through external factors (epidermis, artificial)."[38] Moholy's haptically based design theory, at this point, appears as a general and comparative theory of surfaces.

The surfaces of art, too, enter into the photographically supported view of this theory. One of the illustrations in the German original of *The New Vision*, for example, exemplifies the phenomenon of texture via "various silk linings." Arranged one on top of the other like the individual images of a strip of film, the fabric samples' different weaving patterns almost become graspable (fig. 4.6). Later in the book, painted surfaces are presented photographically in a similar way. Possibly inspired by Aleksandr Rodchenko's

Black on Black series of facturist paintings, Moholy in three circular cut-out photographs presents "different surface treatments of the same oil paint on the same background." Light coming in from the side highlights the facture of these painting samples. According to Moholy, "The three examples are a proof of the statement that the manner of applying the paint, the motion of the brush gives different light effects therefore different color values."[39]

Published in 1947, Moholy's major work, *Vision in Motion*, takes up and elaborates on these observations concerning the connection between texture and light. In reading this book at the end of the 1940s, McLuhan thus receives not just a well-informed "resume of the Bauhaus program with its superb methods for training the senses"[40] but also, at the same time, a comprehensive introduction to an aesthetics of materials and surfaces. Moholy's book, in fact, opens up a broad perspective on the "visual 'tactilism'" of the arts and of media,[41] and it is this perspective, precisely, that McLuhan will adopt in his theory of television.

Vision in Motion, too, discusses the role of photography in capturing and presenting surface qualities. As if he had the illustrations from his earlier books before his eyes, Moholy writes, "There is the incisive sharpness of camera portraits pitted with pores and furrowed by lines; the air view of a ship at sea moving through waves that seem frozen in light; the chiseled delicacy of an ordinary sawn block of wood; the close-up of a woven tissue; the whole of rarely observed details of structure, texture and facture of whatever objects we choose within the realm of the traditional, monocular viewing and rendering of the world."[42] A wealth of new illustrations is meant to show how nourishing the "visual food . . . photography provides" is in engaging with the arts.[43] Besides "tactile charts," dramatically staged by lateral lighting, we encounter sharply drawn photographs of shiny "hand-sculptures" in precious wood, on which every pore seems to be visible. Aerial photographs of different landscapes appear as abstract patterns of traces, while close-ups of sculptures, also lit from the side to great effect, display the texture of their surfaces almost too clearly.[44]

It is against this background that Moholy revisits the texture of oil paintings. With comparative black-and-white photographs of van Gogh's, Cézanne's, and Seurat's brushwork, he draws attention to the different qualities of the painting surfaces (fig. 4.7). The arrangement of these photographs, incidentally, takes up the strip-like montage Moholy had used already in his Bauhaus days to present the different surfaces of silk fabrics and tactile materials.[45]

The accompanying text describes the different "brush textures" in van Gogh, Cézanne, and Seurat so vividly that the surfaces of the paintings seem to become sculptures in their own right. Thus Moholy writes about the way van Gogh applied paint to the canvas: "The pigment appeared as relief casting a shadow, while the edges were touched by light."[46] This view of paintings as reliefs or sculptures goes back to the Bauhaus Vorkurs just as much as it announces McLuhan's theory of television.

TV Pointillism

Understanding Media discusses the particular properties of the TV image at length. In doing so, McLuhan focuses on two aspects with tactile connotations. They concern, first—and entirely in keeping with Moholy—the texture of the television image. According to McLuhan, the TV image consists of small pictorial dots; it is "a mosaic mesh of light and dark spots."[47] The tactile aspect, briefly put, is that the emergence of this mosaic is traced back to the electronic scanning procedure of the TV camera.

The second particularity of the TV image for McLuhan is that it is a tube or ray image. It is an image projected from behind onto a coated glass surface. The TV image "appears by light *through*, not light *on*," as would be the case for the page of printed book, for example. Here the tactile aspect is that the TV image does not simply confront viewers but includes them in a kind of radiant envelope. It functions, as McLuhan puts it in evoking Malraux's photographic museum of the history of art, as a "housing-without-walls."[48] In this sense, though, television is not as much an extension of the sense of touch but, like clothing, an extension of the skin.

Just how much this analysis of the TV image is indebted to the plastic illustrations in Moholy's book is apparent, first, in McLuhan's interest in the qualities of surfaces in general. In referring to written records before the age of print, for example, McLuhan mentions the "diffuse texture" of medieval manuscripts; with regard to current fashion, he speaks of a contemporary "preference for coarse heavy textures and sculptural shapes in dress"; and in discussing cubist paintings and collages, he describes a "dramatic conflict of patterns, lights, textures."[49]

Then he turns in a similar way to the surface character of the TV image. For him, the particularity of this image shows itself first of all in the medium's predilection for motifs that appeal to the sense of touch. Given the low resolution of television images in the 1960s, these are, according to McLuhan, primarily rough textures. Hence television "takes kindly to the varied and rough textures of Western saddles, clothes, hides, and shoddy match-wood bars and hotel lobbies," whereas high-resolution cinematic film "is at home in the slick chrome world of the night club and the luxury spots of the metropolis." McLuhan even uses this approach to try and explain the outcome of the presidential debate between Nixon and Kennedy. On television, he says, "Nixon's sharp intense image" had no chance against the "blurry shaggy texture of Kennedy."[50]

But McLuhan does not remain on the level of motifs. Relying on Moholy, he subsequently inscribes the tactile aspect in the material constitution of this kind of image. Insisting, in *Understanding Media*, on the TV image being a mosaic of light and dark spots, he time and again refers to Seurat's pointillist paintings, whose texture is analyzed in *Vision in Motion*.

Moholy already had given this analysis a turn very much of interest to media theory. According to him, the pointillists following Seurat juxtapose "small color dots" to provoke in viewers the illusion of a wide vibrant field of colorful lights. For Moholy, the kind of image thus produced is to be understood in analogy with another, a technical procedure of image production: "At the end of the last century, Signac, Gross and especially Seurat preconceived the method of color photography as a new medium of expression by working with light effects."[51]

McLuhan takes up this argument but adapts it to his object and his purposes. In *Understanding Media*, he thus declares, at first in general terms, that "Cézanne or Seurat, or Rouault . . . provide . . . an indispensable approach to understanding TV." Elsewhere he goes so far as to call Seurat a "prophet of TV." He then takes up the connection established by Moholy between pointillism and photography: "In the daguerreotype process there was the same stippling or pitting with minute dots that was echoed later in Seurat's *pointillisme*, and is still continued in the newspaper mesh of dots that is called 'wire-photo.'" And then he includes television in this description: "The stipple of points of Seurat is close to the present technique of sending pictures by telegraph, and close to the form of the TV image or mosaic made by the scanning finger."[52]

As soon as the aspect of pointillist texture has come to the fore, it no longer matters to McLuhan whether the dots of the image are produced by hand (as in painting) or by a camera (as in photography or television). In other words, his analysis is "symmetrical" in Latour's sense of the term. Independently of whether it has come about artificially or naturally, that is, in a human or a nonhuman way, the primary focus is on the qualities of images' respective "epidermis." It is on this condition, precisely, that movements of the brush on the canvas can be set in analogy with the scanning process in the television camera. In both cases, accordingly, we are dealing with tactilely produced images (fig. 4.8).[53]

At this point, however, it also becomes clear just how much the black-and-white photographs from Moholy's books intervene in McLuhan's theorizing. The description of the television image as a mesh of light and dark spots rather summarily suppresses the difference between Seurat's color paintings and 1960s black-and-white TV images. As a result, the television image in McLuhan appears to be remarkably static. It is not a movement image and does not draw viewers into the temporal structure of its broadcasting. Instead, it appears as a snapshot.

A Diaphanous Image

These static aspects are even reinforced when McLuhan moves to a discussion of the second characteristic of television images. In explaining the qualities of this kind of image, where light is coming "through," however, he temporarily suspends his references to the Bauhaus. McLuhan instead refers, via the painter, wall decorator, and experimental filmmaker André Girard, to the symbolist Georges Rouault.

Girard was Rouault's only student, and both were friends with the philosopher Jacques Maritain, whose importance for McLuhan I have already mentioned. In the United States during the postwar years, Maritain had been active on behalf of both artists, and it is likely that McLuhan, too, came to know of them via Maritain. Maritain, for example, wrote the introduction to the 1953 Rouault retrospective at the Museum of Modern Art in New York, and in the same year he authored an enthusiastic commentary on Girard's design for the glass windows in St. Ann Chapel in Palo Alto, California (fig. 4.9).[54]

In the late 1950s, Girard began experimenting with painted films he produced by directly applying paint on 70 mm film (fig. 4.10). He contributed several such films to the CBS show *Lamp unto My Feet*, broadcast on Sundays, among them a filmic representation of the life and passion of Jesus Christ.

In addition, Girard's films, accompanied by music and explained by lectures given by the artist, were screened at American universities. In February 1960, for instance, Girard showed his films *The Tell-Tale Heart* and *The Life of St. Patrick* at Boston College and gave a lecture, “Rouault as I Knew Him”—a tribute to his recently deceased teacher, who had worked not only as painter and graphic artist but also as creator of stage sets and church windows.[55]

As McLuhan reports in his essay “Inside the Five Sense Sensorium,” Girard declared in this connection that it had really been Rouault who had fired his enthusiasm for the medium of television: “For Rouault made his effects as if by light *through*, rather than by light *on*, as occurs in stained glass. In fact, says Girard, Rouault was the painter of television before TV.”[56] These remarks are one reason why Rouault repeatedly appears in *Understanding Media* as an artist who, like Seurat, makes significant contributions to understanding the TV image.

The connections thus made between television technology and religious art are far from random. In *The Gutenberg Galaxy*, too, McLuhan refers to a religious context to discuss the difference between light “through” and light “on.” There, however, a different medium initially takes center stage: alphabetic writing.

According to McLuhan, medieval illuminated manuscripts allowed for a completely different form of transmission than the printed pages of the Gutenberg Bible in early modernity. The splendidly decorated manuscripts of the Middle Ages, which, read aloud, produced an entire “ballet” of gestures and attitudes in the reader, clearly had a much more tactile orientation than the uniform, linear typography of the printed page that instilled quiet, visually oriented reading. The lavishly designed manuscripts urged medieval readers not to focus on individual letters or words but, as it were, to look through the text to grasp not the letter but the “spirit” of the divine message. According to McLuhan, the reader’s task was thus to “release the light from within the text” rather than simply decipher a text by the light of a lamp.[57]

Not just medieval manuscript culture, the author of *The Gutenberg Galaxy* goes on to explain, but entire architectures at that time were working with the principle of light shining through. The obvious example McLuhan cites in this context is that of Gothic cathedrals. Not least with regard to their stained glass windows, he describes these church buildings as monumental architectures, in which light is not used as lighting for individual segments of interior space but serves as an active design principle that ultimately makes even the walls appear “diaphanous” or transparent.[58]

Evoking the work of art historians such as Otto von Simson and Erwin Panofsky, McLuhan explains that in the Middle Ages, believers in such an edifice did not reservedly, as if from a distance, observe the divine light emanating from a specific source. Rather, they were completely surrounded by light, immersed in it. Thus, Gothic cathedrals already created the media conditions for the "depth involvement" that, according to McLuhan, also characterizes present-day television.[59]

In *Understanding Media*, these discussions form the background against which it becomes possible to see in television a potential for a "liturgical revival" of contemporary culture.[60] The diaphanous character of the TV image, according to McLuhan, opens up completely new possibilities for shaping the cultural space. He follows Teilhard in connecting the "event" of the discovery of electromagnetic waves with the expectation that they will bring about an "etherized" commonality, but it is Girard's television experiments that he credits with actually producing this new form of community. To a certain extent, television here loses its ethereal character and indeed becomes an expansion of the skin: "painting with light is a kind of housing-without-walls," as McLuhan summarizes the point with reference to Girard's experimental films.[61]

The contexts of this analysis, however, might not be quite as religious at they might at first seem. For here, McLuhan, in addition to Girard, refers to the "landscape by light through" by György Kepes, a former assistant of Moholy-Nagy's who also adhered to Bauhaus ideals.[62] Already in Weimar, the Bauhaus had workshops for glass and mural painting, and on the Bauhaus stage, experiments were conducted with "reflected light displays" that were projected from behind onto a transparent canvas, that is, presented via light through. Moholy himself worked intensively with diaphanous image supports such as film, glass, and plexiglass, such that it is not surprising that in *Vision in Motion*, he repeatedly speaks of "painting with light." In this connection, Moholy even speculates about "a mural art of this age" that in his view would "most probably" emerge from "photography, cinema, and television."[63]

As a matter of fact, as early as 1919, the architect who had brought Moholy to the Bauhaus in the 1920s had made reference to the Gothic cathedrals. In the Bauhaus program, Gropius speaks of the "great building" as the ultimate goal of the newly founded art and architecture school, choosing Feininger's depiction of a radiant church as its programmatic title page (fig. 4.11). Shortly after the opening of the Bauhaus, the architect also declared that the work done at this institution "must find its crystalline expression in a great *Gesamtkunstwerk*. And this great total work of art, this cathedral of the future, will then shine with its abundance of light into the smallest objects of everyday life."[64]

Given this vision—inspired in turn by the visionary glass architectures of Bruno Taut, Paul Scheerbart, and others—McLuhan's description of the light architectures created by the television image is indeed only consistent. Even his talk of television as a technically enhanced and commercially viable version of the Bauhaus agenda becomes more plausible.

The Electric Cave

McLuhan expands and generalizes his analysis of the television image as a surface composed of individual points penetrated by light from behind in a series of further observations on the tactile aspects of electric media. Here, too, artistic and art historical contextualizations play an important role. In *Understanding Media*, the assessment that electricity is primarily tactile and only incidentally visual and auditory, for example, is followed by the statement that "the electric form of pervasive impression is profoundly tactile and organic, endowing each object with a kind of unified sensibility, as the cave painting had done." And *The Gutenberg Galaxy*, too, makes a connection between tactile-electric media and prehistoric art: "It is necessary to understand the close interrelation between the world and art of the cave man, and the intensely organic interdependence of men in the electric age."[65]

Such match cuts, which—as in Kubrick's *2001: A Space Odyssey*—seamlessly join prehistory and future, evidently play in a different register than the comparison between the diaphanous TV image and the stained glass windows of Gothic cathedrals. Ultimately, however, they, too, remain with the referential framework of Bauhaus aesthetics, only that now, the anchor is not Moholy but Giedion.

As stark as the contrast might seem between the subject matter of Giedion's early treatise on the dominance of mechanization and his study on the origin of art, the topic of the first volume of *The Eternal Present* was neither completely new for Giedion, nor did it constitute a break with earlier interests of his. For, at least in the Weimar phase of the Bauhaus, the endeavor to discover the foundations of creative design and use them as a starting point for a new aesthetics was by no means limited to the practical tactile exercises in the preliminary course. It also included an exploration of the "Art of Primitive Peoples and of Prehistory." Besides Eckart von Sydow's eponymous book, in any case, Gropius had the Bauhaus library stocked with works such as Carl Einstein's *Afrikanische Plastik* (*African Sculpture*), Herbert Kühn's study *Malerei der Eiszeit* (*Ice Age Painting*), and Adolf Stiegelmann's presentation of the Altamira cave as a *Kunsttempel des Urmenschen* (*Art Temple of Prehistoric Man*).[66]

Yet once again, the first programmatic articulation of an interest in the aspects of art thus invoked is Moholy's. As early as 1929, in *von material zu architektur*, he explains the second stage of the development of sculpture, which according to him is characterized by the "modeled (hollowed-out) block," with the help of illustrations he takes, without commentary, from Sydow's book on prehistoric art. He presents the *Venus of Menton* as a stone "modeled according to a previous plan—not in the sense of a representation true to life, but in the sense of the tool, the material, and the abstract idea."[67]

The shaping of the stone thus does not intervene profoundly but stops at the tactile surface of the stone. According to Moholy, there are analogous procedures to be found in contemporary sculpture. Immediately following the photograph of the *Venus of Menton* are similarly "modeled" sculptures by Archipenko and Brâncuşi.

Such combinations of the archaic and the modern take up and develop a photographic rhetoric that avant-garde publications like *Der blaue Reiter* and *Der Querschnitt* experimented with in the 1910s and that can be found, in the 1920s and 1930s, in books by Le Corbusier and Amédée Ozenfant, for example, or in the journal *Documents* edited by Carl Einstein and Georges Bataille.[68]

Via Moholy, this visual rhetoric also finds its way into the treatise on modern sculpture that Giedion's wife, Carola Giedion-Welcker, published in 1937. In this book, which McLuhan cites in *The Gutenberg Galaxy*, prehistoric Venus figures stand side by side with plastic works by Jean Arp, and Bronze Age megalith formations are juxtaposed with sculptures by Giacometti.[69]

Yet it was Giedion's studies on prehistoric art and architecture that subordinated the photographic juxtaposition of prehistory and modernity to a clearly defined argumentative purpose. After the end of the Second World War, Giedion set out and "search[ed] for the unchanging elements of human nature" and found a "real inner affinity . . . between the longings of the man of today and the longings of primeval man, crystallized in signs and symbols on the cavern walls" (fig. 4.12).[70]

In *The Beginnings of Art*, Giedion successfully stages the "eternal present" that became visible from this perspective by using photographs to juxtapose prehistoric finger drawings in clay found in the cave at Pech-Merle with an engraving by Georges Braque or the animal reliefs, also prehistoric, from the Abri Murat cave with a drawing by Paul Klee.[71] McLuhan picks up on such pictorial montages when he puts the art of cave dwellers in parallel with forms of experience of the electric age—not without reminding readers, incidentally, that the television image is really "an abstract work of art on the pattern of a Seurat or Rouault."[72]

Giedion himself points out just how important photography is for his form of historiography. Right at the beginning of his essay "Space Conception in Prehistoric Art," which thanks to McLuhan appears in *Explorations* (and was later included, in revised form, in *The Beginnings of Art*), he highlights the contributions of the photographs by Hugo P. Herdeg, "one of the best Swiss photographers," and his colleague Achille Weider to the reconstruction of this conception of space. For if, as Giedion explains, "the root of primeval art" is that it has "no relation to the horizontal or vertical," then photography facilitates capturing this decisive feature with precision because it makes possible a permanent detachment of the gaze from the usual standpoint and habitual stance of human viewers. It allows, as the later version of the essay included in the book puts it, for "seeing things without 'relation to myself.'"[73]

Besides contributing to the discovery of what McLuhan would later call "multidirectional space orientation" in auditory-tactile environments (and what Deleuze and Guattari, going back to the context of *Explorations*, would refer to as the visual tactility of "smooth space"),[74] the photographs taken under Giedion's direction served above all to capture and display the particular structures and textures of prehistoric art. As a matter of fact, McLuhan's comparison between the tactility of electric media and cave paintings becomes concretely plausible only once the aspect of the surface is taken into account. Giedion, too, was convinced that photography played an important if not decisive role here. Like Moholy, he supposed that such photographic records would be able to aid in developing a new culture of touch and materiality; for that reason, they could also aid in fostering a new, haptically oriented conception of prehistoric art.[75]

The structure of Giedion's studies on prehistoric art and architecture is in fact guided by the systematic approach Moholy followed in investigating the transition "from material to architecture." Just as Moholy in the eponymous volume proceeds from superficial textures and factures via plastic volumes to built spaces, so Giedion some thirty years later begins with scratch marks and imprints on cave walls, continues with images, reliefs, and sculptures, and finally reaches the first comprehensive architectures, namely huts, houses, and temples. The Vorkurs, it seems, exerts its influence even here.

This is apparent in the role of photography as well. Giedion's complaint in the *Explorations* article about the poor quality of the photos of cave art in circulation does indeed read like a repeat of the criticism Wölfflin had voiced at the end of the nineteenth century about some photographs of Roman sculptures.[76] Thus Giedion writes, "Nothing is more destructive of the true values of primeval art than the glare of electric light in this realm of eternal night. . . . The engraved lines, and even the coloured surfaces, lose their intensity under a strong direct light, and sometimes disappear altogether." Yet it immediately becomes clear that the issue is not, as it is in Wölfflin, finding the "right" angle—this right angle precisely does not exist for Giedion. What he is calling for instead is visualizing the specific qualities of surfaces: "Only a soft side-lighting—lumière frisée—can awaken their [the lines' and images'] original strength. Only by this means can the fine veining of the drawings be seen unsmothered by their rough background."[77]

Giedion knew exactly what he was talking about. As part of the preparations for his cave expeditions in the early 1950s, he had visited the electrical engineer and experimental photographer Harold E. Edgerton at MIT, seeking advice on the best lighting equipment for Herdeg and Weider to use. He tells his friend, the Harvard archaeologist Hallam L. Movius Jr., about the result in a letter from August 1952: "The Carpenter master light [spotlight] is by far the best apparatus to examine prehistoric pictures 'à la lumière frisante' [in oblique light]."[78]

The effect of using these spotlights is exemplarily visible in the photographs Herdeg took of the monumental horse reliefs at Cap Blanc. Even in the printed book they impress with their tactile look (fig. 4.13).[79]

The Woman with the Horn

Gideon discusses at length photography's potential for bringing out the complex structures and textures of prehistoric art, using a prominent example, the so-called *Venus of Laussel*. This relief was discovered in a rock shelter near Marquay in the Dordogne *département*. It shows a female figure who with her right hand holds up a horn as her left hand rests on her bulging belly. While Giedion had long been familiar with this relief thanks to art historical publications such as Sydow's *Art of Primitive Peoples and of Prehistory* (fig. 4.14), he returned time and again to the *Woman with the Horn* in the course of working on the texts and images for *The Beginnings of Art*.

In fact, he visited the "small museum" near Bordeaux that then housed the relief twice: first in October 1950, when under Herdeg's direction a first set of photos was taken, then in September 1953, after it had turned out that these pictures, "though good," were "not satisfactory" for the purposes of the book publication (fig. 4.15). In a letter to the director of the museum, Giedion explains his special interest in the *Woman with the Horn*: "I intend to place the Venus of Laussel at the center of my book about the continuity of human nature, for historical but also for artistic reasons."[80]

When almost ten years later, in 1962, the first American edition of *The Beginnings of Art* comes out, the relief does not stand at the center but rather serves as the vanishing point, as it were, of the entire presentation. According to Giedion, it is "the most vigorously sculptured representation of the human body in the whole of primeval art."[81] That is, this work of art fully depicts, for the first time, what constitutes the real point of reference of Giedion's history of continuity: the human in its eternal present. At this point, too, "the longings of the man of today and the longings of primeval man" meet again. The observation, at least, that one decisive characteristic of postwar art is a "return to the human figure" can be found in the new edition of her study on modern sculpture that Carola Giedion-Welcker publishes around the same time.[82]

Giedion painstakingly prepared the prominent placement of the *Venus of Laussel* in the first volume of *The Eternal Present*. As early as 1957, when, giving the A. W. Mellon Lectures in the Fine Arts, he provides a first overview of his research, he talks about the *Woman with the Horn* right from the beginning. As the manuscript of the first lecture shows, he specifically inserted a passage to illustrate the transition from engraved lines and paintings to sculpture with this example. In a manner recalling Moholy, he, at this point and in other notes, traces the particular form of the relief back to a particular conception of the material: "*The rock is treated like an elastic material*." At the same time, Giedion also already criticizes the pictures of the work of art in circulation: "The usual photographs of the Venus of L[aussel] do not express its artistic spirit. The Venus appears their [*sic*] like flattened in a plane."[83]

To obtain an appropriate depiction of the *Woman with the Horn*, Giedion in preparing the book publication proceeded very carefully. In detailed layout sketches, he prescribed the reproduction of no fewer than five different views of the relief on a total of four print pages (figs. 4.16 and 4.17). In addition to a frontal detail view of the head and the horn, in which strong side lighting makes the outlines of the sculpture stand out, these include two total views from a side angle. One of them, which is looking onto the relief from above, shows, according to Gideon, how the backward-leaning head "seems to be reclining as though on a cushion"; another, a side view from below, is meant to convey how the relief would have been seen in its "original position" on the rock. At this point, the "indifferent position toward any kind of direction" the German text evokes in the context of cave *painting* is suspended.[84]

Giedion seems to have been happy with the second photograph in particular (fig. 4.18). In the American edition of *The Beginnings of Art*, it is reproduced in black and white in the text and once more in color on a separate plate. In the German-language and other European editions, this color photograph even serves as the cover image. And that is not all. To demonstrate the plastic intensity of the Venus relief and the particular quality of the photographs made at his behest, Giedion also includes a reproduction of one of the frontal-view photographs as a negative example to show how the *Woman with the Horn* is "usually reproduced in art books and on postcards." In the main text, he does not hold back: "The Venus of Laussel . . . occurs in every history of art but is always reproduced directly from the front. This view makes this highly plastic relief appear as flat as a pancake and greatly reduces its artistic intensity."[85]

It is this intensity that he tries to convey not only via the new photographs but also in his descriptive text: "The figure and the block are inseparably interlocked. In the position selected by the artist for this relief, the block had a slight overhang, so that the figure swelled forward gently. When seen from the side, the curve appears as taut as a strung bow. . . . No part of this figure is without vitality. The bison horn with its hunting notches, which would normally be depicted entirely in one plane, curves sculpturally, clinging to and emphasizing the curve of the block."[86] The way in which the structure and texture of the block of stone entered into the elaboration of the *Woman with the Horn* thus becomes the aspect guiding Giedion's analysis. He also brings it to bear in the *Explorations* essay where, toward the end, he describes a flexible way of dealing with surfaces as an additional characteristic of the prehistoric conception of space. As in the case of space, Giedion here does not explicitly speak of tactility. But the context makes clear that that is precisely what is at issue.

Prehistoric art, on this view, is essentially founded on a "freedom of approach to all surfaces."[87] It is based on a constant change of surfaces that become the starting point and frame of reference of creative design in the most varied of ways and on the most varied of occasions: "Whether the structure or shape of the surface be smooth, curved, or puckered, one can always recognize paleolithic man's ability to use it to the full." Giedion describes this procedure as an artful hugging or *embracing of contours* and explains that in French, such a use of rocks' natural shape is indeed called *épouser les contours*.[88]

McLuhan seems to have paid particular attention to this description. Fascinated with tactility as the main mode of perception of the nonliterate anyway, he immediately saw the connections with his observations of the texture of clothes, manuscripts, and TV images. *The Gutenberg Galaxy* even quotes Giedion's formula, "épouser les contours," and follows up with a statement aimed at the present day: "Our rediscovery of a passion for contours is inseparable from the recognition of precise interdependence and function, and of all forms as organic."[89]

In speaking of "the recognition . . . of all forms as organic," McLuhan describes the position of a morphologist interested in art and media, a position assumed equally by the humans of the electric age and the cave artists. This position, in Giedion's terms, is the result of a creative reaction of prehistoric humans to their natural surroundings. For McLuhan, who also discerns a creative moment there, it "is thrust upon us by the electromagnetic wave technology."[90]

This is the real basis for putting electric media and cave art in parallel. It consists in supposing that electric media follow the principle of épouser les contours. In *Understanding Media*, too, McLuhan draws on Giedion's suggestive formula. Reasserting the notion that electricity is primarily tactile, he expands the statement about the TV camera constantly scanning its surroundings with its "scanning finger" to *all* electric (pictorial) media. Be it the wirephoto or television, all electronic media "caress the contours of every kind of being by . . . multiple touches." From McLuhan's point of view, this is true even of the "digital computer" he usually pays little attention to, since the computer, too, "with its multiple yes–no dots and dashes," scans its surroundings.[91]

Electronic media—to summarize McLuhan's once again symmetrical observations—thus work in the same way as the authors of prehistoric cave art. They do not engage in incisive fashioning but in a careful modeling, an embracing of contours. Electric media, and television chief among them, are surface media par excellence.

Photography and Historiography

The *Venus of Laussel* holds a horn in her hand. Like the discoverer of the relief, Jean-Gaston Lalanne, Gideon, too, assumed that the carvings discernible on the horn are "hunting notches." We do not know what McLuhan thought about them. With the exception of a comparison between today's radio and age-old "tribal horns," the horn for him was not a medium that warranted any closer attention.[92]

More recent research on the *Venus of Laussel* conceives of the notches on the horn differently than Giedion and earlier authors. It sees them as temporal markers. Thirteen lines are visible, which is said to be a reference to the lunar months or the menstrual cycle. Some authors even go so far as to see a half moon in the horn the *Venus of Laussel* is holding in her hand.[93]

The connection between horn and time thus evoked leads us back to the question of historiography. McLuhan's media theory, I argued, shows television in the rearview mirror of photography. The black-and-white photographs of differently structured surfaces of bodies and things, paintings and sculptures, walls and reliefs he encountered in reading Moholy and Giedion prompted him to take a closer look at the texture of the TV image.

The paradoxical result was, on the one hand, a further amplification of the spiritualization of the sense of touch already prepared in the Thomist and Jesuit references of McLuhan's writings. Although he does bring in Bauhaus pedagogy to counterbalance the psychologization of the sense of touch, his recourse to Moholy's and Giedion's photographs leads him to conceive of tactility not as bodily touch but as a visual phenomenon, as the result of a "touching seeing" that can be done with the eye but also with the camera.

That, however, is only one consequence. For, on the other hand, the dominance of photography in McLuhan leads to a far-reaching withdrawal of time. Because his investigation is oriented by photographically captured and reproduced textures of surfaces, the TV image appears less as a dynamic entity than as a static construct. To be sure, McLuhan stresses that the TV camera, unlike the photo camera, does not aim at the isolated moment but performs a "continuous scanning action."[94] Nonetheless, from the viewpoint of texture, the television image loses many attributes of a movement-image or time-image. Instead, it becomes a space-image that is at the same time an image-space, a visual envelope that leads, not least because it is first assembled from dots, to a certain form of architecture, not unlike the way in which stones are assembled to form a house.

Yet more or less the same can be said about McLuhan's notion of history as a whole. What he is offering is not so much a historiography of media, which would in fact investigate the changes in the impressions of modernity brought about by media, as it is a survey of historical snapshots. Prompted by the photographs he found in the publications by Moholy and Giedion, the author of *Understanding Media* in this synopsis ultimately assumes a simultaneity of all epochs—and accordingly, like Giedion, a substantial constancy of human experience. In this survey, television can join the Bauhaus but also Gothic architecture and cave painting. Prehistory meets the present just as much as early modernity meets late modernism. In this sense, McLuhan already says that we have never been modern.

The productivity of this approach, however, is immense. McLuhan's media theory assembles a previously unheard-of wealth of examples to have them shed light on each other. On the one hand, one might say that this endows his presentation of media effects with pointillist traits of its own. It consists of a multitude of dots that are barely graspable in their details but in the synoptic view yield a picture.

On the other hand, one might say about *Understanding Media* what McLuhan, with a critical intention, notes about Moholy's magnum opus, *Vision in Motion*: "The book swarms with brilliant insights into parallel effects and intentions between the most diverse activities of contemporary science, photography, engineering, art and literature. . . . A view of obsolescent farm equipment will provide a striking counterpoint to the vision of Léger, intercellular photography suddenly links up with stream of consciousness, and *Finnegans Wake* appears as the encyclopedic filter for old knowledge and new hunches."[95] According to McLuhan, this "vortex of interfused interests and activities" can be mastered only by the intervention of a "serious teacher" whose thinking—like that of Joyce or Giedion—is securely anchored in traditional knowledge.[96]

As author of *Understanding Media*, however, he himself proceeds differently. To link his diverse and varied examples, he relies on the fundamental assumption that there is no essential difference between light and matter. Yet this assumption, too, points back to photography. Although the conception of photography as an indexical sign based on physical contact with the signified would have to wait for later theorists,[97] McLuhan already supposes that the reflection of rays of light is, at bottom, a phenomenon of touch.

That is why for him *scanning* always also means *touching*, independently of whether this scanning is done by the human eye or camera technology. The ungraspable thus encounters the palpable; one transitions to the other. Not unlike medieval metaphysics or modern physics, McLuhan's presentation has light appear as a form of matter, and the sense of touch, accordingly, dissolves in the life of the mind. This, if you like, is McLuhan's version of Dalí's "nuclear mysticism," which, also under Catholic auspices, leads to a metaphysics of not touching.

Ultimately, in McLuhan, even history turns into light. "All ages are contemporaneous" is the quotation from Ezra Pound, whom McLuhan much admired, that Giedion places at the beginning of the first volume of *The Eternal Present*.[98] Giedion thus sums up his own conception of history, which is indebted to a largely detached view on the archive of photography. This view is also at the basis of McLuhan's media theory. Certainly, many of his observations and claims—for example, the famous thesis about the "global village"—are suggestive even with regard to today's mobile and connected media. Given the ever-increasing presence of the most varied of scanning devices (body scanners, book scanners, barcode scanners, and so on), however, his discussion of how television images envelop and penetrate their viewers appears to be especially relevant—even if this media theory hardly captures the historical particularities of the impressions of modernity.

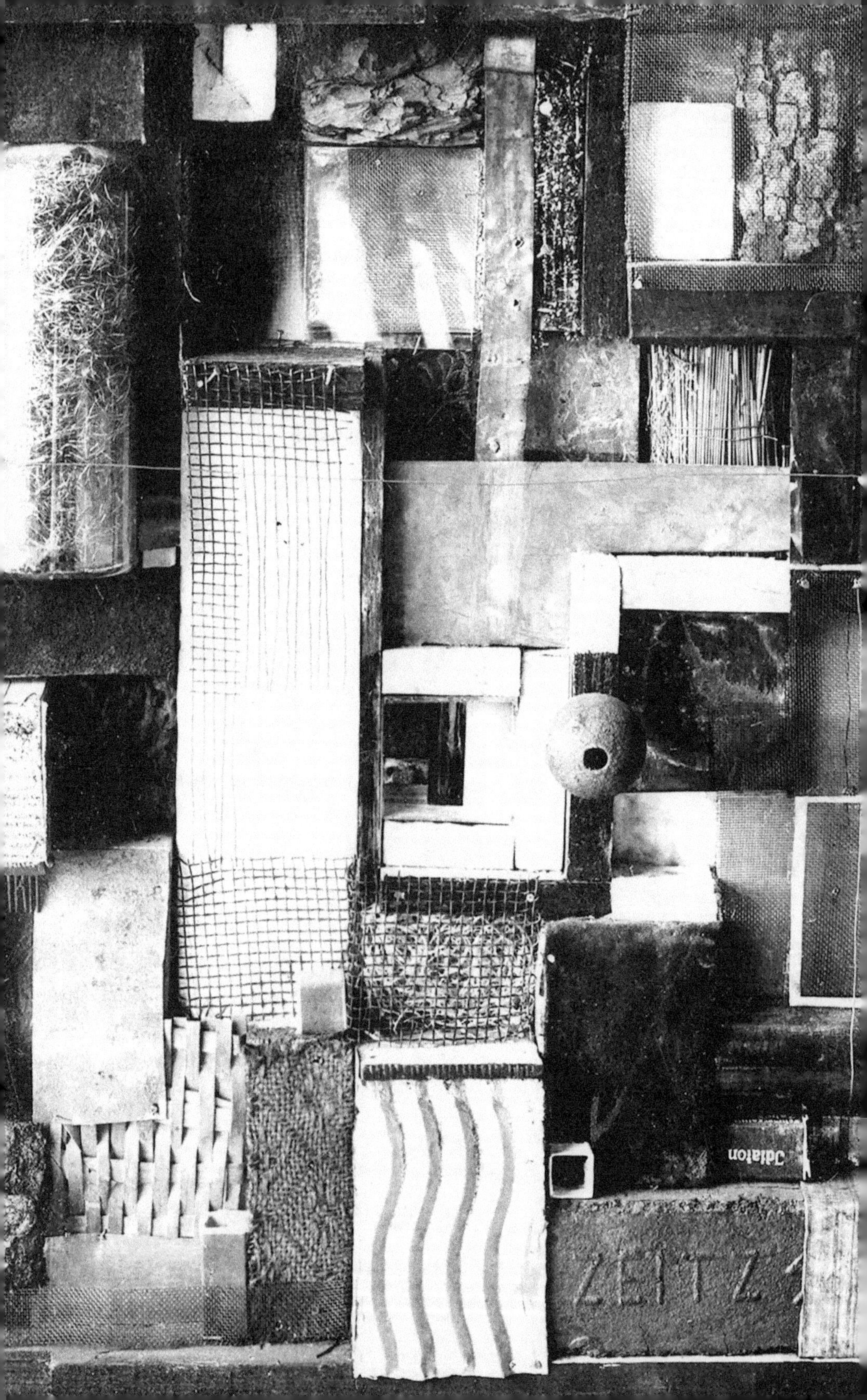
ZEITZ

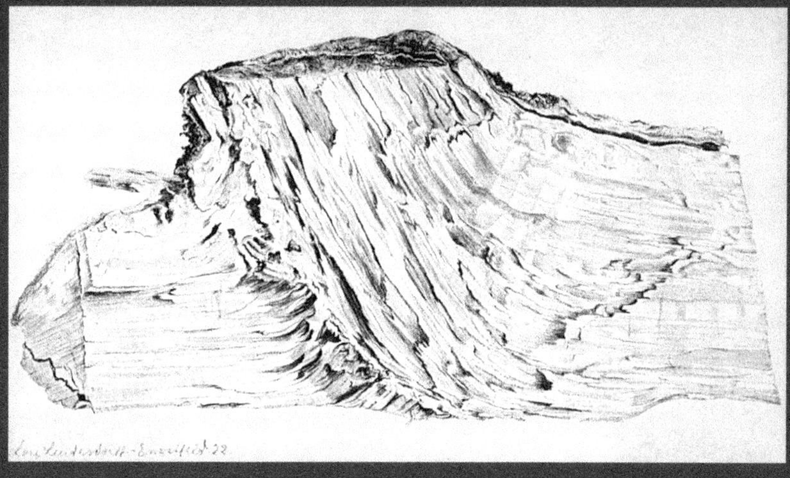

FIGURE 4.1

"Zeichnerische Darstellung der charakteristischen Eigenschaften einer Materie (Holz). Übungsaufgabe zur Entwicklung des Auges als des rezeptiven Sinnes und des Tastsinnes als des produktiven Sinnes (L. Leudersdroff-Engstfeld)." Exercise from Itten's *Vorkurs* (ca. 1920). Bauhaus-Universität Weimar. Archiv der Moderne.

FIGURE 4.2

"Kombination einfachster Materialien zur Entwicklung des Tastsinnes und Beobachtung des subjektiven Materialgefühls (E. Dieckmann)." Exercise from Itten's *Vorkurs* (ca. 1920). Bauhaus-Universität Weimar. Archiv der Moderne.

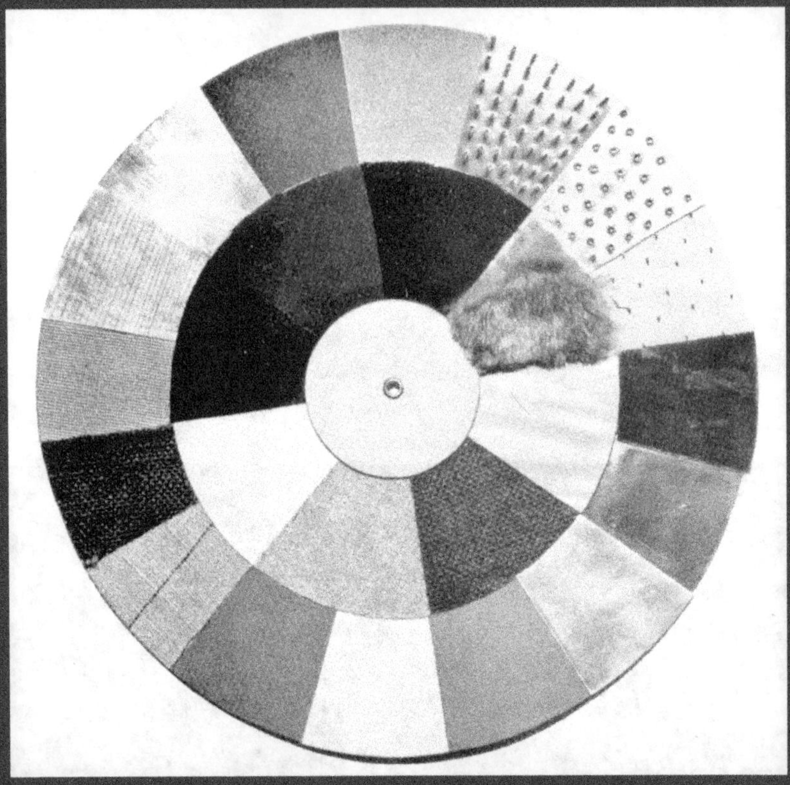

FIGURE 4.3
"Zweizeilige, drehbare tasttafel mit nebeneinander liegenden kontrastierenden taktilischen werten von weich zu hart, von glatt zu rauh (W. Kaminski)." Exercise from Moholy-Nagy's *Vorkurs* (ca. 1925).

FIGURE 4.4
László Moholy-Nagy, "holzstruktur" (from Moholy-Nagy, *von material zu architektur*, 1929).

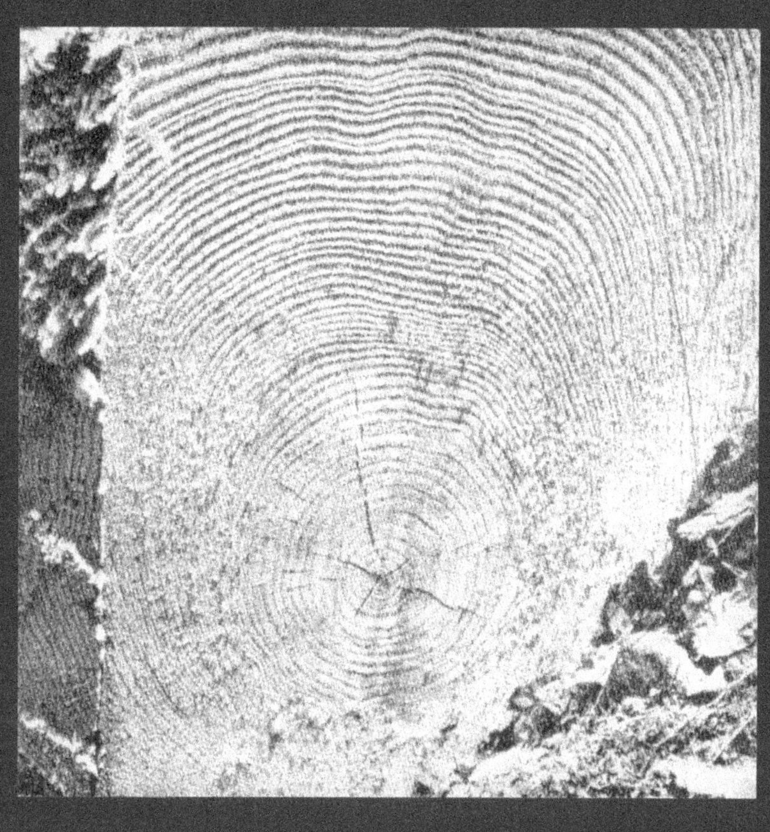

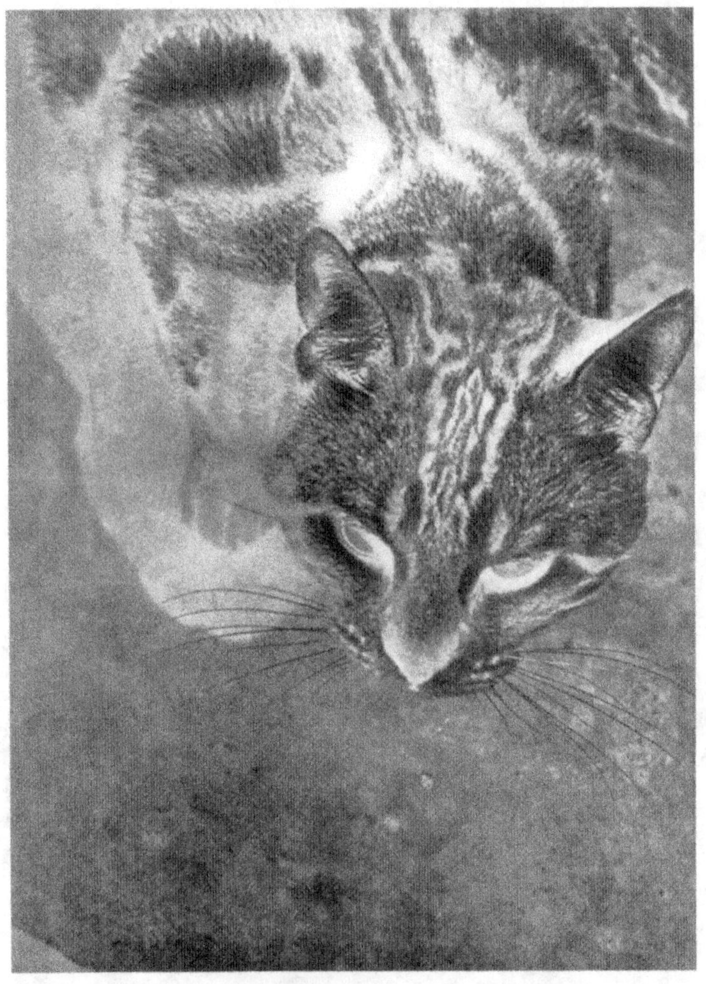

foto: moholy-nagy

abb. 22 textur. das fell einer katze. (negativ)

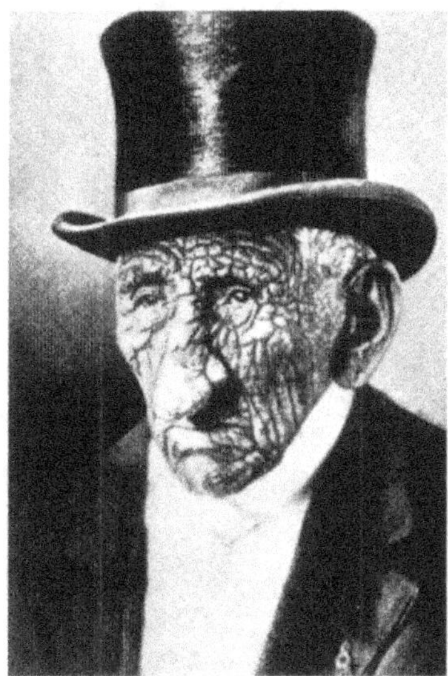

foto: weltspiegel

abb. 23 textur
ein 130 jähriger amerikaner von minnesota

im grunde ist diese fotografie eine zeitrafferaufnahme der epidermiswandlung: eine flugzeugaufnahme der zeit.

abb. 24 textur
ein fauler, mit pilzen besetzter apfel

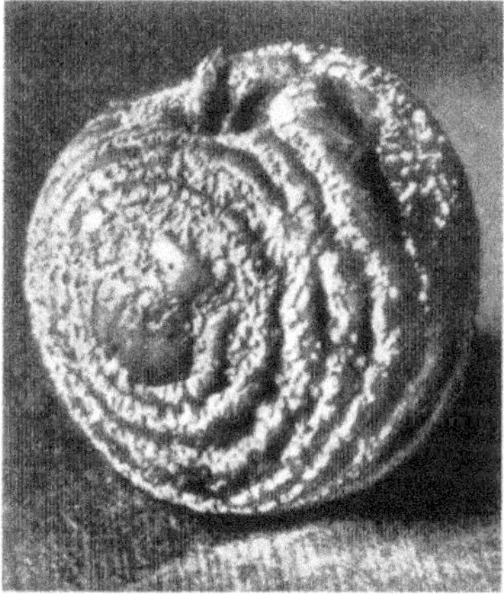

foto: haus und garten

6 moholy-nagy

41

FIGURE 4.5

László Moholy-Nagy, texture as organic epidermis (from Moholy-Nagy, *von material zu architektur*, 1929).

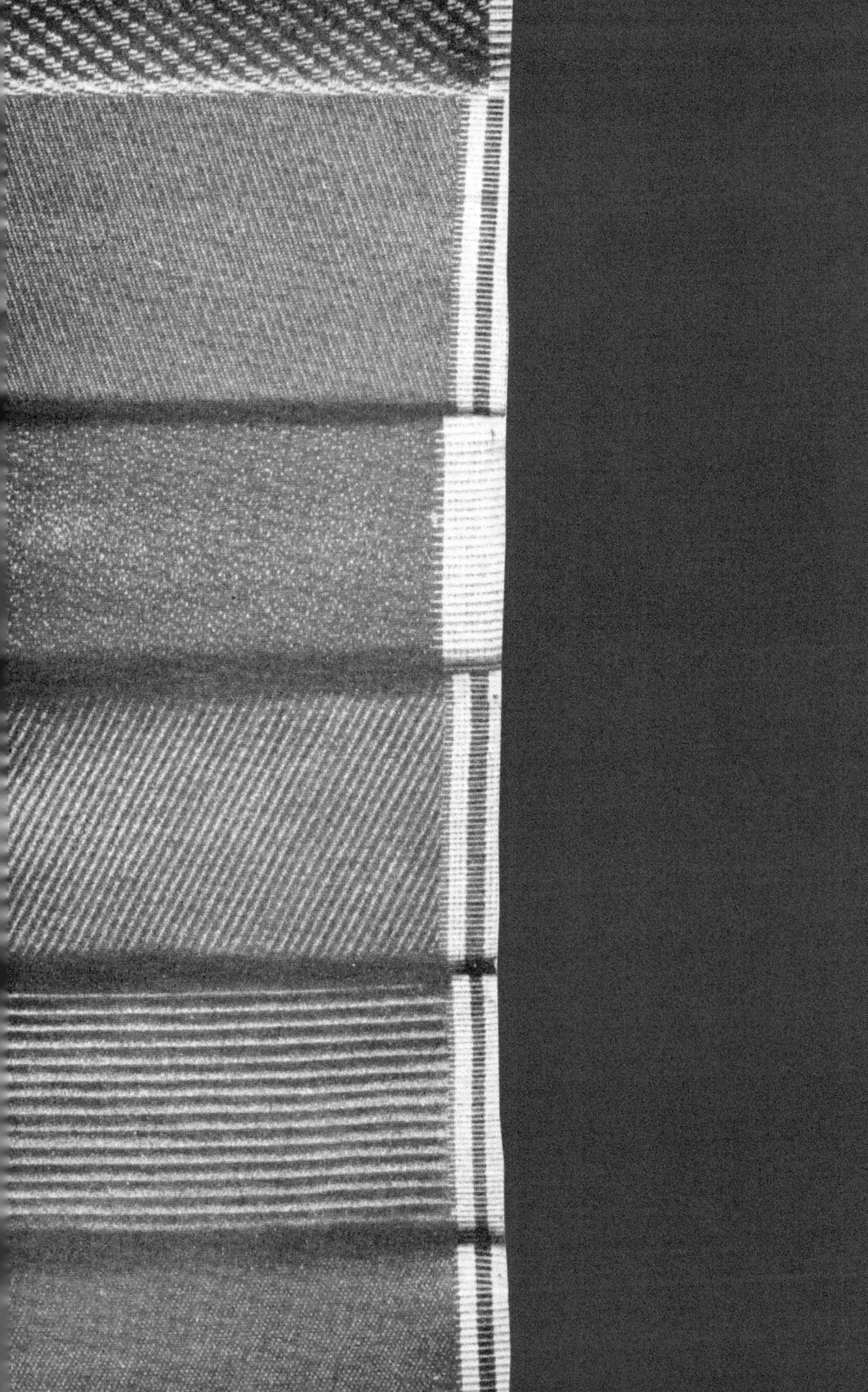

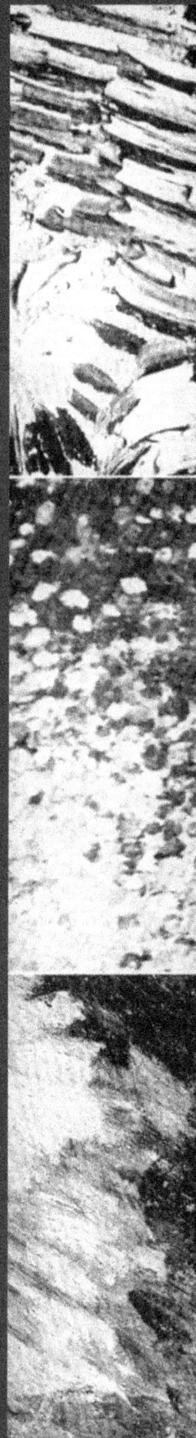

FIGURE 4.6

László Moholy-Nagy, “textur verschiedener futterseiden” (from Moholy-Nagy, *von material zu architektur*, 1929).

FIGURE 4.7

Close-ups of brush textures by (1) van Gogh, (2) Seurat, and (3) Cézanne (from Moholy-Nagy, *Vision in Motion*, 1947).

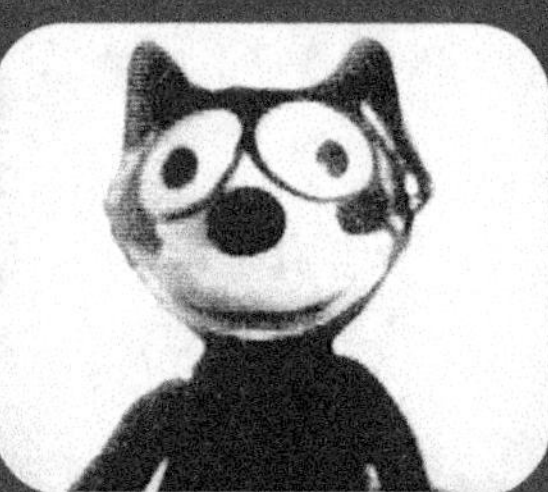
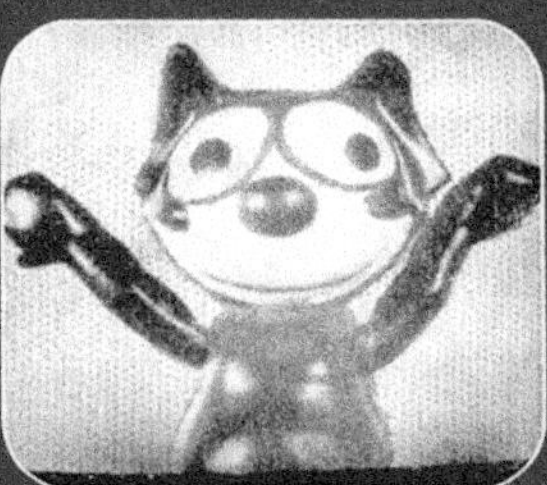

FIGURE 4.8
The changing quality of US television images. *Left*: a mechanically produced image with 60 scan lines from 1929; *middle*: an electronically produced image from 1936 with 343 lines; *right*: an electronically produced image from 1937 with 441 lines. The 1944 account in *Life* magazine is one of few texts to speak of the television camera's "scanning finger."

FIGURE 4.9
André Girard, sketch for a glass window in St. Ann Chapel in Palo Alto. Screen print (1953).

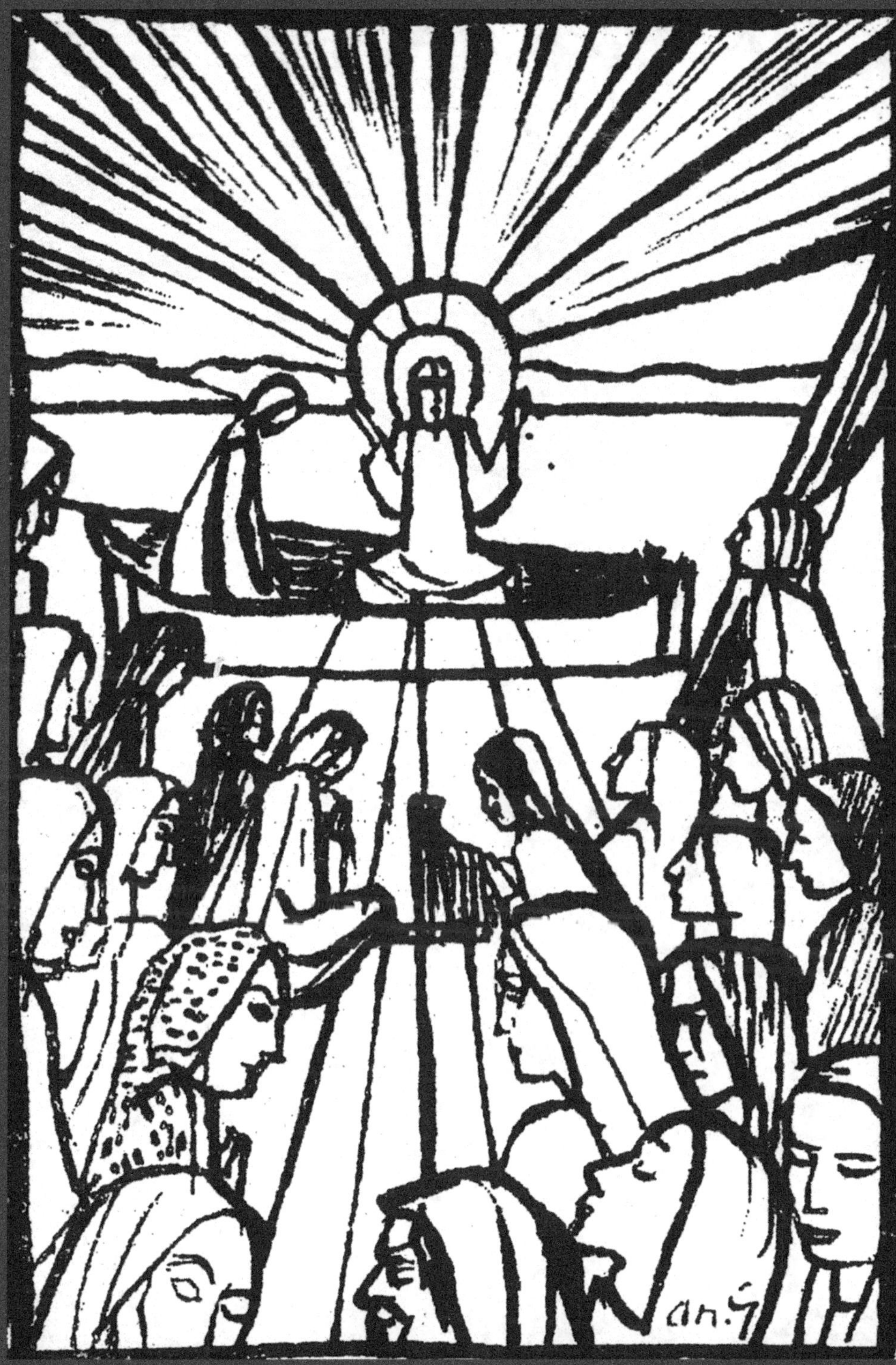

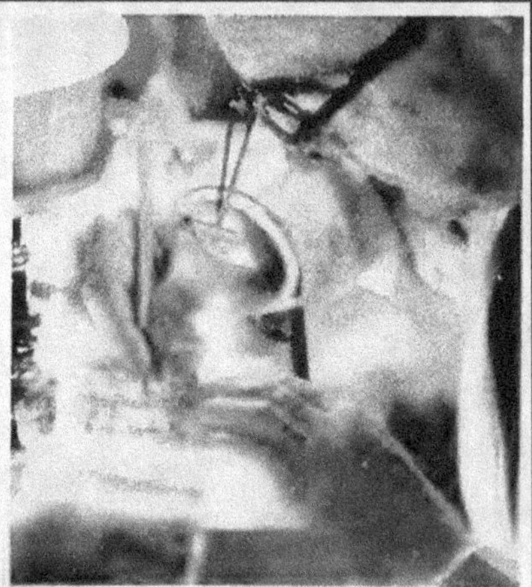

'Painting on light' not easy

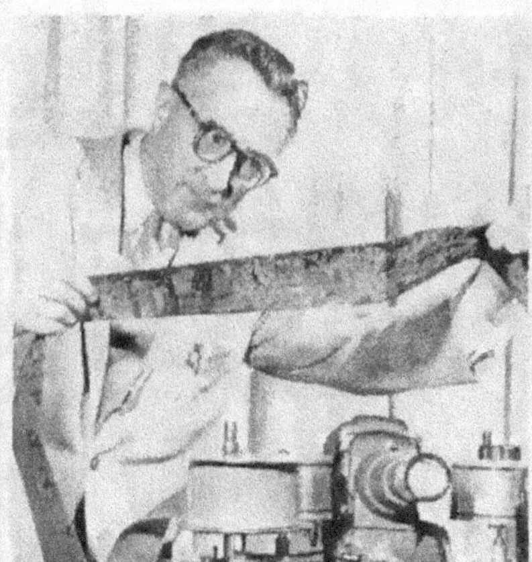

Artist Girard inspects 70mm film

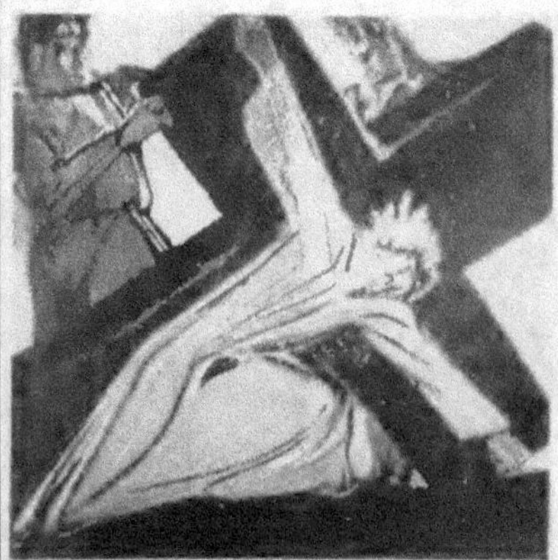

Excerpt from new tv art

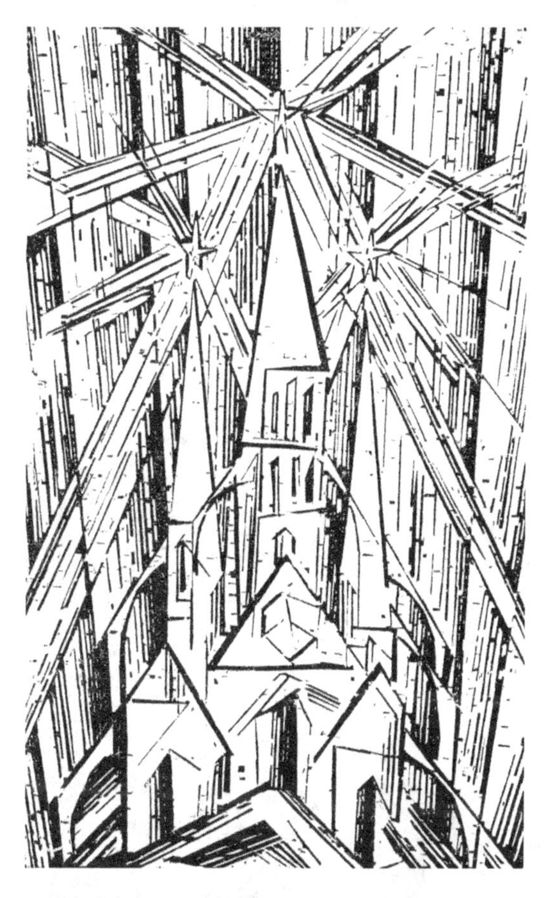

FIGURE 4.10

André Girard working on an experimental film (ca. 1959).

FIGURE 4.11

Lyonel Feininger, *Kathedrale* (1919). Woodcut on the title page of the Bauhaus program.

of enigmatic significance. But, taken all in all, Pech-Merle is the most magical of the prehistoric caverns. Even in recent years, amazing new discoveries have been made: scenes with fabulous animals—a lioness-queen, for example—never seen in any other place.

In the center—if one can use this expression for the complicated subterranean caverns of Pech-Merle—there is a high vaulted hall with a fantastic rock pillar and stalactites. This natural setting was perfectly adapted to form a great sanctuary in which different parts, at different levels, were used by men (maybe even by different races), at different periods, to create their own sacred shrines—without ever disturbing the shrines created by bygone generations. How long the religious use of this cavern continued, whether four, five, or ten thousand

plan after 538

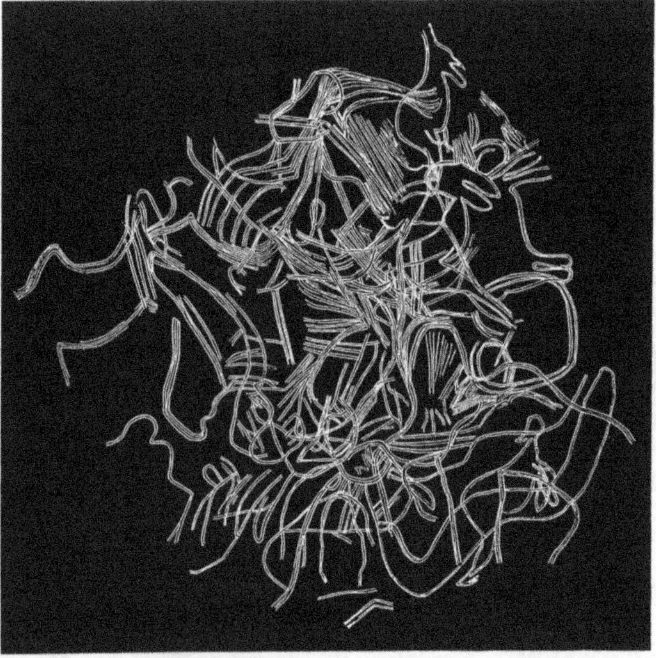

Drawing by Lemozi (in negative; cf. fig. 18)

FIGURE 4.12

Juxtaposition of prehistoric and modern art.

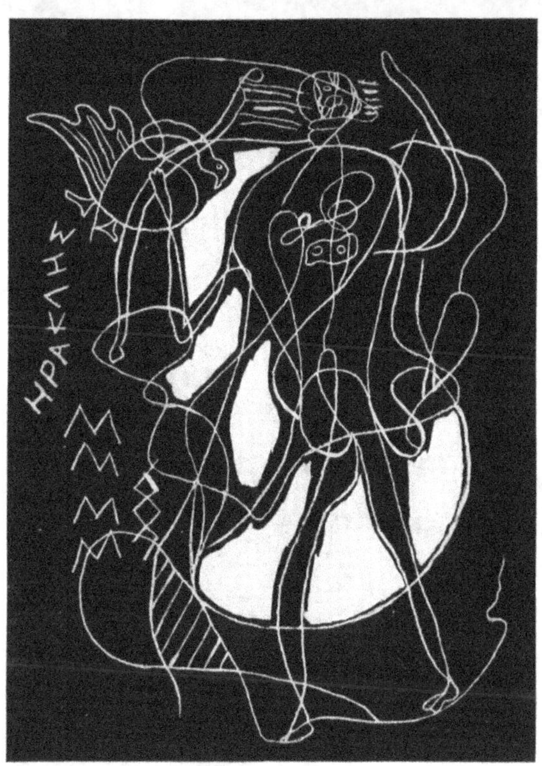

19. GEORGES BRAQUE: *"Hercules and the Stymphalian Birds." Engraving in blackened plaster, 1932*

years—from the Aurignacian until the Magdalenian period or even later—it is useless to ask.

The background of this high hall is perforated by two natural galleries. On the ceiling of the upper gallery is spread a large-scale manifestation of one of man's earliest artistic experiments. Rightly did the Abbé Lemozi baptize the place the Hall of the Hieroglyphs. No other document of Aurignacian times exists which expresses the fundamental conceptions of the time with such intensity. To our eyes, especially at first glance, this ceiling with its crisscross lines

53

Left: negative copy of finger drawings in the cave at Pech-Merle; *right*: Georges Braque, *Heraklès* (from Sigfried Giedion, *The Beginnings of Art*, 1962).

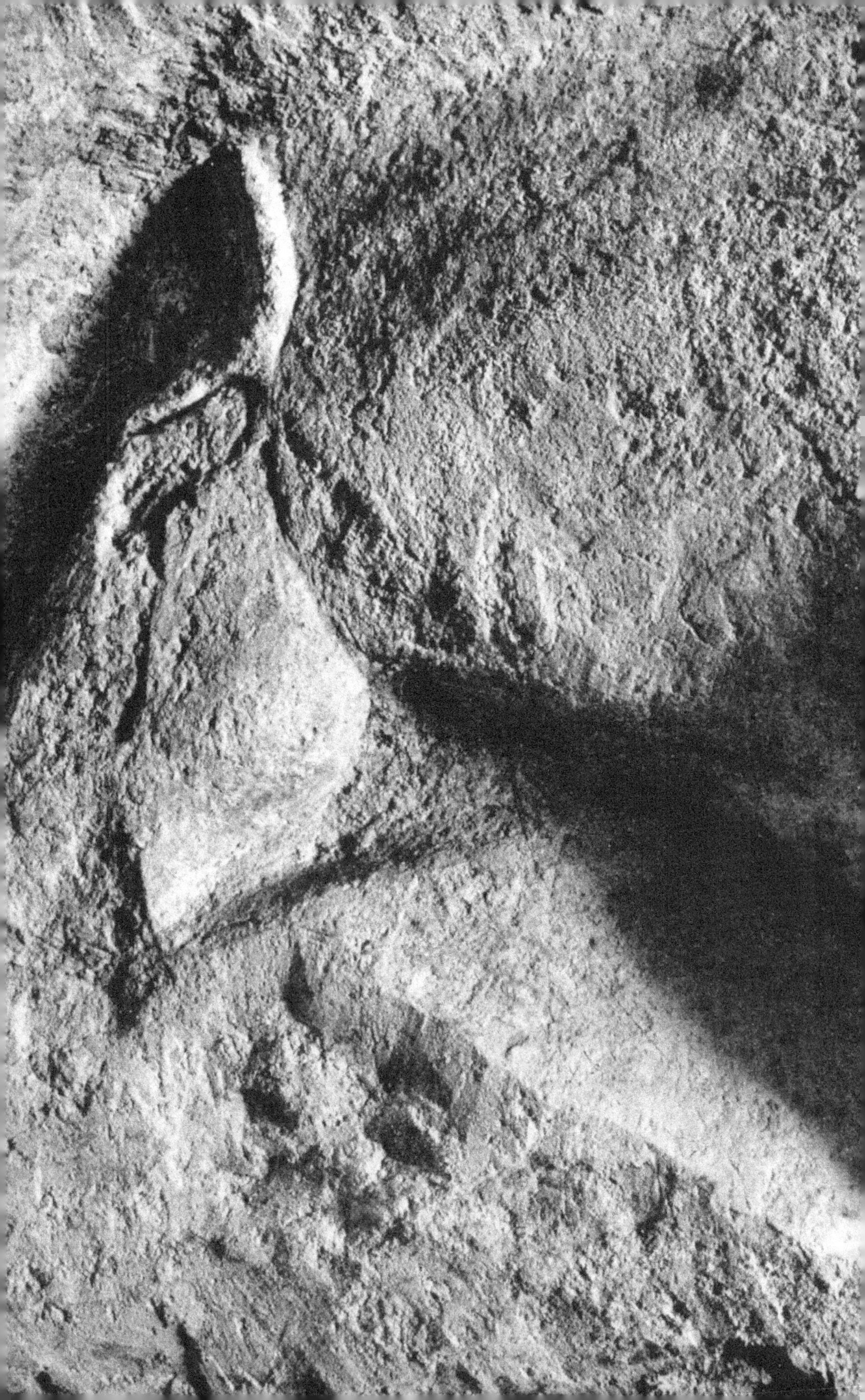

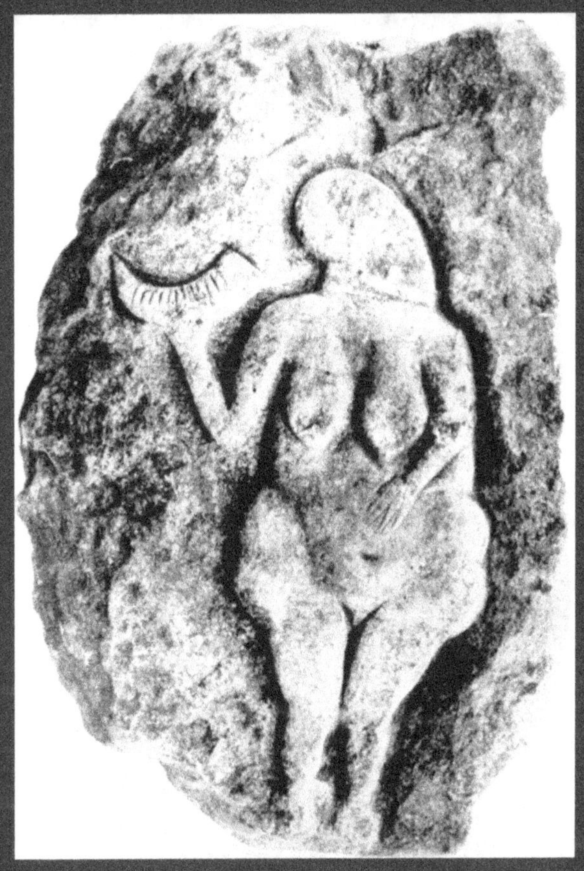

FIGURE 4.13

Hugo P. Herdeg, photograph of a relief in the semicave at Cap Blanc (from Sigfried Giedion, *The Beginnings of Art*, 1962).

FIGURE 4.14

"Weibliche Figur von Laussel in der Dordogne" (from Eckart von Sydow, *Die Kunst der Naturvölker und der Vorzeit*, 1925).

Aufnahmen
nach Original
J. F. Cheron. Bordeaux

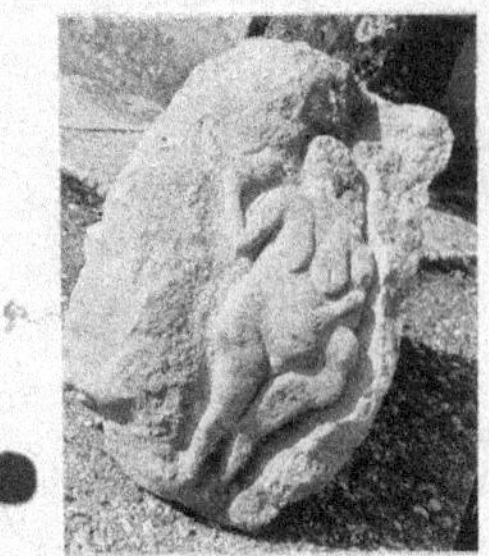

Haar mit Einschnitten
undeutlich.
Figur ist sehr im Profil
& nach hinten geneigt.

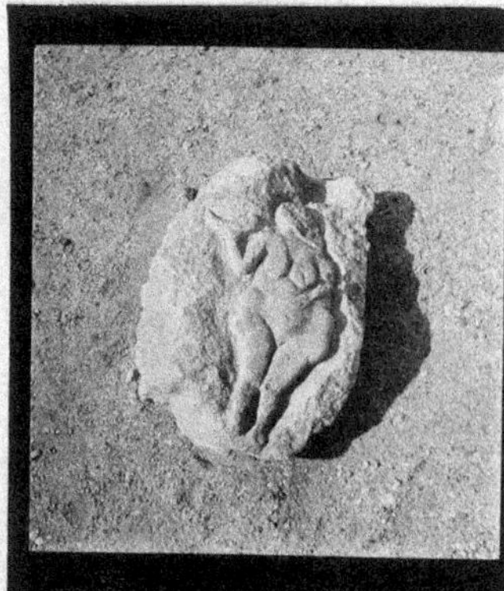

? Kopieren.
an sehr konventioneller
Gesichtspunkt.

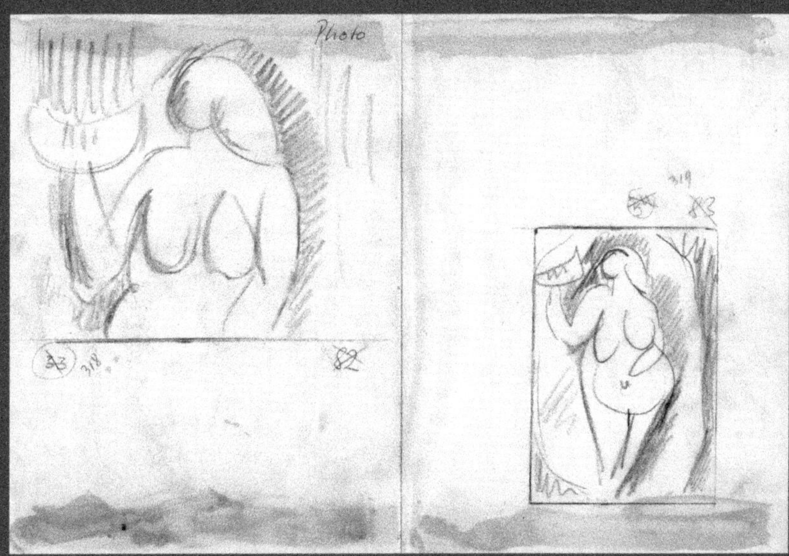

FIGURE 4.15

Hugo P. Herdeg, trial shots of the *Venus of Laussel* with Giedion's comments (ca. 1950). "*Photographs of original / Dr. Charon. Bordeaux* / horn with incisions / blurred. / figure too much in profile/ & inclined backward. // ?Copy. / too much like conventional / point of view." Courtesy ETH Zürich, gta Archive, Giedion Papers.

FIGURE 4.16

Sigfried Giedion, layout sketch for a double page on the *Venus of Laussel* (ca. 1960).

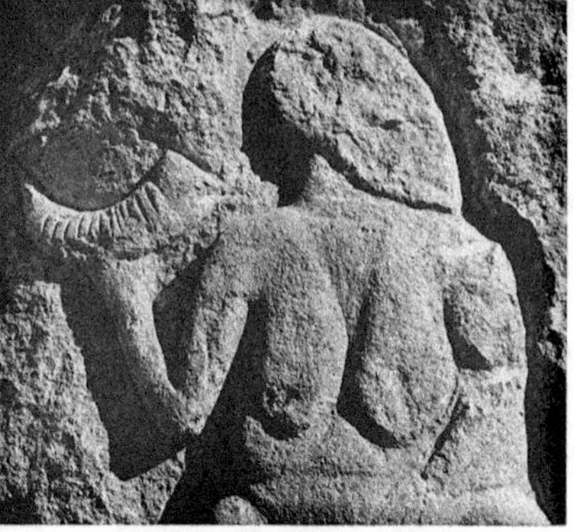

320. LAUSSEL: *Detail of the upper part of the "Venus of Laussel," the right arm raising a bison horn in the air*

In this relief of a standing man a new development seems to be inaugurated, destined not to be followed up in prehistoric art. Like the reclining female figures of La Magdeleine (Tarn), it is one of those precocious announcements of the human mind which, from time to time, emerge and then fade away. Its unique quality will be compared in our second volume with an Egyptian wood relief of Hesy-ra, one of the earliest realizations of the full power of Egyptian sculpture. ⊲ 482

The standing man from the Solutrean period and the Egyptian relief from the Third Dynasty (around 2600 B.C.) are both depicted in the boxer's stance, with

476

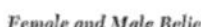
Female and Male Reliefs

body turned to the right and left shoulder advanced. Both have the head and the legs shown in profile. Both are naked, except for a girdle, a feature often preserved in solemn rituals from prehistoric times. In Mesopotamia the priests entered the presence of the deity completely naked, except for a narrow girdle similar to that worn by the standing man of Laussel.

The female figures at La Magdeleine

For the Magdalenian era, the two large female figures at La Magdeleine (Tarn) ⊲ 481, 482
are in their way unique just as the Venus of Laussel is for the foregoing period. Now, however, all physical robustness has disappeared. The figures lie, light as a breath, upon the rock face. They are so delicately modeled that they continually elude the eye, and it is easy to understand that they lay unnoticed by the generations of prehistorians who excavated at the entrance to the cavern (Bétirac,
1954, pp. 125–26). A classic Magdalenian engraving of a horse is situated im- ⊲ 479

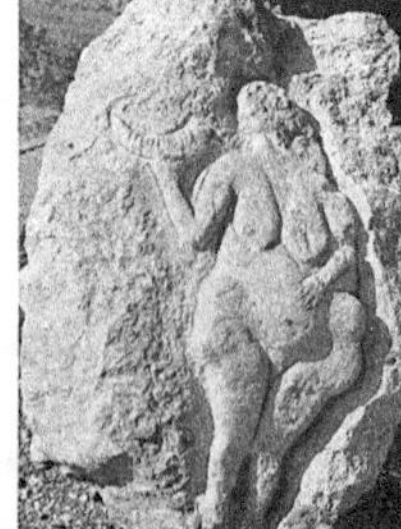

321. LAUSSEL: *The block hewn from the rock face, showing the head of the "Venus of Laussel" reclining as though on a cushion*

477

FIGURE 4.17

Multiple views of the *Venus of Laussel* (from Sigfried Giedion, *The Beginnings of Art*, 1962). Courtesy ETH Zürich, gta Archive, Giedion Papers.

FIGURE 4.18

Achille Weider, definitive photograph of the *Venus of Laussel* (from Sigfried Giedion, *The Beginnings of Art*, 1962).

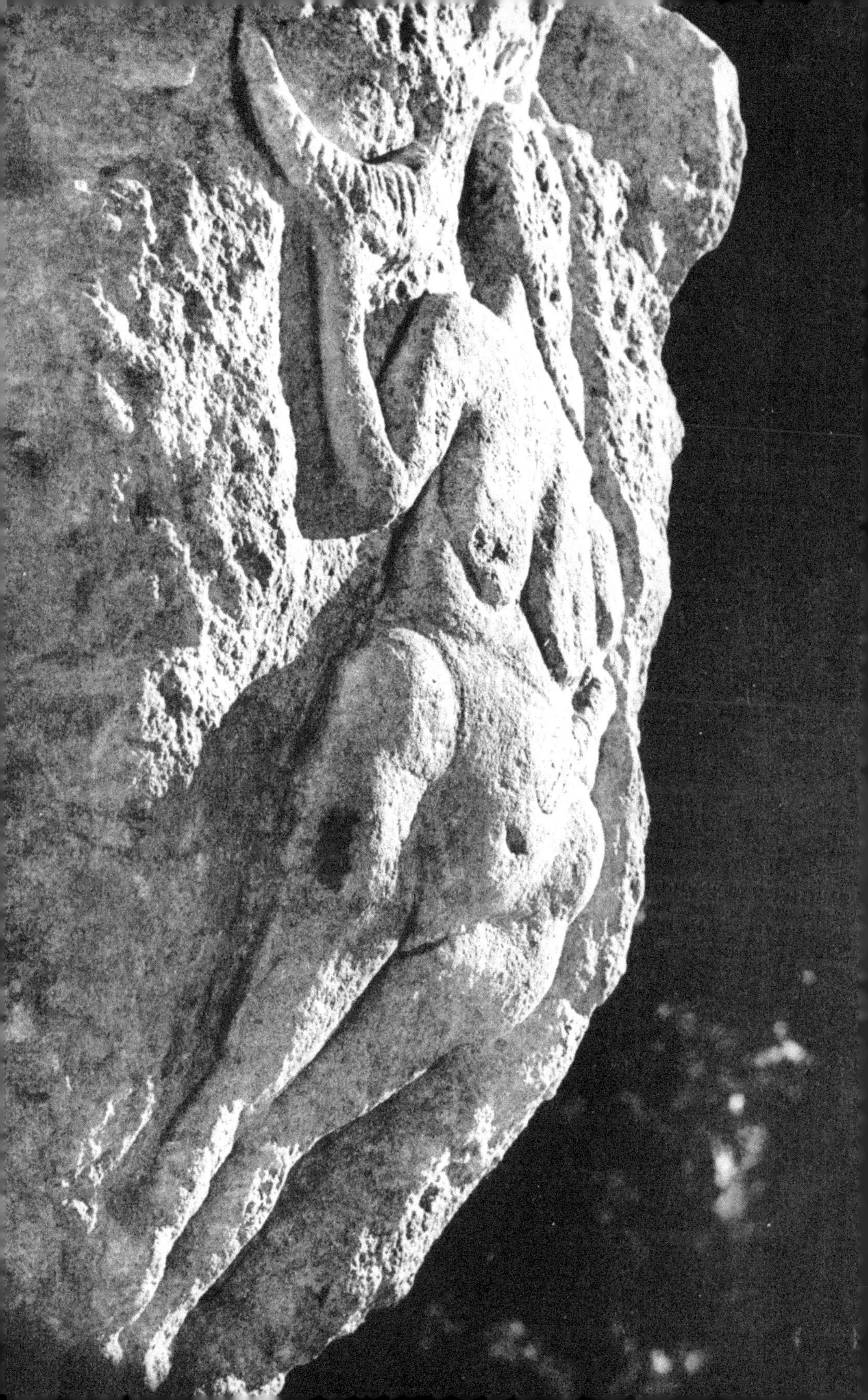

FIVE

Horn and Time

In this room, the American author Thomas Pynchon and the South African artist William Kentridge meet. The room is filled with post horns from various epochs and with bullhorns of various kinds. Lying in a glass case is the manuscript fragment for the anti-IBM musical *Minstral Island* Pynchon was working on at the end of the 1950s. Standing next to it are two of the kinetic sculptures Kentridge constructed for his *documenta* project, *The Refusal of Time.* On tripods, they combine Duchampian bicycle wheels, wind instruments, and concertinas. On the walls hang some paintings by Remedios Varo that Pynchon refers to in his novel *The Crying of Lot 49*. Visible on screens are excerpts from Kentridge's films and performances. The motto of this room comes from the *Encyclopaedia Da Costa*. It reads: "[ECRAN] SCREEN. Usually a quadrangular surface, material unimportant, stretched over a frame and intended to be interposed between a cause and its effect."[1]

The constellation has become familiar. In Thomas Pynchon's *The Crying of Lot 49*, objects and media have an agency of their own. This is made clear from the very first scene. The domestic environment the protagonist, Oedipa Maas, walks into is populated by technical entities that act like organisms. The moment she enters the living room, Oedipa has the "greenish dead eye of the TV tube" stare at her. Later, she experiences how, "so out of nothing," the "screaming" of the telephone in the living room turns an "instrument" that a second ago had been "inert" into an extremely active apparatus emitting a multitude of voices. Similarly, a "whitewashed bust" standing on a very narrow shelf in a different bedroom threatens to develop a life of its own and thereby endanger the human agents in its proximity.[2]

Ultimately, every machine in this world, which Pynchon situates in early 1960s California, is inhabited by a small demon that can be brought to life, provided one looks at it "sensitively" enough. Every surrounding in which Oedipa and the other characters move seems to be endowed with a soul. Every piece of land, every *lot*, is not just a car or a parking lot but also always the object of a negotiation, appraisal or, precisely, a lot to be auctioned that, the very next moment, can turn out to be a fateful lot, the lot, for example, of only apparently having escaped Lot's city of Sodom.

In this Californian wonder world, even madness and the limit between madness and reason are inscribed in things. For example, a can of hair-spray falls down, explodes, and, "hissing malignantly," propels itself "swiftly about the bathroom." What appears as wild and crazy, however, turns out to be reasonable and calculated: "The can knew where it was going"—just like "God or a digital machine."

That is also why it does not come as a surprise that the inhabitants of this world are not only able to talk to the material culture surrounding them but that these objects understand them, even if they do not respond: "You're so sick, Oedipa, she told herself, or the room, which knew."[3]

It does not take long until objects' and media's life of their own is explained, in terms clearly reminiscent of McLuhan, by referring to technical objects as expansions or extensions of the human body. Waiting for her husband to return from his job as a disc jockey, Oedipa looks back on his former work as a used car salesman. The cars in which Wendell "Mucho" Maas traded back then appear as "motorized, metal extensions" of individual bodies, even of entire families. A car, the book tells us, is nothing but an "automotive projection of somebody else's life."[4]

As the novel unfolds, it becomes clear that this describes not just a static, formal relationship between body and technics but also a behavior or function symmetrically distributed among human and nonhuman agents. At one end, there is a machine called "projector," which the English professor Emory Bortz uses to show Oedipa some dirty pictures allegedly meant to help her in her research. At the other end, there is a stage artist Oedipa meets, named Randolph Driblette, who claims to work like "the projector in the planetarium" since his theater productions create entire universes. Situated between these two extremes is Oedipa's psychiatrist, Dr. Hilarius, who demands projective behavior from his patients, subjecting them to procedures such as the Rorschach Test or the Thematic Apperception Test (TAT).[5] Extension or projection here turn out be processes.

A closer look shows the very name of the city in which much of the action unfolds finds a place on this spectrum. Evoking San Francisco, "San Narciso" is not just one of the excitingly superficial puns Pynchon fills his novel with. The name also points to the thesis—also by McLuhan—that people are hypnotized or anaesthetized by media the way Narcissus is hypnotized by the mirrorlike surface of the water on which he beholds his own image. The relevant chapter in *Understanding Media* is called "The Gadget Lover: Narcissus as Narcosis."[6]

And indeed, the inhabitants of San Narciso that Oedipa encounters in the course of the novel seem to be anaesthetized in a variety of ways, by alcohol and narcotics, by beat music and fashion, by haircuts that block their vision, or—making the obvious step from an individual propensity for projection to the "sensitives'" notion of relationship—by developing a paranoia. The effects of the Cold War and McCarthyism, of course, make such paranoia seem like the most up-to-date mode of the Californian perception of the world.

It is in this setting that Oedipa is charged with executing the will of her recently deceased ex-lover Pierce Inverarity. Her first task is to make an inventory of the riches Inverarity has left behind, a difficult task given how complicated his business involvements were. Not unlike Soho Eckstein, the character thought up by Kentridge,[7] Pierce Inverarity stands for citywide property ownership, dubious development activities, and wide-ranging stock investments. In fact, Inverarity's possessions turn out to spread so widely that Oedipa wonders whether, in the end, his "legacy was America" itself.[8]

In the course of her inquiries, Oedipa quickly distances herself from the dominant culture of extension and projection. To be sure, after meeting Driblette, she wonders, "Shall I project a world?"[9] But the question is clearly rhetorical because by that point, she has long been aware of just how deceptive the extensions of man are. Already in her time with Inverarity, this knowledge announced itself in a feeling. Being together with her former lover, "she had noticed the absence of an intensity, as if watching a movie, just perceptibly out of focus, that the projectionist refused to fix."[10]

This lack of emotional focus reflected in her former lover's name—at least according to one reading that sees "Pierce Inverarity" as an association of *to pierce* and *inveracity*[11]—is translated into a tactile sensation, a "sense of buffering, insulation."[12] As the story develops, Oedipa seeks to escape this "buffering" as much as the insincere, inveracious piercings or quasi-intensities.

In living with her husband, the former used car salesman, her vague feeling transforms into a specific conception of the fact of projection. Thanks to Mucho Maas's experiences and stories, Oedipa comes to see that extensions are not to be thought of simply as *extensions* but also as *excretions* of the human body. A car, accordingly, is not only a means of transportation, shiny chrome on the outside, soft upholstery on the inside, extended by a human organ—the foot, McLuhan would say. Simultaneously, the vehicle functions as "condensed exhaust, dust, body wastes."[13]

Cars thus are not simply a human technology but also always the waste of a society, and just how telling, literally, this waste can be is what Oedipa learns when she encounters the secret postal system W.A.S.T.E., where trash cans serve as mailboxes. Not only the medium, the waste, too, is the message.

From the perspective of this media ecology, even objects and media that do not at first appear as extensions of man can turn out to be waste, human waste, even, as in the case of the Beaconsfield brand of cigarettes, in whose filters the ash of incinerated human bones is used. In this sense, McLuhan's notion of extension turns out be rather ideological. As Oedipa recognizes clearly, this notion reinforces the erroneous belief that what capitalist society provides in terms of commodities really represents extensions or projections of life. She shares with her husband fundamental doubts about a culture and society that reduces the human being, like a random customer in a used car lot, to "exchang[ing] a dented, malfunctioning version of himself for another, just as futureless, automotive projection of somebody else's life."[14]

It is these "endless rituals of trade-in," this "endless, convoluted incest" in which Oedipa is entangled thanks to her former relationship with Inverarity but from which she has already begun to distance herself thanks to her marriage. This distancing progresses in the course of the novel. Oedipa will separate from her husband as she tries to get a better, or at least clearer, understanding of how the capitalist incest works. The leitmotif of this endeavor can be found in something she says to her psychiatrist. She resolutely asserts to Dr. Hilarius that "she didn't want to get hooked in any way."[15]

In depicting Oedipa's search, Pynchon's novel in many respects follows the schema of detective stories à la Raymond Chandler, even if at the end, no perpetrator is caught and no clear evidence is secured. The detective story, moreover, is only one of the models on which the novel is based and which it transforms. Some of the themes that dominate *The Crying of Lot 49*, the mysterious task and the secret inscriptions, recall the novels of Roussel, which also feature stories that are nestled into each other, are reflected and varied in songs and fantastic inventions, and mutually explain each other—without reaching any final resolution.

Besides evoking many aspects of the literature of the beat generation, Pynchon's novel also alludes to the figure of the Benjaminian flaneur. Time and again, Oedipa sets out to read the city as text and to decipher the scripts and signs spread out across the urban space. As in Aragon, whom Benjamin so admired, in Pynchon, public announcements, signs, and banners intervene in the texture of the text. The cover of the first edition underlines the connection thus established with surrealism. As in Man Ray's and Helen Levitt's photographs showing chalk graffiti on the walls of houses, this cover shows a chalk drawing of the muted horn on a wall (fig. 5.1).

Pynchon reaffirms such associations when, at the end of the first chapter, he refers to a painting by the surrealist Remedios Varo to describe Oedipa's preliminary alternative conception of the notion of extension.[16] Varo's 1961 painting *Bordando el Manto terrestre* (*Embroidering Earth's Mantle*) shows a group of six "frail girls," sitting like a group of lacemakers locked up in a tower. Supervised by a "Great Master," they embroider a fabric that flows through slit windows into the surrounding landscape or, rather, produces the surrounding landscape (fig. 5.2).[17]

This literal connection of inside and outside evidently conceives of the relationship between body and technics differently than McLuhan does. Instead of starting from the clearly outlined figure of the human confronted by objects and media at a safe distance, as it were, it aims for a level of material interweaving that precedes or grounds this relation. Humans and machines are referred back to a surface or envelope, an "earth's mantle," that links them both, prior as it were even to the separation prompted by the amputation of organs.

Accordingly, this fabric, which is not just matter but also text, brings together extensions and excretions on the same plane of consistency. Pynchon's textual fabric does not fundamentally distinguish between technics and trash—and it thereby undermines the alternatives, thematized again and again, of paranoia on the one hand and knowledge on the other, madness and reality, sacred and profane, profound magic and superficial puns.

Oedipa's Epistemology

In such a network, time becomes the decisive factor. Varo's painting suggests as much in representing the alchemist origin of the threads used by the girls in the shape of an hourglass. Pynchon takes up this suggestion when he writes that a lonely girl like Oedipa has "plenty of time to think."[18] Above all, however, he inscribes the motif of temporality deeply in the protagonist's cognitive process.

Oedipa's search follows a time-based epistemology that brings in her corporeality as a crucial medium of knowledge. How her body is affected by different kinds of signs, what, inversely, the body of the signs that affect her would be, and how Oedipa, inversely again, can affect the signs—these are the novel's decisive questions. In keeping with the consistency plane of the earth's mantle, though, this epistemology is articulated not only with respect to Oedipa but also by way of the novel's central emblem, the muted post horn.

The first form of time Pynchon describes in this connection is that of suddenness. On her drive to San Narciso, Oedipa associates the view down on the still-distant town with the memory-image of a transistor radio's printed circuit diagram. The passage not only names the result of the association—in both cases, there is "an intent to communicate"—it also emphasizes that from the very first moment of encountering the city, this "revelation" "spr[ings] at" Oedipa, takes her in. Pynchon even ties Oedipa's insight back to a "religious instant" in which—as in Benjamin's shock-like insights—the sacred appears in the profane.[19]

Conversely, the novel demonstrates what the eminently secular precondition for such revelation consists in. The "hierophany" Oedipa experiences is made possible by her having left the flow of car traffic. Her flash-like insight into the significance of communication is due to the fact that she has parked her car on the roadside or in a parking lot so she can look at the city in peace. The epistemological shock here takes place not in the midst of the metropolitan crowd but at a consciously chosen distance from the dominant regime of traffic and speed.

On the text's performative level, the correlate of this form of time is the first appearance of the muted horn that will later turn out to be the identificatory mark of the W.A.S.T.E. system. The hierophanic character with which Pynchon endows Oedipa's first insight corresponds to the sudden way this mark appears in terms of a "hieroglyphics," the word Oedipa uses when she first discovers the sign in question on the wall of a women's restroom in a bar.[20]

Pynchon carefully stages the suddenness of this discovery. He interrupts the flow of type by mounting a hand drawing of the muted horn in the body of the text and thereby momentarily suspending the flow of reading (fig. 5.3). The activity of reading is here confronted with the impression of a body that—as the way the lines are drawn clearly shows—has an ethos of its own, an irreducible singularity. With a view to Remedios Varo's painting, we might even highlight the tactile aspects of this semiotic gesture: the author embroiders a personal pattern onto the fabric of his novel.

The accompanying text, however, points in a different direction. It relies on a distant, matter-of-fact description guided by geometrical forms. The muted post horn, at this point, is not yet recognized as such but appears as an abstract pattern formed by "a loop, triangle and trapezoid." Corresponding to the context of discovery, as it were, the unclear meaning of the figure is associated with "something sexual" and with the "sophisticated fun" evoked on the toilet wall.[21]

The fact that at the beginning of the novel, Oedipa's husband is called "horny" by his boss fits in here but also announces a different conception of the sign.[22] However, its postal aspects only move to the foreground once Oedipa, on visiting the Yoyodyne plant financed by Inverarity, is confronted a second time with the sign in question.

One of the Yoyodyne engineers is doodling the sign on an envelope when Oedipa catches sight of it. Once more, Pynchon underlines the suddenness of this encounter by inserting a hand drawing into the text, a smaller and narrower one this time (fig. 5.4). As if explicitly to highlight the semiotic status of this insertion, it is announced by the remark, "this sign."[23] Later editions, however, blur the traces of this gesture by replacing this and the earlier drawing with identical computer graphics.[24]

At this stage of the plot, in any case, it has become clear that the hieroglyph is a modified post horn. At this point at the latest, it is also clear that in this case, too, as in Oedipa's first glimpse of San Narciso, the impressive suddenness of the encounter with the sign takes place at a distance from a particular regime of speed.

As a matter of fact, in the interaction of postal items, riders, and stage posts, the horn instrument fulfilled a decisive function from the very beginnings of the Thurn und Taxis Post, as the novel goes on to explain in its last third especially: it served in the advance notification of the relay riders waiting in the posts strung along a given route to take over the knapsacks and transport them to the next post (fig. 5.5).[25] The particular speed, and hence also the economic success, of the Thurn und Taxis Post was based on this principle, which is why the horn was included in the family crest already in the early modern period (fig. 5.6).

In Pynchon, the modified horn marks a distance from this acceleration of communication. As we will see in a moment, it is a plugged, silenced post horn; the W.A.S.T.E. system, accordingly, turns out to be a genuinely slow kind of communication.

The moment the link with the post horn has been established, a further form of epistemological time enters the scene. It is the time of announcement or anticipation. During her visit with the philatelic expert Genghis Cohen, who is to appraise the stamp collection Inverarity has left behind, Oedipa has a second insight: she sees, "for the very first time, how far it might be possible to get lost" in the fabric of signs.[26]

This insight is justified in a remarkable passage that draws a parallel between the labor of deciphering and epileptic seizures "announcing" themselves in "an odor, color, pure piercing grace note." We are already familiar with this structure: before it is possible to speak of meaning or of knowledge, there is a certain feeling, a premonition. According to Pynchon, however, the attack itself and with it "what is revealed during the attack" is no longer experienced consciously; it "blaze[s] out, destroying its own message irreversibly." A minute space of time between announcement and event, "the space of a sip of dandelion wine," affords Oedipa insight into a possible disappearance into the realm of signs: "It came to her that she would never know how many times such a seizure may already have visited, or how to grasp it should it visit again. Perhaps even in this last second—but there was no way to tell."[27]

The epileptic "aura" evoked here and elsewhere in the novel has only little to do with the experience Benjamin describes using the same term. Of course, he too works with the motifs of sudden illumination and flaring up,[28] but as we saw, his formula of the aura as "the unique apparition of a distance, however near it may be" emphasizes the spatial aspect of visual experience. Pynchon by contrast stresses the temporal and tactile dimensions of Oedipa's experience. What she calls up, in analogy with her premonitions, is a seizure, a being-seized that, moreover, is announced by a sense of being pierced, a piercing.

Accordingly, the decisive model for knowledge in *The Crying of Lot 49* is not paranoia with its infinite references but intermittent epileptic episodes. In Brian Massumi's terms, we might say that knowledge here becomes a matter of largely autonomous affects, affects that seize the body before the body can become aware of them.[29] Pynchon seems to confirm this elsewhere in the novel when he speaks of "a time differential, a vanishingly small instant in which change had to be confronted at last for what it was, where it could no longer disguise itself as something innocuous like an average rate"—the very opposite of inveracity.[30] These extremely short periods of time, however, are obviously inaccessible to human beings, which is why truth initially eludes them. They are thrown back onto the annunciatory structure of affect.

The confirmation, in the conversation with Cohen, of the association of the sign with the postal system thus also concerns the form of time of delay Oedipa experiences. The post horn, to be sure, sends a message, but this message is peculiarly empty; it merely announces other messages. The signal given by the horn—a sound or a short melody—is a signal that merely points ahead to other signals, to letters or packages. On the one hand, it is precisely this kind of communication of communication that allows for rapid access to sometimes eagerly awaited messages. On the other hand, this structure also allows for delaying access to the messages. In citing the famous formula of the "mail call,"[31] the novel also makes the point that this formula precisely does not mean that a letter has been transmitted and read—only that it has arrived.

The post horn accordingly stands not only for increased speed in delivering messages. It simultaneously symbolizes the kind of delay that in the nineteenth century was called the intermediary time, the interval, or "lost time" of communication: a letter may well have arrived at its destination but that does not mean that it has also been received. Mail and telegraph experts were just as aware of this as the physiologists and psychologists who, around 1850, were interested in the sending of messages within the human body.[32]

The third form of time of Oedipa's epistemology is memory. It results from the peculiarities of epilepsy. Since the epileptic cannot recall the seizure itself, she so to speak only ever receives letters without being able to recall their content, without even being able to recall whether she has read them. The "central truth" thus remains inaccessible. It seems to be too strong, too bright for her memory. In her aimless wandering through the city and the night, however, Oedipa also comes to see that in pursuing her search, she is resisting this systematic withholding: "*She was meant to remember.*"[33]

Memory—however affect-motivated and unreliable it may be—thus becomes the decisive basis for referring the different signs, indications, and scripts of the city to one another—which also means accepting them in their respective temporalities: “Each clue that comes is *supposed* to have its own clarity, its fine chances for permanence.”[34] And even if this form of knowledge is extremely fragile—and indeed, it is immediately questioned—it represents the decisive tool for sorting out the problem of inheritance, the “legacy” of America, to be able to situate itself within the formation of capitalist incest.

This third form of time of knowledge, too, is connected with the post horn—and not only because it distantly resembles the cone in Bergson’s theory of memory. Cohen’s characterization of the small object sticking out from the horn as nothing but a “mute” can be read as a cultural reference to 1950s jazz. As a literary reference, however, it points back much further, namely to the clogged post horn that—taking up a motif in Rabelais[35]—features exemplarily in the fanciful tales attributed to Baron Munchausen.

In Munchausen’s account, a “postilion” riding his carriage in the bitter cold tries in vain to “give a signal with his horn.” Only once he has hung up his horn near the kitchen fire in a stage post do the sounds become audible: “His tunes were frozen up in the horn, and came out now by thawing, plain enough, and much to the credit of the driver.”[36] The post horn here serves as a medium of memory.

Pynchon confirms and affirms the multilayered connections between horn and time on the level of his novel’s content. On the one hand, as noted, the W.A.S.T.E. communication system indicated by the muted post horn appears as an eminently slow system. It is not just Oedipa’s search for this system alone that proceeds sluggishly. The delivery people working for W.A.S.T.E., too, move listlessly and, it seems, aimlessly, like vagrants, through the urban space.[37]

On the other hand, the muted horn is time and again approximated to motifs of intoxication, sexuality, and death that in turn refer to the finitude of human life. Having discovered the sign on the toilet wall in a bar, Oedipa repeatedly suspects it might be “a homosexual sign or something,” that it might, therefore, be “a channel for communication for those of unorthodox sexual persuasion.” But she also has to confront the fact that the sign is occasionally accompanied by the letters DEATH, whose meaning is resolved rather combatively: “DON’T EVER ANTAGONIZE THE HORN.”[38]

This embeds Oedipa’s temporal epistemology in a social context in which time—we might also say, *labor*—is the decisive variable. Ironically refracted, certainly, but no less emphatic, the connection between muted post horn and social time is thematized in one of the stories the novel tells about the genesis of the W.A.S.T.E. system. According to this account, it was a

Yoyodyne executive who, having lost his job to a streamlining measure and contemplating suicide, founded the system as a kind of pastoral service for disappointed lovers. The executive, already doused in gasoline and lighter in hand, discovers that his wife is having an affair with, of all people, the "efficiency expert" responsible for replacing him with a computer. At this point, the efficiency expert mocks his suicidal ex-colleague for his indecisiveness by pointing to the very short times it takes electronic computing machines to reach a decision: "You know how long it would've taken the IBM 7094? Twelve microseconds. No wonder you were replaced."[39]

The fact that humans need more time for their reflections and conclusions than computers do is presented as an important prompt for instituting the W.A.S.T.E. system. In other words, the problem the system addresses is not so much disappointed love but rationalization measures in the workplace that increasingly lead to a dominance of machines over humans. It is the dominance of certain technologies that turns humans into waste.

Pynchon here takes up motifs from his dystopic musical *Minstral Island*, directed against the increasing power of IBM, on which he was working with his fellow Cornell student Kirkpatrick Sale at the end of the 1950s. Pynchon was quite serious about the machine wrecker's attitude mobilized against technology in the unfinished play (and discussed once more later by Sale in a historical study of the Luddites), and its association with the motif of the muted post horn in *The Crying of Lot 49* testifies how serious he was.[40]

For, when the novel later associates "each alienation, each species of withdrawal" with the horn, when the horn stands not for "an act of treason" but rather for the "calculated withdrawal, from the life of the Republic, from its machinery," it also names forms of refusal grounded in the human claim to determining one's own time that opposes the technically and socially dominant forms of labor.[41] In this sense, the muted horn also stands for the counterside of media.

Pynchon affirms this perspective when, in a remarkable 1984 article, he declares that one doesn't need a "German philosopher" (an evident reference to Marx) to oppose the misunderstanding that refusing the machine is always simply a hostility to technology or a dull wrecking of machinery. The Luddites, already, were concerned not simply with destroying spinning machines but with fighting two more general phenomena: "One was the concentration of capital that each machine represented, and the other was the ability of each machine to put a certain number of humans out of work." Ultimately, Oedipa's time-based epistemology is anchored in this struggle, and the muted post horn is the sign guiding her toward possible allies.[42]

The Refusal of Time

Fifty years after the publication of Pynchon's novel, William Kentridge expands and deepens the temporalization of the horn in his installation, *The Refusal of Time*. The "five-channel video with sound, 30 min., with steel megaphones and breathing machine ('elephant')," first shown at *documenta 13*, stages this temporalization against the background of the advance of media communication techniques.[43]

Like Pynchon, Kentridge is interested in the history of media. Given the increasingly globalized infrastructure of the internet, however, his installation's historical point of reference is no longer the traditional postal service but the worldwide network of connections for electrical telegraphy set up by the Western industrial nations in the nineteenth century (fig. 5.7). This network of overhead and submarine cables that included power sources, sending and receiving stations, and an immense number of telegraph poles forms the earth's mantle, as it were, of *The Refusal of Time*, the fabric within which the installation unfolds as a complex arrangement of bodies and movements, words and images, drawings and ideas (fig. 5.8).

The Kassel audience that let itself be enveloped in this mantle found itself in a rather multireferential time-cinema that served simultaneously as dance theater and political arena but also as the artist's studio. In this cave-like multitude that seemed to lie beyond the dominant speed regimes just as much as the parking lot does from which Oedipa first looks out on San Narciso, horns and hornlike instruments—bullhorn, trumpet, tuba—became symbols for a distancing from twenty-first-century globalized internet culture as well as emblems for a time proper to art that, at least in the conception of *documenta*'s artistic director, Carolyn Christov-Bakargiev, is simultaneously a "time of materials."[44]

The setup of the installation was comparatively simple. To the five video channels corresponded five projection areas within a rectangular room located in the old north wing of Kassel's central train station. The projections on the whitewashed brick walls reached from the ceiling almost all the way to the floor. Two video channels each were projected next to each other on the room's longer walls, the fifth on the shorter end. Temporarily also used as split screens, the projection areas served for presenting intermingling film pieces in color as well as black and white that, in Catherine Meyburgh's complex montage, were sometimes running simultaneously but most often staggered in time. At first, only individual things and people were visible that, in ever longer sequences, entered into combinations.

Following a literally explosive alignment, they entered into new forms, ultimately to disappear in the darkness of the cave.

Standing in the middle of the room was a kinetic wooden sculpture. In the lower part of this "breathing machine ('elephant')," two rectangular crates were moving toward and away from each other as if on a short railway track, as if they sought to bring the Kassel train station into the installation's interior. The machine's upper part consisted of a laterally mounted framework of rods moving at a right angle to the crates. The longer section of the three rods, which each had a joint at the lower end, was swaying back and forth, while the upper, shorter segment, also equipped with a joint, moved up and down. The artificial elephant at the center was thus not only breathing, it also moved head and trunk up and down again.

This basic setup distributed the audience in the intermediary space between breathing machine and projection areas. In addition to a few chairs, a number of polished bullhorns on tripods were distributed across this intermediary space. Pointing in different directions (up, down, toward projections, away from them), these hornlike objects not only played the soundtrack accompanying the movement-images: sounds, voices, and the music composed by Philip Miller. As we will see in detail, the horn motif also linked and connected the spatial and pictorial elements of the installation as a whole.

Awaiting visitors in this room was a piece of about half an hour. "Piece" is indeed the right word, for Kentridge's installation was just a snapshot of an artistic process that, prompted by curators, had started in a conversation with the physicist and historian of science Peter Galison, continued in the performance of *Six Drawing Lessons* at Harvard University, manifested itself at one point in an experimental TV version of *The Refusal of Time*, and came to a preliminary end in the staging of *Refuse the Hour*, the theater version of the installation.[45] And indeed, the many layers of the installation only become intelligible when this process of artistic research is taken into account. Kentridge thus demands much more from the observers of his work than letting themselves, for a short while, be decelerated by an experience of art.

This is also apparent in the fact that the installation does *not* present time as an abstract instrument of domination. To be sure, it sees the standardization of time and the acceleration of communication as part of the dialectical history of the Enlightenment, whose "primary political manifestation," according to Kentridge, is colonialism. Taking up Galison's study on Einstein's clocks, this reflects the fact, for example, that the telegraphic transmission of standardized time in the late nineteenth century also served to subject the English and French colonies in Africa to a regime of communication and control.[46]

Time nonetheless appears as a locally anchored and materially as well as corporally bound phenomenon that is not good or evil per se. For that very reason, Kentridge's piece does not begin with an all-powerful clock but with individual objects and people that execute more or less regular movements, such as the initial back and forth of mechanical metronome pendulums running synchronously at first before deciding to make music together; the pacing and standing still of the artist in his studio, his sitting down and getting up as he looks at and discards pieces of paper, looks at them anew, discards them anew; or—inversely, as it were—the turning of pages in old books and atlases as well as in contemporary sketchbooks.

The highlighting of movement blurs the difference between human and nonhuman actors. A signaling tree from the age of optical telegraphy transforms into a dancing body. The big belly of a man dressed entirely in white comes bouncing at us as a globe. The artist, whose voice is heard reading time stamps, becomes a "talking clock."[47] The order of metamorphosis, which in the series *Drawings for Projection* (1989–99) had led to a cat becoming a telephone or a coffee pot becoming a mineshaft, has thus made way for a regime of cinematics that combines the most varied of entities. The "general equivalent" on which Rosalind Krauss considers the fluid transformations in Kentridge's filmed charcoal drawings to be based here appears in the form of rhythmized and clocked movements.[48]

Images, too, are subjected to this regime. That is the media-technical precondition of the entire piece, but it is also explicitly stressed as the piece unfolds. Apparently randomly scattered newspaper shreds thus combine to form a female figure that, at first, dances, turns, stretches, and bends over but then becomes an espresso maker and, the next moment, a (clock) pendulum. A scattered mass of black paper flakes forms the image of a typewriter to immediately dissolve and transform into a woman lying down, who again dissolves and moments later appears as a bullhorn (fig. 5.9). One particularly impressive sequence is in the style of the *Drawings for Projection* and shows how optical telegraph lines turn into the cable network of electrical telegraphy to then quickly transition to the global transmission of electromagnetic waves. It is hard to think of a more succinct way of presenting the technological history of the "etherized" being-together Teilhard and McLuhan speak of.[49]

Kentridge further intensifies the explicit references to the movement-image when he shows short action sequences in black and white that are formally reminiscent of the silent movie era. The jerking of the filmic images converts the objects and people up to now shown separately into temporally conditioned combinations and confrontations: a man returns home from work earlier than expected and surprises his wife with a lover. A brass band is giving a wild concert and yet seems to follow a precise rhythm.

Other sequences make it clear that such dynamic assemblages of objects and people are also at the basis of the production and distribution of standardized time. In an observatory, an astronomer is looking at a model of planetary orbits while his assistant is looking through a telescope to take precise time measurements. Next to them, a mechanic is working in a control room for a system of electric clocks that allows for sending the observatory's time signals to schools, factories, or entire cities (fig. 5.10). In the adjacent map room, a cartographer is painting on a white globe while in a telegraph office, two workers are operating a concertina-like air pressure machine used to send pneumatic dispatches and time signals.

But there is resistance to this work with and on time as well. Not far from the observatory, an anarchist couple is manufacturing a bomb. Shortly afterward, an explosion rocks all the rooms. Telegrams and maps, book pages and images are swirling through the air the way the black paper flakes did earlier.

This commotion brings dancers—and especially Dada Masilo—onto the scene who take possession of the space of science and technology with their twirling dresses. It quickly becomes clear, however, that there is no easy victory over time. Via movement, time not only manifests in clocks and telegraphs, it is also inscribed in dance and in music, in language and in images.

At least this is what the end of the piece suggests, which shows a series of shadows wandering across all five projection screens. At a slow pace, a dark train of people and objects is moving into yet another swirl of black paper flakes. In a kind of exodus, the survivors of the time explosion carry, pull, or push the objects they were manipulating in the course of the piece out into the darkness: clocks, telephones, telegraph posts, showers, typewriters, bicycle wheels, and again and again horns in all imaginable forms and formats: as megaphone, as trombone, as loudspeaker, as tuba (fig. 5.11).

The epilogue makes clear that this darkness is not simply an abyss, a death, or a black hole but stands for a departure or a new start. There, a woman and a globe are dancing jauntily in the map room. This is Kentridge's conception of the dialectic of Enlightenment. It contains insight into "the need for the darkness, for shadow, to be present for anything to be visible"—for only then can they be rearranged.[50]

Air as the Medium of Time

The Refusal of Time thus counters the tendency toward simple deceleration with a complex montage of movement-images. In this context, Kentridge himself speaks of a "messy, overlapping series of films, dances, drawings."[51] The installation further prevents a simple recollection of their time proper (*Eigenzeit*) on the part of observers with a wealth of references to the history of art and culture, including to the artist's earlier work.

The entire setup and especially the shadows at the end of course refer to Plato's cave parable, but equally to Kentridge's *Shadow Procession* of 1999, which in turn refers to Goya's depiction of processions and pilgrimages in the *Pinturas negras*.[52] But we mustn't deceive ourselves: besides such scholarly allusions, the shadow procession also and above all conveys references to the complex, conflictual situation in South Africa. This procession's iconography in fact recalls the political fights and demonstrations Kentridge had already engaged with in the *Drawings for Projection*. The horns visible in both instances, though, do not summarily refer to acts of resistance. They concretely evoke the processions of the Nazareth Baptist or Shembe Church, whose members traditionally play long horn instruments—"vuvuzelas"—during their meetings. Art, politics, and religion thus enter into a complex relationship.[53]

The short action sequences filmed in black and white are similarly multireferential. They do not simply represent an abstract reminiscence of silent movie aesthetics but concretely take up the work of Georges Méliès, as Kentridge already did in *Journey to the Moon* and *7 Fragments for Georges Méliès* (both 2003). The observatory in *The Refusal of Time* certainly alludes to the opening sequence of Méliès's *Voyage dans la lune* (1902). In conjunction with the telegraph office and the map room, however, this observatory is simultaneously a reference to Galison's studies in the history of science, which highlight the significance of such spaces of knowledge for the emergence of Einstein's theory of relativity.[54]

This has nothing to do, though, with an artistic presentation of the history of science. In Kentridge, the material of history instead serves to visualize the present. The artist is fully aware that the "relativist" correction of time signals emitted by satellites today is an essential precondition for the precise functioning of the Global Positioning System (GPS) and other navigation services. He is thus not interested in Einstein's theory as a historical idea but as the contemporary reality of a media technology that—along with many other things—serves to advance the colonization of the world.[55]

There are further references. The metronomes at the beginning of the piece go back to Ligeti's *Poème symphonique* for one hundred metronomes and Man Ray's *Object to Be Destroyed*, also exhibited at *documenta 13*.[56] The dancing telegraph tree, on the one hand, recalls another work of Goya's, the drawing *Telégrafo*, which depicts a man lying upside down on a table, dancing wild signals into the air with his legs. On the other hand, the dance element is to be seen as a reflex reaction to one of the leitmotifs of the 2012 *documenta* that programmatically conceived of itself as a complex "choreography" of the most varied artistic and scientific work.[57]

The anarchist couple, finally, that toward the end fabricates a bomb is a reminiscence of Joseph Conrad's novel *The Secret Agent* about the preparation of a bomb attack on the Greenwich Observatory (and allegedly motivated the antitechnology bombings of Ted Kaczynski, the "Unabomber").[58] Not unlike the post horn symbol in Pynchon, however, the motif of the bombing can also be understood as alluding to the Luddite's machine wrecking.

The innumerable references *The Refusal of Time* holds in store of course run the risk of becoming overbearing. Nonetheless, they only appear to be forced or arbitrary. For insofar as this installation can be conceptualized as a "collage of fragments of different modernisms,"[59] its wealth of references should be tied back to the situated context in which Kentridge has been working for a long time. "There are no long local traditions in Johannesburg," as the artist himself explains.[60] The cultural "bastardy" that characterizes that city as much as the work of art in question is thus not to be regarded as a result of either exaggerated erudition or postmodern arbitrariness but on the contrary as self-confident indications of the historically developed particularity of a geopolitical space.

It may even be possible to go so far as to recognize in this indication a claim to superimposed layers of time, which have been described as a general characteristic of postcolonial existence: "As an age, the postcolony encloses multiple *durées* made up of discontinuities, reversals, inertias, and swings that overlay one another, interpenetrate one another, and envelop one another."[61] The relativity of time would then be nothing but a lived reality of the South African everyday.

This does not yet account for the fact, however, that *The Refusal of Time* on a different level counteracts the centrifugal forces, which it releases with its movement-images. Of course, the centrally placed "breathing machine ('elephant')" also contains an entire bundle of references. On the one hand, it is an explicit homage paid to Beuys's *Honeypump at the Workplace* exhibited at *documenta 6* in 1977, but it also alludes to James Tilly Matthews's "Air Loom," the "breathing machine" that features on the first pages of *Anti-Oedipus*, and similar influencing apparatuses.[62]

Here, too, it is possible and necessary to be more precise. For, as Kentridge has repeatedly explained, the design of his breathing machine takes up a description in Charles Dickens. In *Hard Times*, Dickens observes in a textile factory that "the piston of the steam-engine worked monotonously up and down, like the head of an elephant in a state of melancholy madness."[63] In adopting the comparison to make it the starting point for his breathing machine, Kentridge turns it into a succinct image of the relationships of economic dependence produced and amplified by colonialism (fig. 5.12).

It is this image that significantly contributes to keeping the installation together. On the one hand, the body of the artificial elephant combines with the images on the screens via the shadow play the moving frame rods and crates leave on the images. On the other hand, there are projections of short color film sequences that show the functioning of individual aspects of the machine in the center from close up. In parallel, the connection between the center and the periphery is emphasized via the motif of the horn, which occurs in a gradated manner, as it were.

It appears materially realized, first, in the megaphones distributed around the room on tripods. It is then conveyed acoustically through the accompanying music sounding from these bullhorns. It relies primarily on brass instruments like trumpets, flugelhorns, trombones, and tubas. The horn motif then shows up in the films. First, a tuba appears in the short melodrama during the first third, magically replacing the lover hidden underneath a tablecloth. Next, the bullhorn shows up beside the typewriter and the espresso maker as one of the objects dissolving into black paper flakes. And finally, the horn motif can be found in the form of cone-shaped bonnets or ear protectors on the two dancers whirling through the destroyed clock center.

The prominent role of the horn in the aggregation of the installation as a whole is not a coincidence. Megaphones, speakers, and brass instruments are among the leitmotifs of Kentridge's work, as are cats, the artist's persona, or pages from old books, magazines, and atlases.[64] The horn motif appears repeatedly already in the *Drawings for Projection*. In *Monument* (1990), for example, the sheets of paper from which Soho Eckstein is reading a speech transform into megaphones (fig. 5.13). In *Sobriety, Obesity, and Growing Old* (1991), loudspeakers, ear trumpets, and tuba-like objects populate the landscapes in which Felix Teitlebaum, Eckstein's nemesis and alter ego, lives (fig. 5.14). Simultaneously, these objects can be seen on the roofs of Eckstein's high-rises. In a remarkable sequence, they contribute, like the trumpets at Jericho, to the collapse of the city's buildings and thereby confirm the motif's political connotations.

In a 1999 interview, Kentridge explains that his use of the motif was inspired by paintings by Max Beckmann and photographs of concerts by Italian futurists (figs. 5.15 and 5.16). Another motivation, he says, was a picture of Lenin speaking into a funnel for a recording (fig. 5.17). And yet there is no explicit political positioning associated with this motif. According to Kentridge, the bullhorn is a general cipher for the connection between art and life.[65]

In *The Refusal of Time*, this is to be taken quite literally. In their gradual deployment, the horns refer back to the breathing machine, which indeed represents something like the living center, the lung or the heart of the entire installation. And yet Kentridge is concerned with more than establishing an abstract analogy between the precise ticking of clocks or metronomes and the more or less regular inhaling and exhaling of organisms. The analogy he goes back to is grounded both historically and materially.

The sequence with the black paper flakes makes this clear. Over the rapid brass music accompanying this sequence, Kentridge in his "Springbok Radio Voice" explains that in the nineteenth century, it was not just electricity that was used to send time signals from A to B. Air, too, was employed to that end. In major cities like Paris and Vienna, clock systems were installed that distributed the time, which had been precisely determined in the observatories, across the cities via underground tubes. On public dials and in private homes, the hands moved every time they received a blast of air from the air pressure control center linked to the observatory.[66]

Air here appears as a medium of time, as the "flow" (in Deleuze and Guattari's terms) that always already connects machines and organisms before they confront each other as separate entities. Accordingly, megaphones, speakers, and brass instruments stand for a reappropriation of time by the human body. Against a dominant technology of communication, what McLuhan has called "the scent of time"[67] ties the horns as technical objects back again to the behavior and lived experience of subjects. The question is just what body is thus brought into play: a holistic body or individual, delimited organs that currently are "losing out"—the ear, for example, or the nose, which Kentridge has recently been interested in—or something else entirely?

The Time Proper of Media

Even at this point, viewers of *The Refusal of Time* might feel thrown back to the initial position of Pynchon's Oedipa. Up to now, in Kentridge, too, the horn appears primarily as hieroglyph, as a multireferential sign for "undergrounds"[68] that evidently try to withdraw from a dominant practice without, however, making it clear what this withdrawal consists in and where it leads.

It takes one more metamorphosis to give the horn a more precise meaning. One of the kinetic sculptures built for the installation combines a bullhorn with a Duchampian bicycle wheel (fig. 5.18). Mounted on a tripod next to the wheel, the horn in this metamorphosis switches from the pneumatic to the optical register: while the bicycle wheel stands for the reel (or, as in Duchamp, for the movement-image), the megaphone becomes the lens of a movie camera or a film projector. Unlike Pynchon, Kentridge in fact has few reservations about the mode of projection. Whereas the novelist, as we saw, recognized in projection a strategy of concealment and a state of imprecision, projection in Kentridge is a cipher for the kind of practices that might be able to lead at least the artist-subject out of the Platonic cave of the Enlightenment.

The problem for Kentridge is not projection as such but its social division. "Everyone their own projector" is one of the artist's programmatic slogans directed against any unilateral appropriation and social standardization of projection.[69] And indeed, in his more recent work, the filming or projecting horn appears again and again in the place of the individual human head. *The Refusal of Time*, too, takes up this agenda, since it thematizes not only the significance of the theory of relativity for the globalized media technology of the present but, with equal emphasis on its current relevance, the pre- and early history of cinematography.

Kentridge's installation, in fact, outlines a veritable archaeology of cinema. The procession of shadows stands for the earliest form of projected moving images; the continuous turning of book pages for the flip book; the repeated loops that show the artist walking or getting up and sitting down for the studies of movement by Marey and Muybridge, as well as for views of movement-images conveyed by other optical toys from the prehistory of cinema (stroboscopic discs, phenakistiscopes, etc.).[70] As noted earlier, one part of the silent movie sequences is indebted to the aesthetics of Méliès's films. The dance in the destroyed telegraph office, in turn, is a reprise of the "serpentine dance" à la Loïe Fuller as recorded by the Lumière brothers.

In so doing, Kentridge does not simply place the epoch in which the theory of relativity emerged in parallel with the time in which cinema first came to prominence. What he is particularly interested in are the forms of time that characterize the medium of film to this day. And that also endows the refusal of time symbolized by the horn with a precise meaning.

Cinematography is a form of technical reproducibility. It allows for recording images of movements and of re-presenting them as movement-images. For that reason alone, it acts in the sense of a rejection of standardized time. In Pynchon, memory was the third form of time that Oedipa claimed for herself in her quest for truth. In Kentridge's epistemology of media, it takes the first position.

As early film theory already knew, film is to be understood as "an objectivation of our memory function." But the medium goes far beyond mere repetition. As Hugo Münsterberg goes on to say, film allows for a "remodel[ing]" of "the course of the natural events . . . by the power of the mind." For example, it allows for recording sequences of movements and playing them in reverse. Münsterberg describes the magic of this effect: "The divers jump, feet first, out of the water to the springboard. It looks magical, and yet the camera man has simply to reverse his film and to run it from the end to the beginning of the action."[71]

Just how receptive Kentridge is to this magic can be seen in the way he brings out this manipulation of the time axis repeatedly in *The Refusal of Time*: in the books that rise up from the floor by themselves and land in the hand of the wife caught in flagrante, for example; or in the paper flakes that assemble to form perfect images as by an invisible hand; or in the telegrams that seem to fly up during the serpentine dance although they are really falling down.

In *Six Drawing Lessons*, the artist in this context even speaks of a "utopian impulse of reversals" linked to cinema. The medium thus appears not only as memory but beyond that as a kind of compensation that can reach back in time: "An action done can be undone. A tear forward becomes a repair backward."[72] It is precisely this kind of possibility that turns cinema into a refusal of time.

The decisive point, now, is that the times proper of cinema, according to Kentridge, are not accessible by simply watching a movie. Nor are they simply "embodied" by the medium; they do not go without saying, as it were. For the artist, the specific times of cinematography manifest themselves in the first place through work in the artist's or the film studio, a labor that brings out concretely the combination of machines and organisms.

With technical and bodily means, this labor explores the space between the represented and representation. Its real territory, however, is the space between different kinds of representation, in other words, the counterside of media. Ever since *Drawings for Projection*, this is what Kentridge's characteristic form of media art has consisted in: "Now it is just this walking back and forth, this constant shuttling between the movie camera on one side of the studio and the drawing tacked to the wall on the other, that constitutes the field of Kentridge's own operation."[73]

In this back-and-forth space, the forms of time that are suddenness and anticipation—which for Oedipa come first and second—are combined and reoriented. On the one hand, Kentridge's interlocking of drawing, filming, and erasing, renewed drawing, renewed filming, and renewed erasing, is a lonely and slow procedure that—unlike conventional animation—largely avoids rationalization and industrialization,[74] just as Oedipa moves out of traffic onto a parking lot. On the other, however, this interlocking prevents images from "springing" at the body only momentarily. Affect is no longer a state passively experienced but manifests, as we might say in Guattari's terms, as a "complex subjective territoriality" that precedes all acts of expression—as the site of a labor, a potential practice that refers to the subject of the artist as much as to the aesthetic object.[75]

Kentridge is thus entirely consistent when he replaces Pynchon's premonition with a form of tentative projection that relies on the combination of machine and organism. *Six Drawing Lessons* develops this systematic approach: "We are talking about a trust placed in the physical. That is, through the physical materials and techniques—drawing, filming, walking—new thoughts, new images, will arise. Being led by the body, rather than simply the mind ordering the body about. Not random action, but action, rehearsal, performance, prompted or demanded by the discipline itself."[76]

Ultimately, it is this "practical epistemology" that the horn motif stands for and that constitutes the core of *The Refusal of Time*. Within its framework, drawing acquires remarkably tactile qualities. According to Kentridge, a drawing is not only the result of "a mixture of making and looking." It is at the same time a screen or a kind of skin between inside and outside: "a drawing is a membrane between the world coming toward us and our projected understanding of the world, a negotiation between ourselves and that which is outside."[77]

The Relativity of Images

Yet not just cinema but the internet, too, has a time proper. Following Kentridge, the time of this medium manifests not only in the coordinated speeds at which the global circulation of data takes place but also in a specific form of permanence or duration. The internet allows for almost global lightning-speed communications, but it is also a universal archive: "It has the pressure of perfect memory. It has the same inevitability as the claim that no keystroke is ever lost, that once done, something cannot be undone."[78]

Such reflections highlight the contemporary relevance of Kentridge's epistemology. Initially, he proceeds the way a scholar in visual studies, or *Bildwissenschaft*, would. He does so only for a short moment, but it is all the more impressive because it leads us back to South Africa. In the sequence from *The Refusal of Time* in which various everyday objects are assembled from black paper flakes to be blown away by the breath of air of time reversed, a rhinoceros appears (fig. 5.19).

Since his earliest work, Kentridge has time and again engaged with this motif.[79] In *The Refusal of Time*, the sight of this primeval-looking animal is evoked, on the one hand, to establish a "connection to a deeply ancient past" and thus to bring out the relativity of time even further.[80] On the other hand, Kentridge knowingly alludes to Dürer's depiction of the rhinoceros to thematize the historical and social conditions of the (non)perception of the foreign, of what is temporally and spatially distant.

Six Drawing Lessons provides a detailed explanation. Clearly picking up on Ernst Gombrich, Kentridge makes the point that our view of the rhinoceros is inextricably linked with the images we have long formed of this animal, even if—like Dürer—we have never seen it alive. Referring to the famous 1515 drawing but also to the more phallocentric albeit less influential 1751 rhinoceros painting by Pietro Longhi, the artist explains how "its very plates of armor [are] weighed down by the history of expectation of what a rhinoceros is, or can become."[81] There is, accordingly, no direct, innocent view, neither on the rhinoceros, nor on Africa. Our seeing is always already shaped by drawings and paintings—and by the media that contributed and still contribute to spreading these images: from the woodcut Dürer relied on via illustrated books, photographs, and films, all the way to the internet.

This yields only a preliminary outline of the contemporary relevance of Kentridge's practical epistemology. Against the onslaught of images, it insists, through patient drawing, erasing, and redrawing—we might say, through repeating, remembering, and working through—on grasping and feeling individual ways to authentic images, and it does so independently of whether the starting point was determined by Dürer's *Rhinocerus*, by Méliès's *Voyage dans la lune*, or by the photographs of the Sharpeville massacre that Kentridge found on his father's desk as a child.

For a more precise articulation of his epistemology, Kentridge switches from the visual studies register to that of the history of science. In the sequence about the dancing telegrapher who transforms into an ethereal network of emitters and receivers (fig. 5.20), his voice summarizes the speculations about space, time, and eternity that the German writer and amateur astronomer Felix Eberty published in the 1840s and that a young Albert Einstein read with fascination. The engagement with relativity theory is thus given a new turn. For Kentridge it is no longer the material culture of clock coordination alone that prompted Einstein's epoch-making 1905 essay. It is the much earlier speculations by Eberty on the transmission and storage of images that provided an at least equally important impulse.[82] The relativity of time thus combines with the relativity of images.

In this sequence, Kentridge's voice explains that against the backdrop of contemporary measurements of the speed of light, Eberty had concluded that the entire universe was to be conceived as "a universal archive of images": "Everything that had happened on earth could be found in space. Near a star 2,000 light years away, one could see Jesus Christ on his cross. In the vicinity of a star 500 light years away, one could see Luther pinning his edict on a church door in Wittenberg. Every action, heroic or shameful, every secret deed was there to be found."[83] We know that this notion of an all-comprehending archive of images was prompted by an idea Charles Babbage developed in the Bridgewater fragment, namely that air was to be considered "one vast library" because it contained all the sound waves of the past. Once more, then, we encounter the air as the medium of time. We also know that around 1900, Eberty's reflections were expanded in terms of a cosmic cinema. Science writers like Camille Flammarion, but philosophers like Henri Bergson, too, picked up on the notion that the light reflected off the earth sends a continuous stream of images into the universe, and turned it into the popular notion of a "cinema in the skies" or the philosophical conception of matter as a dynamic totality of images.[84]

Kentridge takes up these reflections and observations to describe the status of images in the age of mobile internet use: "We are all constantly broadcasting ourselves, not just here on stage, but throughout the universe. With each breath we pump out our images and transmit ourselves and traces of ourselves, sending out our images. . . . We are transmitting stations and receiving stations, constantly filled with what reaches us: images, sounds, fragments travelling through the world, through the universe."[85] It is this technological condition of wirelessly sending and receiving to which Kentridge responds with his epistemology: "The air is thick with images."[86] This is aimed at the dominant forms of wirelessness just as much as at the dubious promises of cloud computing and internet balloons. Kentridge is thus not only concerned, in a general way, with a self-determined production of images. Much more specifically, he turns against the global detachment of digital images from the materials, bodies, and landscapes they are based on—a point that can succinctly be made, in conclusion, by way of another etching by Markus Raetz on Roussel's *Impressions of Africa* (fig. 5.21).

Kentridge is not a naive enemy of digitalization or the internet, however. Where the movement-images of his own body are concerned, his practice of performing, recording, and reperforming is evidently possible thanks to the availability of digital movie cameras, and one of his most recent publications allows for expanding the usual way of reading by transforming individual images, via an internet connection and a smartphone used as a kind of magnifying glass, into moving images.

He has recognized, though, that the mobile use of image media constitutes a massive intervention in the connection between subjectivity and time: "And no gesture is so stupid but it is sent out at 186,000 miles per second. The universal archive of images also becomes an overstocked collection of miserable, superfluous images. We are caught between wanting to send ourselves out—*here I am, here I am*—and wanting to hold back, to call back, to annul, and to obliterate every act and so many acts and actions. To undo. To unsay. To unsave. To unremember. To unhappen."[87] For this very reason, his work with and on images aims at producing an affective "territoriality." Kentridge has understood that only the construction of such terrains opens up, in the first place, the possibility of refusing the dominant forms of time in order to determine, to claim, and to assert times of one's own in the bodily interaction of charcoal and paper, printing presses, cameras, and projectors. On the small scale and on the large scale, in his Johannesburg studio as in the city of Johannesburg, this takes place via "a set of material practices, signs, figures, superstitions, images, and fictions."[88]

Also and especially in the age of digitalization, Kentridge insists therefore on an individual, simultaneously technical and bodily culture of dealing with media, a local appropriation of media devices through and across the intermediary spaces they always contain, even if today's devices tend toward black boxing. And in that sense, we may indeed say that the refusal of time that Kentridge in his Kassel installation has so effectively staged with horns and rhinoceroses is based on a "time of materials"—of the materials of the body as well as of the materials of technics.

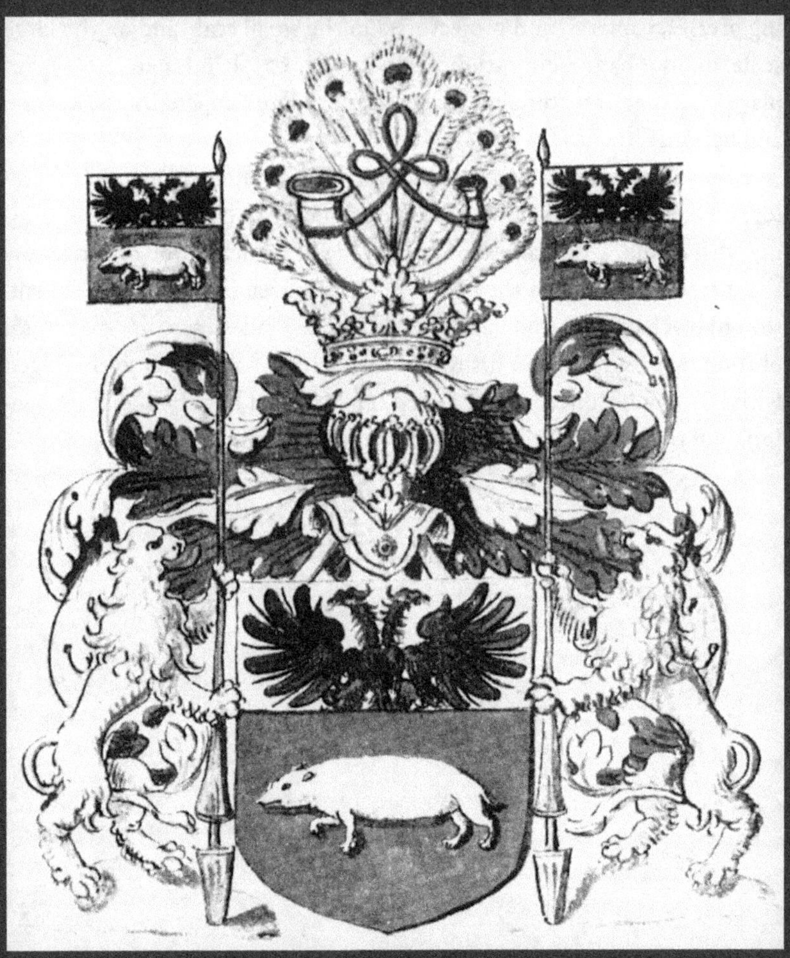

FIGURE 5.6
Early crest of the Thurn und Taxis family (ca. 1534–40). Besides the badger (Italian *tasso*) from which the name derives, the crest features, above the crown, a post horn in front of nine peacock feathers.

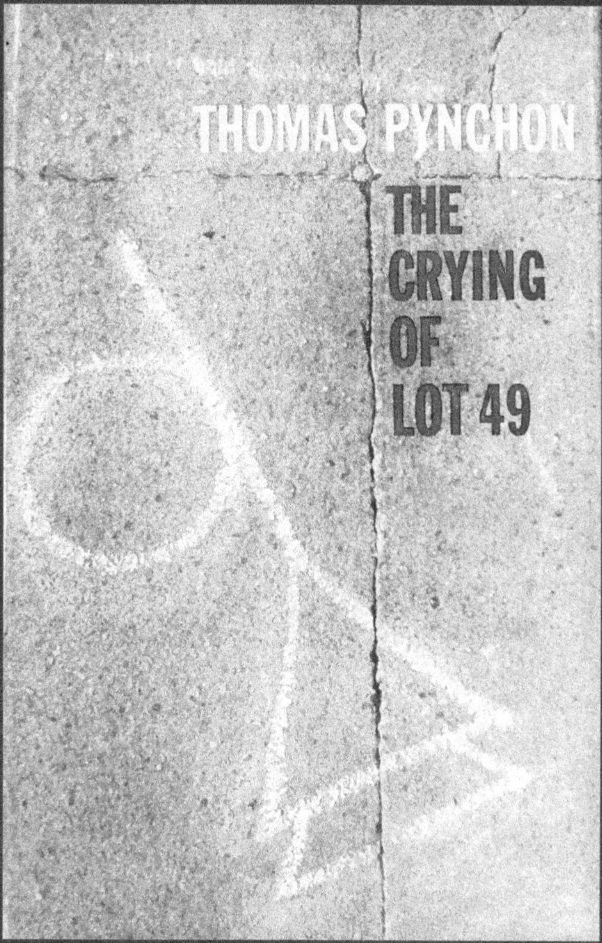

FIGURE 5.1
Cover of the first edition of Thomas Pynchon, *The Crying of Lot 49* (1966).

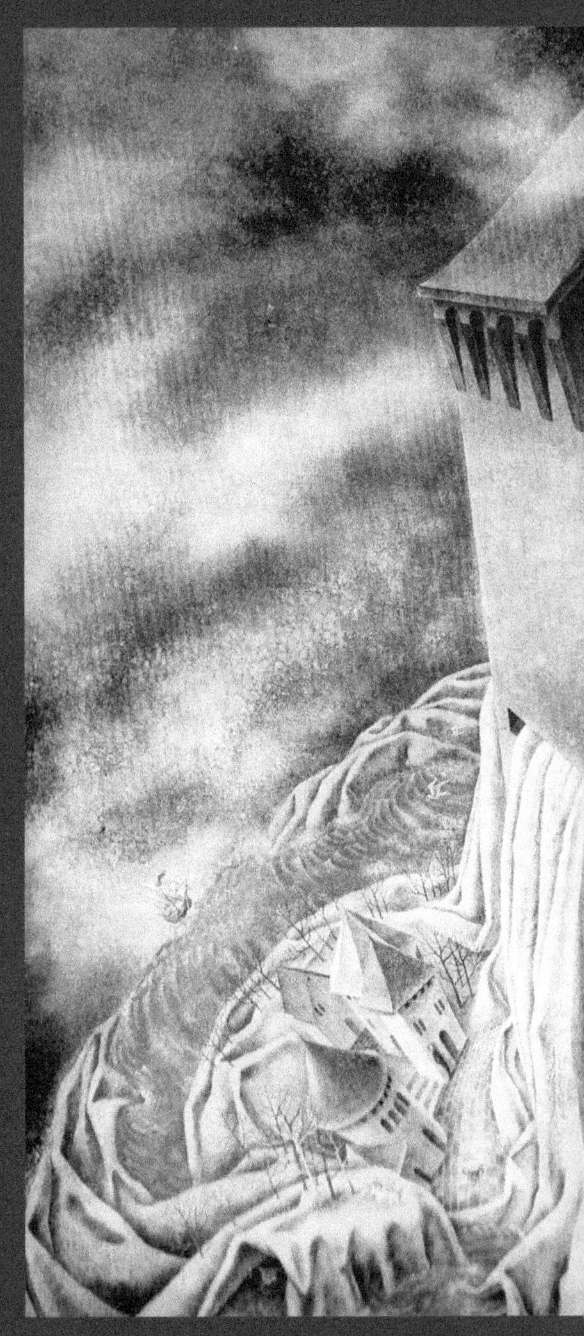

FIGURE 5.2

Remedios Varo, *Bordando el Manto terrestre* (1961).

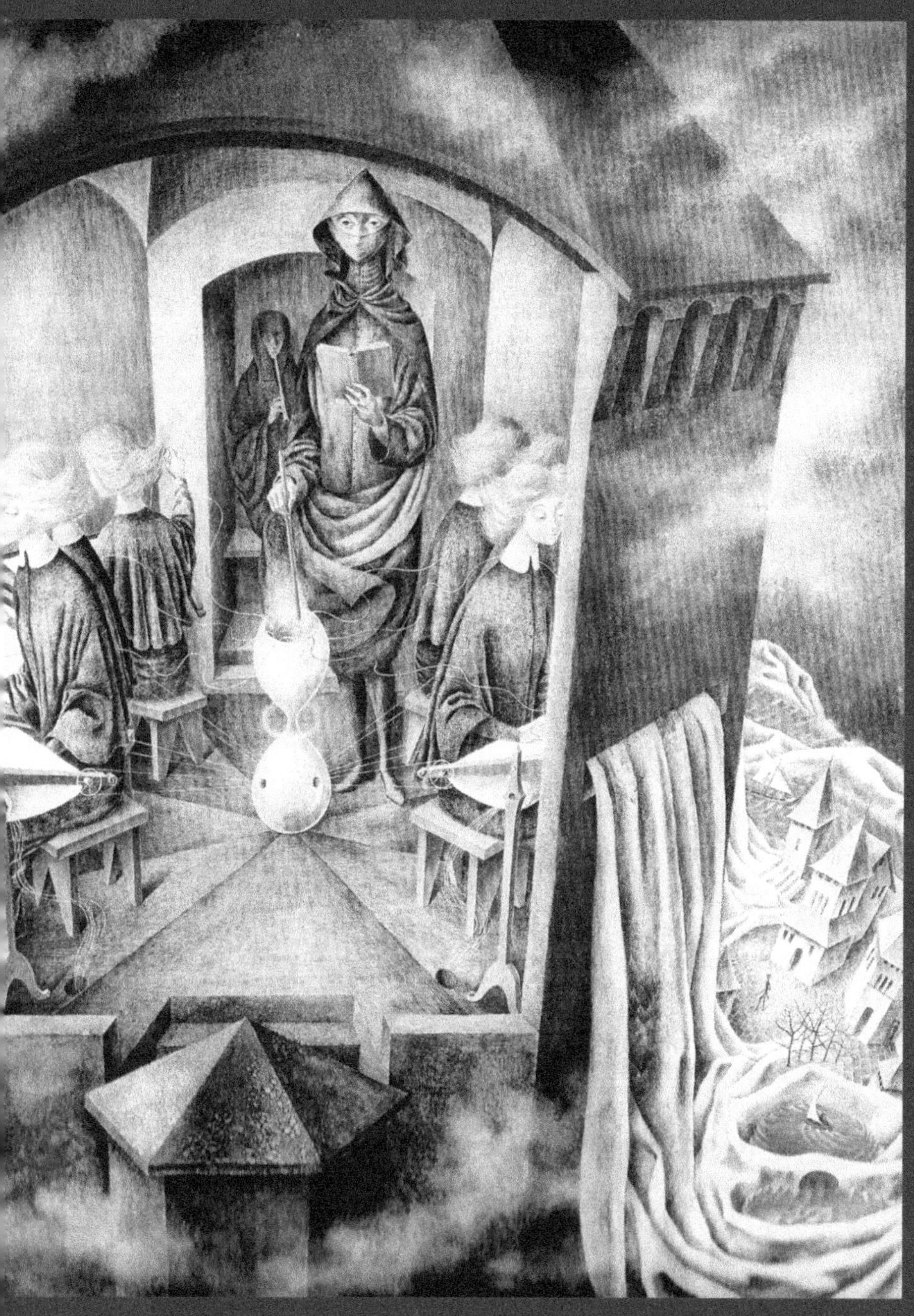

wearing a Yoyodyne badge. What do you make of that?"

"Some inter-office mail run," Oedipa said.

"This time of night?"

"Maybe a late shift?" But Metzger only frowned. "Be back," Oedipa shrugged, heading for the ladies' room.

On the latrine wall, among lipsticked obscenities, she noticed the following message, neatly indited in engineering lettering:

> *"Interested in sophisticated fun? You, hubby, girl friends. The more the merrier. Get in touch with Kirby, through WASTE only, Box 7391, L. A."*

WASTE? Oedipa wondered. Beneath the notice, faintly in pencil, was a symbol she'd never seen before, a loop, triangle and trapezoid, thus:

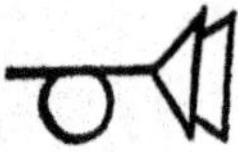

It might be something sexual, but she somehow doubted it. She found a pen in her purse and copied the address and symbol in her memo book, thinking: God, hieroglyphics. When she came out Fallopian was back, and had this funny look on his face.

"You weren't supposed to see that," he told them. He had an envelope. Oedipa could see, instead of a postage stamp, the handstruck initials PPS.

"Of course," said Metzger. "Delivering the mail is a government monopoly. You would be opposed to that."

Fallopian gave them a wry smile. "It's not as rebellious as it looks. We use Yoyodyne's inter-office

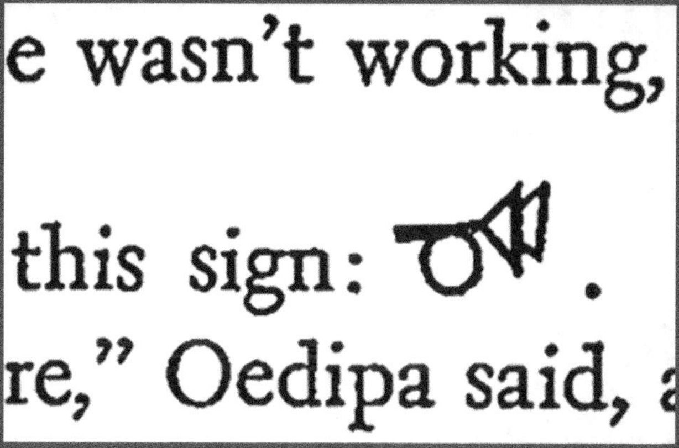

e wasn't working,

this sign: .

re," Oedipa said, a

FIGURE 5.3

The first instance of the muted post horn in Pynchon's novel.

FIGURE 5.4

Detail view of the second muted post horn.

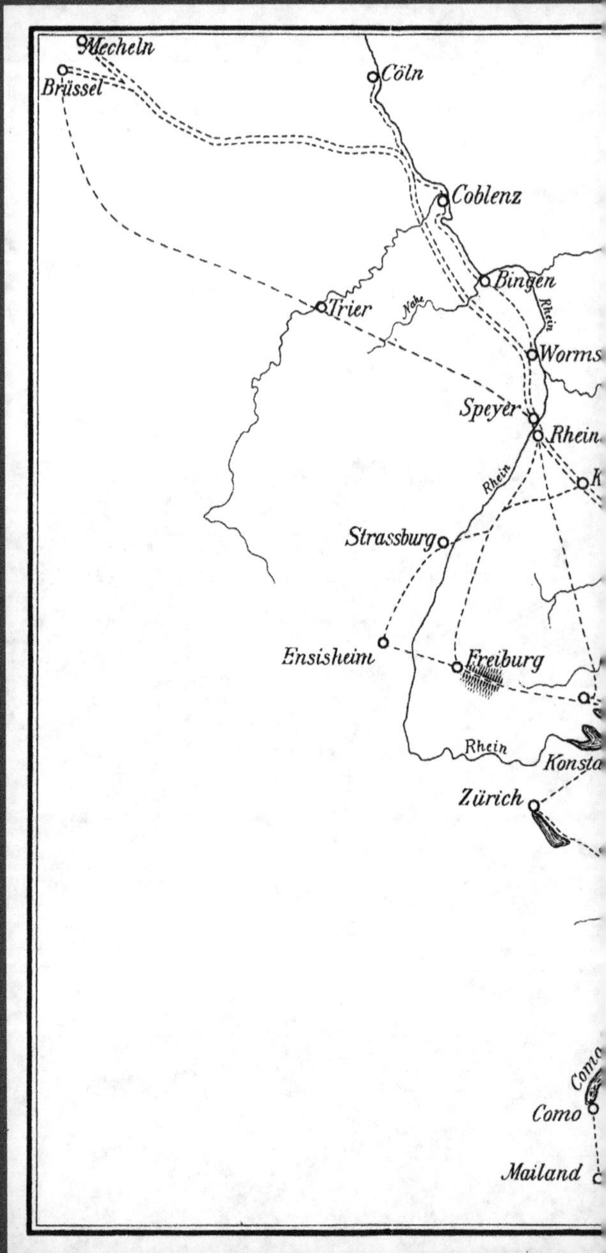

FIGURE 5.5

An early network of communication. The routes of the Thurn und Taxis post, 1490–1520.

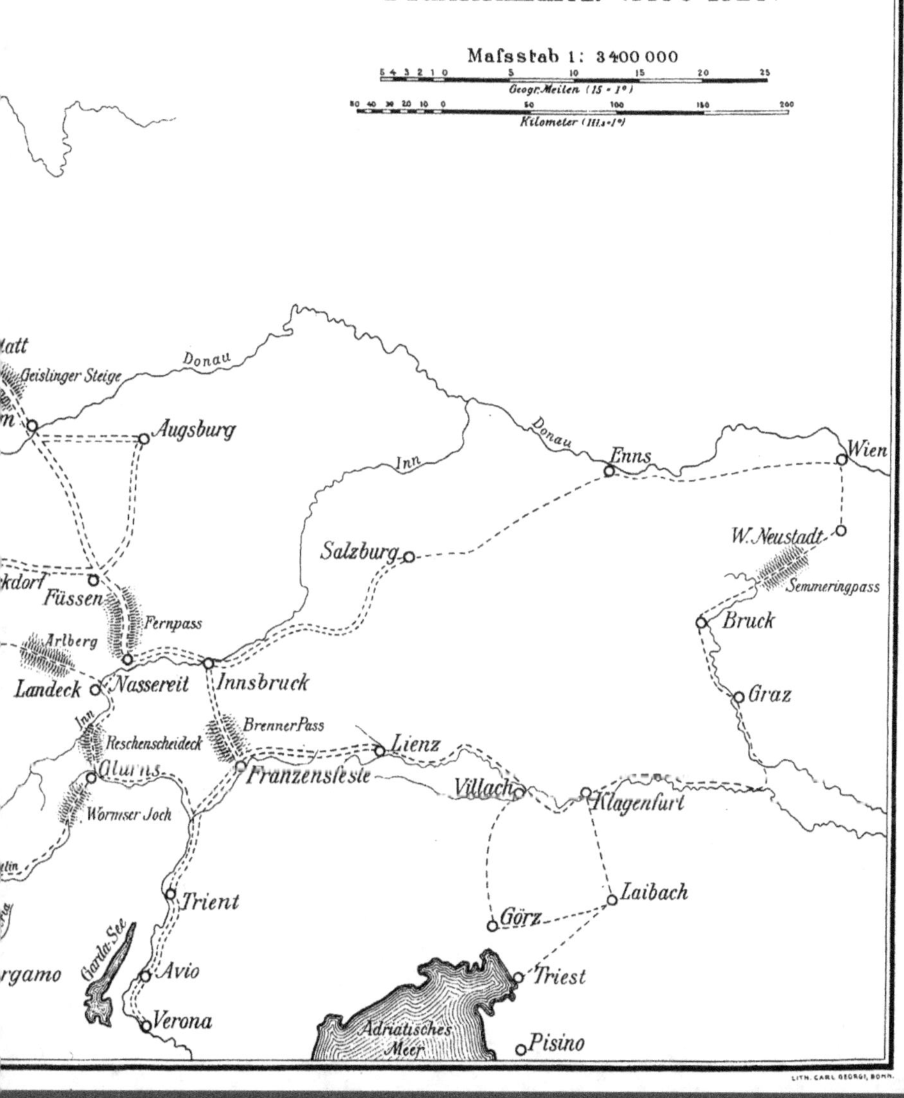

Die deutschen Postkurse unter Maximilian I. (1490-1520)
Mafsstab 1: 3400000
Geogr. Meilen (15 = 1°)
Kilometer
Donau
Geislinger Steige
Augsburg
Inn
Enns
Wien
Salzburg
W. Neustadt
Semmeringpass
Füssen
Fernpass
Arlberg
Bruck
Landeck
Nassereit
Innsbruck
Graz
Brenner Pass
Lienz
Reschenscheideck
Franzensfeste
Villach
Klagenfurt
Wormser Joch
Trient
Laibach
Görz
Garda-See
Avio
Triest
Verona
Adriatisches Meer
Pisino
LITH. CARL GEORGI, BONN.

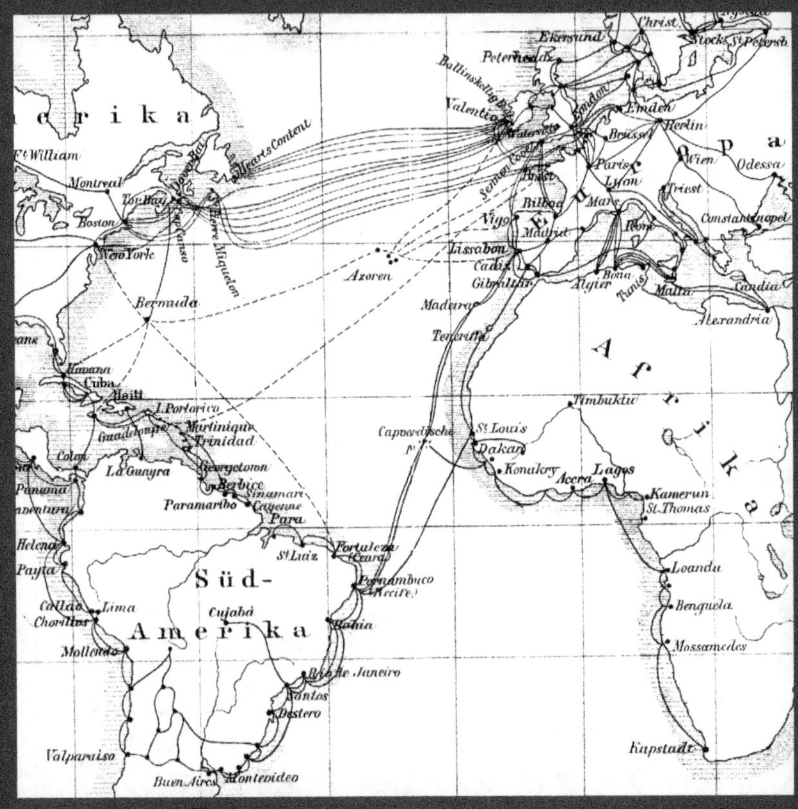

FIGURE 5.6

See earlier.

FIGURE 5.7

"Die wichtigsten Telegraphenverbindungen der Erde," detail (ca. 1900).

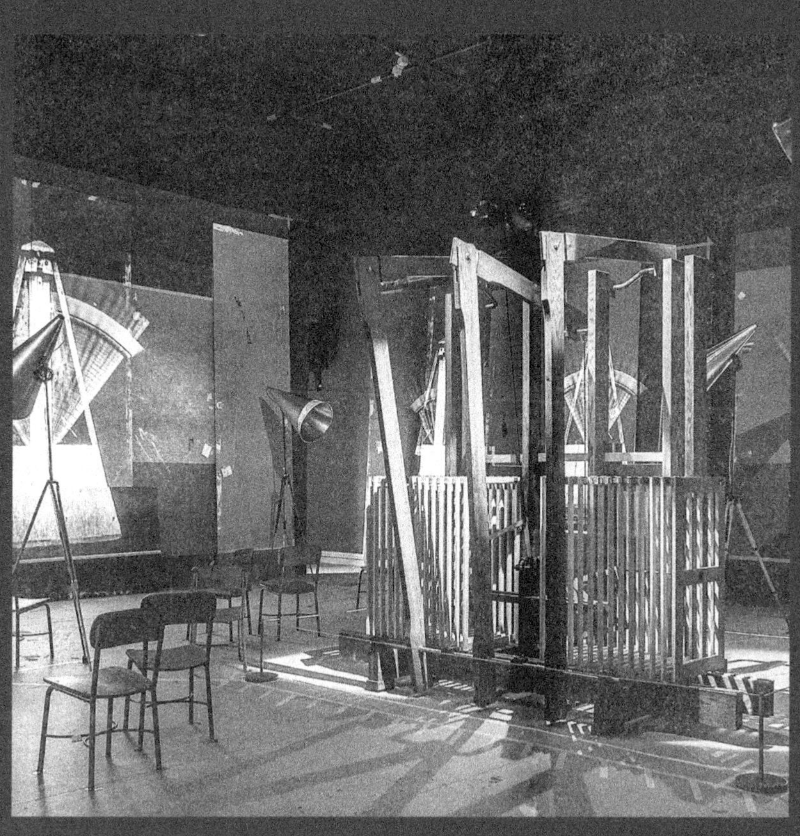

FIGURE 5.8

View of William Kentridge's installation *The Refusal of Time* at the Metropolitan Museum of Art, New York (October 2013–April 2014). Courtesy William Kentridge. © William Kentridge.

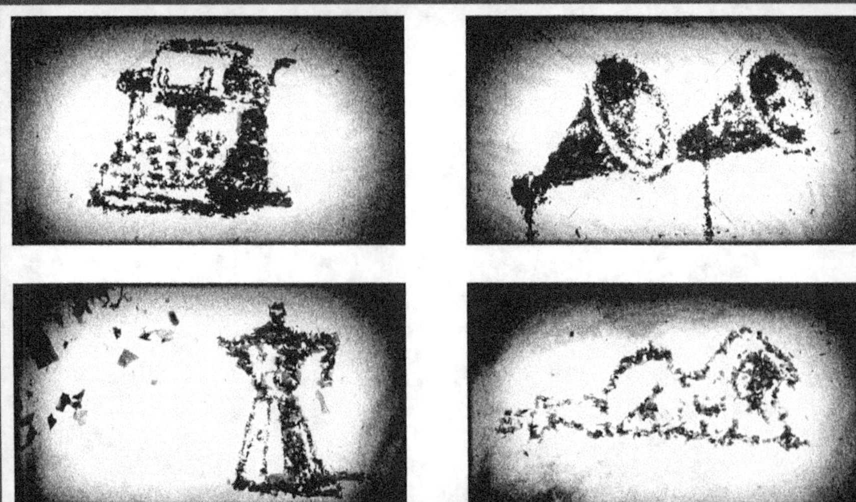

FIGURE 5.9
William Kentridge, four motifs from *The Refusal of Time* (2012). Courtesy William Kentridge. © William Kentridge.

FIGURE 5.10
William Kentridge, still image from one of the "silent film sequences" of *The Refusal of Time* (2012). Courtesy William Kentridge. © William Kentridge.

FIGURE 5.11
William Kentridge, the shadow procession in *The Refusal of Time* (2012). Courtesy William Kentridge. © William Kentridge.

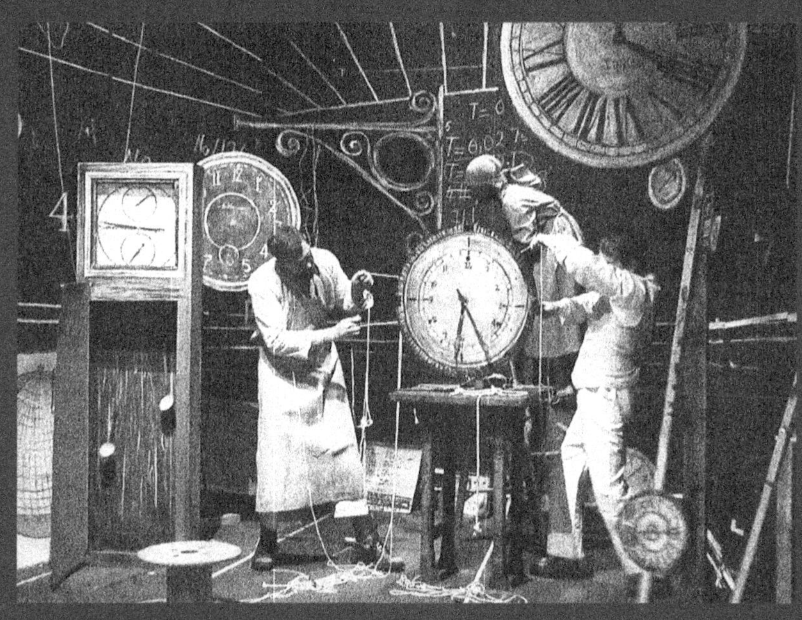

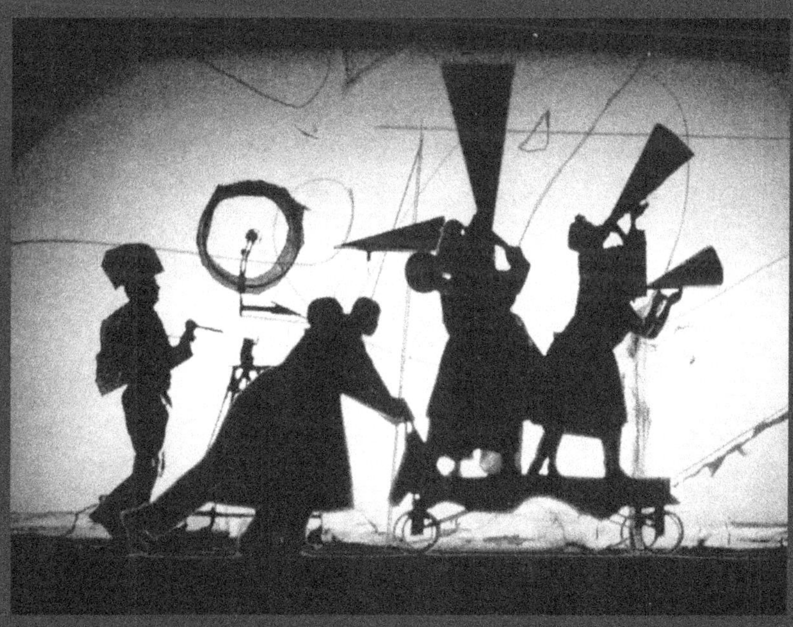

The elephant.

Machine moving "like an elephant in a state of MELANCHOLY MADNESS"

(Hard Times – CD)

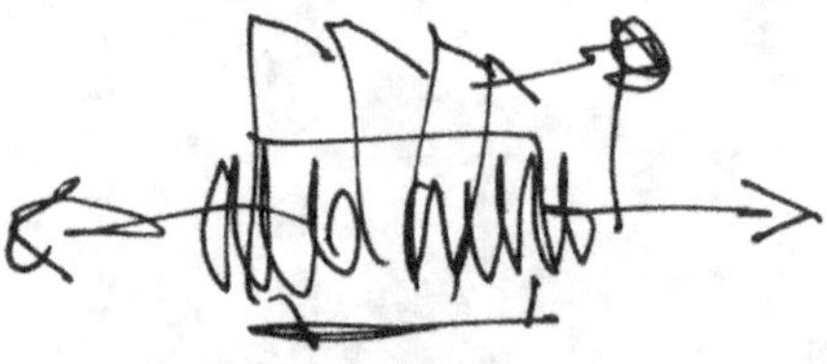

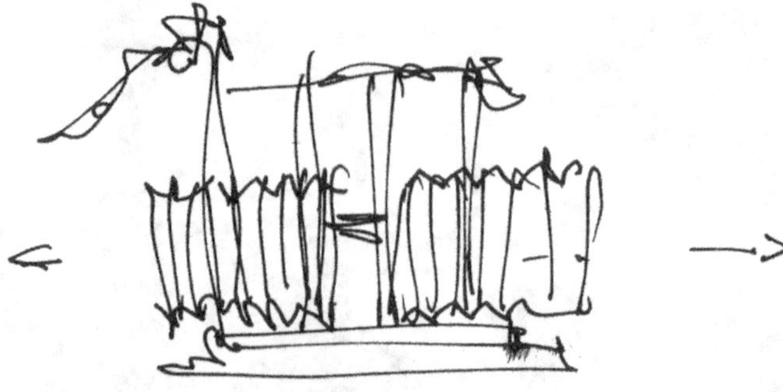

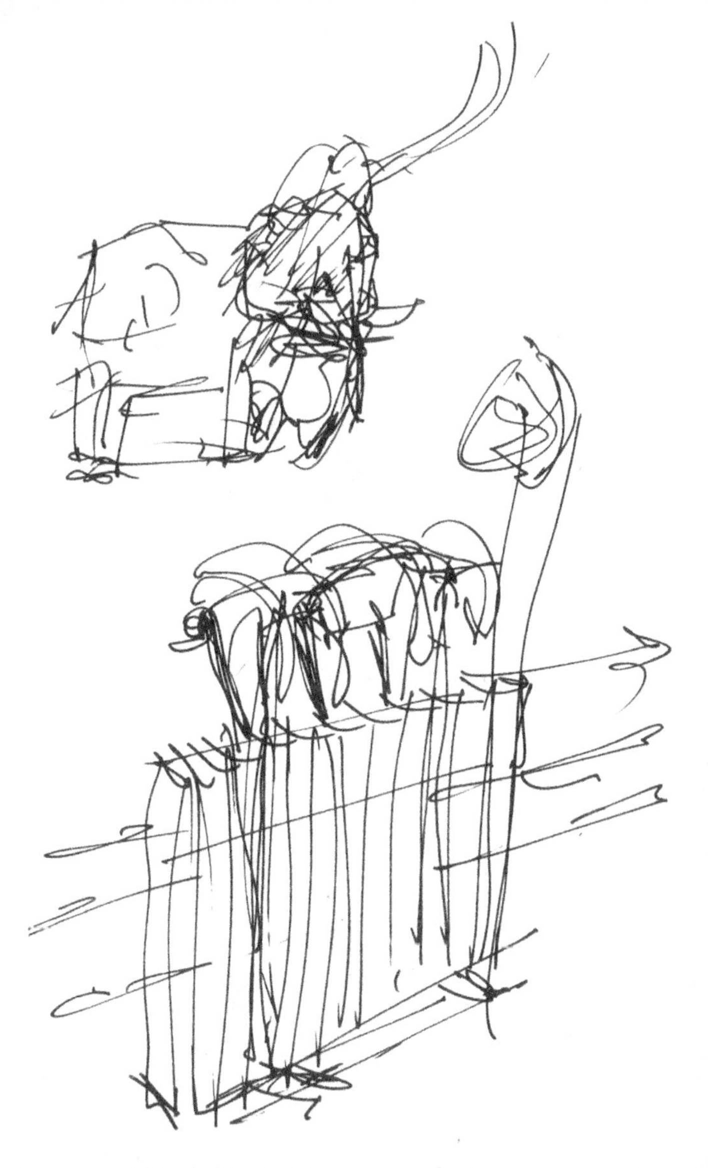

FIGURE 5.12
William Kentridge, sketches for the "breathing machine ('elephant')" of *The Refusal of Time* (2012). "*The elephant*. Machines moving 'like an elephant in a state of MELANCHOLY MADNESS' (Hard Times—C[harles] D[ickens])." Courtesy William Kentridge. © William Kentridge.

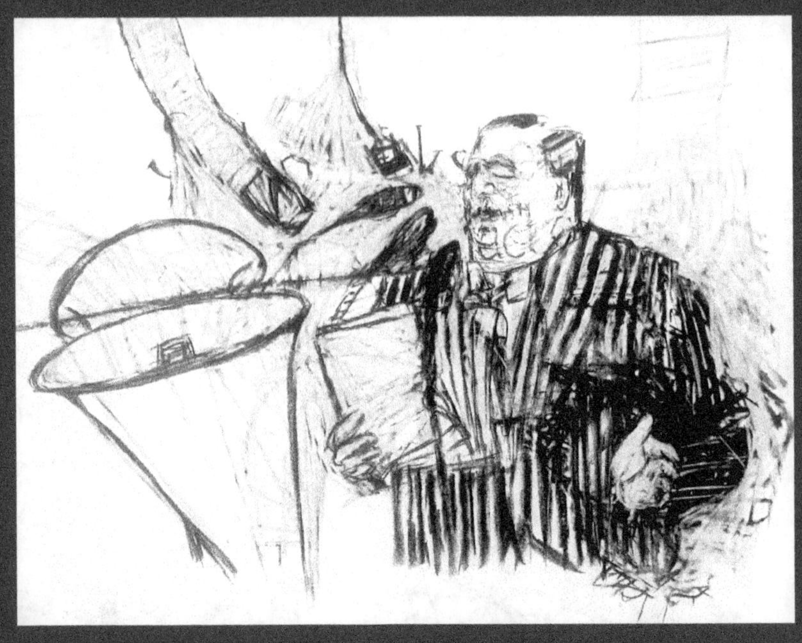

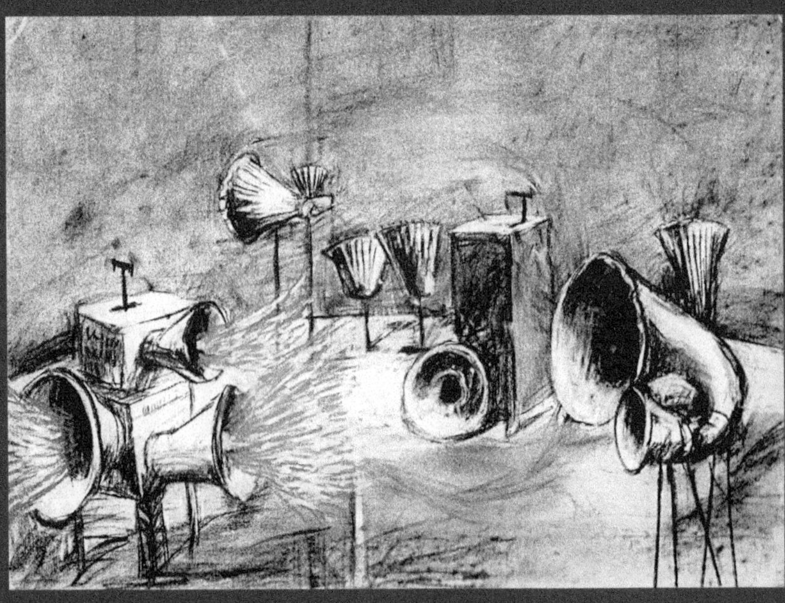

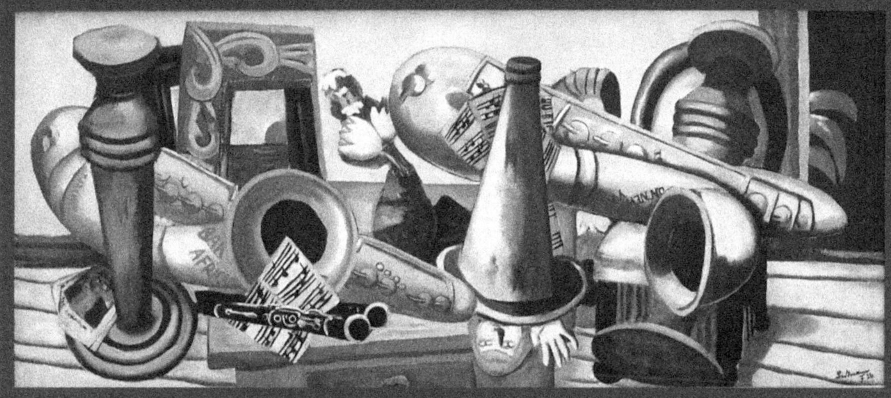

FIGURE 5.13

William Kentridge, drawing for *Monument* (1990). Courtesy William Kentridge. © William Kentridge.

FIGURE 5.14

William Kentridge, drawing for *Sobriety, Obesity, and Growing Old* (1991). Courtesy William Kentridge. © William Kentridge.

FIGURE 5.15

Max Beckmann, *Stillleben mit Saxofonen* (1926). © VG Bild-Kunst, Bonn 2020.

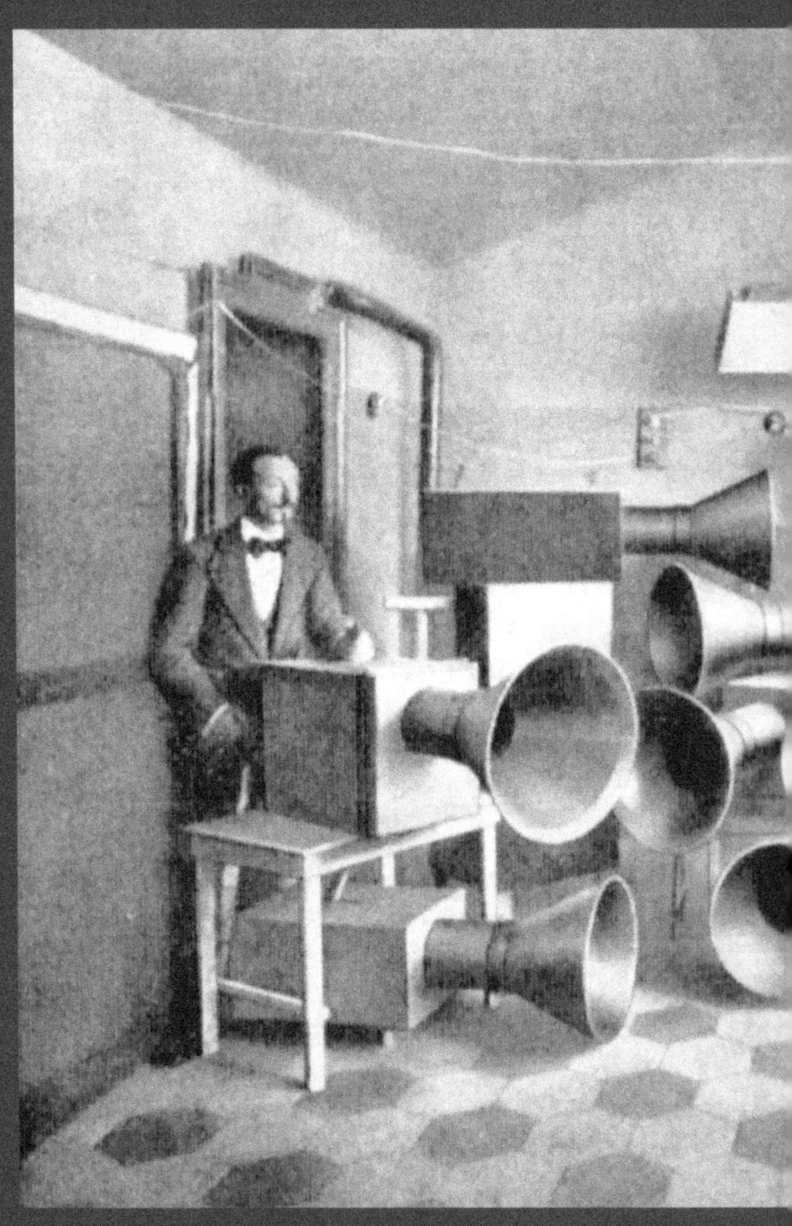

FIGURE 5.16

Luigi Russolo, *Intonarumori* (1913).

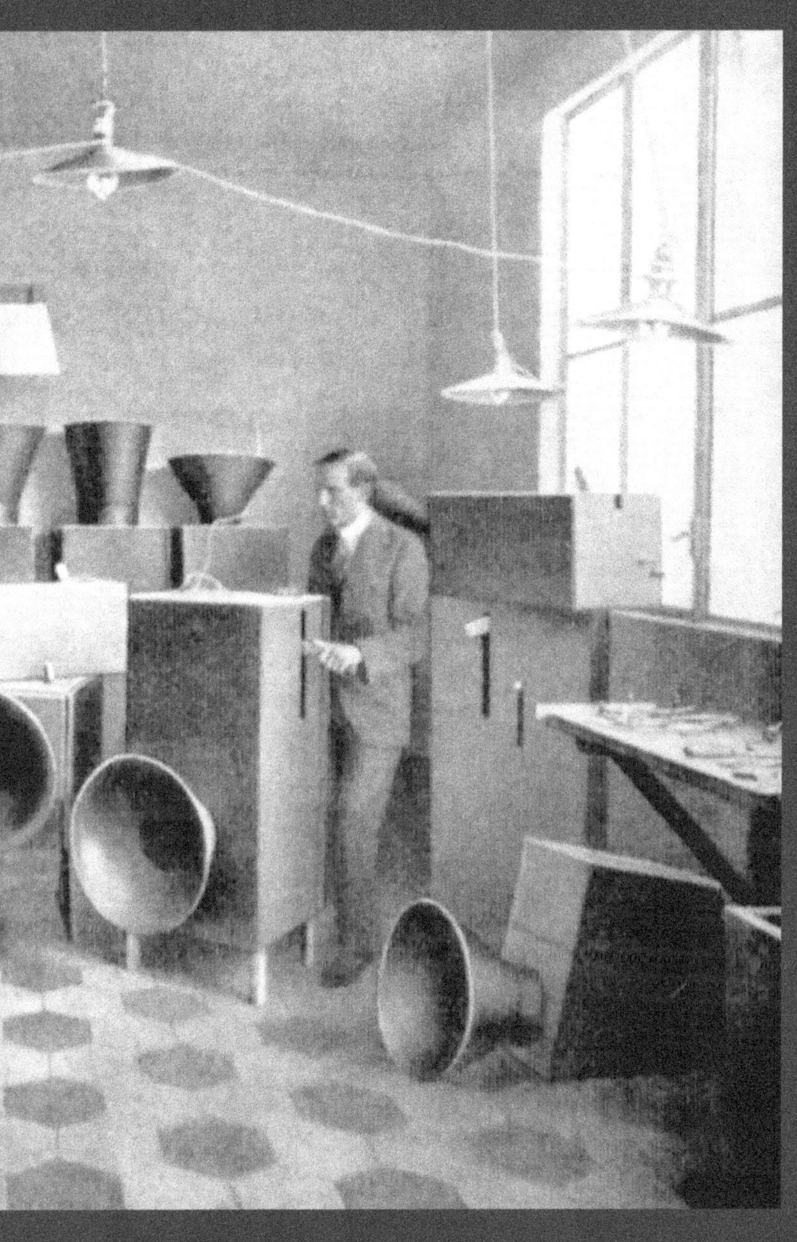

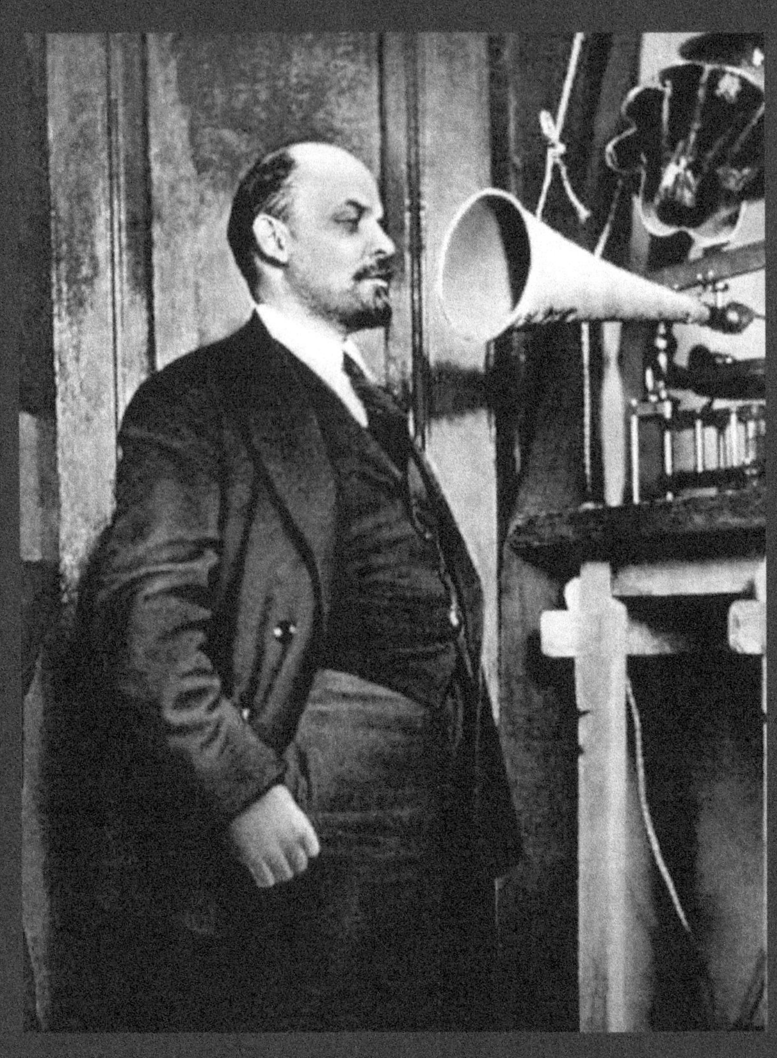

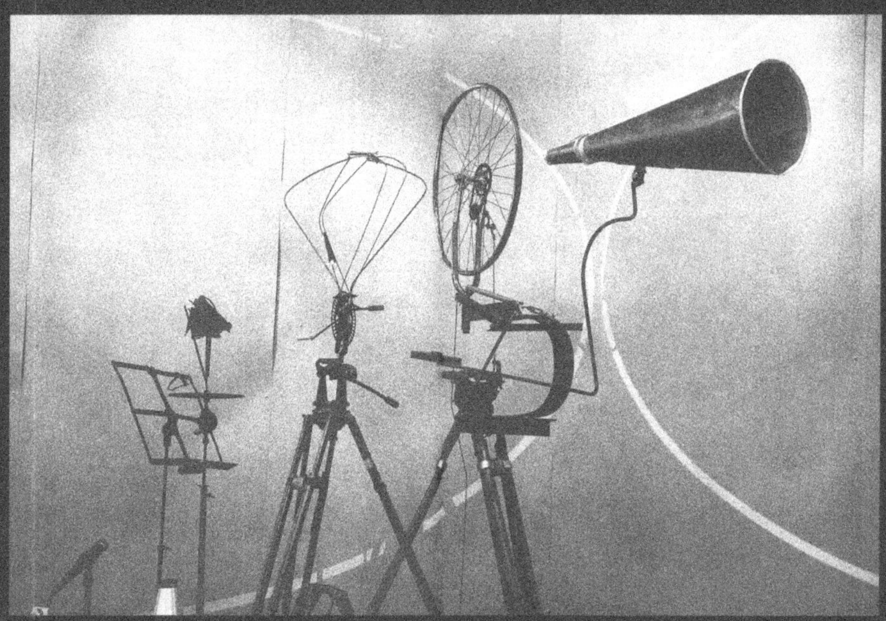

FIGURE 5.17

Lenin making a recording. Photograph taken in the Kremlin, March 29, 1919.

FIGURE 5.18

William Kentridge, kinetic sculpture for *The Refusal of Time* (2012). Courtesy William Kentridge. © William Kentridge.

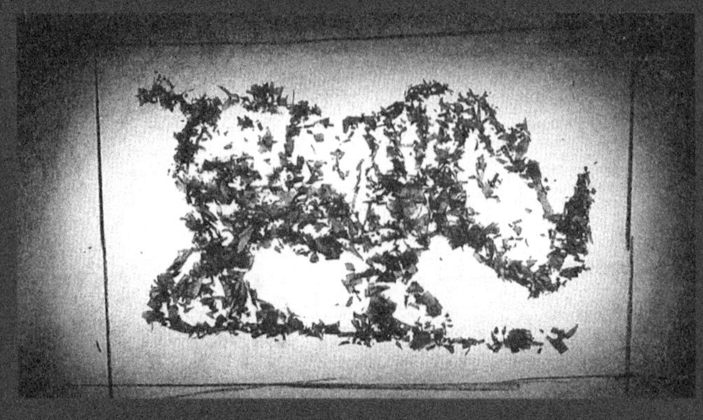

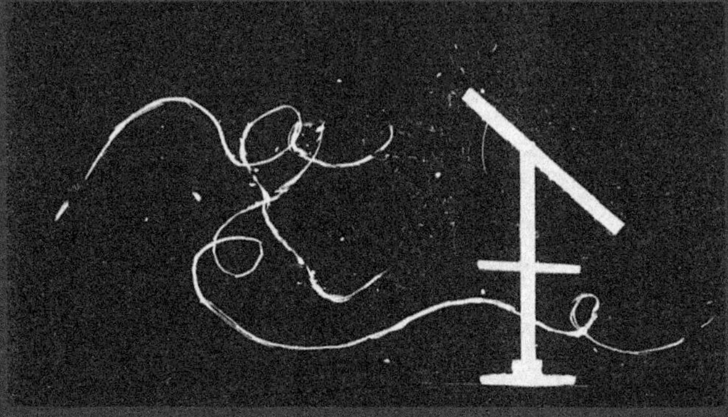

FIGURE 5.19

William Kentridge, motif from *The Refusal of Time* (2012). Courtesy William Kentridge. © William Kentridge.

FIGURE 5.20

William Kentridge, drawing for *The Refusal of Time* (2012). Courtesy William Kentridge. © William Kentridge.

FIGURE 5.21

Markus Raetz, *Ohne Titel* (1980). Etching for Raymond Roussel, *Impressions of Africa.* © VG Bild-Kunst, Bonn 2020.

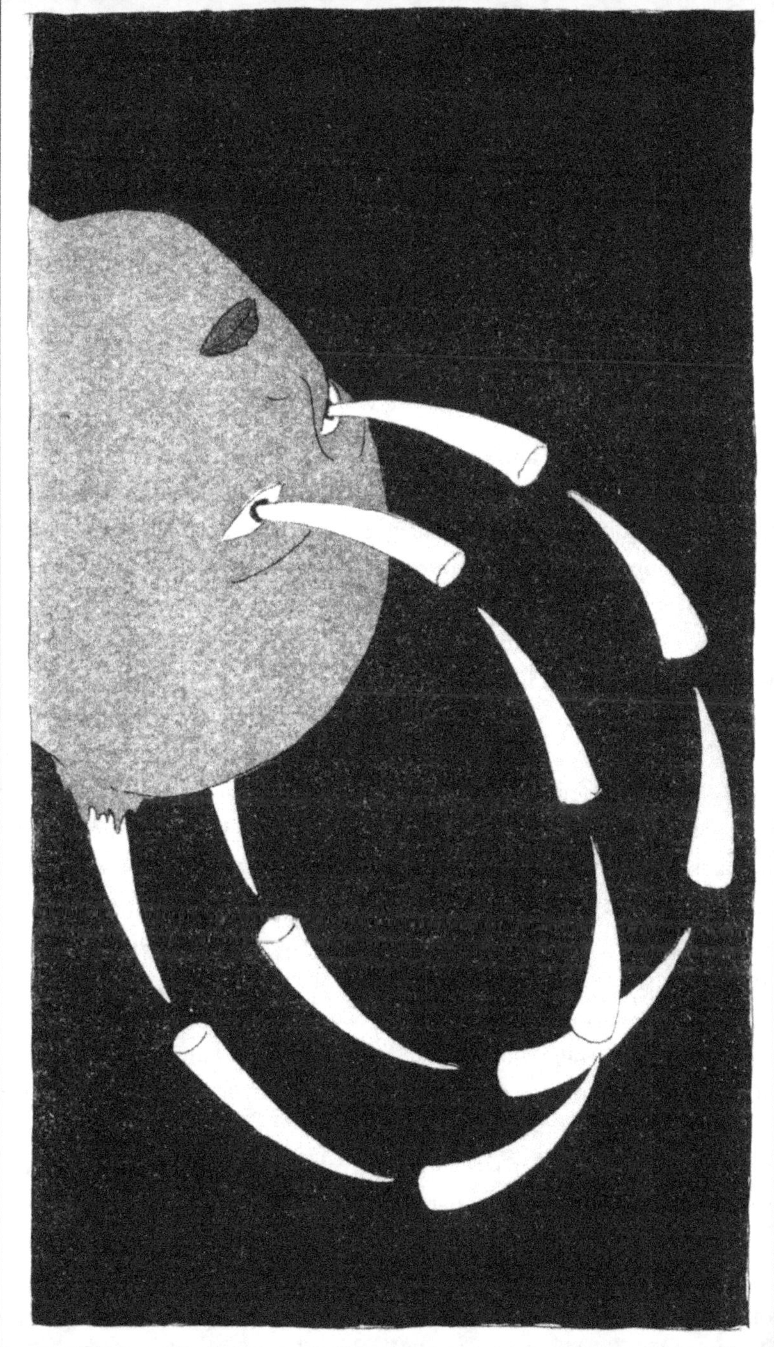

Conclusion

Ionesco was right. We are turning into rhinoceroses. We thought we were enlightened bipeds, smart beings of the upright posture, graceful in our movements, cultivated in our behavior, and always optimally informed in our reflections. Now it turns out that we are something completely different: massive thick-skinned quadrupeds who stampede through cities at amazing speeds, seemingly incapable of considerateness and foresight and who, for the same reason, come to resemble each other more and more.

There is not much consolation in pointing out that in reality rhinoceroses aren't like that at all. The real rhinoceroses are not herd animals, and unlike what their rough exterior might suggest, they are quite sensitive organisms, patient herbivores who have no natural reason to turn against humans. *These* rhinoceroses, however, are threatened by extinction. They are targets of an unbelievably brutal and highly organized criminal trade with their horns that no longer plagues African countries alone but zoological gardens in Europe and North America as well.

What Ionesco did not know, what he could not know: the "hard skin" of the rhinoceros toward which he, smiling, extends his hand in a photo taken at the Zurich zoo is not a natural surface but an artificial epidermis.[1] In the age of mobile and connected media, this skin consists of metal parts and protective screens, of flat TVs and equally flat phones, of tablet computers, smartphones, and wearables that wrap the body like armor.

Sitting inside *this* rhinoceros, which moreover has abruptly evolved from quadruped to quadricycle, are human beings looking at and tapping on screens. Looked at from the inside, every screen appears as a new window onto the world, an opening onto essential information, communications, and interactions. Looked at from the outside, these screens are nothing but protective screens, armor that "users" employ to shield against the outside world, thereby becoming ever more calculable.

This is not meant as a metaphor. As a matter of fact, it is possible to calculate the identity of individual website users from the number, sequence, and rhythm of keystrokes and the movements and taps on pads. Smartphones and cars record and transmit the movement data of their users, which, in combination with data from social networks, email correspondence, and message threads, allows for compiling individual profiles that are much more informative than psychological personality tests. Some years back, a major software firm's advertising slogan was "Where do you want to go today?" Thanks to the combination of data concerning website visits, purchase preferences, and road use, today's IT giants, it seems, are able to answer this question without even having to ask.[2]

The proximity of testing and touching we have encountered again and again in going through our fictional exhibition is thereby redefined: its emphasis lies no longer on the subject testing and exploring an environment it has itself created but inversely on an environment many of whose decisive aspects were created by others and that allows for capturing, studying, and judging every subject that enters it. In this way, the emerging sensor society shifts the conventional boundaries between privacy and publicity, subjectivity and economy, power and reason, while the people inhabiting it seem to have little choice but to turn to "the media" and to recall dystopian conceptions of the future—except that the often-invoked Big Brother is no longer watching the citizens he has turned into customers but is scanning, tracking, and tracing them. *Big Brother is touching you . . .*

The difficulties that arise in trying to describe and critically to reflect on such shifts in media-theoretical terms are due not only to the fact that these developments are taking place right now and rest on highly complex technical foundations. They also arise from the long tradition of writing the history of modernity primarily as a history of optical regimes. From Michel Foucault's "panopticism" via Jonathan Crary's "techniques of the observer" to Bruno Latour's "drawing things together," the emergence and development of modern society has been presented above all as a formation of the eye, of the gaze, and of visibility.[3] The sense of touch has largely been left out in this historiography—the few exceptions include Norbert Elias's remarks on the changing attitude toward bodily touch in early modernity and Klaus Theweleit's attempt at studying the armoring of men's bodies around 1900. As the sense of proximity par excellence, tactility evidently lacks the distant, space-taking, and sovereign controlling momentum that is considered to characterize modernity as a whole. But that, precisely, is beginning to change as sensors, trackers, and tracers spread more and more.[4]

Following the guiding thread of the horn in engaging with the positions of classical media theory, we have encountered a number of examples for a different history of modernity. This is the first result of this study. In Freud, Benjamin, and McLuhan, touching serves as the primary mode of modern subjectivity. Different as these authors' objects, methods, and results obtained may be, they do agree on following the "principle of skin-to-skin closeness,"[5] that is, they presume that human individuals discover their surroundings above all by bodily touching, grasping, and changing them. And although in following this principle, Freud, Benjamin, and McLuhan invoke quite different foundations—biological, psychological, but also theological foundations—they agree that the modern subject is being scanned and touched by its surroundings as well, that it is exposed to the pressure of modernity, that in modernity the subject is confronted with a multitude of impressions and contacts, vibrations and shocks.

Benjamin and McLuhan in particular have reflected on the fact that the changing of media worlds also leads to changes in the tactile behavior of subjects—from an increase in the number of gestures of switching, pushing, and touching to new bodily experiences in driving, swimming, and diving. Simultaneously, they have pointedly shown that increasingly, it is media such as photography, film, and television that, in Benjamin's phrase, "accommodate" us, reach out to and move in on us in the urban space. Film and television images, on their interpretation, hit us with their light beams the way arrows or projectiles hit a living body. They penetrate us, envelop us, and enclose us in entire architectures.

With regard to this counterside of media, McLuhan, in a formula that still hits the mark today, speaks of electric media's "pervasive impression." And although he does not address computers and the internet in any detail, he does not hesitate to see in digital media the starting point of a new form of ecology: "In the age of information, it is information itself that becomes environmental."[6] Already here, then, does the question of media's tactility become a question of media ecologies and media architectures.[7]

Benjamin and McLuhan differ significantly, however, in the way they contextualize the facts they describe historically. In the increasing tactilization of our culture, McLuhan sees the beginning of a new age of holistic perception. At the same time, he regards it as a return to the old, if not prehistoric, ages of the whole human personality's synthetic embeddedness in its environment. This view has a historiographic correlate in the comparatively sweeping assumption that the culture of the present is characterized by the fact that in it, all epochs coexist.

Benjamin furnishes his analysis of tactile experiences in modernity with much more concrete markers. Picking up on Marx, he refers the change in these experiences back to the cultural logic of capitalism. The fact that, thanks to photographic reproductions, works of art are available almost anytime and anywhere; that not only can they be looked at at home or in a library but that in turn, they look back; that ocular muscles transform into shock absorption mechanisms that soften the blow of collisions with cinematic images—all these, according to Benjamin, are experiences that ultimately are defined by the "fantastic form" of capitalist commodity production. In his view, this is the transformation of people into things, namely into commodities, and the transformation of commodities into subject-like, person-like entities that also manifest themselves in the tactile agency of media.

Although Benjamin is one of the most frequently cited media theorists, his observations on the formation of a culture of touch have rarely been taken up in the historiography of modernity. Only Wolfgang Schivelbusch, taking up Marx, Freud, and Benjamin, has made an exemplary attempt to situate tactility in this history. In his famous *Railway Journey*, he develops a theory of "the formation of *an inorganic protective layer due to civilization*" that ties perceptions that come with the spreading of new forms of technology back to the stimulus shield phenomenon.[8] In modernity, then, perception is based no longer simply on the reception of stimuli but at least as much also on protection from them. In this age, perceptions do not become better or more precise when more stimuli are received. What is required instead is a protective filtering—"perceptual unpleasure," as Freud puts it at one point—that ensures the functioning of the process as a whole.[9]

Schivelbusch observes that late nineteenth-century railway passengers who routinely read during the train journey had "a thicker layer of that skin" than passengers during the early years of train travel. Someone for whom the trip in the railway car was still a taxing adventure could not even think of reading. Schivelbusch concludes, "The strength or density of the stimulus shield indicates the strength or density of the stimuli that it receives and . . . the strength or density of these stimuli is an indicator of the prevailing historical stage of civilization."[10] By analogy, it would be possible to determine a kind of stimuli protection coefficient for the way we use mobile connected media today.

While Schivelbusch, following Benjamin, explicitly emphasizes the significance of shock as bodily touch—as push, blow, or collision—the larger share of his analysis does not take place in the register of the haptic but remains within the framework of a historiography centered on optical regimes. His study focuses on the emergence of "panoramic vision."[11] This prioritization of the visual is a function of a certain conception of traveling, but it also has to do with the fact that in Schivelbusch's book, there is no sense of a transition between the tactile activities of the subject and the emergence of technology and media.

Benjamin already limited his discussion of the protective layer city dwellers build up in the obtrusive rush of modernity to the function of consciousness enhancement, and even in Freud, there is no discernible connection between his description of the protective layer enveloping the organism and his reference to the human being as the "prosthetic God" of technicized society.[12]

To bring out this transition, one might, as I have shown, rely on Aby Warburg, who, in some fragments at least, reflects on the link between the ornamental encircling of the body and the production of tools. Yet Warburg considers the fact that humans, "through manipulating or wearing" objects (clothes, instruments, etc.), can "inorganically expand their scope" to be a "tragedy of corporification [*Verleibung*]."[13]

The possibilities for reflection this opens up could easily be pushed even further with Adorno's help: in a remarkable passage on the philosophy of idealism, the author of *Negative Dialectics* compares the subject as such with a rhinoceros. This subject, he writes, "drag[s]" its "protective armor" around like an "ingrown prison" that it "seem[s]—anthropomorphically, at least—to be trying vainly to shed. The imprisonment in their survival mechanism may explain the special ferocity of rhinoceroses as well as the unacknowledged and therefore more dreadful ferocity of *homo sapiens*."[14]

This study has taken a different path. It has opened up to a media art that thematizes the sense of touch from the counterperspective of a productive interlocking of body, image, and technology. This perspective is outlined just as much by the "action experiments" of Rebecca Horn, who with the head, arm, and finger extensions she has built obtains new interpersonal perceptions, as it is by Salvador Dalí's engagement with artificial and natural pictorial surfaces that leads to an artistic practice of an "augmented reality" long before the concept even exists. And William Kentridge's staging of a practical epistemology situated in the tentative back and forth between manual drawing and technical recording assumes this perspective as well. In all these cases, the emergence of and dealing with media is conceived as working with a kind of bodily cortex that can function as instrument and tool but also as ornament and protection and as dress and casing.

But art does not stop there. This is the second result of this study. The works we have looked at not only thematize the passage from corporeality to mediality, they inversely also reflect on the tactility of media that characterizes today's mobile and connected media devices. Raymond Roussel invents a tarot card–insect clock whose light cones painlessly penetrate the human skin. Dalí makes clear to what significant extent "compulsive images" take possession of us such that some paintings seem to pierce viewers like needles.

Rebecca Horn not only invents numerous machines that execute touching movements, she also constructs a *Measure Box* that is able to scan and depict the body on the condition that this body can be locked in and fixed. In Kentridge, this prison of design appears in nineteenth-century garb but at the height of current technology: as a *universal archive of images* to which we have constant and instant access but which simultaneously deprives us of time to breathe because it keeps every conceivable image available and remembers every keystroke made to retrieve it.

This art, too, contributes to accentuating our conception of media in a new way. In that they now manifest themselves as extensions of the body not just analogously but in a literally palpable way, media no longer just appear as central agents of information, communication, and interaction. Just as much, at least, they turn out to be exemplary screens against the world, "formations of *an inorganic protective layer due to civilization*."

Now, every media sociology worth its mettle knows that systems, be they media, people, or institutions, must first obtain closure before they can open up. Phenomena of this kind can be observed among media producers in the form of communications of communications (reporting on other reporting, shows about other shows, and the like), while among media users it manifests in phenomena such as "cocooning" or the formation of information or filter "bubbles" so widely debated in recent years. The motif of the horn allows for confirming and emphasizing such facts on the corporeal level of media usage. It brings out to just what extent media fulfill that function of buffering from which Oedipa Maas, the heroine of Pynchon's novel, *The Crying of Lot 49*, resolutely seeks to withdraw.

Going back once more to Benjamin, we can characterize this phenomenon of closure with more precision. The author of the artwork essay translates his general finding, that capitalism is increasingly tactilized, into a concrete and only apparently paradoxical diagnosis. This diagnosis concerns the *tracelessness* of existence in modernity. According to Benjamin, if a culture that has become tactile entails the "liquidation" of its traditions, then this means nothing else but that there is no longer any solid ground on which the bourgeoisie could leave its trace. It finds itself confronted with its own history-lessness.

The bourgeoisie, Benjamin continues, reacts to this absence of traces by retreating into apartments on whose interior walls made of tapestry, plush, and velvet it can leave clear traces through which it seeks to reassure itself about itself. The state, however, reacts to the tracelessness of modern existence as well. It establishes new kinds of techniques and procedures for "capturing" people: from the installation of house numbers in the streets of the big city via the obligation to carry identification papers to Bertillon's identification procedures that pertain as much to anthropometry as they do to law enforcement.[15]

I cannot insist enough on how relevant this diagnosis is today. What Benjamin outlines is not only a genealogy of the society of control Deleuze had his sights on, which even without house numbers will at every point in time know the exact location of each and every citizen. He also allows us to surmise that the now-dominant use of media refers us to the tracelessness of existence. In concrete terms, it would then, on the one hand, be the protective, screening properties of media that significantly contribute to the use of smartphones, tablet computers, and other media devices precisely because they function as a kind of envelope, armor, or casing. On the other hand, it is just this use that enables the growing control and surveillance of their users. At this point, at the latest, the symmetry of the tactile becomes a dialectic of media use.

The case lining in which today's bourgeoisie is firmly embedded is, of course, no longer made of soft fabric but consists of glass, wired up and lit up from behind, and the case it lines is no longer an opulent apartment but a mobile housing without walls. The status of traces changes accordingly. Benjamin still thought traces on a hylomorphic model. The paradigm for him was the impression the potter's hand leaves on the object she forms.[16] Today, by contrast, the frequency of touching a hard, largely unchanging surface and the repetition of movements in a space divided up into radio cells suffice for us to be identified and addressed.

Borrowing a term from semiotics and recent aesthetics, we might describe this constellation as a multiplication and generalization of *indexical signs*, provided we mean by that, as Charles Sanders Peirce does, signs that emerge from a great proximity or even direct contact between the signified and the signifier.[17] Unlike the traditional fingerprint or the analog photograph, however, the indexical signs produced by today's media devices are symbols from the beginning. What is generated by the proximity of the human body to technics is data that are stored and processed at great distances from this body. Nonetheless, they are indices because they function like continually updated indexes or lists that allow for finding a certain person or a certain thing. They are thus no longer traces in the traditional sense, no longer scattered, permanent impressions in space. The digital traces of the present day are based on a multitude of fleeting impressions in time.

Against this background, we can, by way of conclusion, characterize the tactile agency of mobile and connected media with yet more precision. Insofar as they potentially are "universal archives" (Kentridge), the digital indexes of touch and movement data change the mode of media tactility, as it were. Theirs is not only a punctual scanning and situating of the human body but a downright *suctioning* to it. What long ago Sartre in some memorable pages wrote about the "tactile fascination in the sticky" turns out to be surprisingly relevant in the emerging sensor society: his observations concerning the tactile properties of honey and glue return today via the impalpable space of the digital universal archive.

According to Sartre, the sticky is an entity that can be touched but not grasped; it is "docile" at first but then attaches to the one who touched it: "In one sense it is like the supreme docility of the possessed, the fidelity of a dog who *gives himself* even when one does not want him any longer, and in another sense there is underneath this docility a surreptitious appropriation of the possessor by the possessed."[18]

That almost says it all. The universal archive of touch and movement data endows our media devices with an external stickiness although their surfaces are hard and smooth. This stickiness is all the more insidious for being felt not in space but only in time.

All in all, the work of media art represents an important, perhaps even decisive resource for media theory. This is the third and final result of this study. In fact, the two domains are related much more closely than the current division of disciplines would suggest. As different as their respective analyses, methods, and results may be, both Benjamin and McLuhan refer to a shared foundation shaped by media art. In both cases, the theoretical works of the media art pioneer and former Bauhaus master László Moholy-Nagy and the studies in the history of technology and architecture by Wölfflin's student Sigfried Giedion, also close to the Bauhaus, serve as the basis for engaging with the tactile aspects of photography, film, and television.

Via Moholy and Giedion, the author of the artwork essay, like the author of *Understanding Media*, draws on a context shaped by the discourses of art history on the one hand and an artistic, experimental way of dealing with media on the other. On the one hand, Benjamin and McLuhan are thus able to pick up on discussions by Heinrich Wölfflin and Alois Riegl, Bernard Berenson and Adolf von Hildebrand that starting in the late nineteenth century helped the sense of touch to gain prominence in reflections on art. On the other hand, the two media theorists refer to the tactile exercises and study of materials that in the Bauhaus context led to innovative work with light projections, textiles, and photograms. Indeed, in both Benjamin and McLuhan, Moholy's explanations of these experimental practices in particular lead to a new way of looking at media phenomena and processes.

Given the great resonance of the artwork essay and of *Understanding Media*, this means that an experimental way of dealing with media is an important foundation in the establishment of the discourse we now call media theory. Benjamin's interest in the tactile connection between typography, photography, cinematics, and architecture has its source here just as much as McLuhan's interest in TV's pointillist light architectures does. We might perhaps even go so far as to situate Vilém Flusser's observation on the "surface of images" that are to be scanned in photography and his discussions of "computation's universe of points" in this context. Even the remarkable reflections Deleuze and Guattari have devoted to the relationship between the haptic and the optical under the title "The Smooth and the Striated" go back—via McLuhan—to this context (Riegl, Worringer, Kandinsky, and so on).[19]

It has been important to me to conceptualize this connection of media theory and media art not simply as a discursive link to express that both address similar, often identical, contents. Guided by recent work in the history of science, my goal instead has been, as much as possible, to observe media theorists and media artists *in action*. Artists are not presented here as lonely geniuses, alone with their imagination, sitting in front of the white canvas, just as media theorists are not presented as equally lonely geniuses deriving their original ideas primarily from observing unusual objects (televisions, computers, sensors, etc.). As the examples of Dalí and McLuhan in particular show, we are dealing on both sides with practices that are indeed comparable, that move along a continuum between writing, image, and technology.

In McLuhan, it is above all artistically arranged photographs that get his engagement with the texture of the TV image started and that time and again intervene in the structure of his arguments, whereas Dalí is working largely with scientific books whose illustrations he draws over, copies, and cuts out to turn them into paintings and films. In both cases, these passages through different materials and different semiotics also extend into appearances and performances that in turn make use of media like photography and television. It is in that sense, too, that I have spoken here of the counterside of media. This does not alter the fact that McLuhan became known as a media theorist whereas Dalí became famous as a media artist. But it does show how close and productive the connection is that exists between theoretical and artistic discourses about media. We may assume that this connection will continue to be fruitful in engaging those phenomena and processes that, with Deleuze and Guattari, we can think of as "striations" in our society's smoothed-out tactile spaces.

NOTES

PREFACE

1 Schmidgen, *Das Unbewußte der Maschinen* and *Hirn und Zeit.*

2 Pirsig, *Zen and the Art of Motorcycle Maintenance*, 106.

INTRODUCTION

Epigraphs: Flusser, *Lob der Oberflächlichkeit*, 18; Francis Bacon quoted in Sylvester, *The Brutality of Fact*, 32; Pynchon, *The Crying of Lot 49*, 121.

1 Deleuze, "Postscript on Control Societies," 181.

2 Scoble and Israel, *Age of Context.*

3 Flusser, *Lob der Oberflächlichkeit*, 59. At this point, my reflections converge with those of Jacques Derrida, who writes about the tactility of the computer: "A description is needed of the surfaces, the volumes, and the limits of this new magic writing pad, which exscription touches in another way, with another kind of 'exactitude' or 'punctuality,' precisely, from the keyboard to the memory of a disk said to be 'hard'" (Derrida, *On Touching*, 300). For a media studies perspective, see Lechtermann and Rieger, *Das Wissen der Oberfläche*; for an account from the perspective of historical epistemology, see Dagognet, *Faces, surfaces, interfaces.*

4 Winkler, *Switching, Zapping*; Bardini, *Bootstrapping*; Benthien, *Haut*, 265–79; as well as Paterson, *The Senses of Touch.*

5 Parks, "Points of Departure"; Parisi, "Fingerbombing"; Hayles, "RFID"; and Andrejevic and Burdon, "Defining the Sensor Society." German contributions include, for example, Sprenger and Engemann, *Internet der Dinge.*

6 Plotnick, *Power Button.*

7 Parisi, *Archaeologies of Touch.*

8 Latour, *We Have Never Been Modern.*

9 Kittler, *Gramophone, Film, Typewriter*, xxxix.

10 Benjamin, "On Some Motifs in Baudelaire," 328, modified. See the detailed exposition in Bolz, *Theorie der neuen Medien*, 67–110.

11 McLuhan, *Understanding Media*, 17, 106–18.

12 Benjamin, "The Work of Art in the Age of Its Technological Reproducibility [First Version]," 23. [The term *Stoßdämpfer*, "shock absorber," appears in a passage crossed out by Benjamin and thus not considered in Jennings's translation; see "Das Kunstwerk im Zeitalter seiner technischen Reproduzierbarkeit–Erste Fassung." The first, second, and third version of the essay have been published in English (see references in the bibliography); the fifth version has not.—*Trans.*]

13 McLuhan, *Understanding Media*, 313.
14 [Unlike the more visual English verb *to scan*, the German *abtasten* is primarily tactile. See also below, chapter 4.—*Trans.*]
15 Hildebrand, *The Problem of Form*, 44, 56–58; Kandinsky, *On the Spiritual in Art*, 43; Marinetti, "Tactilism," 198.
16 In this regard, compare Siegfried Zielinski, *Deep Time of the Media*, 1–11, 61. In his excellent study "Taktile Medien," which unfortunately I discovered too late to include in these reflections, Klemens Gruber refers specifically to Benjamin and McLuhan.
17 On all these aspects, see Dagognet, *La peau découverte*.
18 On the history of the horn as instrument, see, for example, Janetzky and Brüchle, *Das Horn*.
19 See Curtis's discussion of "Technology as the Extension of Man" in the work of Kapp, Bergson, and McLuhan (Curtis, *Culture as Polyphony*, 61–79).
20 Flusser, "Von den Möglichkeiten einer Leibkarte"; Flusser, "Skin."
21 Flusser, *Lob der Oberflächlichkeit*, 19.
22 For an overview, see the contributions in the special issue of *Theory, Culture and Society*, "Cultural Techniques," edited by Geoffrey Winthrop-Young, Ilinca Iurascu, and Jussi Parikka.
23 Thacker, *Biomedia*; Mitchell, *Bioart and the Vitality of Media*. Even these studies, however, can claim Flusser to be on their side. As Flusser has shown in his remarkable work on the vampire squid, it is not precisely anthropology but biology that can tell us about the media capacities of a body: "Reality is neither the organism, nor the environment, neither the subject nor the object, neither the ego nor the nonego, but rather the concurrence of both." Ultimately, this is the background that allows us to understand the claim that the characteristic gesture of the present day is the striking of a key. See Flusser and Bec, *Vampyroteuthis infernalis*, 36.
24 Hanson, *Feathers*.
25 Barad, *Meeting the Universe Halfway*, 172.
26 Hayles, "RFID," 48.
27 Serres, *La naissance de la physique*, 134. For an exemplary art historical perspective on embodiment, see Krois, *Bildkörper und Körperschema*.

ONE. THE CAPTURED UNICORN

1 Lucretius, *On the Nature of Things*, 280–81, modified.
2 Roussel, *Locus Solus*, 183. On the gramophonic "groove script," see Moholy-Nagy, "New Forms in Music."
3 Roussel, *Locus Solus*, 189.
4 "I would also like, in these notes, to pay homage to that man of incommensurable genius, namely Jules Verne. My admiration for him is boundless" (Roussel, "How I Wrote Certain of My Books," 19).

5 Roussel, *Locus Solus*, 199.
6 Roussel, *Locus Solus*, 194.
7 Deleuze, "Raymond Roussel, or the Abhorrent Vacuum," 73.
8 See, for example, Horn, "Die Bastille-Interviews I," 29. For unknown reasons, the name of Raymond Roussel was omitted in the English version of this text; see Horn, "The Bastille Interviews I," 21.
9 Marcel Duchamp to Jean Suquet, December 25, 1949, in Duchamp, *Affectionately, Marcel*, 282–84; Ernst, *Écritures*, 51–52; and Ruffa, "Roussel as Read by Dalí." On Dalí, see the detailed discussion in chapter 3.
10 See Horn, "The Bastille Interviews II," 26.
11 Tacke, *Rebecca Horn*.
12 Roussel, *Impressions of Africa*, 36.
13 Roussel, *Impressions of Africa*, 17, 140–42 and 210, 156–59.
14 Universal, the motion picture company, contacted Roussel in the early 1920s to produce a film version of *Impressions of Africa*. It seems that Roussel turned to the filmmaker Alexandre Devarennes with this project in mind. See Piron, "Conversation with John Ashbery," 267.
15 Zweite, "Rebecca Horn's Bodylandscapes," 34.
16 Roussel, *Impressions of Africa*, 372. On the significance of the autobiographical aspects in Rebecca Horn's work, see also Tacke, *Rebecca Horn*, 20–21 and 75–76.
17 See, for example, Engelbach, *Zwischen Body Art und Videokunst*.
18 Bruno, "Innenansichten."
19 Gell, "Vogel's Net" (Gell erroneously refers to "Judith Horn"). On traps and machines, see also Horwitz, "Über die Konstruktion von Fallen und Selbstschüssen"; Mauss, *Manual of Ethnography*, 29 and 45–47; and Blumenberg, *Theorie der Unbegrifflichkeit*, 13–14. On digital media as traps, see Schirrmacher, *Ego*, x–xi.
20 Roussel, *Locus Solus*, 54.
21 Roussel, *Locus Solus*, 54–56, modified.
22 Roussel, *Locus Solus*, 226 and 222. Michel Carrouges was one of the first to insist on the importance of this reprise; see *Les machines célibataires*, 72. See also Tresch, "In a Solitary Place," here 314.
23 Roussel, *Locus Solus*, 215.
24 Roussel, *Locus Solus*, 221 and 227.
25 Bergson, *Matter and Memory*, 19.
26 Bergson, *Matter and Memory*, 196.
27 Bergson, *Matter and Memory*, 196–97.
28 Roussel, *Locus Solus*, 114.
29 Roussel, *Locus Solus*, 53 and 105.
30 Compare Engelbach, *Zwischen Body Art und Videokunst*, esp. 135–40, which explores the significance of the sense of touch in Rebecca Horn's oeuvre.
31 Brock, "Wiederholte Anmerkungen zu Körperplastik und Körperbemalung."
32 Berufsverband Bildender Künstler e.V., "Rebecca Horn."
33 Grosse, *Die Anfänge der Kunst*, 58.
34 Sydow, *Primitive Kunst und Psychoanalyse*, 174.

35 Stephan, *Südseekunst*, 121.

36 Thus Herbert Spencer, for example, writes that "the great diversity of tactual and manipulatory powers possessed by the elephant's proboscis, is not less remarkable than is the creature's high sagacity—a sagacity which, dwelling in so ungainly a body, would otherwise be altogether inexplicable" (*The Principles of Psychology*, 456).

37 Horn and Herzogenrath, *Rebecca Horn*, 34 and 41.

38 McLuhan, *Understanding Media*. See the detailed discussion in chapter 4.

39 Bernard, *An Introduction to the Study*, 5.

40 Horn and Herzogenrath, *Rebecca Horn*, 93, modified.

41 Bernard, *An Introduction to the Study*, 5–6.

42 Horn and Herzogenrath, *Rebecca Horn*, 41, 93, modified.

43 Horn and Herzogenrath, *Rebecca Horn*, 37, modified.

44 Bernard, *An Introduction to the Study*, 21.

45 See Henderson, "Raymond Roussel's *Impressions d'Afrique*."

46 Roussel, *Locus Solus*, 226.

47 Roussel, *Locus Solus*, 209–10 and 137.

48 Roussel, *Locus Solus*, 171.

49 Roussel, *Locus Solus*, 152, 48 and 60–61.

50 Roussel, *Locus Solus*, 214–15.

51 On the notion of "intra-activity," see Barad, *Meeting the Universe Halfway*, 151–52.

52 See Pickering, *Kybernetik und Neue Ontologien*; Pickering, *The Cybernetic Brain*.

53 See Laing, *The Politics of Experience*, 120–37; and Barnes, in Barnes and Berke, *Two Accounts of a Journey through Madness*. For criticism of Laing and Barnes, see Guattari, "The Divided Laing."

54 Documenta 5, "Rebecca Horn," 109.

55 Laing, Phillipson, and Lee, *Interpersonal Perception*, 4.

56 Horn and Herzogenrath, *Rebecca Horn*, 24.

57 Haraway, "A Manifesto for Cyborgs."

58 Rilke, *The Notebooks of Malte Laurids Brigge*, 74–76. See generally Kamper, *Das gefangene Einhorn*, to which the title of this chapter alludes for good reason. On unicorns generally, see Lavers, *The Natural History of Unicorns*.

59 Horn and Herzogenrath, *Rebecca Horn*, 32, modified. Compare, for example, Moholy-Nagy: "Art attempts to establish far-reaching *new relationships* between the known and the as yet unknown optical, acoustical, and other functional phenomena so that these are absorbed *in increasing abundance* [*in bereichernder Steigerung*] by the functional apparatus" (*Painting, Photography, Film*, 30, first emphasis Moholy-Nagy's, second mine).

60 Horn and Herzogenrath, *Rebecca Horn*, 32, modified.

61 Horn and Herzogenrath, *Rebecca Horn*, 29.

62 Horn and Herzogenrath, *Rebecca Horn*, 41.

63 Documenta 5, "Rebecca Horn," 109.

64 Horn and Herzogenrath, *Rebecca Horn*, 24.

65 Bateson, *Perceval's Narrative*, xiv. On this point, see Pickering, *The Cybernetic Brain*, 178. See also Laing, *The Politics of Experience*, 97–98.
66 Laing, *The Politics of Experience*, 20.
67 Laing, *The Politics of Experience*, 18.
68 Laing, *The Politics of Experience*, 18.
69 Heider, *Ding und Medium*. On the way this text is discussed in media studies, see Brauns, *Form und Medium*.
70 Heider, *The Psychology of Interpersonal Relations*, 21.
71 Heider, *The Psychology of Interpersonal Relations*, 23–24.
72 Heider, *The Psychology of Interpersonal Relations*, 24. It is in this sense that Heider distinguishes between "proximal" and "distal stimuli."
73 To take up the title of Heinz von Förster's essay, "Wahrnehmen wahrnehmen."
74 Pickering, *The Cybernetic Brain*, 171–211, quote 211.
75 Horn and Herzogenrath, *Rebecca Horn*, 25.
76 Horn and Herzogenrath, *Rebecca Horn*, 25.
77 Horn and Herzogenrath, *Rebecca Horn*, 25.
78 Horn and Herzogenrath, *Rebecca Horn*, 26–27, modified.
79 Horn and Herzogenrath, *Rebecca Horn*, 26–27.
80 Horn and Herzogenrath, *Rebecca Horn*, 26–27.
81 See, for example, the exhibition catalog *Misura d'uomo* edited by Giulio Barsanti.
82 Laing, *The Politics of Experience*, 53.
83 Horn and Herzogenrath, *Rebecca Horn*, 99.
84 Horn, "The Bastille Interviews I," 16.
85 Moholy-Nagy, *The New Vision*, 1947 ed., 16, modified.
86 Foucault, *Death and the Labyrinth*, 59.
87 Horn, *Buster's Bedroom*, 75.

TWO. IMPRESSIONS OF MODERNITY

1 Moholy-Nagy, *Painting, Photography, Film*, 38.
2 "For three lonely September weeks in 1913 [in fact, 1912—H.S.] I stood every day in the church in front of the statue, studied it, measured it, sketched it, until I captured the understanding for it which I ventured to express in the essay only anonymously." Quoted in Jones, *The Life and Work of Sigmund Freud*, 2:411.
3 For the details, see Jones, *The Life and Work of Sigmund Freud*, 2:407–11; as well as Ilse Grubrich-Simitis's fundamental study, *Michelangelos Moses*.
4 Grubrich-Simitis, *Michelangelos Moses*, 51; as well as Bredekamp, "Michelangelos Moses als Gedankenfilm"; and Vogl, *On Tarrying*.
5 Ginzburg, "Morelli, Freud and Sherlock Holmes."
6 See Jones, *The Life and Work of Sigmund Freud*, 2:407–11; as well as Grubrich-Simitis, *Michelangelos Moses*, 13–23.
7 Freud, *The Moses of Michelangelo*, 213 and 215.

8 Thus, for example, the New Revised Standard Version.

9 Reik, *Probleme der Religionspsychologie: I*, 261. See Grubrich-Simitis, *Michelangelos Moses*, 61; and, moreover, Mellinkoff, *The Horned Moses*, 76–93; Dohmen, *Mose*, 190–208; and Römer, *The Horns of Moses.*

10 Mellinkoff, *The Horned Moses*, 61–75.

11 See Kiening and Beil, *Urszenen des Medialen*, 19–36.

12 See also Hörisch, *Eine Geschichte der Medien*, 51–53.

13 Freud thus agrees with the art historian Henry Thode that the overall conception of the memorial for Julius II aimed at representing "types of human beings" and therefore "excluded a representation of a particular historic episode." See Freud, *The Moses of Michelangelo*, 219–21.

14 Benjamin, "Das Kunstwerk im Zeitalter seiner technischen Reproduzierbarkeit [Fünfte Fassung]" (hereafter "Kunstwerk 5"), 211.

15 Jones, *The Life and Work of Sigmund Freud*, 2:409; as well as Freud and Jones, *The Complete Correspondence*, 183–87. Jones had initiated his discussion with Freud about Michelangelo's sculpture in a letter from October 30, 1912 (165). On the history of plaster casts generally, see Frederiksen and Marchand, *Plaster Casts*. On the plaster cast collections in Vienna, see Weber-Unger, *Gipsmodell und Fotografie*; and Domanig, "Was wurde aus Hansens Glyptothek?"

16 Benjamin, "Kunstwerk 5," 216; and Benjamin, "Little History of Photography," 523.

17 Hildebrand, *The Problem of Form*, 23–24.

18 Freud, *The Moses of Michelangelo*, 211–12 and 220, modified.

19 Simmel, "The Metropolis and Mental Life," 421.

20 See Freud, *The Moses of Michelangelo*, 212 and 215.

21 Freud, *The Moses of Michelangelo*, 218 and 223.

22 Freud, *The Moses of Michelangelo*, 222–23.

23 The reproduction of a photograph of Michelangelo's statue in the essay's first publication bears the caption: "By permission from Robert Langewiesche publishers from the volume 'Michelangelo' in the collection 'Blue Books'" (Freud, "Der Moses des Michelangelo," between pages 16 and 17). The reference is to Sauerlandt, *Michelangelo*, 12.

24 Freud, *The Moses of Michelangelo*, 223.

25 Freud, *The Moses of Michelangelo*, 222–25, modified.

26 Freud, *The Moses of Michelangelo*, 224 and 235, modified. [The term *Wegspur* is Freud's translation of Watkiss Lloyd's *wake.—Trans.*] On this point and more generally, see Weigel, *Literatur als Voraussetzung*, 15–38.

27 Freud, *The Interpretation of Dreams*, 136–45. "My friend R. was my uncle" discusses facial hair's "unpleasing change of colour" from black to gray, which he had also "noticed with dissatisfaction" on himself (138–39).

28 On the semiology and epistemology of the imprint, see Ginzburg, "Morelli, Freud and Sherlock Holmes"; as well as Didi-Huberman, *La ressemblance par contact*. As regards psychoanalysis, see Derrida, "Freud and the Scene of Writing."

29 Freud, *The Moses of Michelangelo*, 222, modified.

30 Jones to Freud, December 23, 1912, *The Complete Correspondence*, 184.

31 Freud, *The Moses of Michelangelo*, 228.
32 Freud, *The Moses of Michelangelo*, 229–30.
33 Freud, *The Moses of Michelangelo*, 221.
34 Freud, *The Moses of Michelangelo*, 233, modified.
35 Freud, *The Moses of Michelangelo*, 233.
36 Freud, *The Moses of Michelangelo*, 233; see also Derrida, "Freud and the Scene of Writing," 265.
37 In the letters, Freud does not shrink from comparing himself directly to Moses; see Grubrich-Simitis, *Michelangelos Moses*, 16–17.
38 Freud, *The Moses of Michelangelo*, 226, emphasis added.
39 Freud, *The Moses of Michelangelo*, 226n1.
40 The plaster cast in the Vienna Academy (shelf mark GM-RE-5) was commissioned in the 1860s from the Vanni workshops in Frankfurt. On the Vannis, see Stutzinger, "Das Geschäft mit der Antike."
41 Jones to Freud, December 23, 1912, *The Complete Correspondence*, 184.
42 Freud to Jones, December 26, 1912, *The Complete Correspondence*, 186; and Freud, *The Moses of Michelangelo*, 228.
43 Grubrich-Simitis, *Michelangelos Moses*, 29–34; as well as Satzinger, "Michelangelos Grabmal Julius' II."
44 See Sauerlandt, *Michelangelo*, 13. It remains unclear why Freud did not include a reproduction of this photograph or of a section of it in the published version of his essay from the beginning. Only the *Standard Edition* and others following it have reproductions of photographs in which the horn on the tablets is visible accompanying the text.
45 Freud, *The Moses of Michelangelo*, 221 and 226, modified, emphasis added.
46 Freud, *The Moses of Michelangelo*, 213.
47 It includes 850 titles; see Benjamin, *Das Passagen-Werk*, 1277–323. The English translation, *The Arcades Project*, does not include a separate bibliography. On "Paris, Capital of the Nineteenth Century," see Benjamin, *The Arcades Project*, 3–13.
48 Péguy, "Un nouveau théologien M. Fernand Laudet." On Benjamin and Péguy, see Tiedemann-Bartels, *Verwaltete Tradition*.
49 Benjamin, *The Arcades Project*, fragment N4,2, 464.
50 Marx, "Economic and Philosophical Manuscripts," 354. Written in 1844, the "Manuscripts" were first published in 1932.
51 Benjamin, *One-Way Street*, 456.
52 Benjamin, "Kunstwerk 5," 209–10.
53 Hellpach, *Nervosität und Kultur*, 33.
54 Benjamin, "On Some Motifs in Baudelaire," 328; Benjamin, "The Work of Art in the Age of Its Technological Reproducibility [First Version]," 32, translations modified; and Benjamin, "Kunstwerk 5," 243.
55 See, for example, Gombrich, *Art and Illusion*, 15–20; as well as Krois, *Bildkörper und Körperschema*, 210–31.
56 On Moholy and Benjamin, see Herbert Molderings, "Fotogeschichte"; and Markus, "Walter Benjamin and the German 'Reproduction Debate.'" On Giedion

and Benjamin, see Brüggemann, "Walter Benjamin und Sigfried Giedion." On Benjamin's links with the aesthetics of constructivism generally, see Schöttker, *Konstruktiver Fragmentarismus*, esp. 148–72.

57 Benjamin, "Little History of Photography," 523 and 527. The first quote comes from Moholy-Nagy's *Painting, Photography, Film*, 27; the second, from his "fotografie ist lichtgestaltung," 5. On the *Film und Foto* exhibition in Stuttgart in 1929, see Moholy-Nagy, "Die wichtigsten Epochen."

58 Moholy-Nagy, *Painting, Photography, Film*, 25.

59 Moholy-Nagy and Giedion met at the Bauhaus exhibition in Weimar in 1923 and maintained a collegial friendship until Moholy's early death in 1947. On the biographical background, see Moholy-Nagy, *Laszlo Moholy-Nagy*; Georgiadis, *Sigfried Giedion*; and Bruderer-Oswald, *Das neue Sehen*. On Giedion and Moholy specifically, see Haus, "Durchspültsein von Luft"; and Lugon, "Le vieux pont."

60 Giedion, *Building in France*, 169; and Benjamin, "Kunstwerk 5," 215.

61 Benjamin, "Kunstwerk 5," 215.

62 Benjamin, "Das Kunstwerk im Zeitalter seiner technischen Reproduzierbarkeit–Zweite Fassung," 89. As in Riegl, "tactical" is to be understood as "tactile." [The sentence is not included in "The Work of Art in the Age of Its Technological Reproducibility: Second Version," where it would find its place in the last paragraph of section XVIII on page 120. On the term "tactical," see also William Jennings's note in his translation of the first version, 37n6.—*Trans.*]

63 Benjamin, *One-Way Street*, 476.

64 Benjamin, "Kunstwerk 5," 245; Benjamin, "The Paris of the Second Empire," 30, modified.

65 Benjamin, "On Some Motifs in Baudelaire," 320; see also 343: "Of all the experiences which made his life what it was, Baudelaire singled out being jostled by the crowd as the decisive, unmistakable experience." On shock as impact, see also Schivelbusch, *The Railway Journey*, 150–58.

66 Benjamin, "On Some Motifs in Baudelaire," 329.

67 Strindberg, *Inferno*, 161.

68 Russolo, "The Art of Noises," 208.

69 Marinetti, "Tactilism."

70 Moholy-Nagy, *The New Vision*, 24.

71 Benjamin, "On Some Motifs in Baudelaire," 328; Benjamin, "Kunstwerk 5," 236 and 213.

72 Benjamin, "The Work of Art in the Age of Its Technological Reproducibility: Second Version," 103. On the "domestic pinacotheca," see Moholy-Nagy, *Painting, Photography, Film*, 25–26.

73 Marx, *Capital*, 63 and 61; Marx, "Economic and Philosophical Manuscripts," 377, modified.

74 Benjamin, "Kunstwerk 5," 228–29n1.

75 Benjamin, "Kunstwerk 5," 213.

76 Benjamin, "Kunstwerk 5," 236 and 246.

77 Benjamin, "Kunstwerk 5," 226n1.

78 Benjamin, "The Work of Art in the Age of Its Technological Reproducibility: Second Version," 104–5; Benjamin, "On Some Motifs in Baudelaire," 337; Benjamin, "Little History of Photography," 512.
79 Lacan, "The Mirror Stage as Formative"; Lacan, *The Four Fundamental Concepts*, 95–96.
80 Benjamin, "On Some Motifs in Baudelaire," 338.
81 Benjamin, "On Some Motifs in Baudelaire," 338.
82 Benjamin, "The Paris of the Second Empire," 32.
83 Baudelaire, "Perte de l'Auréole."
84 Benjamin, "Hashish," 327.
85 Benjamin, "On Some Motifs in Baudelaire," 342; Benjamin, "Letter to Max Horkheimer," 1074; Benjamin, *The Arcades Project*, 7, modified; Benjamin, "Little History of Photography," 517, modified; Benjamin, "Kunstwerk 5," 215; and Benjamin, "Hashish," 328.
86 Benjamin, "Hashish," 327–28.
87 Benjamin, "On Some Motifs in Baudelaire," 354n77; Benjamin, "Translation," 249.
88 Fränkel, "Protokoll," 609 and 614; and Warburg, *Sandro Botticellis "Geburt der Venus,"* 54. See on this point Weigel, *Literatur als Voraussetzung*, 15–38; and Mainberger, "Tragödie der Verleibung."
89 Benjamin, "Hashish," 28.
90 Benjamin, "Hashish," 328.
91 Benjamin, "The Paris of the Second Empire," 26.
92 Benjamin, "Kunstwerk 5," 246; Benjamin, *The Arcades Project*, fragment 14,4, 220.
93 Giedion, *Building in France*, 98.
94 Benjamin, "The Paris of the Second Empire," 26.
95 Benjamin, "The Destructive Character," 542.
96 Giedion, *Mechanization Takes Command*, 366.
97 Benjamin, "The Paris of the Second Empire," 25–26.
98 Benjamin, "The Paris of the Second Empire," 26.
99 Benjamin, "The Paris of the Second Empire," 27.
100 Freud, *Beyond the Pleasure Principle*, 26.
101 Benjamin, "On Some Motifs in Baudelaire," 318.
102 Benjamin, "On Some Motifs in Baudelaire," 318.
103 Benjamin, "On Some Motifs in Baudelaire," 317; compare Freud, *Beyond the Pleasure Principle*, 27.
104 Benjamin, "On Some Motifs in Baudelaire," 317 and 318.
105 Freud, *Beyond the Pleasure Principle*, 27 and 28.
106 Freud, "Negation," 237.
107 Freud, *Beyond the Pleasure Principle*, 26.
108 Freud, "On Narcissism," 75.
109 Haeckel, *Das Protistenreich*, 69. For a detailed discussion, see Schmidgen and Schloegel, "Allgemeine Physiologie."
110 Freud, "Negation," 237; Freud, *Beyond the Pleasure Principle*, 27.
111 Freud, *Beyond the Pleasure Principle*, 27, emphasis added.

112 Freud, *Beyond the Pleasure Principle*, 27.
113 Benjamin, "On Some Motifs in Baudelaire," 319–21.
114 Freud, *Beyond the Pleasure Principle*, 26.
115 Freud, "A Note upon the 'Mystic Writing-Pad,'" 231.
116 Freud, "Negation," 238.
117 Benjamin, "The Paris of the Second Empire," 26.
118 Reik, *Probleme der Religionspsychologie*, 264.
119 Bonaparte, *Über die Symbolik der Kopftrophäen*, 17.
120 Leclaire, "The Dream with the Unicorn."

THREE. RHINOCEROS CYBERNETICS

1 Popitz, *Epochen der Technikgeschichte*, 15–16.
2 Descharnes, *The World of Salvador Dali*, 22–23.
3 In the first third of the TV movie he made with José Montes-Baquer, *Impressions de la Haute Mongolie—Hommage à Raymond Roussel* (1975), Dalí poses next to the Moses statue in his theater museum while the camera moves in ever closer on the statue's fingers grasping the beard.
4 In 1974, Dalí designed prints and the cover for an English edition of Freud's *Moses and Monotheism*. The cover takes up Michelangelo's depiction. See Descharnes and Descharnes, *Dalí*, 225.
5 On Halsman, see Halsman Bello and Bello, *Philippe Halsman*. On the collaboration between Dalí and Halsman, see Feldhaus, *Salvador Dalí und Philippe Halsman*.
6 See King, "Winged Fantasy." King, in this context, highlights the important mediating role of the Catalan philosopher and author Francesc Pujols.
7 Descharnes, *The World of Salvador Dali*, 6.
8 Dalí, "Concerning the Terrifying and Edible Beauty," 200.
9 "Third Eye for Space Explorers"; see also "TV Monocle Gives Extra Eye to Wearer," which discusses other applications, for example in surgery.
10 Descharnes and Néret, *Salvador Dalí*, 547.
11 Descharnes and Néret, *Salvador Dalí*, 557.
12 Bosquet, *Conversations with Dali*, 34 and 100.
13 Dalí, "Anti-matter Manifesto," 366; and Sainsbury, "Chaos and Creation." So far, Dalí's relationship to the sciences has been studied with regard to modern physics: see Weyers, *Salvador Dalís Auseinandersetzung*; Ruffa, Kaenel, and Chaperon, *Salvador Dalí à la croisée*; Taylor, "The Dalí Renaissance"; Taylor, "On the Road"; Parkinson, "How Dalí Learned"; Parkinson, *Surrealism, Art and Modern Science*, 201–17.
14 King, "Rhinoceros Horn"; and Descharnes, *The World of Salvador Dali*, 52.
15 Gibson, *The Shameful Life*, 479; King, "The Prodigious Story"; King, "Crazy Movies That Disappear."
16 Dalí, "Poetry of the Mass-Produced Utility," 57; Dalí, "Saint Sebastian," 21.
17 Dalí, "For the Sitges 'Meeting,'" 66, modified; Dalí, "The Water in Which We Swim," 263; see also Dalí, *Dalí on Modern Art*, 29.

18 On the connections between Bachelard and surrealism, see Parkinson, *Surrealism, Art and Modern Science*, 89–116.
19 Monod-Herzen, *Science et esthétique*; Dalí, "Notes pour l'interprétation," 174; Dalí, "Les idées lumineuses"; Dalí, "The Spectral Surrealism," 312. On the surrealists' appropriation of Monod-Herzen, see Parkinson, *Surrealism, Art and Modern Science*, 86–87. On the history of the science of synthetic biology and biological morphology, see Fox Keller, *Making Sense of Life*.
20 The book was first published in Haakon M. Chevalier's English translation in New York in 1948; the French original version, *50 secrets magiques*, was not published until 1974.
21 On Roussel and Dalí, see Ruffa, "Roussel as Read by Dalí."
22 Bosquet, *Conversations with Dalí*, 23.
23 See Lomas, "'Painting Is Dead,'" esp. 165–69; as well as King, "Crazy Movies That Disappear," 220–22.
24 Dalí, "Mystical Manifesto," 364.
25 Dalí, "Aspects phénoménologiques," 332.
26 Dalí, "Aspects phénoménologiques," 333.
27 Dalí, "Aspects phénoménologiques," 333–34.
28 Dalí, "Aspects phénoménologiques," 334.
29 Dalí, "New General Considerations," 260, Dalí's emphasis.
30 Dalí, "Aspects phénoménologiques," 334.
31 Bosquet, *Conversations with Dalí*, 23.
32 Dalí, "Aspects phénoménologiques," 337.
33 Dalí, "Aspects phénoménologiques," 334–35.
34 Barthes, *Camera Lucida*, 26.
35 Dalí, "Aspects phénoménologiques," 335.
36 Lautréamont, *Les Chants de Maldoror*, canto VI.
37 Dalí, "Aspects phénoménologiques," 334.
38 Dalí, "Aspects phénoménologiques," 335.
39 Dalí, "Aspects phénoménologiques," 336.
40 Dalí, "Aspects phénoménologiques," 336 and 337.
41 Dalí, "Aspects phénoménologiques," 337.
42 Taylor, "Paranoiac-Critical Study," 376.
43 "Dali marie pour se libérer une dentellière et un rhinocéros."
44 Dalí, "Aspects phénoménologiques," 340; and Weart, *Nuclear Fear*, 402.
45 Dalí, "Aspects phénoménologiques," 341.
46 Dalí, "Aspects phénoménologiques," 342.
47 Lacan, *The Psychoses*, 72.
48 Lacan, *Freud's Papers on Technique*, 178.
49 Deleuze and Guattari, *A Thousand Plateaus*, 27, Deleuze and Guattari's emphasis.
50 Tapié, "Extrait de *Dalí*," 363; as well as Descharnes and Descharnes, *Dalí*, 64.
51 Dalí, *Diary*, 37.
52 See Descharnes and Descharnes, *Dalí*, 68–69.
53 Dalí, *Dalí on Modern Art*, 89.

54 King, "Crazy Movies That Disappear," 222.
55 Bosquet, *Conversations with Dalí*, 59 and 58.
56 Dalí, *Diary*, 37–38.
57 Ghyka, *Esthétique*.
58 Ghyka, *The World Mine Oyster*, 322.
59 Ghyka, *Esthétique*, 165–219; and Ghyka, *The Geometry of Art and Life*, 87–110. On the "spiralomania" of Cook, Thompson, similar British authors (Henry Moseley, Arthur Church), and some contemporary artists, see Kemp, *Structural Intuitions*, 79–97.
60 Ghyka, *The World Mine Oyster*, 303.
61 Ghyka, *The World Mine Oyster*, 303.
62 Ghyka, *The World Mine Oyster*, 302.
63 See Dalí's copy of Ghyka, *The Geometry of Art and Life*, Centre d'Estudis Dalinians, Figueres, Fons documental, Biblioteca, no. 16074.
64 Ferrier, *Dali*.
65 Ghyka, *The Geometry of Art and Life*, 91 and 93.
66 Dalí, *50 Secrets*, 181.
67 Ghyka, *The Geometry of Art and Life*, 152 and 149. On Dalí and Leonardo da Vinci, see Lomas, "'Painting Is Dead.'"
68 Ghyka, letters to Salvador Dalí of August 13, 1947, and January 23, 1948, Centre d'Estudis Dalinians, Figueres, Fons documental, Correspondència, nos. 39748 and 41809.
69 Lomas, "'Painting Is Dead,'" 177.
70 Dalí, *50 Secrets*, 178 and 84.
71 Ghyka, *The Geometry of Art and Life*, 33 and 96; Dalí, *50 Secrets*, 77, 175, 179, and 180.
72 Ghyka, *The Geometry of Art and Life*, xi, note 2.
73 Dalí, *50 Secrets*, 185–88; and Thompson, *On Growth and Form*, 389.
74 Thompson, *On Growth and Form*, 945.
75 Thompson, *On Growth and Form*, 387.
76 See Dalí, *50 Secrets*, 98; and Thompson, *On Growth and Form*, 387. On the scientific context of Thompson's work, see Esposito, "Problematic 'Idiosyncrasies.'"
77 Dalí, *50 Secrets*, 181.
78 Wood, *Animate Creation*, 545.
79 Dalí, *50 Secrets*, secret 46 and 43.
80 Canguilhem, "Réflexions sur la création artistique," 179.
81 Thompson, *On Growth and Form*, 874.
82 Whyte, *Aspects of Form*. The volume's bibliography also includes books by Focillon, Ghyka, and Hambidge (247–48).
83 Dalí, "Ecumenical 'chafarrinada' of Velasquez," 30.
84 Dalí, *50 Secrets*, 156.
85 Descharnes and Néret, *Salvador Dalí*, 547.
86 Dalí, *50 Secrets*, 64.
87 See the volume by Descharnes and Prévost, *Gaudi*, which includes, besides a preface by Dalí (9–12), a text by Francesc Pujols, "Gaudi's Artistic and Religious Vision" (220–45).

88 Moholy-Nagy, *The New Vision*, 1947 ed., 25, modified; and Flusser, *Towards a Philosophy of Photography*, 8. See the detailed discussion in chapter 4.
89 Dalí, ". . . The Liberation of the Fingers . . ."
90 Efron, "He Prefers to Watch TV Upside Down," 8.
91 Bosquet, *Conversations with Dalí*, 99.
92 Bosquet, *Conversations with Dalí*, 100, modified.
93 Bosquet, *Conversations with Dalí*, 24.
94 Bosquet, *Conversations with Dalí*, 101, 99, and 34.

FOUR. A SURFACE MEDIUM PAR EXCELLENCE

1 Kittler, *Discourse Networks*, 224.
2 McLuhan, *Understanding Media*, 265; McLuhan, *Gutenberg Galaxy*, 45–46.
3 Nipkow, "Elektrisches Teleskop," 1, emphasis added. On Nipkow and the early history of television, see Zielinski, *Audiovisions*.
4 Marshall McLuhan, letter to Sheila Watson, June 12, 1968, in McLuhan, *Letters*, 353.
5 Marshall McLuhan, letter to Pierre Elliott Trudeau, June 12, 1968, in McLuhan, *Letters*, 354.
6 McLuhan, foreword, xiv. See also Peter Bexte's commentary, "Cadillac und Gebetsmatte."
7 McLuhan, *Understanding Me*, 280.
8 McLuhan, *Understanding Media*, 112; McLuhan, "A Note on Tactility."
9 McLuhan, *Understanding Media*, 327.
10 Benjamin, "Kunstwerk 5," 243. See the detailed discussion above, chapter 2.
11 McLuhan, *Understanding Media*, 313. The quotes are taken from Joyce, *Finnegans Wake*, 349 (where Joyce speaks of the "Charge of the Light Barricade") and 377. McLuhan summarizes the conception of TV's tactile activity thus evoked in his own words as follows: "Light comes through the image at the viewer; the viewer is not a camera, but a screen" (McLuhan and Parker, *Through the Vanishing Point*, 266; similarly McLuhan, *The Gutenberg Galaxy*, 45).
12 McLuhan, *Understanding Media*, 313.
13 For an introduction to the theological aspects of McLuhan's media theory, see his *The Medium and the Light*. On his media Catholicism, see, for example, Wolfe, "McLuhan's New World," 18–25; Marchessault, *Marshall McLuhan*, 35–41; and Kappeler, *Communication Habits for the Pilgrim Church*, 102–11. On the Renouveau catholique, see for example Gugelot, *La conversion des intellectuels*; Schloesser, *Jazz Age Catholicism*, esp. 213–44 on Rouault; and Kühlmann and Luckscheiter, *Moderne und Antimoderne*.
14 See Teilhard de Chardin, *The Phenomenon of Man*, where he writes, among other things, that "however solitary his advent, man emerged from a general groping of the world" (189). For the notion of an "'etherized' universal consciousness," see Teilhard de Chardin, *The Future of Man*, 162.

15 McLuhan, *Understanding Media*, 108, McLuhan's emphasis.

16 Gombrich, *Art and Illusion*. See McLuhan, *Understanding Media*, 12–13, 265–66. On the question of "false depth," see Hildebrand, *The Problem of Form*, 44 and 56–58. See also the introduction to the present book.

17 McLuhan, *Understanding Media*, 250 and 109.

18 On the Bauhaus in Weimar, see Franciscono, *Walter Gropius and the Creation of the Bauhaus*; Hüter, *Das Bauhaus in Weimar*; and Vitale, *Le Bauhaus de Weimar*.

19 McLuhan, "Encyclopedic Unities"; Cavell, *McLuhan in Space*, 113–14; and Gruber, "Taktile Medien."

20 On the relationship between McLuhan and Giedion, see Geiser, "Erziehung zum Sehen"; and Darroch, "Giedion and *Explorations*." On Moholy and McLuhan, see Richard Kostelanetz, "A Mine of Perceptions and Prophecies"; as well as Fiedler and Buschfeld, "Von der Virtualität der Wahrnehmung."

21 Explicit references by McLuhan to the Bauhaus are found above all in *Understanding Media*, 107, 109, 250, and 322. There are numerous references in the journal *Explorations* as well. In volume 8 (1957), for example, McLuhan describes the Bauhaus as a school of synesthesia, and Victor Papanek situates it within the context of European avant-garde movements (also discussing Moholy's first book, *Painting, Photography, Film*).

22 McLuhan, "Inside the Five Sense Sensorium," 50.

23 As Richard Cavell has pointed out, "the work of Moholy-Nagy played a crucial role in McLuhan's aesthetics" (*McLuhan in Space*, 111).

24 McLuhan and Fiore, *The Medium Is the Massage*, 100.

25 McLuhan here relies especially on Edmund Joseph Ryan's dissertation, *The Role of the "Sensus Communis" in the Psychology of St. Thomas*; see McLuhan, *The Gutenberg Galaxy*, 122n31. Although Ryan discusses the role of the sensus communis as a "synthetic sense," he remains largely silent on the question of synesthesia.

26 Teilhard de Chardin, *The Future of Man*, 151 and 162; and Teilhard de Chardin, *The Phenomenon of Man*, 240. See the references to Teilhard in McLuhan, *The Gutenberg Galaxy*, 37. On the ideas of simultaneity and tactility thus evoked, see also Sprenger, *Medien des Immediaten*, 371–78.

27 McLuhan, *Understanding Media*, 322. In his discussion of the Vorkurs, Moholy refers to a number of pedagogical reformers (Pestalozzi, Fröbel, Wyneken) as well as to the educational program developed by Maria Montessori, in which the sense of touch plays a central role. See Moholy-Nagy, *von material zu architektur*, 17. [Not included in the 1947 translation, the reference can be found in the 2005 reissue of the 1938 edition of *The New Vision*, and in *Vision in Motion*, 22–23.—*Trans.*]

28 See generally Wick, *Teaching at the Bauhaus*, 92–130 (on Itten) and 131–63 (on Moholy).

29 On experimental aesthetics in the Soviet Union, see Vöhringer, *Avantgarde und Psychotechnik*, which also discusses the role of the later Bauhaus master Kandinsky.

30 Moholy-Nagy, *von material zu architektur*, 24; Moholy-Nagy, *The New Vision*, 1938 ed., 27.

31 On this point, see also Smith, "Limits of the Tactile and the Optical." These photographs' decisive criterion is not granularity but sharpness; see Moholy-Nagy, "Sharp or Fuzzy?"
32 Moholy-Nagy, *von material zu architektur*, 24n.
33 Benjamin, "Kunstwerk 5," 240.
34 Moholy-Nagy, *von material zu architektur*, 39; Moholy-Nagy, *The New Vision*, 1938 ed., 39.
35 Moholy-Nagy, *Painting, Photography, Film*, 33. See also Hooke, *Micrographia*. Hooke's depictions of different fabrics and individual insects are strikingly similar to some of the photographs in Moholy's books.
36 Moholy-Nagy, *The New Vision*, 1947 ed., 26. On the close relationship between Bauhaus and constructivism, see, for example, the contributions to the exhibition catalog, Finkeldey, *Konstruktivistische Internationale Schöpferische Arbeitsgemeinschaft*.
37 Moholy-Nagy, *von material zu architektur*, 33; Moholy-Nagy, *The New Vision*, 1938 ed., 35 and 40–41.
38 See, for example, Shklovsky, "The Connection between Devices," 53; and Moholy-Nagy, *von material zu architektur*, 33; Moholy-Nagy, *The New Vision*, 1938 ed., 42, amended. On the concept of *faktura* or "facture," see Gaßner, "The Constructivists," 309–10. [Hoffman renders Moholy-Nagy's *Faktur* as "surface aspect." However, given that since the initial publication of her translation in 1932, "facture" has become established as a technical term referring to "the manner in which something (as an artistic work) is made" (*Merriam-Webster*), it is used here throughout.—*Trans.*]
39 Moholy-Nagy, *von material zu architektur*, 42 and 80. On Rodchenko and the problem of faktura, see Gaßner, "The Constructivists," 309–11.
40 McLuhan, "Encyclopedic Unities," 601–2.
41 Moholy-Nagy, *Vision in Motion*, 134.
42 Moholy-Nagy, *Vision in Motion*, 181, modified.
43 Moholy-Nagy, *Vision in Motion*, 181.
44 Moholy-Nagy, *Vision in Motion*, 69, 75, 59, and 220–21.
45 Moholy-Nagy, *von material zu architektur*, 42 and 29.
46 Moholy-Nagy, *Vision in Motion*, 158.
47 McLuhan, *Understanding Media*, 313.
48 McLuhan, *Understanding Media*, 313 (McLuhan's emphasis) and 130. *Museum without Walls* is the title of Stuart Gilbert's 1949 English translation of André Malraux's *Le musée imaginaire*.
49 McLuhan, *Understanding Media*, 317, 122, and 13.
50 McLuhan, *Understanding Media*, 320 and 329.
51 Moholy-Nagy, *Vision in Motion*, 158.
52 McLuhan, *Understanding Media*, 334, 190, and 249; as well as McLuhan and Parker, *Through the Vanishing Point*, 181.
53 If we take the origin of the expression "digital" in *digitus*, "finger," into account, we might even say that we are dealing with digital images in both cases. McLuhan,

however, does not reach this conclusion even though he derives the *digit* from the use of fingers for counting (see the chapter "Number: Profile of the Crowd" in *Understanding Media*, 106–18). See Heilmann, "Digitalität als Taktilität."

54 Maritain, foreword; Maritain, "Visit at St. Ann's Chapel." On Girard's work in St. Ann's Chapel, see Monihan, "The Catholic Art Forum."

55 Other films by Girard include *Sermon on the Mount* and *The Passion and Resurrection*; see National Council of Catholic Men Film Center, *Selected Catholic Films*, 31. On Girard's experimental films, see, for example, "Painting on Light for TV"; and Shanley, "Paintings on Light for the TV Screen." On the lectures about Rouault, see Girard, "Georges Rouault."

56 McLuhan, "Inside the Five Sense Sensorium," 49.

57 McLuhan, *The Gutenberg Galaxy*, 49 and 121.

58 McLuhan, *The Gutenberg Galaxy*, 121. See, for example, Alloa, *Looking through Images*, and Maas, *Diaphan und gedichtet*.

59 McLuhan, *The Gutenberg Galaxy*, 121 and 45; McLuhan, *Understanding Media*, 27.

60 McLuhan, *Understanding Media*, 321.

61 McLuhan, *Understanding Media*, 247 and 130.

62 See McLuhan, *Understanding Media*, 129; and Kepes, "Art and Science."

63 Moholy-Nagy, *Vision in Motion*, 168. On Ludwig Hirschfeld-Mack and Kurt Schwerdtfeger's "reflected light-displays," see Moholy-Nagy, *Painting, Photography, Film*, 79–85.

64 Gropius, "Address to the Students."

65 McLuhan, *Understanding Media*, 249; McLuhan, *Gutenberg Galaxy*, 74.

66 On the library of the Bauhaus in Weimar, see Siebenbrodt and Simon-Ritz, *Die Bauhaus-Bibliothek*.

67 Moholy-Nagy, *von material zu architektur*, 101. [The illustration and accompanying text were not included in *The New Vision*, 1947 ed., where they would find their place on page 43.—*Trans.*]

68 See Fleckner, "Der Kampf visueller Erfahrungen."

69 Giedion-Welcker, *Contemporary Sculpture*, 108–11 and 94–96. On parallels in this context between Giedion and Giedion-Welcker, see also Geiser, "Erziehung zum Sehen," 151–52.

70 Giedion, *The Beginnings of Art*, xix and xx.

71 See Giedion, *The Beginnings of Art*, 51–53 and 74–75.

72 McLuhan, *Understanding Media*, 313.

73 Giedion, "Space Conception," 38 and 50. See also Giedion, *The Beginnings of Art*, 529, 530, and 524. On the foundation of this aesthetics, the "New Vision," in Moholy-Nagy, see Sahli, *Filmische Sinneserweiterung*, 61–79.

74 McLuhan, *The Gutenberg Galaxy*, 76; and Deleuze and Guattari, *A Thousand Plateaus*, 494 and 557n56, referring to Edmund Carpenter's study *Eskimo*, first published in 1959 in a special issue of *Explorations*.

75 The haptic quality of Giedion's photographically supported reconstruction of prehistory is highlighted by Geiser, "Erziehung zum Sehen," 147; and Papapetros, "Modern Architecture and Prehistory," 178.

76 See Wölfflin, "Wie man Skulpturen aufnehmen soll."
77 Giedion, "Space Conception," 47; compare Giedion, *The Beginnings of Art*, 528.
78 Sigfried Giedion, letter to Hallam L. Movius Jr., August 16, 1952, Giedion papers, 43-T-10, p. 12, folder "Korrespondenz," gta Archives, ETH Zurich, Institute for the History and Theory of Architecture (hereafter gta Archives).
79 Giedion, *The Beginnings of Art*, 382–89.
80 Sigfried Giedion, letter to Pierre Charon, August 17, 1953, Giedion papers, 43-T-10, p. 12, folder "Korrespondenz," gta Archives.
81 Giedion, *The Beginnings of Art*, 469.
82 Giedion-Welcker, *Contemporary Sculpture*, xxviii.
83 Sigfried Giedion, "Mellon Lecture ONE, 'Art[,] a Fundamental Experience,' Washington, April 7," 1957, Giedion papers, 43-T-13, hanging folder "Mellon Lectures," gta Archives. There are similar reflections to be found in the letters Giedion exchanged from the beginning of his project with a number of internationally renowned prehistorians, archaeologists, and art historians to establish a central archive for the photographic documentation of prehistoric art. See, for example, Sigfried Giedion, letter to Fernand Lacorre, October 18, 1949, Giedion papers, 43-T-10, p. 12, folder "Prähist. Korrespondenz, 1949–1957," gta Archives.
84 Giedion, *The Beginnings of Art*, 470, 473 (caption for fig. 318), 391; and Giedion, *Die Entstehung der Kunst*, 391.
85 Giedion, *The Beginnings of Art*, 472 (caption for fig. 316) and 469.
86 Giedion, *The Beginnings of Art*, 470–71.
87 Giedion, *The Beginnings of Art*, 529; and Giedion, "Space Conception in Prehistoric Art," 48.
88 Giedion, *The Beginnings of Art*, 402 and 136; and Giedion, "Space Conception in Prehistoric Art," 51.
89 McLuhan, *The Gutenberg Galaxy*, 76.
90 McLuhan, *The Gutenberg Galaxy*, 76.
91 McLuhan, *Understanding Media*, 249.
92 Giedion, *The Beginnings of Art*, 470; and McLuhan, *Understanding Media*, 299.
93 See Marshack, *The Roots of Civilization*, 335; and Cohen, *La femme des origines*, 74.
94 McLuhan, *Understanding Media*, 188.
95 McLuhan, "Encyclopedic Unities," 601. See Moholy-Nagy, *Vision in Motion*, 1947 ed., 132–33, 343, and 344–46.
96 McLuhan, "Encyclopedic Unities," 602.
97 See, for example, Krauss, *Le photographique*, 77.
98 Giedion, *The Beginnings of Art*, vii (the quote is from *The Spirit of Romance*, 1910).

FIVE. HORN AND TIME

1 "[ECRAN] Screen," 110.
2 Pynchon, *The Crying of Lot 49* (hereafter *Crying*), 9–16.
3 Pynchon, *Crying*, 105–8, 37, and 10.

4 Pynchon, *Crying*, 13–14.
5 Pynchon, *Crying*, 154, 79, and 18. In *The Gutenberg Galaxy* in particular, McLuhan uses, in addition to "extension," the terms "externalization" and "exteriorization," which have stronger psychological and procedural connotations.
6 McLuhan, *Understanding Media*, 41–47. On the references to McLuhan, see Abernethy, "Entropy"; and Schaub, *Pynchon*. For a reading of the novel that establishes links with Jean Baudrillard's media theory and Jacques Lacan's theory of language, see Berressem, *Pynchon's Poetics*, 82–118.
7 That is just one parallel. In the most diverse contexts and specific contexts, Pynchon (in *Gravity's Rainbow*) and Kentridge (in *Black Box/Chambre noire*) have also addressed the genocide against the Herero perpetrated by the German colonial power at the beginning of the twentieth century. See Selmeci and Henrichsen, *Das Schwarzkommando*; and Coumans, *Geschichte und Identität*.
8 Pynchon, *Crying*, 178.
9 Pynchon, *Crying*, 82.
10 Pynchon, *Crying*, 20.
11 See Grant, *A Companion to "The Crying of Lot 49,"* 8.
12 Pynchon, *Crying*, 20.
13 Pynchon, *Crying*, 14.
14 Pynchon, *Crying*, 14.
15 Pynchon, *Crying*, 14 and 17–18.
16 On the reference to Remedios Varo, see Colvile, *Beyond and beneath the Mantle*, 47–54; and Mattessich, *Lines of Flight*, 43–69.
17 Pynchon, *Crying*, 21; and Varo, "Comments," 119.
18 Pynchon, *Crying*, 21. On the hourglass, see also Mattessich, *Lines of Flight*, 51.
19 Pynchon, *Crying*, 24.
20 Pynchon, *Crying*, 52.
21 Pynchon, *Crying*, 52.
22 Pynchon, *Crying*, 15.
23 Pynchon, *Crying*, 84.
24 See, for example, Thomas Pynchon, *The Crying of Lot 49* (New York: HarperPerennial, 1999), 38 and 67.
25 In fact, in the earliest evidence for the official installation of the postal service, the Memmingen Chronicle of 1490, we already read that the rider approaching a station blew "a little horn [*hörnlin*]" to announce his arrival to those waiting there; see Behringer, *Thurn und Taxis*, 27. On the media history of the postal service, see Bernhard Siegert's study *Relais*, which mentions Pynchon's novel several times (6, 37, 130, etc.) but refrains from a detailed discussion. See also, generally, Siegert and Krajewski, *Thomas Pynchon*.
26 Pynchon, *Crying*, 95.
27 Pynchon, *Crying*, 95. On epilepsy, see also Colvile, *Beyond and beneath the Mantle*, 61–76; and, picking up on this text, Polednitschek-Veit, "Die epileptische Aura."
28 See, for example, his remarks on the image as "dialectics at a standstill" in Benjamin, *Arcades Project*, fragment N2a3, 462.

29 Massumi, "The Autonomy of Affect." Gary Genosko discusses the connection between affect and epilepsy in *Félix Guattari*, 158–73.
30 Pynchon, *Crying*, 129.
31 Pynchon, *Crying*, 51.
32 For a detailed discussion, see Schmidgen, *The Helmholtz Curves*.
33 Pynchon, *Crying*, 118, Pynchon's emphasis. Mattessich points out that Oedipa's capacity for remembering comes with a suspension of her sense of touch; see Mattessich, *Lines of Flight*, 59–60.
34 Pynchon, *Crying*, 118, Pynchon's emphasis.
35 Rabelais, *Gargantua and Pantagruel*, 829–30. "The Words and cries of men and the women, the pounding of maces . . . all the remaining din of battle froze in the air. And now that the rigour of winter has passed and fine, calm, temperate weather returned, they melt, and can be heard" (829). The motif is also mentioned by Peters, "Helmholtz, Edison, and Sound History," 177.
36 Raspe, *The Singular Travels*, 46–49.
37 Pynchon, *Crying*, 121.
38 Pynchon, *Crying*, 111, 109, and 121.
39 Pynchon, *Crying*, 115.
40 See Gibbs, "A Portrait of the Luddite"; as well as Sale, *Rebels against the Future*.
41 Pynchon, *Crying*, 123 and 124.
42 Pynchon, "Is It O.K. to Be a Luddite?"
43 On the Kassel installation, see Kentridge and Galison, "The Refusal of Time"; as well as Koerner, "Death, Time, Soup," 102.
44 Christov-Bakargiev, "The Dance Was Very Frenetic," 34.
45 Kentridge, *Six Drawing Lessons*; Miller and Kentridge, *The Refusal of Time*, CD of the soundtrack for the installation; Kentridge, Galison, et al., *The Refusal of Time*; and the 2012 TV production, Kentridge et al., *The Refusal of Time*. The installation has since been shown at a number of places, and some institutions, like the Metropolitan Museum of Art, New York, joining up with the San Francisco Museum of Modern Art, have acquired it. See also Holm, "Die Präsenz Poincarés."
46 Galison, *Einstein's Clocks, Poincaré's Maps*, 175–80.
47 Kentridge and Galison, "The Refusal of Time," 108.
48 Krauss, "'The Rock,'" 16.
49 Teilhard de Chardin, *The Future of Man*, 162. On McLuhan's use of Teilhard's notion, see above, chapter 4.
50 Kentridge, *Six Drawing Lessons*, 45.
51 Kentridge, *Six Drawing Lessons*, 188.
52 Kentridge, *Six Drawing Lessons*, 8–9.
53 The title of the relevant section of Miller's soundtrack, "Shembe Death March," is a further indication.
54 See, for example, chapter 5 of Galison, *Einstein's Clocks, Poincaré's Maps*, 221–93.
55 In this sense, Kentridge explains that "it is not so much being fascinated with the ideas of the late nineteenth century, but that it was still such a 'visible' era, in a way in which an electronic era is not. Even if one is talking about contemporary

phenomena, very often an older representation is a better way of drawing it" (Koerner, "Death, Time, Soup," 105).

56 Christov-Bakargiev, "On the Destruction of Art," 284.

57 Christov-Bakargiev, "'The Dance Was Very Frenetic,'" 31; see also Christov-Bakargiev, "Letter to a Friend," where she writes that "in an age of too simple on/off, covered/uncovered dichotomies," it may well be appropriate to "*reperform* . . . the transitional dance of veiling and unveiling" (77).

58 Galison, *Einstein's Clocks, Poincaré's Maps*, 159–60.

59 Kentridge, *Six Drawing Lessons*, 85.

60 Kentridge, *Six Drawing Lessons*, 84.

61 Mbembe, *On the Postcolony*, 14, corrected.

62 Deleuze and Guattari, *Anti-Oedipus*, 1. On the "air loom," see Röske and Brand-Claussen, *Air Loom*. From the perspective of the history of media and technology, what is being evoked here is the "Elephant Clock," a large medieval automaton whose hydraulic system set a complex set of figures into motion to display the time and whose elaborate decoration, simultaneously, articulated a claim to global interconnection. See, for example, Zielinski and Weibel, *Allah's Automata*, 12–27 and 108–9.

63 Dickens, *Hard Times*, 22.

64 McCrickard, *WK: William Kentridge*, 95–103.

65 Christov-Bakargiev, "In Conversation with William Kentridge," 33; and McCrickard, *WK: William Kentridge*, 95.

66 See Galison, *Einstein's Clocks, Poincaré's Maps*, 93–95; see also Schmidgen, *The Helmholtz Curves*, 109–14.

67 McLuhan, *Understanding Media*, 145–56.

68 Pynchon, *Crying*, 124.

69 Kentridge, *Everyone Their Own Projector*.

70 See, for example, Dewitz, *Ich sehe was*; and Mannoni, *The Great Art of Light and Shadow*.

71 Münsterberg, *The Photoplay*, 95, 96, and 35.

72 Kentridge, *Six Drawing Lessons*, 107 and 105.

73 Krauss, "'The Rock,'" 5.

74 See the detailed discussion in Frieling, "Walking and Looking."

75 Guattari, "Refrains and Existential Affects," 210.

76 Kentridge, *Six Drawing Lessons*, 108.

77 Kentridge, *Six Drawing Lessons*, 20 and 76.

78 Kentridge, *Six Drawing Lessons*, 24.

79 See McCrickard, *WK: William Kentridge*, 104–9; as well as Werner, "Bilder auf Wanderung."

80 Kentridge, *Six Drawing Lessons*, 141.

81 Kentridge, *Six Drawing Lessons*, 141. See the discussion in Gombrich, *Art and Illusion*, 81–82; and the commentary in Eco, *A Theory of Semiotics*.

82 See Karl Clausberg's fundamental study, *Zwischen den Sternen*.

83 This part of Miller's soundtrack is called "A Universal Archive of Images."

84 See Clausberg, *Zwischen den Sternen*, 97–102. Eberty's speculations still echo in Barthes's remark that the photograph of a deceased person "touches" the viewer "like the delayed rays of a star" and in Deleuze's conception of a cinema embedded in the "universal undulation, universal rippling" of image-matter; see Barthes, *Camera Lucida*, 81; and Deleuze, *Cinema 1*, 66.

85 Miller and Kentridge, "A Universal Archive of Images."

86 Kentridge, *Six Drawing Lessons*, 25.

87 Miller and Kentridge, "A Universal Archive of Images."

88 Mbembe, *On the Postcolony*, 15.

CONCLUSION

1 Ionesco, "Rhinoceros," 97; the photograph is table 2 in Ionesco, *Die Nashörner*.

2 See Franke, Hankey, and Tuszyinski, *Nervous Systems*.

3 Foucault, *Discipline and Punish*, 195–228; Crary, *Techniques of the Observer*; and Latour, "Visualisation and Cognition."

4 Elias, *On the Process of Civilisation*, 123–33; and Theweleit, *Male Fantasies*. Drawing on media studies, David P. Parisi has made a plea for a history of tactile modernity: see Parisi, "Tactile Modernity"; Parisi, *Archaeology of Touch*, 99–150.

5 Negt and Kluge, *History and Obstinacy*, 148–59.

6 McLuhan, *Understanding Media*, 249; and McLuhan and Parker, *Through the Vanishing Point*, 251.

7 For recent work in this direction, see, for example, Fuller, *Media Ecologies*; and Heibach, *Atmosphären*.

8 Schivelbusch, *The Railway Journey*, 166–67.

9 Freud, *Beyond the Pleasure Principle*, 11.

10 Schivelbusch, *The Railway Journey*, 165 and 166–67.

11 Schivelbusch, *The Railway Journey*, 165.

12 Freud, *Civilization and Its Discontents*, 92.

13 Warburg, "Tragödie der Verleibung," 580–81. [This passage was not included in Michael P. Steinberg's translation, *Images from the Region of the Pueblo Indians of North America*.—*Trans*.] In commenting on Warburg's discussion, Sabine Mainberger implicitly reflects our horn problem, writing that "instruments and clothes, like hair, are intimately connected with the body and yet are something other, alien to the body, nonorganic that humans do not livingly feel [*lebendig fühlt*]: 'body parts without pain'" (Mainberger, "Tragödie der Verleibung," 123).

14 Adorno, *Negative Dialectics*, 180.

15 Benjamin, "The Paris of the Second Empire," 27.

16 Benjamin, "On Some Motifs in Baudelaire," 316.

17 Peirce's conception of indexical signs is complex and changes over time. Among the examples he gives of this kind of signs around 1910 are clocks, barometers, and yardsticks, but also the legends on geometrical figures: "Geometricians mark

letters against the different parts of their diagrams and then use these letters to indicate those parts"; see Peirce, "Logic as Semiotic," 108–9. In that sense it is by far not enough to see in analog photography an exemplary indexical sign, as Rosalind Krauss does; see Krauss, *Le photographique*, 77.

18 Sartre, *Being and Nothingness*, 776 [translation modified; compare Barnes's note on *visqueux*, 770n34—*Trans.*].

19 Flusser, *Towards a Philosophy of Photography*, 8; Flusser, *Lob der Oberflächlichkeit*, 11; as well as Deleuze and Guattari, *A Thousand Plateaus*, 474–500 and 351–423 (the explicit reference to McLuhan is on p. 360).

BIBLIOGRAPHY

Abadie, Daniel, ed. *Salvador Dalí: Rétrospective 1920–1980*. Paris: Centre Georges Pompidou, 1980.

Abernethy, Peter L. "Entropy in Pynchon's *The Crying of Lot 49*." *Critique* 14, no. 2 (1972): 18–33.

Ades, Dawn, ed. *Dalí: The Centenary Retrospective*. New York: Rizzoli, 2004.

Adorno, Theodor W. *Negative Dialectics*. Translated by E. B. Ashton. London: Routledge and Kegan Paul, 1973.

Alloa, Emmanuel. *Looking through Images: A Phenomenology of Visual Media*. Translated by Nils F. Schott. New York: Columbia University Press, 2021.

Andrejevic, Mark, and Mark Burdon. "Defining the Sensor Society." *Television and New Media* 16, no. 1 (2015): 19–36.

Barad, Karen. *Meeting the Universe Halfway: Quantum Physics and the Entanglement of Matter and Meaning*. Durham, NC: Duke University Press, 2007.

Bardini, Thierry. *Bootstrapping: Douglas Engelbart, Coevolution, and the Origins of Personal Computing*. Stanford, CA: Stanford University Press, 2000.

Barnes, Mary, and Joseph Berke. *Two Accounts of a Journey through Madness*. New York: Harcourt Brace Jovanovich, 1971.

Barsanti, Giulio, ed. *Misura d'uomo: Strumenti, teorie e pratiche dell'antropometria e della psicologia sperimentale tra '800 et '900*. Florence: Istituto e Museo di Storia della Scienza, 1986.

Barthes, Roland. *Camera Lucida: Reflections on Photography*. Translated by Richard Howard. New York: Hill and Wang, 1981.

Bateson, Gregory, ed. *Perceval's Narrative: A Patient's Account of His Psychosis, 1830–1832*. Stanford, CA: Stanford University Press, 1961.

Baudelaire, Charles. "Perte de l'Auréole." *Le Spleen de Paris*, no. 46. In *Œuvres complètes*, edited by Claude Pichois, vol. 1, 352. Paris: Gallimard, 1975.

Behringer, Wolfgang. *Thurn und Taxis: Die Geschichte ihrer Post und ihrer Unternehmen*. Munich: Piper, 1990.

Benjamin, Walter. *The Arcades Project*. Edited by Rolf Tiedemann. Translated by Howard Eiland and Kevin McLaughlin. Cambridge, MA: Harvard University Press, 2003.

Benjamin, Walter. "The Destructive Character." Translated by Edmund Jephcott. In *Selected Writings*, vol. 2, part 2, 541–42.

Benjamin, Walter. *Gesammelte Schriften*. Edited by Rolf Tiedemann and Hermann Schweppenhäuser. 7 vols. Frankfurt: Suhrkamp, 1972–89.

Benjamin, Walter. "Hashish, Beginning of March 1930." Translated by Rodney Livingstone. In *Selected Writings*, vol. 2, part 1, 327–30.

Benjamin, Walter. "Das Kunstwerk im Zeitalter seiner technischen Reproduzierbarkeit–Erste Fassung." In *Werke und Nachlaß*, vol. 16, 7–51.

Benjamin, Walter. "Das Kunstwerk im Zeitalter seiner technischen Reproduzierbarkeit–Zweite Fassung." In *Werke und Nachlaß*, vol. 16, 52–95.

Benjamin, Walter. "Das Kunstwerk im Zeitalter seiner technischen Reproduzierbarkeit [Fünfte Fassung]" ["Kunstwerk 5"]. In *Werke und Nachlaß*, vol. 16, 207–55.

Benjamin, Walter. Letter to Max Horkheimer, April 16, 1938. In *Gesammelte Schriften*, vol. 1, part 3, 1072–75.

Benjamin, Walter. "Little History of Photography." Translated by Rodney Livingstone et al. In *Selected Writings*, vol. 2, part 2, 507–30.

Benjamin, Walter. *One-Way Street*. Translated by Edmund Jephcott. In *Selected Writings*, vol. 1, 444–88.

Benjamin, Walter. "On Some Motifs in Baudelaire." Translated by Harry Zohn. In *Selected Writings*, vol. 4, 313–55.

Benjamin, Walter. "The Paris of the Second Empire in Baudelaire." Translated by Harry Zohn. In *Selected Writings*, vol. 4, 3–92.

Benjamin, Walter. *Das Passagen-Werk*. In *Gesammelte Schriften*, 4th ed., edited by Rolf Tiedemann and Hermann Schweppenhäuser, vol. 5, 1277–323. Frankfurt: Suhrkamp, 1996.

Benjamin, Walter. "Translation—For and Against." Translated by Edmund Jephcott. In *Selected Writings*, vol. 3, 249–52.

Benjamin, Walter. *Walter Benjamin: Selected Writings*. Edited by Michael W. Jennings, Howard Eiland, and Gary Smith. Cambridge, MA: Harvard University Press, 2005.

Benjamin, Walter. *Werke und Nachlaß: Kritische Gesamtausgabe*. Vol. 16: *Das Kunstwerk im Zeitalter seiner technischen Reproduzierbarkeit*. Edited by Burkardt Lindner et al. Berlin: Suhrkamp, 2012.

Benjamin, Walter. "The Work of Art in the Age of Its Technological Reproducibility [First Version]." Translated by Michael W. Jennings. *Grey Room*, no. 39 (spring 2010): 11–38.

Benjamin, Walter. "The Work of Art in the Age of Its Technological Reproducibility: Second Version." Translated by Edmund Jephcott and Harry Zohn. In *Selected Writings*, vol. 3, 101–33.

Benthien, Claudia. *Haut: Literaturgeschichte—Körperbilder—Grenzdiskurse*. 2nd ed. Reinbek: Rowohlt, 1999.

Bergson, Henri. *Matter and Memory*. Translated by Nancy Margaret Paul and W. Scott Palmer. New York: Macmillan, 1911.

Bernard, Claude. *An Introduction to the Study of Experimental Medicine*. Translated by Henry Copley Greene. New York: Schuman, 1949.

Berressem, Hanjo. *Pynchon's Poetics: Interfacing Theory and Text*. Urbana: University of Illinois Press, 1993.

Berufsverband Bildender Künstler e.V., ed. "Rebecca Horn." In *Junge Hamburger Künstler: Gruppenarbeiten und Einzelarbeiten*. Hamburg: n.p., 1970.

Bexte, Peter. "Cadillac und Gebetsmatte: McLuhans TV-Gemälde." In *McLuhan neu lesen: Kritische Analysen zu Medien und Kultur im 21. Jahrhundert*, edited by Derrick de Kerckhove, Martina Leeke, and Kerstin Schmidt, 323–37. Bielefeld: Transcript, 2008.

Blumenberg, Hans. *Theorie der Unbegrifflichkeit*. Frankfurt: Suhrkamp, 2007.

Bolz, Norbert. *Theorie der neuen Medien*. Munich: Raben, 1990.

Bonaparte, Marie. *Über die Symbolik der Kopftrophäen: Eine psychoanalytische Studie*. Leipzig: Internationaler Psychoanalytischer Verlag, 1928.

Bosquet, Alain. *Conversations with Dali*. Translated by Joachim Neugroschel. New York: Dutton, 1969.

Brauns, Jörg, ed. *Form und Medium*. Weimar: VDG, 2002.

Bredekamp, Horst. "Michelangelos Moses als Gedankenfilm: Freuds Ambivalenz gegenüber der Kinematographie." In *Kino im Kopf: Psychologie und Film seit Sigmund Freud*, 31–37. Berlin: Bertz + Fischer, 2006.

Brock, Bazon. "Wiederholte Anmerkungen zu Körperplastik und Körperbemalung (Aus Anlass der Veröffentlichung von Arbeiten Rebecca Horns)." *Interfunktionen* 8 (January 1972): 49–55.

Bruderer-Oswald, Iris. *Das neue Sehen: Carola Giedion-Welcker und die Sprache der Moderne*. Bern: Benteli, 2007.

Brüggemann, Heinz. "Walter Benjamin und Sigfried Giedion oder die Wege der Modernität." *Deutsche Vierteljahrsschrift für Literaturwissenschaft und Geistesgeschichte* 70 (1996): 443–74.

Bruno, Giuliana. "Innenansichten: Die Anatomie der Brautmaschine." In *Rebecca Horn*, edited by Nationalgalerie Berlin, 93–111. Ostfildern: Hatje Cantz, 1994.

Canguilhem, Georges. "Réflexions sur la création artistique selon Alain." *Revue de métaphysique et de morale* 57 (1952): 171–86.

Carrouges, Michel. *Les machines célibataires*. Paris: Arcanes, 1954.

Cavell, Richard. *McLuhan in Space: A Cultural Geography*. Toronto: University of Toronto Press, 2002.

Caws, Mary Ann, ed. *Manifesto: A Century of Isms*. Lincoln: University of Nebraska Press, 2001.

Christov-Bakargiev, Carolyn. "The Dance Was Very Frenetic, Lively, Rattling, Clanging, Rolling, Contorted, and Lasting for a Long Time." In Christov-Bakargiev, *Documenta (13)*, 30–45.

Christov-Bakargiev, Carolyn, ed. *Documenta (13): The Book of Books*. Ostfildern: Hatje Cantz, 2012.

Christov-Bakargiev, Carolyn. "In Conversation with William Kentridge." In *William Kentridge*, edited by Dan Cameron, Carolyn Christov-Bakargiev, and J. M. Coetzee, 6–35. New York: Phaidon, 1999.

Christov-Bakargiev, Carolyn. "Letter to a Friend." In Christov-Bakargiev, *Documenta (13)*, 74–79.

Christov-Bakargiev, Carolyn. "On the Destruction of Art—or Conflict and Art, or Trauma and the Art of Healing." In Christov-Bakargiev, *Documenta (13)*, 282–95.

Clausberg, Karl. *Zwischen den Sternen: Lichtbildarchive; Was Einstein und Uexküll, Benjamin und das Kino der Astronomie des 19. Jahrhunderts verdanken*. Berlin: Akademie, 2006.

Cohen, Claudine. *La femme des origines: Images de la femme dans la préhistoire occidentale*. Paris: Belin-Herscher, 2003.

Colvile, Georgiana M. M. *Beyond and beneath the Mantle: On Thomas Pynchon's "The Crying of Lot 49."* Amsterdam: Rodopi, 1988.

Coogan, Michael D., et al., eds. *The New Oxford Annotated Bible with the Apocryphal/Deuterocanonical Books: New Revised Standard Version*. Augm. 3rd ed. Oxford: Oxford University Press, 2007.

Coumans, Sandra T. J. *Geschichte und Identität: "Black Box/Chambre Noire" von William Kentridge*. Berlin: Regiospectra, 2011.

Crary, Jonathan. *Techniques of the Observer: On Vision and Modernity in the Nineteenth Century*. Cambridge, MA: MIT Press, 1990.

Curtis, James M. *Culture as Polyphony: An Essay on the Nature of Paradigms*. Columbia: University of Missouri Press, 1978.

Dagognet, François. *Faces, surfaces, interfaces*. Paris: Vrin, 1982.

Dagognet, François. *La peau découverte*. Le Plessis-Robinson: Institut Synthelabo, 1993.

Dalí, Salvador. "Anti-matter Manifesto." 1959. In *Collected Writings*, 366–67.

Dalí, Salvador. "Aspects phénoménologiques de la méthode paranoïaque-critique." In *Oui*, edited by Robert Descharnes, new augm. ed., 332–42. Paris: Denoël, 2004.

Dalí, Salvador. *The Collected Writings of Salvador Dalí*. Edited and translated by Haim Finkelstein. Cambridge: Cambridge University Press, 1998.

Dalí, Salvador. "Concerning the Terrifying and Edible Beauty of Art Nouveau Architecture." 1933. In *Collected Writings*, 193–200.

Dalí, Salvador. *Dalí on Modern Art: The Cuckolds of Antiquated Modern Art*. Translated by Haakon M. Chevalier. New York: Dial, 1957.

Dalí, Salvador. *Diary of a Genius*. Edited by Michel Déon. Translated by Richard Howard. Garden City, NY: Doubleday, 1965.

Dalí, Salvador. "Ecumenical 'chafarrinada' of Velasquez." *Art News* 59, no. 10 (February 1961): 30 and 55.

Dalí, Salvador. *50 Secrets of Magic Craftsmanship*. Translated by Haakon M. Chevalier. New York: Dial, 1948.

Dalí, Salvador. "For the Sitges 'Meeting.'" 1928. In *Collected Writings*, 64–66.

Dalí, Salvador. "Les idées lumineuses." *L'usage de la parole* 1, no. 2 (February 1940): 24–25.

Dalí, Salvador. ". . . The Liberation of the Fingers . . ." 1929. In *Collected Writings*, 99–101.

Dalí, Salvador. "Mystical Manifesto." 1951. In *Collected Writings*, 363–66.

Dalí, Salvador. "New General Considerations Regarding the Mechanism of the Paranoiac Phenomenon from the Surrealist Point of View." 1933. In *Collected Writings*, 256–62.

Dalí, Salvador. "Notes pour l'interprétation du tableau: 'La persistence de la mémoire.'" 1931. In *Salvador Dalí: Rétrospective 1920-1980*, edited by Daniel Abadie, 174. Paris: Centre Georges Pompidou, 1980.

Dalí, Salvador. "Poetry of the Mass-Produced Utility." 1928. In *Collected Writings*, 57–59.

Dalí, Salvador. "Saint Sebastian." 1927. In *Collected Writings*, 19–24.

Dalí, Salvador. "The Spectral Surrealism of the Pre-Raphaelite Eternal Feminine." 1936. In *Collected Writings*, 310–14.

Dalí, Salvador. "The Water in Which We Swim." 1935. In *Collected Writings*, 262–65.

"Dali marie pour se libérer une dentellière et un rhinocéros." *Paris Match*, no. 319 (May 7–14, 1955): 78.

Darroch, Michael. "Giedion and *Explorations*: Confluences of Space and Media in Toronto School Theorization." In *Media Transatlantic: Developments in Media and Communication Studies between North America and German-Speaking Europe*, edited by Norm Friesen, 63–87. Basel: Springer, 2016.

Deleuze, Gilles. *Cinema 1: The Movement-Image*. Translated by Hugh Tomlinson and Barbara Habberjam. London: Bloomsbury, 2013.

Deleuze, Gilles. "Postscript on Control Societies." In *Negotiations, 1972–1990*, translated by Martin Joughin, 177–82. New York: Columbia University Press, 1995.

Deleuze, Gilles. "Raymond Roussel, or the Abhorrent Vacuum." Translated by Michael Taormina. In *Desert Islands and Other Texts, 1953–1974*, edited by David Lapoujade, 72–73. Los Angeles, CA: Semiotext(e), 2004.

Deleuze, Gilles, and Félix Guattari. *Anti-Oedipus: Capitalism and Schizophrenia*. Translated by Robert Hurley, Mark Seem, and Helen R. Lane. Minneapolis: University of Minnesota Press, 1983.

Deleuze, Gilles, and Félix Guattari. *A Thousand Plateaus: Capitalism and Schizophrenia*. Translated by Brian Massumi. Minneapolis: University of Minnesota Press, 1987.

Derrida, Jacques. "Freud and the Scene of Writing." In *Writing and Difference*, translated by Alan Bass, 246–91. London: Routledge, 2001.

Derrida, Jacques. *On Touching—Jean-Luc Nancy*. Translated by Christine Irizarry. Stanford, CA: Stanford University Press, 2007.

Descharnes, Robert. *The World of Salvador Dali*. London: Macmillan, 1962.

Descharnes, Robert, and Nicolas Descharnes. *Dalí—The Hard and the Soft—Spells for the Magic of Form—Sculptures and Objects*. Translated by Christopher Jones. Azay-le-Rideau: Eccart, 2004.

Descharnes, Robert, and Gilles Néret, eds. *Salvador Dalí, 1904–1989: The Paintings*. Translated by Michael Hulse. Cologne: Taschen, 1994.

Descharnes, Robert, and Clovis Prévost. *Gaudi: The Visionary*. Rev. ed. New York: Viking, 1982.

Dewitz, Bodo von, ed. *Ich sehe was, was Du nicht siehst! Die Sammlung Werner Nekes*. Göttingen: Steidl, 2002.

Dickens, Charles. *Hard Times*. 2nd ed. Edited by George Ford and Sylvère Monod. New York: Norton, 1990.

Didi-Huberman, Georges. *La ressemblance par contact: Archéologie, anachronisme et modernité de l'empreinte*. Paris: Minuit, 2008.

Documenta 5. "Rebecca Horn." In *Documenta 5: Befragung der Realität—Bildwelten heute*, catalog 16, 109–10. Kassel: Documenta, 1972.

Dohmen, Christoph. *Mose: Der Mann, der zum Buch wurde*. 2nd ed. Leipzig: Evangelische Verlagsanstalt, 2013.

Domanig, Andrea. "Was wurde aus Hansens Glyptothek? Zur Geschichte der Gipsabgusssammlung an der Akademie der bildenden Künste Wien." In *Theophil Hansen: Ein Resümee*, edited by Beatrix Bastl, Ulrike Hirhager, and Eva Schober, 75–96. Weitra: Bibliothek der Provinz, 2013.

Duchamp, Marcel. *Affectionately, Marcel: The Selected Correspondence of Marcel Duchamp*. Edited by Francis M. Naumann and Hector Obalk. Translated by Jill Taylor. Amsterdam: Ludion, 2000.

Eco, Umberto. *A Theory of Semiotics*. Bloomington: Indiana University Press, 1976.

"[ECRAN] Screen." In *Encyclopaedia Acephalica*, edited by Robert Lebel and Isabelle Waldberg, translated by Iain White. London: Atlas, 1995.

Efron, Edith. "He Prefers to Watch TV Upside Down: Salvador Dali, a Genius and 'Madman,' Tells What He Thinks of the Medium." *TV Guide* 16, no. 23 (June 8, 1968): 7–10.

Elias, Norbert. *On the Process of Civilisation: Sociogenetic and Psychogenetic Investigations*. Translated by Edmund Jephcott. The Collected Works of Norbert Elias, vol. 3. Dublin: University College Dublin Press, 2012.

Engelbach, Barbara. *Zwischen Body Art und Videokunst: Körper und Video in der Aktionskunst um 1970*. Munich: Schreiber, 2001.

Ernst, Max. *Écritures*. Paris: Gallimard, 1970.

Esposito, Maurizio. "Problematic 'Idiosyncrasies': Rediscovering the Historical Context of D'Arcy Wentworth Thompson's Science of Form." *Science in Context* 27, no. 1 (2014): 79–107.

Feldhaus, Anna. *Salvador Dalí und Philippe Halsman: Das gemeinsame Werk*. Heidelberg: Kehrer, 2015.

Ferrier, Jean-Louis. *Dali: Léda atomica*. Paris: Télécip/Denoël-Gonthier, 1980.

Fiedler, Jeannine, and Ben Buschfeld. "Von der Virtualität der Wahrnehmung im 20. Jahrhundert: Ein Gespräch zwischen László Moholy-Nagy und Marshall McLuhan." In *Über Moholy-Nagy: Ergebnisse aus dem Internationalen László Moholy-Nagy Symposium*, edited by Gottfried Jäger and Gudrun Wessing, 181–88. Bielefeld: Kerber, 1997.

Finkeldey, Bernd, ed. *Konstruktivistische Internationale Schöpferische Arbeitsgemeinschaft, 1922–1927: Utopien für eine europäische Kultur*. Stuttgart: Hatje, 1992.

Fleckner, Uwe. "Der Kampf visueller Erfahrungen: Surrealistische Bildrhetorik und photographischer Essay in Carl Einsteins Zeitschrift *Documents*." In *Begierde im Blick: Surrealistische Photographie*, edited by Uwe Fleckner, 23–31. Ostfildern: Hatje Cantz, 2005.

Flusser, Vilém. *Lob der Oberflächlichkeit: Für eine Phänomenologie der Medien*. Bensheim: Bollmann, 1993.

Flusser, Vilém. "Skin." *Flusser Studies* 2 (2006). http://www.flusserstudies.net/sites/www.flusserstudies.net/files/media/attachments/flusser-skin02.pdf.

Flusser, Vilém. *Towards a Philosophy of Photography*. Translated by Anthony Mathews. London: Reaktion, 2000.

Flusser, Vilém. "Von den Möglichkeiten einer Leibkarte." In *Lab: Jahrbuch der Künste und Apparate*, edited by Kunsthochschule für Medien, 115–24. Cologne: König, 2000.

Flusser, Vilém, and Louis Bec. *Vampyroteuthis infernalis: A Treatise with a Report by the Institut Scientifique de Recherche Paranaturaliste*. Translated by Valentine A. Pakis. Minneapolis: University of Minnesota Press, 2012.

Förster, Heinz von. "Wahrnehmen wahrnehmen." In *Aisthesis: Wahrnehmung heute oder Perspektiven einer anderen Ästhetik*, edited by Karlheinz Barck, 434–43. Leipzig: Reclam, 1990.

Foucault, Michel. *Death and the Labyrinth: The World of Raymond Roussel*. Translated by Charles Ruas. New York: Continuum, 2004.

Foucault, Michel. *Discipline and Punish: The Birth of the Prison*. Translated by Alan Sheridan. New York: Vintage, 1979.

Fox Keller, Evelyn. *Making Sense of Life: Explaining Biological Development with Models, Metaphors, and Machines*. Cambridge, MA: Harvard University Press, 2002.

Franciscono, Marcel. *Walter Gropius and the Creation of the Bauhaus in Weimar: The Ideals and Artistic Theories of Its Founding Years*. Urbana: University of Illinois Press, 1971.

Franke, Anselm, Stephanie Hankey, and Marek Tuszyinski, eds. *Nervous Systems: Quantified Life and the Social Question*. Leipzig: Spector, 2016.

Fränkel, Fritz. "Protokoll des Meskalinversuchs vom 22. Mai 1934." In Walter Benjamin, *Gesammelte Schriften*, vol. 6, 607–16.

Frederiksen, Rune, and Eckart Marchand, eds. *Plaster Casts: Making, Collecting, and Displaying from Classical Antiquity to the Present*. Berlin: De Gruyter, 2010.

Freud, Sigmund. *Beyond the Pleasure Principle* (1920). Translated by James Strachey. In *Standard Edition*, vol. 18, 1–64.

Freud, Sigmund. *Civilization and Its Discontents*. Translated by Joan Riviere. In *Standard Edition*, vol. 21, 57–154.

Freud, Sigmund. *The Interpretation of Dreams* (First Part). Translated by James Strachey. In *Standard Edition*, vol. 4, 136–45.

Freud, Sigmund. "Der Moses des Michelangelo." *Imago* 3, no. 1 (1914): 15–36.

Freud, Sigmund. *The Moses of Michelangelo*. Translated by Alix Strachey. In *Standard Edition*, vol. 13, 209–38.

Freud, Sigmund. "Negation." Translated by Joan Riviere. In *Standard Edition*, vol. 19, 233–39.

Freud, Sigmund. "A Note upon the 'Mystic Writing-Pad' (1925 [1924])." Translated by James Strachey. In *Standard Edition*, vol. 19, 225–32.

Freud, Sigmund. "On Narcissism: An Introduction (1914)." Translated by C. M. Baines. In *Standard Edition*, vol. 14, 67–102.

Freud, Sigmund. *The Standard Edition of the Complete Psychological Works of Sigmund Freud*. Edited by James Strachey et al. London: Hogarth, 1953–74.

Freud, Sigmund, and Ernest Jones. *The Complete Correspondence of Sigmund Freud and Ernest Jones, 1908–1939*. Edited by R. Andrew Paskauskas. Cambridge, MA: Harvard University Press, 1993.

Frieling, Rudolf. "Walking and Looking: Technology and Agency in William Kentridge's Film Work." In *William Kentridge: Five Themes*, edited by Mark Rosenthal, 154–69. New Haven, CT: Yale University Press, 2009.

Fuller, Matthew. *Media Ecologies: Materialist Energies in Art and Technoculture*. Cambridge, MA: MIT Press, 2007.

Gale, Matthew, ed. *Dalí and Film*. New York: MoMA, 2007.

Galison, Peter. *Einstein's Clocks, Poincaré's Maps: Empires of Time*. New York: Norton, 2003.

Gaßner, Hubertus. "The Constructivists: Modernism on the Way to Modernization." Translated by Jürgen Riehle. In *The Great Utopia: The Russian and Soviet Avant-Garde, 1915–1932*, edited by Solomon R. Guggenheim Museum et al., 298–319. New York: Guggenheim, 1992.

Geiser, Reto. "Erziehung zum Sehen: Kunstvermittlung und Bildarbeit in Sigfried Giedions Schaffen beidseits des Atlantiks." In *Sigfried Giedion und die Fotografie: Bildinszenierungen der Moderne*, edited by Werner Oechslin and Gregor Harbusch, 142–57. Zurich: gta, 2010.

Gell, Alfred. "Vogel's Net: Traps as Artworks and Artworks as Traps." *Journal of Material Culture* 1, no. 1 (March 1996): 15–38.

Genosko, Gary. *Félix Guattari: A Critical Introduction*. New York: Pluto, 2009.

Georgiadis, Sokratis. *Sigfried Giedion: Eine intellektuelle Biographie*. Zurich: gta, 1989.

Ghyka, Matila. *Esthétique des proportions dans la nature et dans les arts*. Paris: Gallimard, 1927.

Ghyka, Matila. *The Geometry of Art and Life*. New York: Sheed and Ward, 1946.

Ghyka, Matila. *The World Mine Oyster: The Memoirs of Matila Ghyka*. London: Heinemann, 1961.

Gibbs, Rodney. "A Portrait of the Luddite as a Young Man." *Denver Quarterly* 39, no. 1 (2004): 35–42.

Gibson, Ian. *The Shameful Life of Salvador Dalí*. London: Faber and Faber, 1997.

Giedion, Sigfried. *The Beginnings of Art*. Vol. 1 of *The Eternal Present: A Contribution on Constancy and Change*. London: Oxford University Press, 1962.

Giedion, Sigfried. *Building in France, Building in Iron, Building in Ferroconcrete*. Translated by J. Duncan Berry. Santa Monica, CA: Getty Center for the History of Art and the Humanities, 1995.

Giedion, Sigfried. *Die Entstehung der Kunst*. Vol. 1 of *Ewige Gegenwart: Ein Beitrag zu Konstanz und Wechsel*. Cologne: DuMont Schauberg, 1965.

Giedion, Sigfried. *Mechanization Takes Command: A Contribution to Anonymous History*. New York: Oxford University Press, 1948.

Giedion, Sigfried. "Space Conception in Prehistoric Art." *Explorations* 6 (1956): 38–55.

Giedion-Welcker, Carola. *Contemporary Sculpture: An Evolution in Volume and Space*. 3rd rev. ed. Translated by Mary Hottinger-Machy, Sonja Marjasch, and Joyce Wittenborn. New York: Wittenborn, 1961.

Ginzburg, Carlo. "Morelli, Freud and Sherlock Holmes: Clues and Scientific Method." Translated by Anna Davin. *History Workshop*, no. 9 (Spring 1980): 5–36.

Girard, André. "Georges Rouault: My Friend and Teacher." *The Critic* 20, no. 2 (October–November 1961): 15–21.

Gombrich, Ernst H. *Art and Illusion: A Study in the Psychology of Pictorial Representation*. Princeton, NJ: Princeton University Press, 1960.

Grant, J. Kerry. *A Companion to "The Crying of Lot 49."* Athens: University of Georgia Press, 2008.

Gropius, Walter. "Address to the Students of the Staatliche Bauhaus, Held on the Occasion of the Yearly Exhibition of Student Work in July 1919." In Hans Maria Wingler, *The Bauhaus: Weimar, Dessau, Berlin, Chicago*, edited by Joseph Stein, translated by Wolfgang Jabs and Basil Gilbert, 36. Cambridge, MA: MIT Press, 1976.

Grosse, Ernst. *Die Anfänge der Kunst*. Freiburg: Mohr, 1894.

Grube, Gernot, Werner Kogge, and Sybille Krämer, eds. *Schrift: Kulturtechnik zwischen Auge, Hand und Maschine*. Munich: Fink, 2005.

Gruber, Klemens. "Taktile Medien: Theorien aus der Vorgeschichte: Dreieinhalb Vereinfachungen." *Maske und Kothurn* 62, no. 2–3 (2016): 207–34.

Grubrich-Simitis, Ilse. *Michelangelos Moses und Freuds 'Wagstück': Eine Collage*. Frankfurt: Fischer, 2002.

Guattari, Félix. "The Divided Laing." Translated by Gary Genosko. In *The Guattari Reader*, edited by Gary Genosko, 37–41. Oxford: Blackwell, 1996.

Guattari, Félix. "Refrains and Existential Affects." In *Schizoanalytic Cartographies*, translated by Andrew Goffey, 203–14. New York: Bloomsbury, 2012.

Gugelot, Frédéric. *La conversion des intellectuels au catholicisme en France, 1885–1935*. Paris: CNRS, 1998.

Guggenheim Museum, ed. *Rebecca Horn*. New York: Guggenheim, 1994.

Haeckel, Ernst. *Das Protistenreich: Eine populäre Übersicht über das Formengebiet der niedersten Lebewesen*. Leipzig: Günther, 1878.

Halsman Bello, Jane, and Steve Bello, eds. *Philippe Halsman: A Retrospective*. Boston: Little, Brown, 1998.

Hanson, Thor. *Feathers: The Evolution of a Natural Miracle*. New York: Basic Books, 2012.

Haraway, Donna. "A Manifesto for Cyborgs: Science, Technology, and Socialist Feminism in the 1980s." In *The Haraway Reader*, 7–45. New York: Routledge, 2004.

Haus, Andreas. "Durchspültsein von Luft." In *Sigfried Giedion und die Fotografie: Bildinszenierungen der Moderne*, edited by Werner Oechslin and Gregor Harbusch, 74–87. Zurich: gta, 2010.

Hayles, Katherine. "RFID: Human Agency and Meaning in Information-Intensive Environments." *Theory, Culture and Society* 26 (2009): 47–72.

Heibach, Christiane, ed. *Atmosphären: Dimensionen eines diffusen Phänomens*. Paderborn: Fink, 2012.

Heider, Fritz. *Ding und Medium*. Edited by Dirk Baecker. Berlin: Kadmos, 2005.

Heider, Fritz. *The Psychology of Interpersonal Relations*. New York: Wiley, 1958.

Heilmann, Till A. "Digitalität als Taktilität: McLuhan, der Computer und die Taste." *Zeitschrift für Medienwissenschaft* 3, no. 2 (October 2010): 125–34.

Hellpach, Willy. *Nervosität und Kultur*. Berlin: Räde, 1902.

Henderson, Linda Dalrymple. "Raymond Roussel's *Impressions d'Afrique*, Marcel Duchamp's *Large Glass*, and the Lure of Early Twentieth-Century Science and Technology." In Piron, *Locus Solus*, 146–60.

Hildebrand, Adolf. *The Problem of Form in Painting and Sculpture*. Edited and translated by Max F. Meyer and Robert Morris Ogden. New York: Stechert, 1907.

Holm, Michael Juul. "Die Präsenz Poincarés." In William Kentridge, *Thick Time: Installationen und Inszenierungen*, 81–86. Munich: Hirmer, 2016.

Hooke, Robert. *Micrographia, or Some Physiological Descriptions of Minute Bodies Made by Magnifying Glasses, with Observations and Inquiries Thereupon*. 1665. Reprint, New York: Classics of Science Library, 1995.

Hörisch, Jochen. *Eine Geschichte der Medien: Vom Urknall zum Internet*. Frankfurt: Suhrkamp, 2004.

Horn, Rebecca. "Die Bastille-Interviews I, Paris 1993: Rebecca Horn im Gespräch mit Germano Celant." In *Rebecca Horn*, edited by Nationalgalerie Berlin, 23–31. Ostfildern: Hatje Cantz, 1994.

Horn, Rebecca. "The Bastille Interviews I, Paris 1993: Rebecca Horn with Germano Celant." In *Rebecca Horn*, edited by Guggenheim Museum, 14–23. New York: Guggenheim, 1994.

Horn, Rebecca. "The Bastille Interviews II, Paris 1993: Rebecca Horn with Stuart Morgan." In *Rebecca Horn*, edited by Guggenheim Museum, 24–31. New York: Guggenheim, 1994.

Horn, Rebecca. *Buster's Bedroom: A Filmbook*. Zurich: Parkett, 1991.

Horn, Rebecca, and Wulf Herzogenrath. *Rebecca Horn: Zeichnungen, Objekte, Fotos, Video, Filme*. Cologne: Kölnischer Kunstverein, 1977.

Horwitz, Hugo Theodor. "Über die Konstruktion von Fallen und Selbstschüssen." 1924. In *Das Relais-Prinzip: Schriften zur Technikgeschichte*, edited by Thomas Brandstetter and Ulrich Troitzsch, 117–46. Vienna: Löcker, 2008.

Hüter, Karl-Heinz. *Das Bauhaus in Weimar: Studie zur gesellschaftspolitischen Geschichte einer deutschen Kunstschule*. Berlin: Akademie-Verlag, 1976.

Ionesco, Eugène. *Die Nashörner: Erzählungen, Erinnerungen, Gedanken über das Theater*. Zurich: Arche, 1960.

Ionesco, Eugène. "Rhinoceros." Translated by Jean Stewart. In *The Colonel's Photograph*, 75–98. New York: Grove, 1969.

Janetzky, Kurt, and Bernhard Brüchle. *Das Horn: Eine kleine Chronik seines Werdens und Wirkens*. Bern: Hallwag, 1977.

Jones, Ernest. *The Life and Work of Sigmund Freud*. 2 vols. London: Hogarth, 1955.

Joyce, James. *Finnegans Wake*. London: Faber and Faber, 1960.

Kamper, Dietmar. *Das gefangene Einhorn: Texte aus der Zeit des Wartens*. Munich: Hanser, 1983.

Kandinsky, Wassily. *On the Spiritual in Art*. Edited by Hilla Rebay. New York: Solomon R. Guggenheim Foundation, 1946.

Kappeler, Warren A. *Communication Habits for the Pilgrim Church: Vatican Teaching on Media and Society*. New York: Lang, 2009.

Kemp, Martin. *Structural Intuitions: Seeing Shapes in Art and Science*. Charlottesville: University of Virginia Press, 2016.

Kentridge, William. *Everyone Their Own Projector*. Valence: Cudel, 2008.

Kentridge, William. *Six Drawing Lessons*. Cambridge, MA: Harvard University Press, 2014.

Kentridge, William, et al. *The Refusal of Time*. TV broadcast. 3sat, September 15, 2012.

Kentridge, William, and Peter Galison. "The Refusal of Time." In Christov-Bakargiev, *Documenta (13)*, 104–13.

Kentridge, William, Peter Galison, Philip Miller, Catherine Meyburgh, and Dada Masilo. *The Refusal of Time*. Paris: Barral, 2012.

Kepes, György. "Art and Science." *Explorations* 1 (1953): 77–84.

Kiening, Christian, and Ulrich Johannes Beil. *Urszenen des Medialen: Von Moses zu Caligari*. Göttingen: Wallstein, 2012.

King, Elliott H. "Crazy Movies That Disappear." In *Dalí and Film*, edited by Matthew Gale, 214–29. New York: MoMA, 2007.

King, Elliott H. "The Prodigious Story of the Lacemaker and the Rhinoceros." In Taylor, *The Dalí Renaissance*, 190–204.

King, Elliott H. "Rhinoceros Horn." In *Dalí*, edited by Dawn Ades, 456. New York: Rizzoli, 2004.

King, Elliott H. "Winged Fantasy with Lead Feet: The Influence of Llullism and Hiparxiologi on Dalí's Mysticism." In *Persistence and Memory: New Critical Perspectives on Dalí at the Centennial*, edited by Hank Hine, William Jeffett, and Kelly Reynolds, 189–93. Milan: Bompiani, 2004.

Kittler, Friedrich A. *Discourse Networks 1800/1900*. Translated by Michael Metteer and Chris Cullens. Stanford, CA: Stanford University Press, 1990.

Kittler, Friedrich A. *Gramophone, Film, Typewriter*. Translated by Geoffrey Winthrop-Young and Michael Wutz. Stanford, CA: Stanford University Press, 1999.

Koerner, Margaret K. "Death, Time, Soup: A Conversation with William Kentridge and Peter Galison." In *William Kentridge: No, It Is! Exhibitions and Performances*, 102–14. Cologne: König, 2016.

Kostelanetz, Richard. "A Mine of Perceptions and Prophecies." In *Moholy-Nagy*, edited by Richard Kostelanetz, 206–14. New York: Praeger, 1970.

Krauss, Rosalind. *Le photographique: Pour une théorie des écarts*. Translated by Marc Bloch and Jean Kempf. Paris: Macula, 1990.

Krauss, Rosalind. "'The Rock': William Kentridge's *Drawings for Projection*." *October* 92 (Spring 2000): 3–35.

Krois, John M. *Bildkörper und Körperschema: Schriften zur Verkörperungstheorie ikonischer Formen*. Edited by Horst Bredekamp and Marion Lauschke. Berlin: Akademie, 2011.

Kühlmann, Wilhelm, and Roman Luckscheiter, ed. *Moderne und Antimoderne: Der Renouveau catholique und die deutsche Literatur*. Freiburg: Rombach, 2008.

Lacan, Jacques. *The Four Fundamental Concepts of Psychoanalysis*. Edited by Jacques-Alain Miller. Translated by Alan Sheridan. New York: Norton, 1998.

Lacan, Jacques. *Freud's Papers on Technique 1953–1954*. Edited by Jacques-Alain Miller. Translated by John Forrester. New York: Norton, 1991.

Lacan, Jacques. "The Mirror Stage as Formative of the *I* Function as Revealed in Psychoanalytic Experience." In *Écrits: The First Complete Edition in English*, translated by Bruce Fink, Héloïse Fink, and Russell Grigg, 75–81. New York: Norton, 2005.

Lacan, Jacques. *The Psychoses 1955–1956*. Edited by Jacques-Alain Miller. Translated by Russell Grigg. New York: Norton, 1997.

Laing, Ronald D. *The Politics of Experience and The Bird of Paradise*. London: Penguin, 1990.

Laing, Ronald D., Herbert Phillipson, and A. Russell Lee. *Interpersonal Perception: A Theory and a Method of Research*. New York: Springer, 1966.

Latour, Bruno. "Visualisation and Cognition: Drawing Things Together." *Avant: Trends in Interdisciplinary Studies* 3 (2012): 207–60.

Latour, Bruno. *We Have Never Been Modern*. Translated by Catherine Porter. Cambridge, MA: Harvard University Press, 1993.

Lautréamont, Comte de. *Les Chants de Maldoror*. Chêne-Bourg: La Baconnière, 2011.

Lavers, Chris. *The Natural History of Unicorns*. New York: HarperCollins, 2009.

Lechtermann, Christina, and Stefan Rieger, eds. *Das Wissen der Oberfläche: Epistemologie des Horizontalen und Strategien der Benachbarung*. Zurich: Diaphanes, 2015.

Leclaire, Serge. "The Dream with the Unicorn." In *Psychoanalyzing: On the Order of the Unconscious and the Practice of the Letter*, translated by Peggy Kamuf, 70–87. Stanford, CA: Stanford University Press, 1998.

Lomas, David. "'Painting Is Dead—Long Live Painting!' Notes on Dalí and Leonardo." In Taylor, *The Dalí Renaissance*, 153–89.

Lucretius. *On the Nature of Things*. Translated by William Henry Denham Rouse. Revised by Martin Ferguson Smith. Cambridge, MA: Harvard University Press, 2002.

Lugon, Olivier. "Le vieux pont, l'historien et le nouveau photographe." In *Le pont transbordeur de Marseille: Moholy-Nagy*, edited by François Bon, Olivier Lugon, and Philippe Simay, 7–33. Paris: Ophrys, 2013.

Maas, Renate. *Diaphan und gedichtet: Der künstlerische Raum bei Martin Heidegger und Hans Jantzen*. Kassel: Kassel University Press, 2015.

Mainberger, Sabine. "Tragödie der Verleibung: Zu Aby Warburgs Variante der Einfühlungstheorie." In *Gefühl und Genauigkeit: Empirische Ästhetik um 1900*, edited by Jutta Müller-Tamm, Henning Schmidgen, and Tobias Wilke, 105–35. Munich: Fink, 2014.

Malraux, André. *Le musée imaginaire*. Genève: Skira, 1947.

Malraux, André. *Museum without Walls*. Translated by Stuart Gilbert. New York: Pantheon, 1949.

Mannoni, Laurent. *The Great Art of Light and Shadow: Archaeology of the Cinema*. Exeter: University of Exeter Press, 2000.

Marchessault, Janine. *Marshall McLuhan: Cosmic Media*. London: Sage, 2005.

Marinetti, Filippo Tommaso. "Tactilism." Translated by R. W. Flint and Arthur A. Coppotelli. In *Manifesto: A Century of Isms*, edited by Mary Ann Caws, 197–200. Lincoln: University of Nebraska Press, 2001.

Maritain, Jacques. Foreword to *Rouault: Retrospective Exhibition*, 3–4. New York: Museum of Modern Art, 1953.

Maritain, Jacques. "Visit at St. Ann's Chapel." In *André Girard*, 3–10. New York: Carstairs Gallery, 1953.

Markus, György. "Walter Benjamin and the German 'Reproduction Debate.'" In *Moderne begreifen: Zur Paradoxie eines sozio-ästhetischen Deutungsmusters*, edited by Christine Magerski, Robert Savage, and Christiane Weller, 351–64. Wiesbaden: Deutscher Universitäts-Verlag, 2007.

Marshack, Alexander. *The Roots of Civilization: The Cognitive Beginnings of Man's First Art, Symbol, and Notation*. Mount Kisco, NY: Moyer Bell, 1991.

Marx, Karl. *Capital: A Critical Analysis of Capitalist Production: London 1887*. Translated by Samuel Moore and Edward Aveling. In *Karl Marx Friedrich Engels Gesamtausgabe* II/9, edited by Waltraud Falk, Hanna Behrend, Marion Duparré, Hella Hahn, and Frank Zschaler. Berlin: Dietz, 1990.

Marx, Karl. "Economic and Philosophical Manuscripts." 1844. Translated by Gregor Benton. In *Early Writings*, 279–400. London: Penguin, 1992.

Massumi, Brian. "The Autonomy of Affect." In *Parables for the Virtual: Movement, Affect, Sensation*, 23–45. Durham, NC: Duke University Press, 2002.

Mattessich, Stefan. *Lines of Flight: Discursive Time and Countercultural Desire in the Work of Thomas Pynchon*. Durham, NC: Duke University Press, 2002.

Mauss, Marcel. *Manual of Ethnography*. Edited by N. J. Allen. Translated by Dominique Lussier. New York: Berghahn, 2009.

Mbembe, Achille. *On the Postcolony*. Translated by A. M. Berrett et al. Berkeley: University of California Press, 2012.

McCrickard, Kate. *WK: William Kentridge*. London: Tate, 2012.

McLuhan, Marshall. "Encyclopedic Unities." Review of *Vision in Motion* by László Moholy-Nagy and of *Mechanization Takes Command* by Siegfried Giedion. *Hudson Review* 1, no. 4 (Winter 1949): 599–602.

McLuhan, Marshall. Foreword to *The Interior Landscape: The Literary Criticism of Marshall McLuhan*, edited by Eugene McNamara, xiii–xiv. New York: McGraw-Hill, 1971.

McLuhan, Marshall. *The Gutenberg Galaxy: The Making of Typographic Man*. Toronto: University of Toronto Press, 2011.

McLuhan, Marshall. "Inside the Five Sense Sensorium." *Canadian Architect* 6, no. 6 (1961): 49–54.

McLuhan, Marshall. *Letters of Marshall McLuhan*. Edited by Matie Molinaro, Corinne McLuhan, and William Toye. Toronto: Oxford University Press, 1987.

McLuhan, Marshall. *The Medium and the Light: Reflections on Religion*. Eugene, OR: Wipf and Stock, 2010.

McLuhan, Marshall. "A Note on Tactility." In McLuhan and Parker, *Through the Vanishing Point*, 263–66.

McLuhan, Marshall. *Understanding Media: The Extensions of Man*. Cambridge, MA: MIT Press, 1994.

McLuhan, Marshall. *Understanding Me: Lectures and Interviews*. Edited by Stephanie McLuhan. Cambridge, MA: MIT Press, 2003.

McLuhan, Marshall, and Quentin Fiore. *The Medium Is the Massage: An Inventory of Effects*. New York: Bantam, 1967.

McLuhan, Marshall, and Harley Parker. *Through the Vanishing Point: Space in Poetry and Painting*. New York: Harper, 1968.

Mellinkoff, Ruth. *The Horned Moses in Medieval Art and Thought*. Berkeley: University of California Press, 1970.

Miller, Philip, and William Kentridge. *The Refusal of Time*. CD recording, 2012.

Mitchell, Robert. *Bioart and the Vitality of Media*. Seattle: University of Washington Press, 2010.

Moholy-Nagy, László. "fotografie ist lichtgestaltung." *Bauhaus* 2, no. 1 (1928): 2–9.

Moholy-Nagy, László. "New Forms in Music: Potentialities of the Phonograph." In Krisztina Passuth, *Moholy-Nagy*, 291–92. London: Thames and Hudson, 1987.

Moholy-Nagy, László. *The New Vision and Abstract of an Artist*. New York: Wittenborn, Schultz, 1947.

Moholy-Nagy, László. *The New Vision: Fundamentals of Bauhaus Design, Painting, Sculpture, and Architecture, with Abstract of an Artist*. 1938. Translated by Daphne M. Hoffman. Reprint, Mineola, NY: Dover, 2005.

Moholy-Nagy, László. *Painting, Photography, Film*. Translated by Janet Seligman. Cambridge, MA: MIT Press, 1987.

Moholy-Nagy, László. "Sharp or Fuzzy?" In Krisztina Passuth, *Moholy-Nagy*, 306–9. London: Thames and Hudson, 1985.

Moholy-Nagy, László. *Vision in Motion*. Chicago: Theobald, 1947.

Moholy-Nagy, László. *von material zu architektur*. Mainz: Kupferberg, 1968.

Moholy-Nagy, László. "Die wichtigsten Epochen aus der Geschichte der Fotografie." *Das Werk* 16 (1929): 260–67.

Moholy-Nagy, Sibyl. *Laszlo Moholy-Nagy, ein Totalexperiment*. 1950. Reprint, Mainz: Kupferberg, 1972.

Molderings, Herbert. "Fotogeschichte aus dem Geist des Konstruktivismus: Gedanken zu Walter Benjamins 'Kleiner Geschichte der Photographie.'" In *Die Moderne der Fotografie: Aufsätze und Essays*, 155–80. Hamburg: Philo Fine Arts, 2008.

Monihan, William J. "The Catholic Art Forum, St. Mary's Cathedral, and André Girard: An Oral History Conducted in 1982 by Micaela DuCasse." In *Renaissance of Religious Art and Architecture in the San Francisco Bay Area, 1946–1968*, 1–20. Berkeley: Regional Oral History Office of the Bancroft Library, 1985.

Monod-Herzen, Édouard. *Science et esthétique: Principes de morphologie générale*. Paris: Gauthier-Villars, 1927.

Münsterberg, Hugo. *The Photoplay: A Psychological Study*. New York: Appleton, 1916.

National Council of Catholic Men Film Center. *Selected Catholic Films, 1962–1963*. New York: National Council of Catholic Men, 1963.

Negt, Oskar, and Alexander Kluge. *History and Obstinacy*. Edited by Devin Fore. Translated by Richard Langston et al. New York: Zone, 2014.

Nipkow, Paul. "Elektrisches Teleskop." German Imperial Patent no. 30105, issued January 15, 1885.

"Painting on Light for TV: Artist Andre Girard Readies CBS-TV Film." *Broadcasting*, March 23, 1959, 101.

Papapetros, Spyros. "Modern Architecture and Prehistory: Retracing *The Eternal Present* (Sigfried Giedion and André Leroi-Gourhan)." *RES: Anthropology and Aesthetics*, no. 63/64 (Spring/Autumn 2013): 173–89.

Parisi, David P. *Archaeologies of Touch: Interfacing with Haptics from Electricity to Computing*. Minneapolis: University of Minnesota Press, 2018.

Parisi, David P. "Fingerbombing, or 'Touching Is Good': The Cultural Construction of Technologized Touch." *Senses and Society* 3, no. 3 (2008): 307–27.

Parisi, David P. "Tactile Modernity: On the Rationalization of Touch in the Nineteenth Century." In *Media, Technology, and Literature in the Nineteenth Century*, edited by Colette Colligan and Margaret Linley, 189–213. London: Ashgate, 2011.

Parkinson, Gavin. "How Dalí Learned to Stop Worrying about Surrealism and Love the Bomb." In Taylor, *The Dalí Renaissance*, 71–85.

Parkinson, Gavin. *Surrealism, Art and Modern Science: Relativity, Quantum Mechanics, Epistemology*. New Haven, CT: Yale University Press, 2008.

Parks, Lisa. "Points of Departure: The Culture of US Airport Screening." *Journal of Visual Culture* 6, no. 2 (2007): 183–200.

Paterson, Mark. *The Senses of Touch: Haptics, Affects and Technologies*. Oxford: Berg, 2007.

Péguy, Charles. "Un nouveau théologien M. Fernand Laudet." In *Œuvres en prose, 1909–1914*, edited by Marcel Péguy, 893–1095. Paris: Gallimard, 1961.

Peirce, Charles Sanders. "Logic as Semiotic: The Theory of Signs." In *Philosophical Writings*, edited by Justus Buchler, 98–119. New York: Dover, 1955.

Peters, John Durham. "Helmholtz, Edison, and Sound History." In *Memory Bytes: History, Technology, and Digital Culture*, edited by Lauren Rabinovitz and Abraham Geil, 177–98. Durham, NC: Duke University Press, 2004.

Pettigrew, James Bell. *Design in Nature*. London: Longmans, Green, 1908.

Pickering, Andrew. *The Cybernetic Brain: Sketches of Another Future*. Chicago: University of Chicago Press, 2010.

Pickering, Andrew. *Kybernetik und Neue Ontologien*. Translated by Gustav Roßler. Berlin: Merve, 2007.

Piron, François. "Conversation with John Ashbery." In Piron, *Locus Solus*, 263–71.

Piron, François, ed. *Locus Solus: Impressions of Raymond Roussel*. Translated by Ian Monk. Madrid: Turner, 2011.

Pirsig, Robert M. *Zen and the Art of Motorcycle Maintenance: An Inquiry into Values*. 1974. Perennial Classics. Reprint, New York: HarperCollins, 2000.

Plotnick, Rachel. *Power Button: A History of Pleasure, Panic, and the Politics of Pushing*. Cambridge, MA: MIT Press, 2018.

Polednitschek-Veit, Ulrich. "Die epileptische Aura als zentrale Metapher in Thomas Pynchons *The Crying of Lot 49*." In *"Das ist eine alte Krankheit": Epilepsie in der Literatur*, edited by Dietrich von Engelhardt, Hansjörg Schneble, and Peter Wolf, 225–36. Stuttgart: Schattauer, 2000.

Popitz, Heinrich. *Epochen der Technikgeschichte*. Tübingen: Mohr, 1989.

Pynchon, Thomas. *The Crying of Lot 49*. Philadelphia: Lippincott, 1966.

Pynchon, Thomas. "Is It O.K. to Be a Luddite?" *New York Times*, October 28, 1984. http://www.nytimes.com/books/97/05/18/reviews/pynchon-luddite.html.

Rabelais, François. *Gargantua and Pantagruel*. Translated by M. A. Screech. London: Penguin, 2006.

Raspe, Erich Rudolf. *The Singular Travels, Campaigns, Voyages, and Sporting Adventures of Baron Munnikhouson, commonly pronounced Munchausen* [etc.]. 2nd ed. Oxford: Smith, 1786.

Reik, Theodor. *Probleme der Religionspsychologie: I. Theil: Das Ritual*. Leipzig: Internationaler Psychoanalytischer Verlag, 1919.

Rilke, Rainer Maria. *The Notebooks of Malte Laurids Brigge*. Translated by Robert Vilain. Oxford: Oxford University Press, 2016.

Römer, Thomas. *The Horns of Moses: Setting the Bible in Its Historical Context*. Translated by Liz Librecht. Paris: Collège de France, 2013. https://books.openedition.org/cdf/3013.

Röske, Thomas, and Bettina Brand-Claussen, eds. *Air Loom: Der Luft-Webstuhl und andere gefährliche Beeinflussungsapparate*. Heidelberg: Wunderhorn, 2006.

Roussel, Raymond. "How I Wrote Certain of My Books." Translated by Trevor Winkfield. In *How I Wrote Certain of My Books and Other Writings*, edited by Trevor Winkfield, 3–28. Boston: Exact Change, 1995.

Roussel, Raymond. *Impressions of Africa*. Translated by Mark Polizzotti. Champaign, IL: Dalkey Archive, 2011.

Roussel, Raymond. *Locus Solus*. Translated by Rupert Copeland Cuningham. New York: New Directions, 2017.

Ruffa, Astrid. "Roussel as Read by Dalí: Imaginative Rationales and Figures of Genius." In Piron, *Locus Solus*, 205–15.

Ruffa, Astrid, Philippe Kaenel, and Danielle Chaperon. *Salvador Dalí à la croisée des savoirs*. Paris: Desjonquères, 2007.

Russolo, Luigi. "The Art of Noises (Excerpt), 1913." Translated by R. W. Flint and Arthur A. Coppotelli. In *Manifesto: A Century of Isms*, edited by Mary Ann Caws, 205–11. Lincoln: University of Nebraska Press, 2001.

Ryan, Edmund Joseph. *The Role of the "Sensus Communis" in the Psychology of St. Thomas Aquinas*. Carthagena, OH: Messenger, 1951.

Sahli, Jan. *Filmische Sinneserweiterung: László Moholy-Nagys Filmwerk und Theoie*. Marburg: Schüren, 2006.

Sainsbury, Helen. "Chaos and Creation." In *Dalí and Film*, edited by Matthew Gale, 206–13. New York: MoMA, 2007.

Sale, Kirkpatrick. *Rebels against the Future: The Luddites and Their War on the Industrial Revolution*. Reading, MA: Addison-Wesley, 1995.

Sartre, Jean-Paul. *Being and Nothingness: A Phenomenological Essay on Ontology*. Translated by Hazel E. Barnes. New York: Washington Square, 1992.

Satzinger, Georg. "Michelangelos Grabmal Julius' II. in S. Pietro in Vincoli." *Zeitschrift für Kunstgeschichte* 64 (2001): 177–222.

Sauerlandt, Max. *Michelangelo*. Düsseldorf: Langewiesche, 1911.

Schaub, Thomas H. *Pynchon: The Voice of Ambiguity*. Urbana: University of Illinois Press, 1981.

Schirrmacher, Frank. *Ego: The Game of Life*. Translated by Nick Somers. Cambridge: Polity, 2015.

Schivelbusch, Wolfgang. *The Railway Journey: The Industrialization of Time and Space in the Nineteenth Century*. Berkeley: University of California Press, 1986.

Schloesser, Stephen. *Jazz Age Catholicism: Mystic Modernism in Postwar Paris, 1919–1933*. Toronto: University of Toronto Press, 2005.

Schmidgen, Henning. *The Helmholtz Curves: Tracing Lost Time*. Translated by Nils F. Schott. New York: Fordham University Press, 2014.

Schmidgen, Henning. *Hirn und Zeit: Die Geschichte eines Experiments, 1800–1950*. Berlin: Matthes und Seitz, 2014.

Schmidgen, Henning. *Das Unbewußte der Maschinen: Konzeptionen des Psychischen bei Guattari, Deleuze und Lacan*. Munich: Fink, 1997.

Schmidgen, Henning, and Judy Johns Schloegel. "Allgemeine Physiologie, experimentelle Psychologie und Evolutionstheorie: Einzellige Organismen in der psychophysiologischen Forschung, 1877–1918." In *Der Hochsitz des Wissens: Das Allgemeine als wissenschaftlicher Wert*, edited by Michael Hagner and Manfred D. Laubichler, 239–74. Zurich: Diaphanes, 2006.

Schöttker, Detlev. *Konstruktiver Fragmentarismus: Form und Rezeption der Schriften Walter Benjamins*. Frankfurt am Main: Suhrkamp, 1999.

Scoble, Robert, and Shel Israel. *Age of Context: Mobile, Sensors, Data and the Future of Privacy*. North Charleston, SC: Patrick Brewster, 2014.

Selmeci, Andreas, and Dag Henrichsen. *Das Schwarzkommando: Thomas Pynchon und die Geschichte der Herero*. Bielefeld: Aisthesis, 1995.

Serres, Michel. *La naissance de la physique dans le texte de Lucrèce*. Paris: Minuit, 1977.

Shanley, John F. "Paintings on Light for the TV Screen." *New York Times*, December 13, 1959, X21.

Shklovsky, Victor. "The Connection between Devices of *Syuzhet* Construction and General Stylistic Devices." 1919. Translated by Jane Knox. In *Russian Formalism: A Collection of Articles and Texts in Translation*, edited by Stephen Bann and John E. Bowlt, 48–71. New York: Barnes and Noble, 1973.

Siebenbrodt, Michael, and Frank Simon-Ritz, eds. *Die Bauhaus-Bibliothek: Versuch einer Rekonstruktion*. Weimar: Bauhaus-Universität Weimar, 2009.

Siegert, Bernhard. *Relais: Geschicke der Literatur als Epoche der Post, 1751–1913*. Berlin: Brinkmann und Bose, 1993.

Siegert, Bernhard, and Markus Krajewski, eds. *Thomas Pynchon: Archiv—Verschwörung—Geschichte*. Weimar: VDG, 2003.

Simmel, Georg. "The Metropolis and Mental Life." 1903. In *The Sociology of Georg Simmel*, edited and translated by Kurt H. Wolff, 409–24. Glencoe, IL: Free Press, 1950.

Smith, T'ai. "Limits of the Tactile and the Optical: Bauhaus Fabric in the Frame of Photography." *Grey Room* 25 (Fall 2006): 6–31.

Spencer, Herbert. *The Principles of Psychology*. London: Longman, Brown, Green, and Longmans, 1855.

Sprenger, Florian. *Medien des Immediaten: Elektrizität—Telegraphie—McLuhan*. Berlin: Kadmos, 2012.

Sprenger, Florian, and Christoph Engemann, eds. *Internet der Dinge: Über smarte Objekte, intelligente Umgebungen und die technische Durchdringung der Welt*. Bielefeld: Transcript, 2015.

Stephan, Emil. *Südseekunst: Beiträge zur Kunst des Bismarck-Archipels und zur Urgeschichte der Kunst überhaupt*. Berlin: Reimer, 1907.

Strindberg, August. *Inferno*. In *Inferno and From an Occult Diary*. Translated by Mary Sandbach. Harmondsworth, UK: Penguin, 1979.

Stutzinger, Dagmar. "Das Geschäft mit der Antike: Die Gipsformer Marco, Antonio und Valentin Vanni." In *Begegnungen: Frankfurt und die Antike*, edited by Marlene Herfort-Koch, Ursula Mandel, and Ulrich Schädler, 253–61. Frankfurt: Arbeitskreis Frankfurt und die Antike, 1994.

Sydow, Eckart von. *Primitive Kunst und Psychoanalyse: Eine Studie über die sexuelle Grundlage der bildenden Künste der Naturvölker*. Leipzig: Internationaler Psychoanalytischer Verlag, 1927.

Sylvester, David. *The Brutality of Fact: Interviews with Francis Bacon*. London: Thames and Hudson, 2002.

Tacke, Alexandra. *Rebecca Horn: Künstlerische Selbstpositionierungen im kulturellen Raum*. Cologne: Böhlau, 2011.

Tapié, Michel. "Extrait de *Dalí*." 1957. In *Salvador Dalí: Rétrospective 1920-1980*, edited by Daniel Abadie, 362–63. Paris: Centre Georges Pompidou, 1980.

Taylor, Michael R. "The Dalí Renaissance." In Taylor, *The Dalí Renaissance*, 1–36.

Taylor, Michael R., ed. *The Dalí Renaissance: New Perspectives on His Life and Art after 1940*. New Haven, CT: Yale University Press, 2008.

Taylor, Michael R. "On the Road with Salvador Dalí: The 1952 Nuclear Mysticism Lecture Tour." In Taylor, *The Dalí Renaissance*, 53–70.

Taylor, Michael R. "Paranoiac-Critical Study of Vermeer's 'Lacemaker.'" In *Dalí*, edited by Dawn Ades, 376. New York: Rizzoli, 2004.

Teilhard de Chardin, Pierre. *The Future of Man*. Translated by Norman Denny. New York: Image Books/Doubleday, 2004.

Teilhard de Chardin, Pierre. *The Phenomenon of Man*. Translated by Bernard Wall. New York: HarperPerennial, 2008.

Thacker, Eugene. *Biomedia*. Minneapolis: University of Minnesota Press, 2004.

Theweleit, Klaus. *Male Fantasies*. Translated by Chris Turner, Erica Carter, and Stephen Conway. Minneapolis: University of Minnesota Press, 1987.

"Third Eye for Space Explorers." *Popular Electronics* 17, no. 1 (July 1962): 84.

Thompson, D'Arcy Wentworth. *On Growth and Form*. New ed. Cambridge: Cambridge University Press, 1945.

Tiedemann-Bartels, Hella. *Verwaltete Tradition: Die Kritik Charles Péguys*. Freiburg: Alber, 1986.

Tresch, John. "In a Solitary Place: Raymond Roussel's Brain and the French Cult of Unreason." *Studies in History and Philosophy of Biological and Biomedical Sciences* 35 (2004): 307–32.

"TV Monocle Gives Extra Eye to Wearer." *Radio-Electronics* 33, no. 9 (September 1962): 50.

Varo, Remedios. "Comments by Remedios Varo on Some of Her Paintings." In *Remedios Varo: Catálogo razonado/Catalogue raisonné*, 4th ed., edited by Ricardo Ovalle and Walter Gruen, 111–20. Mexico City: Era, 2008.

Vitale, Elodie. *Le Bauhaus de Weimar, 1919–1925*. Liège: Mardaga, 1989.

Vogl, Joseph. *On Tarrying*. Translated by Helmut Müller-Sievers. London: Seagull, 2011.

Vöhringer, Margarete. *Avantgarde und Psychotechnik: Wissenschaft, Kunst und Technik der Wahrnehmungsexperimente in der frühen Sowjetunion*. Göttingen: Wallstein, 2007.

Warburg, Aby. *Images from the Region of the Pueblo Indians of North America*. Translated by Michael P. Steinberg. Ithaca, NY: Cornell University Press, 1995.

Warburg, Aby. *Sandro Botticellis "Geburt der Venus" und "Frühling."* 1893. In *Werke in einem Band*, 39–123.

Warburg, Aby. "Tragödie der Verleibung." In *Werke in einem Band*, 580–81.

Warburg, Aby. *Werke in einem Band*. Edited by Martin Treml, Sigrid Weigel, and Perdita Ladwig. Berlin: Suhrkamp, 2010.

Weart, Spencer R. *Nuclear Fear: A History of Images*. Cambridge, MA: Harvard University Press, 1988.

Weber-Unger, Simon, ed. *Gipsmodell und Fotografie im Dienst der Kunstgeschichte 1850–1900*. Vienna: Wissenschaftliches Kabinett, 2011.

Weigel, Sigrid. *Literatur als Voraussetzung der Kulturgeschichte: Schauplätze von Shakespeare bis Benjamin*. Munich: Fink, 2004.

Werner, Elke Anna. "Bilder auf Wanderung und in Verwandlung." In *Double Vision: Albrecht Dürer/William Kentridge*, edited by Klaus Krüger, Andreas Schalhorn, and Elke Anna Werner, 80–90. Munich: Sieveking, 2015.

Weyers, Frank. *Salvador Dalís Auseinandersetzung mit den Naturwissenschaften*. Aachen: Mainz, 1995.

Whyte, Lancelot Law, ed. *Aspects of Form: A Symposium on Form in Nature and Art*. London: Lund Humphries, 1951.

Wick, Rainer K. *Teaching at the Bauhaus*. Ostfildern: Hatje Cantz, 2000.

Winkler, Hartmut. *Switching, Zapping: Ein Text zum Thema und ein parallellaufendes Unterhaltungsprogramm*. Darmstadt: Häusser, 1991.

Winthrop-Young, Geoffrey, Ilinca Iurascu, and Jussi Parikka, eds. "Cultural Techniques." Special issue, *Theory, Culture and Society* 30, no. 6 (2013).

Wolfe, Tom. "McLuhan's New World." *Wilson Quarterly* 28, no. 2 (Spring 2004): 18–25.

Wölfflin, Heinrich. "Wie man Skulpturen aufnehmen soll." *Zeitschrift für bildende Kunst*, n.s., 8, no. 12 (December 1896): 294–97.

Wood, John G. *Animate Creation: Popular Edition of "Our Living World,"* vol. 6. Revised by Joseph B. Holder. New York: Hess, 1898.

Zielinski, Siegfried. *Audiovisions: Cinema and Television as Entr'actes in History*. Translated by Gloria Custance. Amsterdam: Amsterdam University Press, 1999.

Zielinski, Siegfried. *Deep Time of the Media: Toward an Archaeology of Hearing and Seeing by Technical Means*. Translated by Gloria Constance. Cambridge, MA: MIT Press, 2006.

Zielinski, Siegfried, and Peter Weibel, eds. *Allah's Automata: Artifacts of the Arab-Islamic Renaissance (800–1200)*. Ostfildern: Hatje Cantz, 2015.

Zweite, Armin. "Rebecca Horn's Bodylandscapes: Ten Observation about the Race of Feelings and Drawing in Post-mechanical Times." Translated by Matthew Partridge. In *Rebecca Horn: Bodylandscapes. Drawings, Sculptures, Installations 1964–2004*, edited by Hans Werner Holzwarth, 13–43. Ostfildern: Hatje Cantz, 2004.

INDEX

Note: Page locators in italics refer to figures.

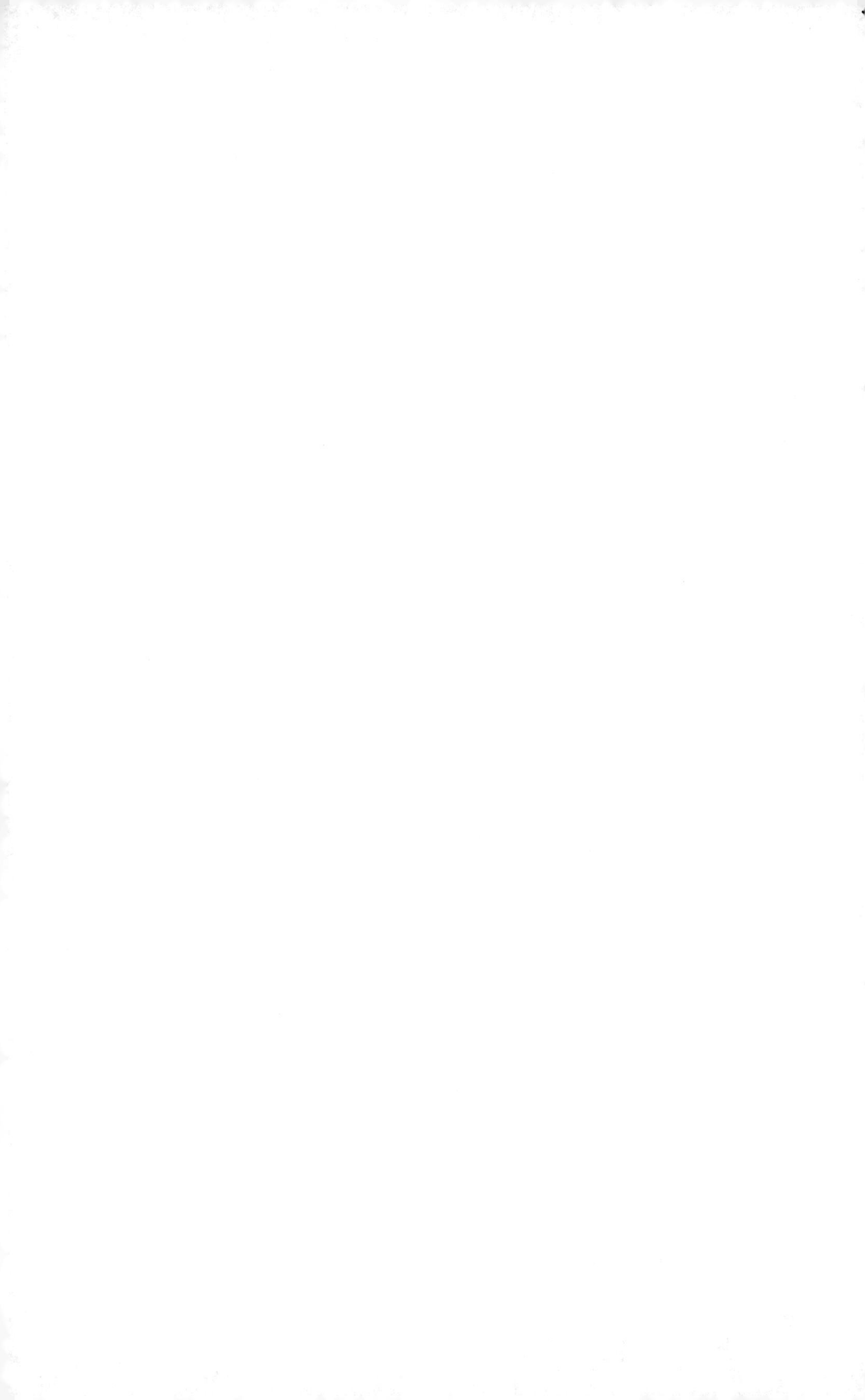

www.ingramcontent.com/pod-product-compliance
Lightning Source LLC
LaVergne TN
LVHW010603100826
845148LV00014B/2830

* 9 7 8 1 4 7 8 0 1 7 7 2 1 *